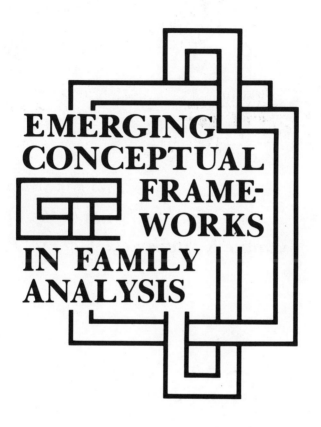

EMERGING CONCEPTUAL FRAME-WORKS IN FAMILY ANALYSIS

*Praeger Studies on
Changing Issues in the Family*
Suzanne K. Steinmetz, *General Editor*

With a New
Introduction
for the 1980s

EMERGING CONCEPTUAL FRAME-WORKS IN FAMILY ANALYSIS

EDITED BY
F. IVAN NYE
FELIX M. BERARDO

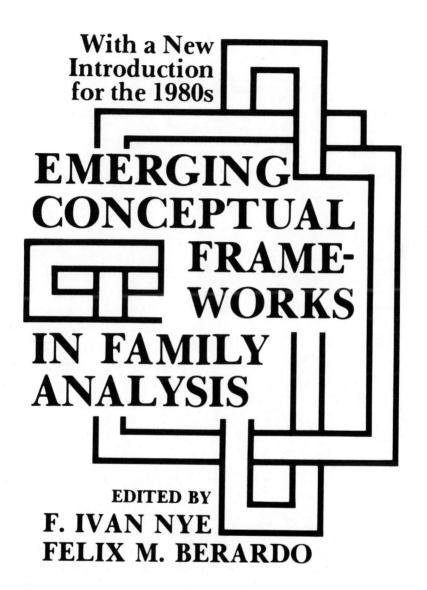

PRAEGER

PRAEGER SPECIAL STUDIES • PRAEGER SCIENTIFIC

Library of Congress Cataloging in Publication Data

Nye, Francis Ivan, 1918-   ed.
    Emerging conceptual frameworks in family analysis.

    (Praeger studies on changing issues in the family)
    Includes bibliographies and index.
    1. Family. I. Berardo, Felix M. II. Title.
III. Series.
HQ734.N9 1981   306.8   80-28823
    ISBN 0-03-057043-3 (pbk.)

29, 019

Published in 1981 by Praeger Publishers
CBS Educational and Professional Publishing
A Division of CBS, Inc.
521 Fifth Avenue, New York, New York 10175 U.S.A.

23456789 052 98765432

Printed in the United States of America

FOREWORD

Emerging Conceptual Frameworks, when it was first published in 1966, quickly became a major source of stimulation for the application of theory to family research and a mechanism for the systematic study of the family. As Nye and Berardo noted in their original introduction, "Family sociologists prior to 1960 had seldom asked publicly, what is and is not theory?" Their statement could easily have been applied to family psychologists, home economists, social workers, family therapists, or others studying family behavior.

Growing out of a 1960 paper by Hill and Hansen, "The Identification of Conceptual Frameworks Utilized in Family Study," *Emerging Conceptual Frameworks* provided the student and professional with a comprehensive compendium of 12 conceptual frameworks. Judging by the activity in family theory over the last decade, the authors have certainly fulfilled their initial goal of stimulating the examination of family behavior from various perspectives.

Unfortunately, the book went out of print in 1973. Coming during a period of increased productivity and growth in the numbers of family "theorists," this event left a distinct void in the literature. While there existed a large handbook with chapters devoted to theory, several monographs using a specific theoretical perspective, and most recently, a two-volume handbook on family theory, these sources tended to be either too limited in outlook to serve students in a basic theory course or too sophisticated— designed to provide resources for the professional researcher and theorist rather than the novice. Furthermore, several of these volumes have also gone out of print in recent years.

Although the original publisher discontinued *Emerging Conceptual Frameworks,* this has not stopped its use for ten years by scholars who have devised ingenious methods for sharing the few obtainable copies. The fact that this book is still considered a major influence for graduate students developing their skills in family theory is certainly a factor behind our desire to initiate the *Changing*

Issues in the Family monograph series with a new edition of this important volume.

This volume, however, represents more than a simple reprinting. The introduction prepared for this edition provides the reader with material on five additional currently-emerging frameworks that are likely to influence family theory in the 1980s. Two of these, conflict and exchange theory, have been widely applied to the family theory during the 1970s. General systems, while popular in sociology and other social science disciplines, has not been as widely utilized.

Similarly, transactional analysis, although popular among professionals and laypersons, has only in the last year been used systematically to delineate the central concepts and basic assumptions in family theory. Social individualism, likewise, is only beginning to emerge. The further explication of these frameworks is an important task for the 1980s.

The profession has now reached a level of sophistication in which it is recognized that research must be grounded in theory. Thus, it is appropriate that the first volume of a series of research monographs be a volume on theory. As editor of this series, I am pleased that this classic is initiating *Changing Issues in the Family*. Family theorists—both established professionals and students—will have the opportunity to examine all 17 conceptual frameworks and evaluate their ability to explain family behavior during the coming decades.

Suzanne K. Steinmetz

PREFACE
TO THE FIRST EDITION

In including *emerging* in the title of this volume, we emphasize the recency of this intellectual development in family analysis. The methodology of conceptual frameworks is still (and we think appropriately) subject to continued review and experimentation. For example, the reader will find that we have not attempted to employ all elements of a framework as outlined by Hill and Hansen. Besides making some minor additions to the framework, we have also chosen to place different emphasis on its various elements.

More importantly, what constitutes a framework worthy of explication is a current and lively issue. Seven, five, and four frameworks have been selected as the appropriate number in prior papers. We understand that still another manuscript including six is being prepared. Because one of our major objectives was to create a volume usable for reference, we have included all that we think may be relevant to the interests of a substantial number of scholars and students. The result has been the delineation of eleven frameworks. The several prominent scholars who have read this volume in typescript have all proposed a total number of frameworks both different from each other and from ours. We anticipate, therefore, a continued lively debate concerning the number and identity of the most significant frameworks for viewing the family. We have no regrets that we have elected to delineate a larger number of frameworks representative of a wider variety of disciplines than have some of our colleagues. In fact, we feel that it might have been useful to attempt two more—a population framework and one stating the development of the psychodynamic school in anthropology.

In still another sense we can see an emergent characteristic in conceptual frameworks, that of delineation of concepts and statement of basic assumptions. We have provided both, but with no illusions that they will prove entirely adequate. Both the scholars who employ the concepts and make the assumptions and the writers who review and revise the conceptual frameworks have a continuing task in improving their clarity, adequacy, and usefulness.

Finally, concerning general objectives, we started with the idea of creating a reference source for the scholar and a learning aid for the advanced student. Our primary objective was not innovation, although we have innovated at some points in pursuit of these objectives. Instead, we have attempted to make the highly abstract notion of conceptual frameworks concrete and real, to the end that scholars and advanced students can really work with them. Insofar as we have achieved this and to the extent we stimulate the continued development of conceptual frameworks, we shall have succeeded in our task.

F. I. N.
F. M. B.

CONTENTS

INTRODUCTION
TO THE 1981 EDITION

The original edition of *Emerging Conceptual Frameworks* (1966) provided a systematic framework for the development of nine disciplinary and two professional frameworks for the study of the family. It has enjoyed a broad use in graduate seminars, by students studying for preliminary examinations, and for personal reference by theoretical and empirical scholars. The fact that the original publisher stopped printing it in 1973 did not stop its use.

Our motivation for developing a systematic statement of the major subdisciplinary, disciplinary, and professional frameworks was the need for communication. At Florida State University the Interdisciplinary Ph.D. Program in Marriage and the Family had drawn in professionals from such varied specialties as psychoanalytic social work, religion, vocational agriculture, law, home economics, and sociology. We found a formidable problem in communication among people accustomed to almost completely different sets of concepts. We felt that if these various sets of concepts were set down together with their accompanying sets of basic assumptions, the "language" of each would become much more apparent to the others and, therefore, communication between and among schools of thought would be facilitated. Certainly this has occurred during the decade and a half since its publication.

DIRECTIONS OF THE STUDY
SINCE THE MID-1960s

This volume was originally conceived in the early 1960s, a period in which structure-functionalism was enjoying its greatest popularity. True, theorists had difficulty developing meaningful, testable hypotheses from this framework, but they were able to employ it for general, discursive descriptions of family functions and family change. Uneasily coexisting with structure-functionalism was the symbolic interaction perspective, represented by a loose set of concepts and assumptions. Empirical research that seemed to belong better in this framework than elsewhere was plentiful, but most family research had not employed symbolic interaction in any self-conscious manner.

Development continued in the psychoanalytic study of the family and in the anthropological framework, as well as in an almost residual category labeled the socio-psychological framework. There was little research using the situational or institutional frameworks. Much activity was present in the legal and religious frameworks, but this was largely unrelated to the work in the socio-psychological and sociological disciplines and specialties. The economic framework continued to generate research, but like symbolic interaction, it usually employed concepts selectively and seldom consciously delineated them or the basic assumptions accompanying them (Becker, 1974; Bivens, 1976).

By the end of the decade, family scholarship had begun to change, just as the family itself began to change. Zetterberg was probably one of the most dynamic catalysts. In his book, *On Theory and Verification* (1965), Zetterberg argued that structure-functionalism was not a theory at all, but a loose group of concepts. Consequently, it had not and could not logically generate meaningful, testable hypotheses. He offered a concrete model for theory development at the middle or mini-theory range. A list of empirically oriented scholars gladly responded to his injunction—"go forth, develop fruitful theories and multiply." Thus, the late 1960s saw the birth of many empirically-based theories.

Emerging Frameworks

During the late 1960s and early 1970s a growing number of scholars were elaborating a variety of conceptual frameworks. Black scholarship moved into a conflict frame of reference and the language of oppression and of revolution appeared in the analysis of the black family. At the same time, a reborn feminist movement began to portray females as an oppressed minority and to use the same set of conflict concepts and assumptions (Bart, 1971).

Parallel to the increased use of conflict concepts, exchange theory began to be employed in family study. Although the original application, limited largely to noninstitutional dyadic relationships, was hardly useful in family study, scholars in the late 1960s and early 1970s began to elaborate and extend it into a dynamic approach in family research. Systems theory, too, received more attention from family scholars, as did social individualism, an unstated framework that is now in the process of being delineated, and transactional analysis, a streamlined version of psychoanalytic theory.

EXCHANGE OR CHOICE AND EXCHANGE THEORY

At the time the 11 frameworks were chosen for development, some consideration was given to including one that has come to be identified as exchange theory. The decision was negative because family scholars up to that time had devoted little attention to it and had employed it even less. Yet, by 1965 when our manuscript went to press, some work had been done. Waller's (1938) famous rating-dating hypothesis was intrinsically an exchange formulation. Blood and Wolfe (1960) employed the concept of rewards in their theory of family power. Farber (1964) also used the reward concept freely in his theory of permanent availability. McCall (1966) found this conceptual approach useful in his historical analysis of courtship practices in the United States.

Unfortunately, in explicating exchange theory, Homans (1961) only employed it to explain choices in dyads and triads in relationships largely outside the normative structure. Thus, it was not clear that the seminal concepts of rewards, costs, outcomes, comparison level, and comparison level alternatives could be appropriately applied to family behavior and social structure. Heer's (Glick, Heer, and Beresford 1963) specific application of its concepts to spousal power was among its earliest uses in the family. The work of Richer (1968), Edwards (1969), and Lederer and Jackson (1969) testified to its increasing popularity. Bartz and Nye (1970) started with an empirical theory model and concluded with an application of exchange theory to the research on early marriage.

The decade of the 1970s witnessed important changes in the structure of the theory. Simpson (1972) called attention to the fact that the concepts delineated by Thibaut and Kelley (1959) are much broader than the applications to behaviors made by them or by Homans (1961). In fact, there are no obvious limits to the theory. Burns (1973) extended the theory to friendship relationships— relationships bearing many similarities to marriage. He also specified exchanges of costs between adversaries. Ekeh (1974) further extended it to sequential exchanges, exchanges of the individual with groups, and finally, through generalized reciprocity, to exchanges between the individual and society.

Throughout all of this theoretical development and broader application in the first half of the 1970s, the label "exchange theory" persisted. Finally, Heath (1976) challenged this label by showing that exchanges between individuals are only a small part of social life. He termed the broad domain of decision making "choice" and showed that the basic concepts of exchange theory are equally useful in all choices or decisions, regardless of whether or not these involve person-to-person relationships. However, Heath (1976) wrote of theories of choice, rather than of *a* general theory of choice applicable to perhaps an unlimited number of substantive problems. Nye (1978, 1979) took the latter stance: that a general theory of behavior and social structure could be constructed from the basic concepts of Thibaut and Kelley as elaborated by other theorists. He employed the label choice and exchange theory to identify this very broad theory.

Meanwhile, another group of psychologists and sociologists was employing the theory under laboratory conditions (Emerson, 1976), to test very limited, very specific theories that included family behavior.

By the close of the 1970s, there was a considerable increase in the number of publications employing this theory. Several examples can be found in Burgess and Huston (1979) and in Burr, Hill, Nye, and Reiss's (Eds.) *Contemporary Theories About the Family*, Vol. I and II (1979). For example, in his chapter "Choice, Exchange and the Family" Nye (1979) uses choice and exchange theory to develop numerous propositions. For example, the following relate to employed wives and mothers:

1. The younger the child, the more rewards it supplies the mother in exchange for the mother's care.
2. The younger the youngest child, the greater the economic cost of child care for families with employed mothers.
3. The younger the youngest child in the family, the greater the share of housekeeping and child care tasks that will be borne by the father and older children in families with employed mothers.
4. The younger the youngest child, the more likely that maternal employment will be opposed by the father and older siblings.
5. The younger the youngest child, the more likely that the mother will experience guilt feelings when leaving the child.

6. The younger the youngest child, the more sanctions will be experienced from kin and neighbors if the mother works.
7. The younger the youngest child, the less the free "disposable time" available to the employed mother.
8. The greater the number of minor children in the home, the greater the financial expenditure to hire housekeeping and day-care services.
9. The greater the number of minor children, the greater the proportion of housekeeping and child care tasks performed by fathers and older children of employed mothers.
10. The greater the number of minor children at home, the less free "disposable time" is available to employed mothers.
11. The greater the number of minor children at home, the more likely that the father and children will oppose the employment of the mother.
12. The greater the number of minor children at home, the more likely that negative sanctions will be imposed on the employed mother by kin and neighbors.
13. The greater the number of children at home, the stronger the guilt feelings of mothers in taking employment.
14. The greater the number of minor children at home, the greater the total positive affect received by mothers from children for services she provides for them.

When these examples of research are added to the growing number of family books that are employing the theory, it appears that the exchange framework is beginning to be employed extensively by family scholars.

Finally, there is the question of the proper label for this theory. *Exchange* describes only part of it, but *choice and exchange* may be awkward. Perhaps *social choice theory* would be better, since choice includes exchange. It is interesting to note, too, that Homans, in his Introduction to Burgess and Huston (1979) has written that it would have been more useful to have stated the concepts of exchange theory as a broad underlying theory of society, rather than limiting it to interpersonal exchanges.

GENERAL SYSTEMS THEORY

General systems theory has attracted family scholars for more than a decade. Cook (1973), for example, has argued that

Any social organization can be subjected to a system analysis. The family as a form of social organization has been and continues to be in need of a more integrative and fertile approach to identify, conceptualize and analyze its own set of linkages and relationships. . . . systems theory easily lends itself to clarification and elucidation of the heretofore muddied areas of family life, so that rather than viewing real life family situations as mystifying, disorganized and disunified phenomena, it is possible to cut to the core of situations by grasping the basic components, reducing the seeming chaos to order.

However, other critics note that it may be more "general" than "theory." (See Broderick and Smith, 1979, for a discussion of the current status of general systems theory in family research and theory building.)

The general idea of systems theory has been in evidence for some time; see, for example, Hall and Fagan's (1967) discussion of the basic concepts. Buckley (1967) gave it tremendous impetus by indicating its potential for the analysis and understanding of social behavior. More recently, Broderick and Smith (1979) have analyzed and applied it to family data. Yet, even they have stopped short of offering a theory of family behavior. Why has a framework that seemed to offer so much produced so little? And, if its record is so sterile, what is the justification for including it here?

Such basic concepts as system, subsystem, input, output, feedback, rules of transformation, strata hierarchies, boundary, environment morphogenesis, and morphostasis offer a substance and culture-free set of concepts for organizing and describing events. (It is this characteristic of the model that has attracted many scholars.) Nevertheless, as useful as it may be for describing and mapping social systems, it has generated few salient, testable hypotheses about social behavior.

A current paper (Cotton and Oransky, 1980), however, promises to break this intellectual deadlock. Besides defining central concepts, the authors have listed ten basic assumptions of the theory. From some of these assumptions, they have been able to develop a hierarchy of propositions ranging from universal propositions that are true for all matter, to general propositions at the institutional (family) level, to testable hypotheses about family behavior. Examples of their propositions relating to the family include:

1. Families that process more information more efficiently will [prosper], other things being equal, compared to families lacking information input.
2. The family that has developed a highly organized structure will more effectively process information than less organized families.
3. The family that can process more information will be able to maintain successful interaction with more external systems than the family processing less information.
4. Middle-class families are more likely to have individual family members realize their individual goals than lower-class families.
5. Families that have higher levels of education will have higher standards of living.
6. Individuals [with supportive] family relationships will satisfy their needs and attain their goals more efficiently than individuals separated from supportive relationships.
7. Individuals without supportive relationship networks will be less likely to prosper.
8. Families in which members choose, or are encouraged, to be [excessively] separated, will be less functional than families in which members are more closely involved, other things being equal.
9. Families in which members are enmeshed in the family, to the exclusion of individual development, will be less functional than families where individual movement is possible, other things being equal.
10. Families in which the distance between members is at neither extreme ([too] enmeshed or disengaged) will be more functional.

They also assume that human systems have needs and goals and that systems with more information are more efficient at meeting these needs and achieving these goals. Education is seen as a major source of such information. Likewise, families in which members communicate well within the systems have more information and, as a consequence, are more successful in meeting needs and reaching goals. Furthermore, effective communication between systems increases information, which leads to more effectiveness in meeting needs and achieving goals.

Implicit in the above discussion is the assumption that a frame-work will not be employed extensively in family study unless it has at least some explanatory potential. With the Cotton-Oransky paper it appears that the breakthrough may be near. It is our feeling, therefore, that although systems theory has not stimulated and guided much family research to date, it has a sizable potential and one that may well be realized in the coming decade.

CONFLICT THEORY

Conflict theory, even in its application to the family, has a long history dating from the work of Engels (1902). During the decades when structure-functionalism was dominant a small group of scholars—Simmel (1955), Coser (1956), Sprey (1969)—kept the basic ideas alive. With the 1970s and the blossoming of the activists movements among the black leadership and the women's move-ment, conflict literature moved out of obscurity and became a dominant force in books and articles about marriage and the family.

Although conclusions based on conflict ideology have largely gone untested, they appear to be testable and, certainly, the concepts of the theory can be defined and the basic assumptions stated. Given the volume of publications being written from this perspective and the number of political and administrative decisions being made based on its premises, it would appear that the research to test its conclusions is forthcoming. Therefore, it seems most appropriate to include it in this discussion of conceptual frameworks that are emerging in the study of the family.

Sprey (1979) recently reviewed conflict theory and offered a list of central concepts. These concepts include conflict, competition, consensus, negotiation, bargaining, power, influence, aggression, threats, promises, conflict management, and consequences of con-flict. He employs these concepts to analyze the range of family relationships in mainstream, as well as unusual families (Sprey, 1979).

Farrington and Foss (1977), besides offering a list of concepts, have specified 29 assumptions basic to this approach. Six are assumptions about the nature of society, two focus on the nature of human beings, seven on social interaction and social relationships, and fourteen deal with the nature of the family. Those dealing specifically with the nature of the family are:

1. Like any other social organization or social group, the family does not naturally tend toward a state of equilib-

rium; rather, the maintenance of consensus and cohesion is problematic.

2. Like any other social system, the family is a "system in conflict." Social conflict and social change are natural parts of family life.

3. Certain structural characteristics of families affect (a) the number of underlying conflicts of interest, (b) the degree of underlying hostility, and (c) the nature and extent of expressions of social conflict. The same structural characteristics do not necessarily have the same effect on each of these aspects of conflict; thus, family conflict has a "paradoxical nature."

4. Conflict situations in the family can take the form of (a) opposing interests, (b) incompatible goals, (c) differing values, (d) discrepant role expectations, (e) structural inequalities, (f) a scarcity of resources, or (g) clashes of personality.

5. Family members have differential access to resources and power.

6. This differential access to resources and power results from differing positions in the systems of social stratification, and can be called structural inequality.

7. Due to its system of stratification by sex and age, the family is, to a large extent, a "structure of dominance." The importance of age and sex stratification in the family distinguishes it from other social groups.

8. Like any other social system, the family is largely integrated through coercion.

9. Family members' positions (status), both within society and within the family unit, help determine their interests, goals, values, and needs.

10. Expressions of conflict in families are usually of the mixed-motive variety, in that family members possess not only conflicting, competing interests, but also common, interrelated ones. Hence, destruction or elimination of the other party is usually not a goal.

11. It is necessary to distinguish between (a) conflict avoidance or prevention, (b) conflict regulation or management, and (c) conflict resolution.

12. The absence of conflict expression within a particular family unit cannot be interpreted as implying the happiness and satisfaction of family members.

13. Complete suppression of conflict is likely to have negative consequences for the family unit and/or its members.
14. Each aspect of conflict can have both positive and negative consequences (functions) for its participants and for the larger social system.

SOCIAL INDIVIDUALISM

At the beginning of the 1970s an ideology aimed at a revolution in the social order gained prominence in the United States. At the personal level it exalted the individual and questioned the authority of the state or the group to control and direct individual behavior. However, social commentators found it puzzling. For example, Schneider (1975) wrote that many of the youth of the early 1970s sought to destroy the present social structure but they proposed nothing to replace it. They did not advocate communism, nor were their ideas those of the far right. It appeared that they either assumed that a good, just social structure would spontaneously emerge or that social structure was simply unnecessary. Etzioni (1976) referred to them as anarchists.

Cornille and Harrigan (1980) accepted the challenge to delineate the central concepts and basic assumptions of this framework. In so doing, they traced some of the concepts back to the work of distinguished social psychologists. The scholars of the 1950s and 1960s generally viewed social structure as benign; not perfect, certainly, but perhaps perfectable. Many in the 1970s viewed it as exploitive and oppressive. However, they shared a faith that individuals could find self-actualization without transgressing on the rights of others.

Cornille and Harrigan have selected a number of concepts that they view to be central to the social individualism framework. The reader is likely to recognize several from the works of Maslow and Rogers: awareness, perception, self, self-directed, other-directed, social individual, self-actualization, needs, basic needs, growth needs, alienation, frustration, focus of evaluation, unconditional positive regard, inner nature, ideal self, threat growth, distortion, defense, openness to experience, and perceived locus of control. Cornille and Harrigan have also delineated fifteen basic assumptions:

1. People are a unity with nature as an open process, influenced by movement toward the common good.

2. Human beings are self preserving and self-enhancing (Rogers, 1959).
3. Human beings tend toward preservation and enhancement of their species.
4. The nature of the person is a process, motivated toward a balanced relationship with the environment. This process, therefore, is inclined toward good.
5. The person is intrinsically social by nature, rooted in the desire for significance or self-esteem. This growth process must take place within social relationships.
6. People have certain needs that must be met if they are to successfully self-actualize (Maslow, 1959).
7. People are in great part motivated by the desire to self-actualize.
8. The desire for self-actualization is motivated by the concept of what the self hopes to become (Miller, 1967:177).
9. People choose behavior (self-directed or other-directed) that they perceive as best actualizing their potential.
10. The means that people employ to satisfy their needs and to self-actualize are in part learned and in part unique manifestations of an internal process.
11. Self-actualization at all levels of needs (basic and interpersonal) is a process that is continuing rather than satisfied or finalized.
12. Perception is subjective, always mediated by the level of actualization of the person at the present time.

This approach has by no means reached the level of a well-defined conceptual framework for the study of marriage and the family. It draws its concepts from a variety of disciplines, especially from the area of psychology. Whether it will ever achieve the status of a full-fledged framework remains open to question. Few would argue, however, that this approach does not have significant implications for both understanding and studying marriage and family living. We suspect, for example, that students of the cohabitation phenomenon would find it useful in both research and analysis. Similarly, analyses and explanations of dual-career families, divorce, and employed wives, etc., might very well benefit from this approach. Because its concepts and assumptions have not yet been fully delineated and specified into a coherent frame of reference, we were tempted to omit it from this discussion. Our decision not to do so was based on the assumption that social individualism will increasingly emerge as a viable framework.

TRANSACTIONAL ANALYSIS: A FRAMEWORK THAT REFUSES TO EMERGE

Perhaps the most influential conceptual framework of the 1960s and at least the early 1970s was transactional analysis. Founded by Berne (1963), it attracted a number of scholars and practitioners who expanded, disseminated, and applied it. With such volumes as Harris's (1967) *I'm O.K., You're O.K.*, the framework reached and influenced millions of lay people, as well as a substantial number of professionals. Institutes and seminars for the training of practitioners came into being throughout the United States (Nye, 1978).

Berne was a psychiatrist influenced by such scholars as Freud, Adler, Jung, and Sullivan (Richards, 1979). Transactional analysis, therefore, has its roots in psychoanalytic theory. However, writers on the subject often refer to it as a method, rather than a theory. Whether or not is is a theory (and we are inclined toward the view that it is), it has concepts and implicit basic assumptions. Some of the more basic concepts include: parent, child, adult, game, stroke, transaction, contamination, script, and contract, What is needed, we think, is a further explication of the framework so that its dimensions, validity, and usefulness can be assessed. Richards (1979) has constructed ten basic assumptions from this literature that have direct applications to the family, thus providing an initial attempt to delineate this framework:

1. That every adult was once a child.
2. That every human being with sufficiently functioning brain tissue is potentially capable of reality testing.
3. That every individual who survives into adult life has had either functioning parents or someone in *loco parentis*.
4. That it is possible to change decisions made earlier.
5. That we are born OK, and that we become "not-OK" by accepting the negative injunctions of our parents. (Later theorists are divided, and some do not seem to care, as the issue has no particular significance for therapy.)
6. That our brain acts as a recorder—capturing every experience from birth (or possibly prior); and these events are intact including our response to them.

7. That we are born with stimulus hunger and without it the infant may become crippled or die (marasmus).
8. That our decisions on how to live are based on our perceptions at that moment.
9. That our perceptions are influenced by past experiences, future aspirations, and more importantly as children, by our levels of cognitive development.
10. That we have a need to structure time in ways designed to achieve a desired level of strokes.

THEORIES WITHOUT CONCEPTUAL FRAMEWORKS

We make the basic assumption that all theories have conceptual frameworks, e.g., concepts that are appropriate and assumptions that are made about the nature of the components involved in the theory. However, in a great deal of the theoretical work appearing in the 1970s theorists have gone directly to the family research and other literature, extracted propositions, and mapped interrelations between the propositions (Burr, 1973; Burr, Hill, Nye, and Reiss, Vol. I, 1979). Rarely do these theorists define concepts or state basic assumptions. (The same might also be said for causal analysis, which ordinarily requires that the theorist state causal relationships, but does not usually include careful attention to conceptualization.) Presumably, all these theoretical efforts could involve the specification of conceptual frameworks. If so, we would have hundreds, possibly thousands, of conceptual frameworks. We do not, however, advocate this. Just as we think a few good general theories are preferable to a thousand very limited, specific ones, so we think that a few good general conceptual frameworks introduce more order and are more parsimonious of everyone's time than a thousand very limited, specific ones.

THE FUTURE OF CONCEPTUAL FRAMEWORKS

Throughout the 1960s, three conceptual frameworks dominated the field of marriage and the family—the structure-functional, the interactional, and the developmental approaches. The first two, in particular, held a commanding lead over the other conceptual frameworks. It is our perception that this pattern has changed with a decline in structure-functionalism and the emergence of conflict and exchange frameworks. We have noted that still other theoretical approaches or frameworks have emerged. Whether they will gain wide acceptance in the field will depend largely upon their ability to generate empirically testable hypotheses and the degree to which they stimulate new concepts and areas of systematic investigation.

Conceptual frameworks were sometimes criticized in the 1970s because they were not theories (Klein, Calvert, Garland and Paloma, 1969). They were not intended to be theories, but devices to map, categorize, and communicate the diverse efforts of family researchers, practitioners, and would-be theorists. The record of the past 15 years will show that they have been most useful in clarifying differences and similarities among the disciplines, subdisciplines, and professions. The need for such mapping, categorization, and communication continues. Thus further work on conceptual frameworks and the use of this or similar volumes seems desirable and likely.

We would anticipate that the five emerging frameworks discussed above will be fully explicated and at least some of them added to the most viable ones from this volume. Will some of those presently included be eliminated from a future revision? It seems likely. The editors welcome comments from readers on these latter points.

REFERENCES

BART, PAULINE B. "Sexism in Family Studies," a special issue of the *Journal of Marriage and the Family*, **33** (Aug. 1971), pp. 733–99.

BARTZ, W. B., and NYE, F. IVAN. "Early Marriage: A Propositional Formulation," *Journal of Marriage and the Family*, **32** (May 1970), pp. 258–69.

BECKER, GARY. "A Theory of Marriage," in T. W. Schultz, ed. *Economics of the Family*. Chicago: University of Chicago Press, 1974.

BERNE, ERIC. *The Structure and Dynamics of Organizations and Groups*. Philadelphia: J. B. Lippincott Company, 1963.

BIVENS, GORDON E. "The Grants Economy and Study of the American Family: A Possible Framework for Trans-Disciplinary Approaches," *Journal of Home Economics Research*, **5** (Dec. 1976), pp. 70–78.

BLOOD, ROBERT O., JR., and WOLFE, D. M. *Husbands and Wives*. New York: Free Press of Glencoe, Inc., 1960.

BRODERICK, CARLFRED B., and SMITH, JAMES. "The General Systems Approach to the Family," in Wesley R. Burr, Reuben Hill, F. Ivan Nye, and Ira L. Reiss, eds. *Contemporary Theories about the Family*, Vol. II. New York: The Free Press, 1979, Ch. 2.

BUCKLEY, WALTER F. *Sociology and Modern Systems Theory*. Englewood Cliffs, N.J.: Prentice-Hall, Inc., 1967.

BURGESS, R. G., and HUSTON, T. L. *Social Exchange in Developing Relationships*. New York: Academic Press, 1979.

BURNS, THOMAS. "A Structural Theory of Social Exchange," *Acta Sociologica*, **16** (1973), pp. 188-208.

BURR, WESLEY R. *Theory Construction and the Sociology of the Family*. New York: John Wiley and Sons, Inc., 1973.

———, HILL, REUBEN, NYE, F. IVAN, and REISS, IRA L. *Contemporary Theories about the Family*, Vol. I and II. New York: The Free Press, 1979.

CHRISTENSEN, HAROLD T. *Handbook of Marriage and the Family*. Chicago: Rand McNally, 1964.

COOK, ELBERT L. "Family Analysis: A General Systems Strategy," *Southern Sociologist*, **3** (Jan. 1973), pp. 3-11.

*CORNILLE, THOMAS A., and HARRIGAN, JOHN. "Social Individualism." Unpublished seminar paper (Florida State University, Department of Home and Family Life, 1980).

COSER, L. A. *The Functions of Social Conflict*. New York: The Free Press, 1956.

*COTTON, S. D., and ORANSKY, K. S. "Systems Theory: Movement from a Conceptual Perspective to a General Theory of the Family." Unpublished seminar paper (Florida State University, Department of Home and Family Life, 1980).

EDWARDS, JOHN N. "Familial Behavior as Social Exchange," *Journal of Marriage and the Family*, **31** (Aug. 1969), pp. 518-26.

EKEH, PETER P. *Social Exchange Theory*. Cambridge, Mass.: Harvard University Press, 1974.

EMERSON, R. M. "Social Exchange Theory," in Alex Inkeles, J. Coleman, and N. Smelser. *Annual Review of Sociology*, Vol. II. Palo Alto, Cal.: Annual Reviews, 1976.

ENGELS, FRIEDRICH. *The Origin of the Family: Private Property and the State*, trans. by Ernest Untermann. Chicago: C. H. Kerr and Company, 1902.

ETZIONI, AMITAI. *Social Problems*. Englewood Cliffs, N.J.: Prentice-Hall, Inc., 1976.

FARBER, BERNARD. *The Family: Organization and Interaction*. San Francisco: Chandler, 1964.

*FARRINGTON, K., and FOSS, J. E. "The Social Conflict Framework." Paper read before theory development workshop at the National Council on Family Relations, 1977.

HALL, A. D., and FAGAN, R. E. "Definitions of Systems," in *Systems Engineering*. New York: Bell Telephone Laboratories, 1967.

HARRIS, THOMAS A. *I'm O.K., You're O.K.* New York: Harper and Row, 1967.

HEATH, ANTHONY. *Rational Choice and Social Exchange*. Cambridge, England: Cambridge University Press, 1976.

HOMANS, GEORGE C. *Social Behavior: Its Elementary Forms.* New York: Harcourt Brace Jovanovich, 1961.

KLEIN, JOHN F., CALVERT, GENE P., GARLAND, T. NEAL, and POLOMA, MARGARET M. "Pilgrim's Progress I: Recent Developments in Family Theory," *Journal of Marriage and the Family,* 31 (Nov. 1969), pp. 677–87.

LEDERER, WILLIAM J., and JACKSON, DON D. *The Mirages of Marriage.* New York: W. W. Norton and Company, 1968.

McCALL, MICHAEL M. "Courtship as Social Exchange: Some Historical Comparisons," in Bernard Farber, ed. *Kinship and Family Organization.* New York: John Wiley and Sons, Inc., 1966. Ch. 17.

NYE, F. IVAN. "Is Choice and Exchange Theory the Key?" *Journal of Marriage and the Family,* 40 (May 1978), pp. 219–35.

———. "Choice, Exchange and the Family," in Wesley R. Burr, Reuben Hill, F. Ivan Nye, and Ira L. Reiss, eds. *Contemporary Theories about the Family,* Vol. II. New York: The Free Press, 1979. Ch. 1.

OPINION RESEARCH CORPORATION. *National Statistical Survey on Runaway Youth.* Princeton, N.J.: Opinion Research Corporation, 1976.

RALLINGS, E. M., and NYE, F. IVAN. "Wife-Mother Employment, Family, and Society," in Wesley R. Burr, Reuben Hill, F. Ivan Nye, and Ira L. Reiss, eds. *Contemporary Theories about the Family,* Vol. I. New York: The Free Press, 1979. Ch. 9.

*RICHARDS, R. "Transactional Analysis as a Conceptual Framework." Unpublished seminar paper (Florida State University, Department of Home and Family Life, 1979).

RICHER, STEPHEN. "The Economics of Child Rearing," *Journal of Marriage and the Family,* 30 (Aug. 1968), pp. 462–66.

RUANO, BETTY, BRUCE, JAMES, and McDERMOTT, MARGARET. "Pilgrim's Progress II: Recent Trends and Prospects in Family Research," *Journal of Marriage and the Family,* 31 (Nov. 1969), pp. 688–98.

SCHNEIDER, LOUIS. *The Sociological Way of Looking at the World.* New York: McGraw-Hill, Inc., 1975.

SIMMEL, GEORG. *Conflict and the Web of Group Affiliation.* New York: The Free Press, 1955.

SIMPSON, R. L. *Theories of Social Exchange.* Morristown, N.J.: General Learning Press, 1972.

SPREY, JETSE. "Conflict Theory and the Study of Marriage and the Family," in Wesley R. Burr, Reuben Hill, F. Ivan Nye, and Ira L. Reiss, eds. *Contemporary Theories about the Family,* Vol. II. New York: The Free Press, 1979. Ch. 4.

———. "The Family as a System in Conflict," *Journal of Marriage and the Family,* 31 (Nov. 1969), pp. 699–706.

THIBAUT, JOHN W., and KELLEY, HAROLD H. *The Social Psychology of Groups.* New York: John Wiley and Sons, Inc., 1959.

ZETTERBERG, HANS L. *On Theory and Verification,* 3rd ed. Totowa, N.J.. The Bedminster Press, Inc., 1965.

*These papers are available from the ERIC Microfiche Collection, National Institute of Education, under the author's name.

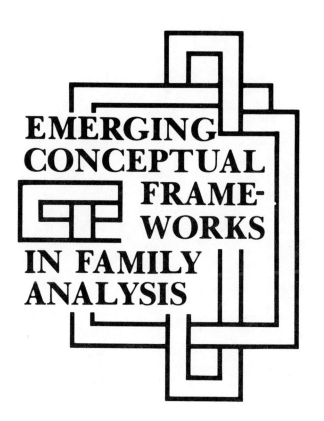

EMERGING CONCEPTUAL FRAME-WORKS IN FAMILY ANALYSIS

chapter I

Introduction

Family sociologists prior to 1960 had seldom asked publicly, What is and is not theory? It is true that the question has been raised by other sociologists, perhaps most succinctly by Merton (1957). Even the more recent review of the status of the study of the family by Goode (Merton *et al.;* 1959) is content with reviewing a few theoretical efforts of past family sociologists. However, he provides at least an implicit definition by stating "the striking fact [is] that no theorist has been able to state, let alone prove, *any set of systematic propositions* about the relations between the family and other institutions. . . ." (Italics supplied.)

It may be possible to make some progress in an intellectual enterprise without defining what is being attempted, but with a number of scholars commencing from different points with different intellectual tools and somewhat different objectives, confusion mounts rapidly, communication is difficult, and results are nonadditive— which is perhaps not an unfair characterization of family theory at the beginning of the 1960's. The "Grand Theories" of Zimmerman, Westermark, and other early theorists were in disuse. Parsons and others taking their cues from his approach to general theory were attempting to classify family behavior by the use of a few concepts; however, these produced little more than descriptions of the "logical" distribution of family behavior among family members. Finally, there were a number of more limited formulations varying from hypotheses such as Waller's Rating and Dating Hypotheses (1938) to Winch's more complex Theory of Complementary Needs (1958).

Just emerging at the turn of the decade and illustrated by Goode's work is the model of theory as a set of interrelated propositions. (By *propositions* we mean statements of relationships between events or properties.) This approach to theory was to be formulated and illustrated more fully by Zetterberg in his third edition of *On Theory and Verification* (1965). Zetterberg also notes that in 1960 there was not a great deal in current sociological use that could properly be labeled theory and, of that being employed, there were at least four different types of materials but no adequate definitions of what these "theories" constituted or what was the nature of their objectives. Zetterberg refers to these as (1) social classics (substantive), (2) sociological criticism, (3) sociological taxonomy, and (4) theoretical sociology.

Although theoretically-inclined family sociologists had until 1960 made only slow and uneven progress in formulating theory, the need for progress was rapidly evolving. The volume of research in the family area following World War II was large and growing. (Nye and Bayer, 1963.) Its sheer volume required systemization. A number of family sociologists, including Goode, Foote, and Hill, shifted their attention in part from research to evaluation and classification schemes. Toward the close of 1960, Hill and Hansen published their paper, "The Identification of Conceptual Frameworks Utilized in Family Study," (1960) which may well constitute a breakthrough *toward* the systematic construction of family theory. They are quick to point out that a conceptual framework does not constitute a theory. However, we believe that the delineation of such frameworks will expedite sound and accumulative development of theory.

THE NATURE OF CONCEPTUAL FRAMEWORKS

The idea of conceptual frameworks has been variously defined and employed. Currently it is referred to by Zetterberg (who is not much interested in it) as a group of concepts employed principally as a classification scheme or taxonomy, the specification of "a small number of definitions which delineate the few aspects of reality with which sociology deals. These definitions, broadly speaking, tell the sociologist what is important for him to pay attention to when he views a human relationship, a group, or a society." (1963, pp. 7–10.) For Zetterberg, such taxonomies are limited primarily to summarizing and inspiring descriptive studies. Hill and Hansen employ the notion of conceptual frameworks more broadly to include five categories of concepts: type of behavior treated, social space in which it occurs, time dimension with which it deals, substantive foci of research, and the basic assumptions which underly research and action.

(Hill and Hansen, 1960.) For the latter authors, the identification of conceptual frameworks is crucial both to the inventory and codification of family research on one hand, and, on the other, to the eventual development and accumulation of research propositions in family study.

The present volume was, to some extent, stimulated by the Hill-Hansen paper, and consequently the present development of the idea of conceptual frameworks bears a relationship to theirs. Our perception of a conceptual framework is the essential or important concepts employed and the basic assumptions which underlie the concepts and to a degree integrate them into a meaningful configuration. Besides what we regard as the core of the framework, we have chosen to consider as relevant a brief history of the development of the framework, the substantive problems on which those who employ it have concentrated, the value judgments or evaluations which have guided those contributing to the framework, and, finally, the impact which work done in this framework has had on research, theory, counseling and action programs. This idea of conceptual frameworks is not radically different from that of Hill and Hansen. It attempts something less detailed in the classification of concepts and in dealing with social time and space. It places somewhat more emphasis on basic assumptions as providing the integrating content of the framework and it attempts considerably more illustration and description. The treatment of values (although limited in scope) and the evaluation of the framework is explicit in the Nye-Berardo treatment whereas the former is not treated and the latter tends toward the incidental in the Hill-Hansen analysis.

Of the Zetterberg, Hill-Hansen, and Nye-Berardo ideas of conceptual frameworks, it can be said that a limited group of definitive concepts is central to each. To Zetterberg it apparently is no more than a group of concepts, usually employed in a classificatory scheme. To Hill and Hansen it is, first, a group of related concepts which can fruitfully be broken down into more homogeneous subgroups of concepts and, second, one which involves dimensions of time and space. The principal addition in the Nye-Berardo scheme is the emphasis on the underlying assumptions. These are seen as the connecting links in conceptual frameworks. We also give more prominence to the substantive concerns of those employing the framework and we give specific, if limited, attention to the value positions of the authors. Although not ignoring social time and space entirely, we do not treat them formally as do Hill and Hansen.

It may be concluded then, that both the Hill-Hansen and Nye-Berardo formulations involve considerably more than the Zetterberg definition. The former two deal, in general, with the same elements of a classification scheme but differ considerably in emphasis and in whether an element receives formal or informal treatment in the design.

CONCEPTUAL FRAMEWORKS AND RESEARCH

Concepts are in our estimation the most important of all sociological research tools. It must be admitted, however, that to date this potential has not been realized, since attention is usually focused on sampling techniques and manipulation of the data. Lack of attention to conceptualization and the relationship of working definitions to concepts has led to the development of inadequate measures of family properties. Conceptual frameworks providing adequate definitions of concepts would have reduced these measurement difficulties. Another way in which conceptual frameworks can facilitate the research process is by providing an "armory" of ideas. No researcher thinks of all the possible variables that might be employed in dealing with a problem. A review of the conceptual frameworks in his field would likely suggest some variables that would otherwise be overlooked.

In the study of the family, scholars from several disciplines and from a number of schools within disciplines have done and are doing research, theory-building, and counseling. Frequently it is important that a researcher not only know the substantive results of research done by someone employing another framework but also that he understand the essential concepts being employed and the principal assumptions on which the researcher proceeds. This is essentially a matter of effective communication between scholars who speak a different language with respect to concepts and make different implicit assumptions concerning the original nature of man, the socialization process, the part played by unconscious motivations, cultural and subcultural influences, and many other factors considered important to family behavior. It is problematic that, in the present development of knowledge in the behavioral sciences, the presence of numerous competing "languages" is only vaguely sensed and, even if their existence is understood, there is no adequate and convenient way for a scholar to become informed concerning the intellectual content of the other frameworks.

Even more difficult for the researcher to learn are the assumptions made by those employing various other frames of reference. On occasion the researcher may have identified them, but more frequently they are only implied and must be deduced from the variables he employs and interpretive statements he makes. Often the researcher is not entirely aware himself of the assumptions which must be made in his approach to a problem. For example, Freudian analysis assumes the original antisocial nature of the human being, whereas most sociological analyses begin with the assumption that it is asocial while some social-psychological frames of reference seem to assume that it is social. (See Chapter 7.) The nature of this basic assumption has a great deal of bearing on the type of concepts developed, the types of hypotheses posed, the theory developed, and the interpretations made from the data.

It is felt, therefore, that the delineation of the conceptual frameworks relevant to the study of the family can contribute to research by:

1. Making it explicit that a number of different frameworks exist and represent varied perspectives for viewing family behavior.
2. Providing a listing and definition of the central concepts of each framework so that these are readily available to the researcher.
3. Making explicit the implicit underlying assumptions of each framework.
4. Providing a bibliography of research done employing each frame of reference, that will afford the researcher convenient access to the relevant literature.

CONCEPTUAL FRAMEWORKS AND THEORY

The term *theory* has been employed in a variety of ways. Our view of it stems from Zetterberg (1963). He states that "I want to pursue sociological theory in the sense of systematically organized, law-like propositions about society and social life." The problem in such pursuit appears to be finding an adequate number of lawlike propositions relating to a given problem which would permit the formulation of significant hypotheses with a high rate of positive affirmation. Zetterberg acknowledges that sociologists can point to few theories based on these criteria. The writers are unable to describe one theory in the area of the family in which the propositions are lawlike.

It is our feeling that conceptual frameworks are a useful first step in theory-building in that they introduce an element of orderliness into research processes and findings. They are a useful tool in the development of propositions which will stand the tests of replication by other researchers and application to other populations with different cultures or subcultures. In short, we suggest that conceptual frameworks are necessary for good research and that good research is, in turn, necessary for the development of valid theory.

PLAN OF THE VOLUME

This book developed from a graduate seminar on conceptual frameworks offered by the senior editor in the spring of 1963. The seminar was inspired by the need for sociologists, psychologists, social workers, and economists and others to communicate with each other and with the faculty in an interdivisional graduate program. The strategies in developing the frameworks owe much to the Hill-Hansen (1960) article on conceptual frameworks. However, the need was felt for a broader treatment than theirs since they had elected to limit themselves to frameworks that deal with the family as a group, that is, sociological frameworks.[1] Our interest included not only this but also a broader set of behavior such as dyadic relationships between family members, impact of family or family-member behavior on the socialization or behavior patterns of family members, the welfare of family members, and the impact of other institutions on family or family-member behavior. This delineation transcended the treatment of family behavior as group behavior.

The criteria for inclusion of a conceptual framework are that it

1. Have a major commitment to the study of family roles, the family as a group, family relationships and/or their impact on the socialization and functioning of the child.

[1] The present book is essentially a parallel development to the conceptual frameworks chapters in Harold T. Christensen (ed.), *Handbook of Marriage and the Family* (Chicago: Rand McNally & Company, 1964). Although the Christensen volume appeared before this one, the plan of this volume and drafts of its chapters were completed before the other one appeared. One chapter of the Christensen book was available to the authors in draft form while the parallel chapter was being written for this book. Reference is made to that fact in the appropriate chapter in this volume.

2. Have developed a substantial body of concepts employed in such study.
3. Have a distinctive set of assumptions concerning the individual, society, and/or family relationships.

Employing these criteria, a broad analysis of social science and related fields was undertaken with the result that 11 frameworks were identified. Four were drawn from sociology, one partly from sociology and partly from child development, two from psychology, and one each from economics, religion, law, and anthropology.

Considerable discussion preceded and followed the selection of the frameworks. Those already identified by Hill and Hansen were included on the grounds that previous work justified it. The psychoanalytic, economic, and anthropological frameworks employ numerous distinctive concepts and distinguishable underlying assumptions. The social-psychological framework appeared somewhat lacking in cohesion, but is important because of its distinctive psychological concepts and assumptions and because it has produced an important body of research. The religious and legal frameworks have not been related closely to the others listed above but they, no less than the others, have distinctive groups of concepts and underlying assumptions concerning the nature of the family—which form the basis for many counseling and action programs.

Each of the eleven frameworks is presented in a chapter following a common outline which starts with (1) a note on the historical development of the framework, (2) foci of study (that is, substantive content), (3) concepts, (4) basic assumptions, (5) product, or impact on family study, (6) value orientation of scholars, (7) a restatement of the framework, (8) an evaluation of its contributions, contradictions, and inadequacies, and (9) an annotated bibliography.

The use of the same outline for describing all conceptual frameworks produces some strains since it was composed with primary reference to the frameworks that have generated extensive research. Even the stresses that become evident in its use, however, may perform a latent function in throwing into sharper contrast the preoccupations, objectives, and strategies of the several disciplines and professions.

Our objective throughout has been to mirror faithfully and accurately the concepts, assumptions, and products of the several frameworks. In order to accomplish this, contributors were asked to include all concepts, assumptions, and scholars' works which they felt belonged in that framework. This naturally resulted in considerable overlap in the frameworks, especially the sociological. This overlap was accepted because in our judgment it best represents the intellectual world of those employing the framework. Most of the frameworks share a number of concepts and assumptions with some other framework, and several scholars of the family at different times in their lives have employed significant portions of more than one framework. Since conceptual frameworks do, in fact, overlap, our formulation includes this overlapping characteristic. The present volume is essentially a model of what conceptual frameworks *are*, rather than what they might be under hypothetical circumstances.

We are under no illusions that the final word on conceptual frameworks is provided in this book. On the contrary, we feel that the development of this intellectual approach is still in its formative stages and that the present volume is a pioneer one with the shortcomings of such enterprises. We are convinced, however, that conceptual frameworks bring some order from the chaos that has characterized the study of man and his relations to his fellows. This volume is offered as a step in such development.

In a period of increasing specialization and increasing preoccupation with immediate problems in the several behavioral sciences and professions, the present volume is offered to the continued interest in knowing and understanding something outside of the day-to-day intellectual preoccupations of individual scholars and their immediate associates. Its contributors include sociologists, psychologists, lawyers, religious scholars, and economists. Because of the far-flung intellectual area covered in this book, which extends beyond the personal competence of the editors, we have enlisted the assistance of ten distinguished scholars, George P. Murdock, Norman W. Bell, John Sirjamaki, Sheldon Stryker, Eleanor S. Boll, George Simpson, John T. Greene, Roy H. Rodgers, Frederica Carleton, and Seward Hiltner, each of whom has employed a given conceptual framework in making his own intellectual contribution, as a consulting editor for the respective appropriate frameworks. This has afforded a degree of protection against dealing with content which must, in some instances, be relatively unfamiliar territory. We are grateful for these contributions, which are indicated specifically in the particular chapters on which the editorial consultants served.

We are grateful also to Hans Zetterberg and Jessie Bernard for reading the manuscript and offering both encouragement in its over-all concept and criticism for specific inadequacies. These inadequacies have not been entirely overcome, but the book is materially better for their reactions. Acknowledgment is also made to the stimulus of the Inter-Divisional Program in Marriage and Family Living at Florida State University, with which the editors as well as the contributors were at one time associated, and which convinced the senior editor of the need for a comprehensive volume on conceptual frameworks.

Special thanks are offered to Washington State University for providing support for the completion of the project, and especially to Walter L. Slocum, Lowell Rasmussen, Mark T. Buchanan, and Wallis Beasley for their interest in and willingness to support an intellectual enterprise which defied classification into any specialized, well-defined category in the university structure.[2]

REFERENCES

Goode, William J. "The Sociology of the Family," in Robert K. Merton, Leonard Broom, and Leonard S. Cottrell, Jr. *Sociology Today*. New York: Basic Books, Inc., Publishers, 1959, Chap. 7.

Hill, Reuben, and Hansen, Donald A. "The Identification of Conceptual Frameworks Utilized in Family Study," *Marriage and Family Living*, 22 (Nov. 1960), pp. 299–311.

Merton, Robert K. *Social Theory and Social Structure*. New York: Free Press of Glencoe, Inc., 1957.

Nye, F. Ivan, and Bayer, Alan. "Some Recent Trends in Family Research," *Social Forces*, 41 (March 1963), pp. 290–301.

Waller, Willard. *The Family, A Dynamic Interpretation*. New York: The Dryden Press, Inc., 1938.

Winch, Robert F. *Mate Selection*. New York: Harper & Row, Publishers, 1958.

Zetterberg, Hans L. *On Theory and Verification*, 3rd ed. Totowa, N.J.: The Bedminster Press, Inc., 1965.

———. *On Theory and Verification*, 2nd ed. Totowa, N.J.: The Bedminster Press, 1963.

[2] Work on this book was supported in part under Project 1778 of the Agricultural Experiment Stations of Washington State University.

chapter 2

The Anthropological Approach
to the Study of the Family*

Felix M. Berardo

Previous efforts by anthropologists in the field of family and kinship to formally specify their particular frame of reference are
surprisingly few in number and tend to be rather general in nature.
Mead, for example, in commenting on the contemporary American
family "as an anthropologist sees it," notes that anthropological contributions to the study of the family have generally taken the form
of detailed investigations of American culture (1) by anthropologists
trained as ethnologists, (2) on the basis of some of the premises and
methods which have been developed in ethnological research, (3)
through use of diagnostic studies of regularities in American culture
against the background of research in several other cultures, and (4)
through use of anthropological concepts in the theoretical analysis
of American problems. (1948, p. 453.) Unfortunately, Mead did not
attempt to spell out these broad categories of investigation nor to
relate them specifically to family research, but concentrated primarily on a description of various aspects of family patterns in the
United States at mid-twentieth century.

* Grateful acknowledgment is made of the contribution of George Peter
Murdock, who served as editorial consultant for this framework and who
read and critically reviewed the manuscript prior to its final revision. Many,
although not all, of his suggestions have been incorporated into the final
manuscript. Inadequacies and errors in the chapter as published, however, are
entirely the responsibility of the author and the editors.

In his discussion of "an anthropological approach to family studies," Lewis comes to the conclusion that the discipline has in fact neglected this field. "Anthropologists have developed no special methodology for family studies and to my knowledge there is not a single published study in the entire anthropological literature of a family as a unit." (1950, p. 470.) Lewis, of course, made this statement over a decade ago and was referring primarily to case-history investigations of particular families in various societies or cultures. Nonetheless, certain of his remarks are explicitly related to the present analysis, especially those concerning the comparison between anthropological and sociological treatment of the family:

> If sociological studies of the family have tended to be of the segmental, specific problem type, the work of the anthropologist has been of the opposite kind, that is, generalized descriptions with little or no sense of problem. In most anthropological community studies, the family is presented as a stereotype. We are told not about a particular family but about the family life in general. . . . And always the emphasis is upon the formal aspects of the family rather than upon the content and variety of actual family life. (pp. 470–71.)

The anthropologists, then, are criticized for presenting what is considered to be an unduly mechanical and static picture of the relationship between the individual, his family, and his culture.

In his own research on Mexican families over the past fifteen years, Lewis has employed a variety of related approaches which, in his opinion, may be combined to provide a rounded and integrated anthropological study of family life. The description of these approaches is extremely brief, however, and specific information regarding the make-up of the conceptual frameworks involved is not provided:

> The first or topical approach applies most of the conceptual categories used in the study of an entire community to a single family. The data on the family are organized and presented under the headings of material culture, economic life, social relations, religious life, interpersonal relations, and so on. From a great mass of information based upon living with the family, interviews, and extended observation, the aspects of the family and of the individual members of the family are reconstructed.

This approach is analytical and has the advantage of permitting comparisons between family cultures and the larger culture outside the family.

A second approach is the Rashomon-like technique of seeing the family through the eyes of each of its members. This is done through long, intensive autobiographies of each member of the family. This gives more insight into the individual psychology and feeling tone as well as an indirect, subjective view of family dynamics. This type of material would probably be most useful to the psychologist. Its methodological advantage derives from the independent versions of similar incidents in family life which amount to a check on the validity and reliability of the data.

The third approach is to select for intensive study a problem or a special event or crisis to which the family reacts. The way a family meets new situations is revealing particularly of many latent aspects of family psychodynamics; it also points up individual differences.

A fourth approach to the study of the family as a whole is through detailed observation of a typical day in the life of the family. To give depth and meaning to this approach it must be combined with the other three. (1959, pp. 3–4.)

Lewis has effectively utilized the latter approach in combination with the others, most noticeably in his *Five Families* (1959), *The Children of Sanchez* (1961), and, more recently *Pedro Martinez* (1964).

In previous as well as more recent attempts to identify conceptual frameworks utilized in family research, Hill associates the field of social anthropology with the structure-functional frame of reference, "which views the family as a social system, has its roots in anthropology and sociology, and is rapidly winning adherents in the United States and Europe." (Hill and Hansen, 1960, pp. 299–311.) Since the rationale for this association is not provided, we shall examine the matter below in some detail in an effort to more adequately relate these streams of family theory and research.

Cultural and Social Anthropology

In the behavioral-science literature one frequently encounters the terms *cultural anthropology* and *social anthropology* being used interchangeably, with the implication that they are one and the same. It should be pointed out, however, that many anthropologists, especially those identified with the English and American schools of thought, are by no means in complete agreement with this position.[1] The subject does have some bearing on the manner in which the family is to be theoretically conceived, and for this reason it appears important that the distinction be clarified.

American cultural anthropology is typically subdivided into the separate but complimentary areas of ethnology and ethnography, the former generally characterized as "the comparative study of culture and the investigation of theoretical problems that arise out of the analysis of custom," and the latter as "the description of individual cultures." (Herskovits, 1949, p. 9.) However, certain English and American scholars refer to cultural anthropology as social anthropology, in which case "ethnology becomes the description of individual cultures [and] . . . social anthropology is assigned something of the role we give ethnology." (*Ibid.*) Evans-Pritchard in his treatment of British theoretical social anthropology (1952, p. 3) and Levi-Strauss, the outstanding French theorist, have made a similar distinction. (1963, p. 2.) The field of ethnology is conceded to have had its major development in the United States, where primary emphasis was placed upon culture history and culture process. Social anthropology, on the other hand, is viewed largely as a product of British anthropology, and has emphasized social structure and function as its major concepts. (Eggan, 1954, p. 743.)

The orientation of social anthropology traces its beginnings to the early theoretical formulations of Malinowski and Radcliffe-Brown, the latter demonstrating

> how social behavior is keyed to structure. In particular, he rescued kinship from the morass in which it had been left by Morgan and Rivers—as a set of survivals from which earlier forms of marriage and kin groups could supposedly be inferred —and showed that nomenclature, patterns of kinship behavior, marriage rules, and aggregates of kinsmen tend to be related to one another in consistent ways within any social system. (Murdock, 1951, p. 469.)

[1] For some recent comments concerning the distinction between social and cultural anthropology, see Levi-Strauss (1963) and Beattie (1964).

Contemporary British social anthropologists, lead by Firth and Fortes and their students, have continued to emphasize the structure-functional conceptual framework.[2] They have their counterparts in the United States in the works of Linton, Warner, Whyte, West, Arensberg, Kimball, and others.

American ethnologists, on the other hand, with their interest in culture history and culture process, tend to utilize a more general and less explicit "theory" of culture: "Assuming culture to be their province, most anthropologists," according to Murdock, "feel free to explore its every ramification . . . to study the processes by which it grows (culture change), is transmitted from one generation to the next (education and socialization), and is spread geographically (diffusion or cultural borrowing), and are thus driven irresistibly to an interest in history, psychology, and geography." (1951, p. 471.) The basic assumptions underlying this general theory of culture have been variously stated. Murdock, for instance, has identified seven assumptions which, for convenience and without elaboration may be compressed into this statement: Culture is learned, inculcated (that is, transmitted), social, ideational, gratifying, adaptive, and integrative. (1940, pp. 364–69.) Herskovits has compiled a similar list of propositions which, taken together, form his theory of culture.[3] Such general theories are apparently compatible with a wide variety of approaches to family life in American anthropology. In particular, they appear quite amenable to those anthropologists employing a psychological frame of reference. (See Appendix 1.)

Proponents of culture theory often view themselves at variance with the functionalism of social anthropology. Thus, for example, Murdock, in reviewing British social anthropology, accuses the latter of (1) concentrating exclusively on kinship and subjects directly

[2] Fortes' remark that "social structure is not an aspect of culture but the entire culture of a given people handled in a special frame of theory," is perhaps the most explicit, even though extreme, statement of this position. (1953), p. 23. It appears that Davis has taken essentially the same position in his well-known essay, "The Myth of Functional Analysis as a Special Method in Sociology and Anthropology" (1959), p. 757.

[3] Herskovits has presented these propositions: (1) culture is learned; (2) culture derives from the biological, environmental, psychological, and historical components of human existence; (3) culture is structured; (4) culture is divided into aspects; (5) culture is dynamic; (6) culture is variable; (7) culture exhibits regularities that permit its analysis by the methods of science; (8) culture is the instrument whereby the individual adjusts to his total setting and gains the means for creative expression. (1949), p. 625.

related thereto,[4] such as marriage, property, and government, (2) exhibiting an almost complete disinterest in history, and (3) showing considerable indifference to psychology. (1951, pp. 467–69.) He comes to the "startling conclusion" that "they are actually not anthropologists, but professionals of another category"; that "in their fundamental objectives and theoretical orientation they are affiliated rather with sociologists"; and that "like other sociologists, they are interested primarily in social groups and the structuring of interpersonal relations, rather than culture, and in synchronic rather than diachronic correlations." (p. 471.) British social anthropologists themselves consider their discipline to be separate and distinct from that of American ethnologists. (Evans-Pritchard, 1952, p. 4.)

There have been attempts to reconcile the different points of view as evidenced, for instance, in the suggestion by Eggan that the "structural point of view makes possible a superior organization and interpretation of the cultural data; and good monographs may well be related to this point of view . . . we need to adopt the structural-functional approach of British social anthropologists and integrate it with our traditional American interest in culture process and history." (1954, p. 745.) Eggan further suggests that American anthropologists cultivate more intensely the middle range of theory proposed by Merton.

The preceding analysis, admittedly brief, leads to the conclusion that there are essentially two major anthropological approaches to family study: (1) the structure-functional framework, exemplified by the social anthropologists and (2) the institutional frame of reference characteristic of cultural anthropologists. Hill and Hansen evidently take a similar position with respect to social anthropology,

---

[4] Social anthropologists recognize this emphasis. Note, for example, the recent commentary by Beattie: "Social anthropologists are sometimes accused of concerning themselves overmuch with the refinements and complexities of kinship terminologies. . . . But there are good reasons for this concern. Very few of the interpersonal relationships which make up a Western European's social world are kinship ones. Kinship plays little or no part in his relations with his friends, his employers, his teachers, his colleagues, or in the complex network of political, economic and religious associations in which he is involved. But in many smaller-scale societies kinship's social importance is paramount. Where a person lives, his group and community membership, whom he should obey and by whom he is obeyed, who are his friends and who his enemies, whom he may and may not marry, from whom he may hope to inherit and to whom pass on his status and property—all these matters and many more may be determined by his status in a kinship system." (1964), p. 93.

but they identify the institutional approach with the disciplines of sociology and historical sociology, with no specific reference to cultural anthropology. (1960, pp. 299–311.) An examination of the properties of the institutional framework which they delineate, however, and in particular the concepts they list as belonging to this approach, reveals a heavy reliance upon cultural anthropology. Herskovits provides sufficient documentation for the latter statement in his *Man and His Works: The Science of Cultural Anthropology* (1949). In it the reader will find ample citations and illustrations of several major terms depicted by Hill and Hansen as belonging to the sociological-institutional approach.

It is not necessary to belabor the point, but merely to raise it.[5] Three alternatives are suggested: (1) there is an institutional framework peculiar to sociology or (2) there is an institutional framework peculiar to cultural anthropology or (3) the frame of reference is common to both disciplines as a result of historical and interdisciplinary developments. Sirjamaki's recent presentation of the institutional approach to study of the family would seem to favor the latter alternative. (In Christensen, 1964, pp. 33–50.) Whatever the case, it appears further clarification is needed on this point.[6] Since the present analysis concentrates on the structure-functional approach of social anthropology, no further attempt is made here.

Social Anthropology: A Structure-Functional Approach

There is a certain consensus that the field of social anthropology—often referred to as *comparative sociology*—is based upon sociological conceptions and anthropological data. That is to say, its

> theoretical orientation is properly with sociology rather than with anthropology, for the comparative sociologist is concerned with social explanation, rather than cultural, [and] . . . tries to derive generalizations about behavior of persons in groups, rather than about cultural continua; to seek both the sociological imperatives that operate irrespective of particular cultures and the sociologically derived variations between cultural forms." (Goldschmidt, 1953, p. 287.)

[5] Mead's comment on the contributions of anthropology to the study of the family, to which we referred on page 1, for example, would seem to apply to cultural anthropology.

[6] The theoretical discussion by Duncan and Schnore on differentiating the "cultural, behavioral, and ecological perspectives" may be helpful in this connection. (1959), pp. 132–46.

Theoretically, societies are viewed as functioning wholes, all the parts of which are closely interrelated. To evaluate any particular subunit or system such as the family, one must (1) indicate its place in the society as a whole, (2) show its relation to other subsystems, and (3) attempt to specify the particular functions that it performs in promoting the existence of society. The essence of this approach is captured in an early statement by one of its original proponents, Bronislaw Malinowski, who remarked how the functionalist point of view "aims at the explanation of anthropological facts at all levels of development by their function, by the part which they play within the integral system of culture, by the manner in which they are related to each other within the system, and by the manner in which this system is related to the physical surroundings." (1926, pp. 132–33.) A contemporary exponent of British social anthropology, Evans-Pritchard, has expressed a similar notion:

> A total social structure, that is to say the entire structure of a given society, is composed of a number of subsidiary structures or systems, and we may speak of its kinship system, its economic system, its religious system, and its political system. . . . The social activities within these systems or structures are organized round institutions such as marriage, the family, markets, chieftainships, and so forth; and when we speak of the functions of these institutions we mean the part they play in the maintenance of the structure. (1952, p. 20.)

It is this type of perspective which has served as the theoretical background for a number of recent studies in England on marriage, the family, and kinship, such as those conducted by Firth and his associates in 1956.

The approach has been characterized as holistic, and its major interest lies in what has been termed *macrosocial organization*. It involves what Hill has called *macrofunctionalism*, which concerns itself with the family—as opposed to individual families—as an abstraction useful in institutional analysis. As Hill and Hansen have observed (1960), the functionalist approach to the family is broad:

> the framework posits both an internal system for regulating relations within the family and an external system for dealing with the transactions between the family and non-family events. The framework thus encompasses the interplay between (1) the

family and collateral systems like the school, the occupational world, and the market place, and (2) the transactions between the family and the smaller sub-groups of the husband-wife dyad, the sibling cliques, and the individual personality systems of family members.

In this framework, then, the family is perceived as an open system sensitive to external influences and transactions (the family treated as a dependent variable) as well as a system which tends to maintain its boundaries (the family treated as a closed system). Social anthropological investigations lean heavily toward the former viewpoint, that is, treating the family in relation to external factors. In this connection, "the individual family member is viewed more as a reactive bundle of statuses and roles than as an active, action initiating person." (*Ibid.*)

FOCI OF STUDY

Homans has stated that in studying primitive kinship one crosses the line that divides sociology from social anthropology. (1950, p. 192.) Social anthropologists have, for the most part, concentrated their efforts on investigations of primitive or communal societies which are typically small, with a relatively simple division of labor and a limited differentiation of roles.[7] In such societies, immediate families and larger kinship groups often nearly exhaust the group memberships and constitute the important units within the society as a whole. Anthropological investigations have often revealed that in this type of social structure behavior is regulated primarily by custom or tradition. The family—or some larger kinship group—is taken to be the most significant social unit to which individuals belong, and the majority of any one individual's roles and relationships are viewed as being heavily dependent upon such membership.[8]

---

[7] The characteristics of such a community in its "ideal" state have been summarized by Chinoy: "In the communal society social roles are inclusive rather than segmental, social relationships are personal and intimate, and there are comparatively few sub-groups other than family and kinship units. In this typically small, isolated, non-literate and homogeneous society, with a strong sense of group solidarity, tradition permeates all aspects of life and the range of alternative patterns of behavior open to individuals is inevitably restricted." (1961), p. 89.

[8] See Chinoy's comments on how numerous anthropological investigations have revealed the difficulty of distinguishing economic, political, and religious institutions and roles from those of marriage and the family in such societies. (1961), p. 106.

Social anthropologists focus on the *formal aspects* of the systems of marriage and the family, such as composition, residence rules, kinship obligations, parental-authority patterns, marriage forms and regulations, separations, and so on, and attempt to trace the structural implications of these aspects for the community as a whole. Thus, Fortes, in discussing the study of marriage, states: "A complex and fundamental problem in the comparative sociology of marriage is that of the regulations, conditions and criteria governing the choice of a spouse and the procedure of espousal entailed thereby. For everything connected with marriage is directed to this outcome." (1962, p. 2.) In analyzing the manner in which marriages are terminated, for example, and the frequency with which this occurs, the social anthropologist concerns himself with distinguishing the pattern of divorce which characterizes a society and tracing the ways in which this is related to other features of the social system. He deals with such questions as: who initiates divorce, at what point in a person's life divorce is most likely to occur, the reallocation of rights and obligations which follow divorce, the available alternatives, and the spatial correlates of divorce. (Goody, in Fortes, 1962, pp. 14–54.)

The social anthropologist also engages in analyses of the nature of affinal roles and relationships and their connection with other institutions. In a recent investigation, for example, Harris attempts "to seek out the interconnection between the form of affinal relationships on the one hand and, on the other, the distribution of affinal ties —between the *how* and *who* of affinity," and "the interconnection between the dominant forms of affinal relationships as related to the age-status system on the one hand and other features of the social structure on the other." (In Fortes, 1962, pp. 55–87.)

More often than not, however, the social anthropologist will choose to focus primarily on the kinship system at large, attempting to gain some understanding of its underlying principles and the structural implications of these principles. (Olderogge, 1961.) Firth has commented on the theoretical importance of such analyses: "The study of kinship is a perennial theme for the social anthropologist. An understanding of the kinship system in any society is essential as clues to the working of some of the most fundamental relationships—sexual, marital, economic, in that society. It also may be of prime importance in the process of socialization, in developing patterns of reaction to authority and in providing important symbols for the moral evaluation of conduct." (1956, p. 11.) In a similar vein, Radcliffe-Brown's introductory statement to *African Systems of Kinship and Marriage* aptly conveys the importance of this aspect of social organization to social anthropological inquiries concerning family life:

> In these essays I have referred to "Kinship systems." The idea is that in a given society we can isolate conceptually, if not in reality, a certain set of actions and interactions amongst persons which are determined by the relationships of kinship and marriage, and that in a particular society these are interconnected in such a way that we can give a general analytical description of them as constituting a system. The theoretical significance of this idea of systems is that our first step in an attempt to understand a regular feature of a form of social life . . . is to discover its place in the system of which it is a part. (1950, p. 6.)

It should be noted that the quotation also contains certain assumptions regarding the framework under discussion, and these assumptions shall be examined more fully in the appropriate section below.

In sum, it may be said that the social anthropologist concerns himself with a variety of problems revolving around the institutionalized forms in which human groups are organized, how the group members conventionally seek their mates, the lines along which such mating is permitted, and the resulting family structures, as well as how these primary groupings proliferate into the broader units of social organization.

Comparative Analysis

A related and integral aspect of the anthropological approach to family study is the comparative method. In an early statement by Mead, the comparative analysis is viewed as an attempt to arrive at a general understanding of an institution of universal occurrence—such as the family—by a "critical comparative study of its various manifestations in differing cultures at different periods in history." (1932, p. 23.) According to Mead, this method may further serve as a "useful corrective of attempts to theorize upon the family's loss of functions; for the comparative student will realize that the family has had many and various functions, of varying degrees of social importance, as it has occurred in different types of culture." (*Ibid.*)

Social anthropologists engage in comparative analyses of related cultural forms, such as the comparison of forms of marriage and divorce, to provide clues to the function any specific form may serve in a given society. "The essence of the comparative method in social anthropology is that comparison is made between items of behavior in different major social units, with the object of establishing types and seeing variants from them." (Firth, 1951, p. 18.) Perhaps more to the point, the comparative method allows concise testing of specific hypotheses, illustrated by Murdock's study (1950) of family stability in non-European societies.

Comparison may be carried out either on the quantitative or qualitative levels of analysis. The former type of comparative method is illustrated by Murdock's well-known *Social Structure* (1949) which concentrates on family and kinship organization in relation to the regulation of sex and marriage. Here the emphasis is on cross cultural investigation of a large sample of societies in terms of a limited number of traits or variables by means of statistical analysis.[9]

A second type of comparative approach is illustrated in *African Systems of Kinship and Marriage*, edited by Radcliffe-Brown and Forde. In the introduction to this volume, the authors propose that:

Analysis . . . is a procedure that can only be applied to something that is in itself a whole or synthesis. By it we separate out, in reality or in thought, the components of a complex whole and thereby discover the relation of these components to one another within the whole. To arrive at an understanding of kinship systems we must use comparison and analysis in combination by comparing many different systems with one another and by subjecting single systems to systematic analysis.

A study of kinship systems all over the world by this method reveals that while there is a very wide range of variation in their superficial features there can be discovered a certain small number of general structural principles which are applied and

[9] For more recent and statistically sophisticated analyses along these lines see Homans and Schneider (1955), Schneider and Gough (1961), and Gouldner and Peterson (1962). The latter study, for example, is an exploratory analysis of data from seventy-one primitive societies and has the following objectives: "(1) It seeks to identify fundamental dimensions or subsystems common to such societies, and (2) To examine some of their relations to each other, thus to see them systematically, and (3) To assess the relative importance of these dimensions. (4) It aims to pursue the above objectives with a systematic body of empirical data derived from the Human Relations Area Files and with statistical methods, rather than calling upon random anecdotal materials or impressionistic insight." p. 1.

combined in various ways. It is one of the first tasks of a theoretical study of kinship to discover these principles by a process
of abstractive generalization based on analysis and comparison.
(1950, p. 2.)

The method proposed here has tended to take a highly qualitative
form emphasizing analytical description of the systems under investigation, with considerably less emphasis on statistical procedures
for mobilizing the data and arriving at generalizations. The general
assumption underlying this method is perhaps most simply expressed
by Timasheff: "Qualitatively, if two social situations could be found
differing by the presence or absence of a particular trait or partial
structure, the differential consequences of this dissimilarity for the
survival and prosperity of the total system may be established."
(1957, p. 229.)

Social anthropologists, of course, can and do utilize both quantitative and qualitative methods at the same time, and a variety of
comparative techniques have been described and suggested in the
literature. Discussions by Schapera (1953), Eggan (1954), and
McEwen (1963), are particularly recommended in this connection.
McEwen's remarks are especially revealing regarding attempts by
social anthropologists to validate their findings.

CONCEPTS

Anthropologists employ a plethora of significant concepts in their
analysis of the family and society. Many of these concepts have pro-
liferated into the general language of the behavioral sciences; for
example, those relative to the forms of marriage, such as monogamy
and polygamy, or to the rules of marriage, such as endogamy and
exogamy. Others have been found to be quite amenable to interdisciplinary research on family life. And still others remain unique
to the field itself. Consequently, only a limited selection of the major
concepts utilized by contemporary social anthropologists are presented in the form of definitions or illustrations taken directly from
the literature; others have been simply listed.[10]

An attempt has also been made to loosely group those concepts

[10] The concepts cited should be viewed as representative rather than exhaustive. For a recent publication in which some of the major terms peculiar to
social anthropology are presented and discussed, see Mair (1963). A list of
concepts and definitions specifically related to the study of kinship is provided
by Zelditch, in Faris (1964), pp. 716–17.

which would ordinarily be found occurring together in the analysis of a particular subsystem, such as the family. Finally, it must be noted that there is a good deal of terminological debate among anthropologists regarding nomenclature. The conceptualization of the family, for example, has often been subject to debate.[11] It is obvious, therefore, that some of the definitions and/or illustrations presented do not necessarily have complete consensus among family and kinship specialists. With the latter precaution in mind, we may proceed.

CONCEPTS	DEFINITION AND/OR ILLUSTRATIONS
Family Nuclear family Extended family (joint) Family of orientation Family of procreation	The family, as distinguished from the more embracing kinship structure, consists of a group made up of "adults of both sexes at least two of whom maintain a socially approved sexual relationship, and one or more children, own or adopted, of the sexually cohabiting adults." (Murdock, 1949.)
	"The unit of structure from which a kinship is built up is the group which I call an 'elementary family,' consisting of a man and his wife and their child or children. . . . The existence of the elementary family creates three special kinds of social relationship, that between parent and child, that between children of the same parents (siblings), and that between husband and wife as parents of the same child or children. . . ." (Radcliffe-Brown, 1941.)
	"But certain important groupings depend upon bilateral and also affinal kinship, and are frequently associated with common residence. The best known and most widespread grouping founded on kinship is the extended family, sometimes called the joint family because of their common claims to land and certain kinds of property. The extended family is a group founded on kinship and locality, and resulting from the

[11] An overview of this question including pertinent references regarding the definitions and functions of the family may be found in Zelditch, in Faris (1964), pp. 680–82. His remarks concerning the disparity between the sociologists' use of the term *extended family* and the anthropological definition of this concept are also of interest.

rules of patrilocal or matrilocal marriage. It is a socially recognized group of individual families living together in close association, which are bound together by the fact that either: (A) The men in each of the individual families are genealogically related in the male line (the patrilineal or patrilocal extended family); or (B) The women in each of the individual families are genealogically related in the female line (the matrilineal or matrilocal extended family)." (Piddington, 1950.)

Conjugal family system
Consanguineal family system

A system in which the conjugal ties are given preponderant importance is called a *conjugal* family system; one in which ties to blood kin are emphasized is called *consanguine:* "In societies organized upon the conjugal basis we can picture the authentic functional family as consisting of a nucleus of spouses and their off-spring surrounded by a fringe of relatives. In those organized on the consanguine basis we can picture the authentic family as a nucleus of blood relatives surrounded by a fringe of spouses." (Linton, 1936.)

Marriage and parenthood
  Exogamy
  Endogamy
  Levirate
  Sororate
  Hypergamy
  Hypogamy
  Monogamy
  Polygamy
  Polygyny
  Polyandry

Marriage consists of the rules and regulations which govern the relationships between spouses. Such rules define how the relationship shall be established or terminated, the expectations and obligations it entails, and the persons who are eligible to enter such a relationship. "Marriage cannot be defined as the licensing of sexual intercourse but rather the licensing of parenthood." (Malinowski, 1930.)

"If we regard marriage as a relationship not just between individuals, but also, at least potentially, between groups, then an important distinction is that between endogamy and exogamy. The terms . . . simply mean that one must 'marry in' or 'marry out'; that is, inside or outside of a social group to which one belongs. Since the terms

CONCEPTS	DEFINITION AND/OR ILLUSTRATIONS

are relative, it is necessary when using them to define the group within which, or outside of which, one must marry." (Beattie, 1964.)

"Under the levirate, when a man dies his widow becomes the wife of one of his brothers. In some communities a man must marry his deceased brother's wife, in others he may waive the right. . . . The term sororate is a somewhat ambiguous one, being used in three different senses by various writers to refer to: (a) the rule whereby a man who marries a woman has a preemptive right to marry also her younger sisters as they reach maturity; (b) the rule whereby if a man wishes to marry more than one wife, the subsidiary wives must be sisters of his first wife; (c) the rule whereby if a man marries and his first wife dies, then his wife's kinfolk are under an obligation to provide him with another wife, particularly if the first wife had died childless." (Piddington, 1950.)

Kinship systems
  Descent systems
    Patrilineal (unilateral)
    Matrilineal (unilateral)
    Bilateral
    Ambilineal

From the point of view of the individual, kinship refers to "any relationship . . . to another through his father and mother. All kinship ties thus derive from the family, that universal and fundamental group which everywhere and in some way or another incorporates the institution of marriage." (Evans-Pritchard, 1951.)

"A kinship system is therefore a network of social relations which constitute part of that total network of social relations which is the social structure. The rights and duties of relatives to one another are part of the system and so are the terms used in addressing or referring to relatives." (Radcliffe-Brown, 1950.)

"A rule of descent affiliates an individual at birth with a particular group of relatives with whom he is especially intimate and

CONCEPTS	DEFINITION AND/OR ILLUSTRATIONS

from whom he can expect certain kinds of services that he cannot demand of non-relatives, or even of other kinsmen. The fundamental rules of descent are only three in number: patrilineal descent, which affiliates a person with a group of kinsmen who are related to him through males only; matrilineal descent, which assigns him to a group consisting exclusively of relatives through females; and bilateral descent, which associates him with a group of very close relatives irrespective of their particular genealogical connection to him." (Murdock, 1949.)

Consanguineal groups
Lineage
Sib
Phratry
Moiety
Clan
Kindred

"When the members of a consanguineal kin group acknowledge a traditional bond of common descent in the paternal or maternal line, but are unable always to trace the actual genealogical connections between individuals, the group is called a sib. . . . Occasionally two or more sibs recognize a purely conventional unilinear bond of kinship, more tenuous than that which unites a sib but nevertheless sufficient to distinguish the constellation of sibs from others of its kind. A consanguineal kin group of this higher order is called a phratry. When a society has only two sibs or phratries so that every person is necessarily a member of one or the other, the dichotomy results in so many distinctive features in social structure that a special term, moiety, is applied to them." (*Ibid.*)

Residence rules
Matrilocal
Patrilocal
Bilocal (ambilocal)
Neolocal
Avunculocal

Joint families are often established by means of common residence. "If custom requires the groom to leave his parental home and live with his bride, either in the house of her parents or in a dwelling nearby, the rule of residence is called matrilocal. If, on the other hand, the bride regularly removes to or near the parental home of the groom, residence is said to be patrilocal. It should be emphasized that this rule implies, not

CONCEPTS

DEFINITION AND/OR ILLUSTRATIONS

merely that wife goes to live with her husband, but that they establish a domicile in or near the home of his parents. Some societies permit a married couple to live with or near the parents of either spouse. . . . The rule of residence in such cases is termed bilocal. When a newly wedded couple . . . establishes a domicile independent of the location of the parental home of either partner, and perhaps even at considerable distance from both, residence may be called neolocal. . . . A fifth alternative, which we shall term avunculocal residence, prevails in a few societies which prescribe that a married couple shall reside with or near a maternal uncle of the groom rather than with the parents of either spouse or in a separate home of their own." (*Ibid.*)

Social status
Social roles
Social norms
Social patterns

"The place in a particular system which a certain individual occupies at a particular time will be referred to as his status with respect to that system, and 'role' will be used to designate the sum total of the culture patterns associated with a particular status. It thus includes the attitudes, values, and behavior ascribed by the society to any and all persons occupying this status. It can even be extended to include the legitimate expectations of such persons in other statuses within the same system. Every status is linked with a particular role . . . a role is the dynamic aspect of a status; what the individual has to do in order to validate his occupation of a status." (Linton, 1945.)

Social processes
Social action

Social process is "the operation of the social life, the manner in which the actions and very existence of each living being affect those of other individuals with which it has relations." (Firth, 1951.) Again, social process "is the immense multitude of actions and interactions of human beings, acting as individuals or in combinations or in groups." (Radcliffe-Brown, 1952.)

CONCEPTS	DEFINITION AND/OR ILLUSTRATIONS
	And more recently, "process consists of the manner in which every social organization operates to maintain itself and/or to undergo change due to external pressure or internal impetus." (Hsu, 1959.)

Social relations
Social usages
Sentiments
Social control
  Folkways
  Mores
  Sanctions
	"We can regard these observations as facts of custom—as standardized ways of doing, knowing, thinking and feeling—universally obligatory and valued in a given group of people at a given time. But we can also regard them as facts of social structure. We then seek to relate them to one another by a scheme of conceptual operations different from that of the previous frame of reference. We see custom as symbolizing or expressing social relations—that is, the ties and cleavages by which persons and groups are bound to one another in the activities of social life." (Fortes, 1953.)

	"By a social sanction I meant broadly, any institution a consequence of which is to incline persons occupying certain roles to conform to the norms and expectations associated with these roles . . . any social system must provide some institutionalized means of constraining individuals to at least some degree of conformity to accepted norms." (Beattie, 1956.)

Socialization
  Age-sex categories
  Age grades
  Age sets
  Age classes
	Socialization may be generally defined as "The way in which a society integrates its members and the process by which individuals learn to adapt to their society." (*Dictionary of Anthropology*, 1956.)

	One aspect of social structure is the classification of a society's members on the basis of age and sex. Thus, "membership in associations and statuses within the family organization bear a very close relation to age-sex categories . . . before an individual can assume the status of father in a new conjugal family unit he must belong to the adult male category in the age-sex system." (Linton, 1942.)

CONCEPTS	DEFINITION AND/OR ILLUSTRATIONS
Institution Integration Equilibrium	An institution has been defined as a fairly permanent cluster of social usages. It is a reasonably enduring complex pattern of behavior by which social control is exerted and through which basic social desires or needs can be met. (*Dictionary of Anthropology*, 1956.)
	"A system implies a state of equilibrium in which elements are in mutual dependence. If change is introduced at one point, change follows at another. If the first change is not too great—that is, if it is not so great that destruction of the system ensues—then subsequent changes do not alter the situation out of recognition. Far from it, since the elements are woven into a common whole, the effect of the change is soon dissipated. . . . The system reverts to its former state. It may be said to have thus an equilibrium which it regains after each disturbance." (Arensberg and Kimball, 1948.)
Social structure Social function Social organization Social system Social stratification Social field	"In studying a field of social relations, whether we are using the notions of society, of culture, of community, we distinguish their structure, their function, and their organization. These are separate but related aspects . . . by the structural aspect of social relations we mean the principles on which their form depends; by the functional aspect we mean the way in which they serve given ends; by the organizational aspect we mean the directional activity which maintains their forms and serves their ends." (Firth, 1951.)
	"By social organization (or social structure) is meant the division of society into social groups, based upon conventionally standardized social relations between the individuals concerned. . . . In modern democratic countries most social groups are of the voluntary type, and here we find the most striking contrast with primitive cultures in which the individual's place in the social

CONCEPTS	DEFINITION AND/OR ILLUSTRATIONS
	structure is determined, in general, by such factors as kinship, locality and hereditary social class which cannot be changed except by certain special social mechanisms. (Piddington, 1950.)
Functional prerequisites Social imperatives	*Functional prerequisites* and *social imperatives* refer "broadly to the things that must get done in any society if it is to continue as a group concern, i.e. the generalized conditions necessary for the maintenance of the system concerned." (Aberle, 1950.) A related term is *social imperatives*, by which is meant "those insistent interpersonal problems that every culture must face. For man is committed to living in society, and group life requires certain organizational features through which each individual compromises his personal interests with the demands of others. Social imperatives are then those general organizational features that are requisite to the continuation of social life irrespective of cultural form." (Goldschmidt, 1953.)
Culture Society Community 　Neighborhood 　Village 　Band	The terms *culture, society,* and *community* refer to the most general terms used in the description and analysis of group life; each is commonly used to express the idea of totality. "If society is taken to be an organized set of individuals with a given way of life, culture is that way of life. If society is taken to be an aggregate of social relations, then culture is the content of those relations . . . the term community emphasizes the space-time component, the aspect of living together . . . a body of people sharing in common activities and bound by multiple relations in such a way that the aims of any individual can be achieved by participation in action with others." (Firth, 1951.)

CONCEPTS   DEFINITION AND/OR ILLUSTRATIONS

"a society or a social institution, is not a thing at all. It is a concept, an abstraction from people's observed behavior; and it exists only in the minds of the people who are concerned with it. Whether as members of the society or as investigators of it. . . . It is simply a number of people who are related to one another and to their environment in innumerable ways. When we use the term 'society' in a strict sense we are not referring simply to this human collectivity . . . rather we are referring to the complex of institutionalized interpersonal relationships which bind them together, or to some aspect or aspects of them." (Beattie, 1964.)

BASIC ASSUMPTIONS

Hill and Hansen have suggested that "perhaps the most significant elements in differentiating one frame-work from another are the underlying assumptions which each makes about the nature of man, the family, and society." (1960, pp. 309–11.) In this connection they present a list of five basic assumptions which are felt to be peculiar to the structure-functional approach of sociology and social anthropology, namely:

1. Social conduct is best analyzed for its contribution to the maintenance of the social system or for its nature under the structures of the system.
2. A social human is basically a reacting part of the social system; self-elicited (independent) action is rare and asocial.
3. The basic autonomous unit is the social system, which is composed of interdependent subsystems, (for example, institutions, family systems, and so on).
4. It is possible to profitably study any subunits of the basic system.
5. The social system tends to homeostasis.

Unfortunately, Hill and Hansen do not provide the specific source or give illustrations of the above assumptions; nor do they attempt to elaborate upon them to any extent.

The three basic "postulates" underlying functional analysis as it is expressed by anthropologists were explicitly stated and critically evaluated in a much earlier publication (1949) by Merton: "These postulates hold first, that standardized social activities or cultural items are functional for the entire social or cultural system; second, that all such social and cultural items fulfill sociological functions; and third, that these items are consequently indispensable." (Revised edition, 1957, pp. 19–84.) While many contemporary social anthropologists have either rejected or modified these postulates,[12] one still finds examples of them in the literature. Thus, Evans-Pritchard writes: "A social system has a functional unity. It is not an aggregate but an organism or integrated whole." (1952, p. 54.) Similarly, Fortes has suggested "that a culture is a unity in so far as it is tied to a bounded social structure." (1953, p. 23.)

A fourth assumption holds that a knowledge of the kinship system is necessary for the comprehension of social behavior. In the words of one social anthropologist, "an understanding of the kinship system in any society is essential as a clue to the working of some of the most fundamental relationships—sexual, marital, economic, in that society." (Firth, 1956, p. 11.) The idea here is that kinship systems exhibit regularities and systematic forms which are socially significant and that the nuclear or elementary family is not an isolated unit. In short, the notion of kinship is posited as basic to the study of society.

A fifth assumption is that the history of any society or subsystem of society, such as the family, is unnecessary for understanding its present nature. Thus we are told that "societies are systems, and these systems are natural systems which can be reduced to variables, with the corollary that the history of them is irrelevant." And again, "an institution is not to be understood, far less explained, in terms of its origins, whether these origins are conceived of as beginnings, causes, or merely in a logical sense, its simplest forms." (Evans-Pritchard, 1952, pp. 38–49.) The idea here is that a knowledge of the origin of an institution such as the family cannot tell us how it functions in a society. "To know how it has come to be what it is, and to know how it works, are two different things." (*Ibid.*) Contemporary social anthropologists assume that the study of institutions in their present form must precede any inquiry into their origin and development, if proper conception of their function is to be gained.

[12] See, for example, Beattie (1964), especially Chaps. 3 and 4.

A sixth assumption, noted by Hill and Hansen, and documented here, is that a human being is basically a reacting part of the social system. It is said that "most people are shaped to the form of their culture because of the common malleability of their original endowment. They are plastic to the molding force of the society into which they are born . . . the great mass of individuals take quite readily to the form that is presented to them." (Benedict, 1934, p. 221.) Similarly, Radcliffe-Brown in his presentation of the functionalist perspective notes how such a point of view implies "that we have to investigate as thoroughly as possible all aspects of social life, considering them in relation to one another, and that an essential part of the task is the investigation of the individual and of the way in which he is molded by or adjusted to the social life." (1935, p. 400.)

A seventh and final assumption holds that a knowledge of cultural or societal forms of institutions is necessary for the comprehension of human behavior. It is suggested, for example, that "the chief requirement for a discussion of culture is that it should be based on a wide selection of possible cultural forms. . . . If we are interested in human behavior, we need first of all to understand the institutions that are provided in any society." (Benedict, 1934, p. 29.) A similar notion is apparent in the list of basic assumptions by Hill and Hansen presented earlier in this section, especially number three.

PRODUCT

It is somewhat difficult to assess the theoretical and research contributions of functional social anthropologists to the field of marriage and the family. Social anthropology has been primarily a qualitative discipline, and its studies of the family have been highly descriptive, for the most part, with little emphasis on theory formulation and hypothesis testing. (See Critique and Discussion.)

Nonetheless, the close relationship between social anthropologists and sociology—and their identification with it has resulted in some fruitful contributions. Homans' comment on this relationship in *The Human Group* is of interest.

If we agree that there is only one sociology, a sociology of human organization, we can hardly admit any division between sociology and social anthropology. A social anthropologist is a sociologist of primitive peoples, a sociologist, an anthropologist of civilizations. The anthropologists are indebted to some of the ideas of the earlier sociologists, and the other side of the exchange has been even more rewarding. In many of the social sciences, ideas worked out by anthropologists have been adopted and found fecund, and anthropologists, self-trained in the bush, have gone on to make excellent studies of civilized communities using the techniques of gathering material and analyzing it that they learned among the primitives. This book, for one, leans heavily on their findings and ideas. (1950, pp. 192–93.)

With regard to the "studies of civilized societies," Homans has in mind such works as the *Yankee City* series by W. L. Warner and his associates; *Family and Community in Ireland* by C. M. Arensberg and S. T. Kimball; *Deep South*, by A. Davis, B. Gardner, and M. Gardner; as well as the well-known *Middletown* by the Lynds.

As has been previously noted, social anthropologists apply sociological conceptions to anthropological data. But the reverse is also true. An examination of past as well as current sociological textbooks—in particular the sections dealing with marriage and the family—reveals a heavy reliance upon anthropological conceptions, ethnographic data, and results of comparative analyses. This is especially true in discussions of marriage forms and regulations, functions of the family, premarital practices, duration and dissolution of marital ties, and so on.[13]

Social anthropological emphasis on kinship systems and their functions in the structuring or patterning of familial relations has led to fruitful hypotheses concerning the extended family in Western

[13] Recognition of this close alliance between sociology and social anthropology has prompted Faris to remark: "Social anthropology . . . is mainly sociology, and there is little distinction between the two fields other than that resulting from the accidental and scientifically irrelevant differences in the routes by which the two fields came to their present interests. There is, of course, some practical division of labor in the fact that anthropologists undertake most of the descriptive studies of preliterate societies, although for more than a quarter of a century they have also conducted sociological research on communities in modern civilizations. Also, until recently anthropologists mainly employed their personal skills in recording and interpreting a society as a whole, while sociologists placed somewhat more confidence in the use of technical research methods and their application to problems of considerably smaller scope. At the present time, however, even this distinction is diminishing, and if present trends continue it may soon become pointless to attempt to distinguish between sociology and social anthropology." (1964), p. 31.

civilization. The widely read study by Arensberg and Kimball of the Irish family, for example, and Sussman's sociological research on extended family relations in American communities (1962) got their impetus from social-anthropological demonstrations of the utility of kinship analyses for theory as well as for research.

Social anthropology along with anthropology in general has made an impact on the field of psychology and, in particular, on psychoanalytic theory. (See Appendix 1.) "Recognition of the extent to which the activities of the members of a society are culturally patterned and of the extraordinary range of variation in modal patterns as one moves from society to society led to a veritable revolution in psychological thinking that is still working itself out today." (Smith, in Gillin, 1954, p. 59.) The classic example here is Malinowski's test of the Freudian hypothesis concerning the universality of the Oedipus complex. Malinowski revealed how the manifestation of this phenomenon is dependent upon family structure; his finding that the role of the uncle in Trobiand society is central has lead to a modification of Freud's original statement. In other ways psychological researchers draw upon the comparative data and analyses of social anthropologists for cross-cultural validation of specific hypotheses. This is particularly true of those researchers engaged in so-called culture and personality studies. (See Appendix 1.)

In the areas of culture contact and change, social anthropologists have investigated the impact of Westernization on various societies.[14] This has led in turn to an interest in the concomitant variation in family organization and disorganization. (See Appendix 2.) The manner in which the family in different societies adapts to changing situations has been noted and observed. Such observations have contributed to the general field of social disorganization and have suggested hypotheses in that area. That the methods and approaches developed in social anthropology have made substantial contributions to studies of the family in complex societies is well documented by Eisenstadt (1961).

VALUES

An attempt was made to uncover any outstanding value judgments or value objectives, either implicit or explicit, within the structure-functional framework of contemporary social anthro-

[14] A recent discussion of the social anthropologists' study of social change and its impact on family life may be found in Beattie (1964), Chap. 14.

pologists, especially as this framework relates to the study of the family. The results were, for the most part, negative. The heavy emphasis on kinship does at times project an underlying outlook which views extended relationships other than those organized around the marriage bond as best suited to the welfare of society, the family, and the individual.

THE FRAMEWORK

The structure-functional framework of social anthropology may be briefly summarized, as it deals with the family, in the following manner. Society is viewed as a functioning whole composed of various subsystems or institutions, all of which are closely inter-related. The family and kinship systems must be perceived in terms of their relations or interactions with the other subsystems—economic, political, religious —which make up the total society. When the social anthropologist speaks of the functions of the family he is, in general, referring to the part it plays in perpetuating itself and in maintaining the total social system or structure, that is, society.

The family here is viewed as a social system, and its evaluation must be in terms of its place in the society as a whole and the special functions it performs in the existence of society. This is best accomplished by focusing on the formal aspects of the family and/or kinship systems—composition, residence and inheritance rules, kinship rights and obligations, parental authority patterns, marriage forms and regulations, separations—and tracing the structural implications of these aspects for social relations. The goal is to deduce the underlying structural principles and derive generalizations about behavior of persons in groups which eventually may be useful in comparative analyses.

In focusing on the formal aspects of family and kinship systems, the social anthropologist pays particular attention to the normative patterns evident in the social relations occurring within these systems. Eisenstadt has commented on this aspect of the framework:

> This type of analysis is achieved through the great emphasis on social behavior as related to various norms which are said to be operative in the social structure. Most of the social-anthropological descriptions of social behavior are studies of the ways in which major norms found in these societies are upheld by

individuals, of the interrelationships between these different norms, and of the ways in which these norms influence and regulate the relations between different groups in society. . . . Thus, various norms and the patterns of behavior which uphold them are seen mostly as institutional directives upholding the interrelations among the society and the continuity of the society as a whole. In this way, most anthropological studies combine in one basic model the analysis of social behavior, institutional norms, groups and societies. They explain patterns of social behavior through the analysis of group structure, institutions and "total" societies. (1961, pp. 201–02.)

Eisenstadt cites a considerable amount of substantive research conducted by social anthropologists as illustrations of the application of this to both simple and complex societies.

CRITIQUE AND DISCUSSION

The structure-functional framework of social anthropology has received criticisms primarily with respect to its basic assumptions (Merton, 1957) and its methodological procedures (Murdock, 1954). Among the basic assumptions, the notion of functional unity is viewed as especially vulnerable, particularly in failing to account for the dysfunctional elements. "Anthropologists often cite 'Increased solidarity of the community,' and 'increased family pride' as instances of functionally adaptive sentiments. Yet . . . an increase of pride among individual families may often serve to disrupt the solidarity of a small community." (Merton, p. 27.) It is Merton's contention that the postulate of functional unity is often contrary to fact and has little heuristic value since it diverts attention from possible disparative consequences of various social or cultural items. In this connection, the social anthropologists have been cited for displaying, until very recently, an almost exclusive concern with patterned behavior.[15]

A pertinent methodological weakness in social-anthropological

[15] "To students of man, of course, all behavior is important, patterned or otherwise. It is a serious defect of anthropology that it has traditionally concerned itself so exclusively with the former. Sociology has made a major contribution in calling attention to the latter. That anthropology has learned this lesson is revealed by the increasing attention being paid in ethnographic literature to variations in behavior within the prescribed patterns and to deviant behavior." Murdock (1954), p. 23.

field work, according to Lewis, has been too great a reliance upon relatively few informants to obtain a picture of the society or culture. "The traditional justification of this procedure has been the assumption of the essential homogeneity of primitive or folk societies. But this very presupposition has often affected the methods used and therefore colored the findings." (1950, p. 472.) Further, on theoretical grounds, it has been proposed that the

> unity of the total society cannot be usefully posited in advance of observation. The theoretic framework of functional analysis must expressly require that there be specification of the units for which a given social or cultural item is functional. It must expressly allow for a given item having diverse consequences, functional and dysfunctional, for individuals, for subgroups, and for the more inclusive social structure and culture. (Merton, 1957, p. 30.)

The homogeneity assumption, while perhaps adequate for many nonliterate societies, becomes tenuous and dangerous when moved to the realm of large, complex, and highly differentiated literate societies.[16]

Social anthropology has, by and large, been a qualitative science, and this orientation is reflected in the social anthropologists' treatment of the family. On the purely descriptive level, they "usually deal with observed patterns of social behavior of individuals in different social situations and in different groups, and with statements by individuals of norms which would be appropriate to such different situations." (Eisenstadt, 1960.) The social anthropologist investigating family forms has only rarely concerned himself with problems of sampling design. Nor has he made much use of the interview schedule and other standard research tools. (Beals and Hoijer, 1953, pp. 18–19.) Along these lines it has been admitted that "when it comes to the formulation and testing of hypotheses, anthropologists reveal little comprehension of the requisites of a viable scientific theory and even less of the methods which science has devised for putting such a theory to the test." (Murdock, in Gillin, 1954, p. 27.)

---

[16] Again, it should be emphasized that many contemporary social anthropologists no longer adhere strictly to the postulates examined and criticized by Merton. See, for instance, Beattie (1964), pp. 49–64.

APPENDIX 1. CULTURE AND PERSONALITY

In the preceding pages we have elected to stress structure-functionalism as representing the major frame of reference for family study in anthropology. At least one other school in anthropology, however, should be noted in this connection, namely, culture and personality. This approach is often interdisciplinary in nature, with a primary emphasis on (1) the relationship of culture and the family to the formation of personality and personality structure or (2) descriptions of cultural configurations and personality types and their relation to family life.

Four major foci in the literature on personality and culture have been noted: (1) the study of social and cultural influences reflected in the individual personality; (2) the delineation of group regularities in the personalities of populations in given societies; (3) the specification of causal factors accounting for these observed regularities; and (4) the explanation of interrelations between social systems and observed regularities in personality. (Inkeles, 1955, pp. 577–92.)

There are actually three approaches involved in this frame of reference, each representing different emphases on variant aspects of the same problem: the study of the interaction between the individual and his cultural setting. They are, however, so closely interrelated that for the investigator to frame his research in terms of a single one is perhaps the exception rather than the rule. The schools of psychology that have stimulated the study of the individual in his cultural setting are behaviorism, the Gestalt or configurational school, and psychoanalysis.

CULTURAL-CONFIGURATIONAL
OR
THEMATIC APPROACH

The cultural-configurational or thematic approach is essentially ethnological and seeks to establish the dominant integrative patterns of cultures which encourage the development of certain personality types. The reference here is always to institutions, to the cultural patterns that set the framework within which the predominant personality structures, as manifested by the group, develop. The writings of Sapir, Benedict, and Mead are illustrative of this approach. Thus, for example, Benedict states the significant sociological unit . . . is the cultural configuration. The studies of the family . . . need to be broken up into studies that emphasize the different configurations that in instance after instance have dominated these traits . . . marriage in our own civilization is a situation which can never be made clear as a mere variant of mating and domesticity. Without the clue that in our civilization at large man's paramount aim is to amass private possessions and multiply occasions of display, the modern position of the wife and the modern emotions of jealousy are alike unintelligible. Our attitudes toward children are equally evidences of this same cultural goal. . . . The pattern is not inherent in the parent-child situations, as we so glibly assume. It is impressed upon the situations by the major drives of our culture. (1934, p. 213.)

The basic concept here is that of culture occurring in certain patterns which determine its fabric and are of influence on the lives of family members.

Actual research applying configurational analysis to the specific study of the family is scarce.[17] Yet it continues to be emphasized as an important conceptual framework. Thus Sirjamaki more recently speaks of the cultural analysis of the family in terms of its dominant configurations. He is of the opinion that when these can be specified for the family, it is possible to interpret the basic moral ideas which give the family its distinctive and identifying characteristics.

The concept of the configurations of the culture, and a knowledge of the manner in which these are expressed within an institution, illuminates the study of the family. Configurations reach into the most intimate areas of individual and family behavior; they furnish the meanings and determine right and wrong behavior in courting, in husband-wife and parent-child relationships, in heterosexual social activity, and in ideas about sex. Thus they supply the moral sentiments by which family members are influenced and make explicable the vagaries of their behavior. (1948, p. 465.)

[17] There are problems of measurement, for one thing. Thus Kroeber has stated "this quality of course inheres largely in forms, or interrelations of forms; it can never be adequately formulated in terms of culture content alone. Nor can it be measured or demonstrated. Essentially, it is seizable and definable by subjective empirical approach." (1935), pp. 689–90.

Sirjamaki notes the following configurations appearing in the American family: (1) marriage is a dominant life goal, for men as well as for women, (2) the giving and taking in marriage should be based on personal affection and choice, (3) the criterion of successful marriage is the personal happiness of husband and wife, (4) the best years of life are those of youth and its qualities are most desirable, (5) children should be reared in a child's world and shielded from too early participation in adult woes and tribulations, (6) the exercise of sex should be contained within wedlock, (7) family roles of husband and wife should be based on sexual division of labor, but with the male status being superior, and (8) individual, not familial, values are to be sought in family living. (pp. 465–70.)

A variant of the configurational approach is the so-called thematic approach, suggested by Opler, who states that "a limited number of dynamic affirmations, i.e. themes, can be identified in every culture and . . . the key to the character structure and direction of the specific culture is to be sought in the nature, expression, and interrelationships of these themes." An example of a theme in Apache culture, for instance, is that "men are physically, morally, and mentally superior to women." This theme is said to ramify Apache culture, impinging on family life, for example, in defining familial roles. (1945, pp. 198–206.)

MODAL PERSONALITY APPROACH

The modal personality approach lays emphasis on the reactions of the individual to the cultural setting into which he is born. The aim here is to discern the typical personality structures which on the basis of common experience are to be found in a given society. This approach stresses the individual, especially in his reactions to parental sanctions. It derives from the application of psychoanalysis to the comparative study of broad problems of social adjustment. It represents a development out of the conceptual and methodological scheme of Freud. Its basic assumptions, summarized below by Lindesmith and Strauss (1950, pp. 587–601), clearly reveal the psychoanalytic emphasis:

a. Personality is largely a product of interpersonal relations.
b. An emphasis on the predominant character-forming efficacy of the infant disciplines: bowel and bladder training, nursing, weaning, mothering, restraint of motion, punishment, amount and kinds of frustration, etc.

   c. If post-infantile experiences tend to reinforce the personality trends in infancy, then the resulting adult traits will conform to the infantile pattern.

   d. If later experiences run counter to earlier ones the resulting adult character may be something not predictable from infantile experience alone.

   e. The idea that basic personality patterns are established in the first couple of years of life or in pre-adolescent childhood involves the assumption that personality does not change, or changes only in minor ways, in response to later experiences and cultural influence.

   f. The belief that personality patterns are fixed unconsciously and early involves a corollary assumption that these patterns cannot be directly taught, or that they can be taught only if the childhood training has been favorable.

Studies by Kardiner, Linton, and DuBois are illustrative of this type of analysis. Because of the heavy reliance upon a psychological framework evident in this approach, it has not been pursued to any great extent in the present paper. This is also true of the final approach to be briefly mentioned below.

PROJECTIVE APPROACH

   The projective approach employs the various projective methods of analysis, especially the Rorschach series of ink blots to establish, by induction, the range of personality structures in a given society. Both the individual and the culture are emphasized. Here the technique employed is the outstanding factor; tests are used to assess the personality structures of the individual members of a given group in terms of their enculturation (socialization) to the institutions and values of their culture. The leading proponent of this type of analysis among anthropologists is A. I. Hallowell.

Appendix 2. The Evolutionary Approach

   The evolutionary theorists in anthropology are primarily concerned with cultural change. *Early evolutionists* are characterized by their search for original stages of cultural development, their belief in the universality of certain societal institutions, and their basic assumption of inevitable and unilinear progress. *Modern evolu-*

tionists, in contrast, pass over the question of origins of the various institutions, argue that particular phenomena which recur cross-culturally are not necessarily universal, and insist that evolution is not unilinear but multilinear.

With regard to the family, the early evolutionists concentrated their efforts almost entirely on this institution in the belief that the study of kinship is the primary clue to an understanding of social organization. More recent followers of the evolutionary school reject this study of isolated aspects of societies, such as the family, in favor of an analysis of human societies as functioning wholes. The present focus, therefore, is not upon the family as the primary independent variable, but upon the interrelations of economic, political, and kinship organization. The aim of these investigators is to analyze cultural similarities and cultural differences, and to interpret this analyzation in terms of cultural change.

The original proponents of social evolutionary theory include Tylor, Morgan, McLennan, Briffault, Westermarck, Spencer, and Sumner. The modern evolutionary approach is best exemplified in the works of Childe, White, Steward, Sahlins, and Aberle.

The idea of evolution was a very live issue at the time when both anthropology and sociology were delineated as distinct sciences. As Charles Darwin traced the origin of the species, so did the early social theorists outline the origin of marriage, the family, and other societal institutions. The principal foci of study, therefore, of the first evolutionists were origins and stages of family development. Kinship terminology and kinship organization were also stressed as indicators of cultural progress. The modern evolutionists retain some of these interests but are more likely to emphasize the institutional determinants of kinship organization (economic, political, religious) and the reciprocal influences of kinship and other cultural forms. Of present interest is the study of the distribution of certain family forms and the circumstances under which they occur.

The basic concepts currently employed by the evolutionist school are: social evolution (multilinear, specific, and general), culture and culture types, crosscultural regularities, levels of sociocultural regularities, and levels of sociocultural integration. The family is defined not in terms of the natural family of parents and children, but as an institution, a unit of cooperation, and a vehicle for the transmission of cultures.

The general assumption that underlies the modern evolutionary approach to the study of the family is that family forms are an expression of different levels, or stages, of cultural development. The implication is that forms of the family may be delineated and that cultural stages may be constructed, differentiated, and placed upon some continua of sequential development. "The methodology of evolution . . . postulates that genuine parallels of form and function develop in historically independent sequences of cultural traditions. Second, it explains these parallels by the independent operation of identical causality in each case." (Steward, 1953, p. 315.) By examining the emergence of roughly similar social forms in different societies it might then be possible to arrive at valid conclusions concerning the development of institutional systems and social structures.

The evolutionary approach has had, in the past, a more obvious impact upon family study than it may claim in the present. The early evolutionists were among the first scholars to place primary emphasis upon the family as an element of study. Their analysis of kinship and their crosscultural comparisons of family forms have been of influence in the functional school of anthropology. Such empirical anthropologists as Murdock, Hobhouse, Wheeler, and Ginsberg show in their work an implicit evolutionary approach to the study of the family. Modern evolutionism appears to merge with current functionalism in its emphasis on functional requirements and a holistic approach. Research utilizing the evolutionary framework may still be distinguished, however, by an attempt to arrange societies in a hierarchical series. Such attempts to trace the development of the family are now marked by the greater attention given to empirical validation (statistical and archaeological evidences) rather than the quite arbitrary principles used by the early evolutionists.

Perhaps the most obvious value judgment in the evolutionary framework is exemplified in the work of Leslie White. White asserts that technological progress has been, is now, and always will be the primary indicator of cultural development. Critics of the evolutionary school attack both the concern with stages in evolution and the adoption of technological criteria for the definition of these stages. The evolutionary school is, however, one of the few that deals with major cultural change. It is by means of this broad perspective that workers in this area contribute most to the future understanding of the family.

REFERENCES

ABERLE, DAVID F. "Matrilineal Descent in Cross-cultural Perspective," in David M. Schneider and Kathleen Gough, eds. *Matrilineal Kinship*. Berkeley: University of California Press, 1961.

———, et al. "The Functional Prerequisites of a Society," *Ethics*, **60** (Jan. 1950), pp. 100–11.

ANSHEN, RUTH N., ed. *The Family: Its Function and Destiny*, rev. ed. New York: Harper & Row, Publishers, 1959. Contains a variety of essays on the family in different societies, several of which are by anthropologists. See particularly Ralph Linton, Chap. 3.

ARENSBERG, C., and KIMBALL, S. I. *The Family and Community in Ireland*. Cambridge, Mass.: Harvard University Press, 1940. One of the earliest studies of community life in Western civilization using the social-anthropological approach. Primary emphasis on family and kinship ties.

BEALS, RALPH L., and HOIJER, HARRY. *An Introduction to Anthropology*, 2nd ed. New York: The Macmillan Company, 1959.

BEATTIE, JOHN H. M. *Other Cultures: Aims, Methods and Achievements in Social Anthropology*. London: Cohen & West, Limited, Publishers, 1964.

———. "Social Anthropology," in Alan Pryce-Jones, ed. *The New Outline of Modern Knowledge*. New York: Simon and Schuster, Inc., 1956, pp. 252–78.

BENEDICT, RUTH. "Configurations of Culture in North America," *American Anthropologist*, **34** (Jan.–March 1932), pp. 1–27.

———. "Continuities and Discontinuities in Cultural Conditioning," *Psychiatry*, **1** (May 1938), pp. 161–67.

———. *Patterns of Culture*. New York: The New American Library of World Literature, Inc., 1934.

CHINOY, ELY. *Society: An Introduction to Sociology*. New York: Random House, Inc., 1961.

CHILDE, V. GORDON. *Social Evolution*. New York: Henry Schuman, Inc., Publishers, 1951.

CHRISTENSEN, HAROLD T., ed. *Handbook of Marriage and the Family*. Chicago: Rand McNally & Company, 1964. Contributions by outstanding contemporary scholars in the area of marriage and the family. Chapters on the institutional, structure-functional, interactional, situational, and developmental approaches to family study are especially relevant.

COHEN, ALBERT K. "An Evaluation of 'Themes' and Kindred Concepts," *American Journal of Sociology*, **52** (July 1946), pp. 41–44.

———. "On the Place of 'Themes' and Kindred Concepts in Social Theory," *American Anthropologist*, **50** (July–Sept. 1948), pp. 436–43.

DAVENPORT, W. "Nonunilineal Descent and Descent Groups," *American Anthropologist*, 61 (August 1959), pp. 557–72.

DAVIS, ALLISON, GARDNER, BURLEIGH B., and GARDNER, MARY R. *Deep South*. Chicago: University of Chicago Press, 1941.

DAVIS, KINGSLEY. "Intermarriage in Caste Societies," *American Anthropologist*, 43 (July–Sept. 1941), pp. 376–95.

———. "The Myth of Functional Analysis as a Special Method in Sociology and Anthropology," *American Sociological Review*, 24 (Dec. 1959), pp. 752–72.

DUNCAN, OTIS D. and SCHNORE, LEO F. "Cultural, Behavioral, and Ecological Perspectives in the Study of Social Organization," *American Journal of Sociology*, 45 (Sept. 1959), pp. 132–46.

FARIS, ROBERT E. L. "The Discipline of Sociology," in Robert E. L. Faris, ed. *Handbook of Modern Sociology*. Chicago: Rand McNally & Company, 1964, pp. 1–35.

EGGAN, FRED. "Social Anthropology and the Method of Controlled Comparison," *American Anthropologist*, 56 (Oct. 1954), pp. 743–63. A review and suggested clarification of the various comparative methods utilized in social anthropology.

EISENSTADT, S. N. "Anthropological Studies of Complex Societies," *Current Anthropology*, 2 (June 1961), pp. 201–22. An examination of the contributions and limitations of some of the concepts and approaches of social anthropology to the study of complex societies. Also included are comments on the article by several leading social anthropologists.

EVANS-PRITCHARD, E. E. *Kinship and Marriage Among the Nuer*. London: Oxford University Press, 1951.

———. *Social Anthropology*. New York: Free Press of Glencoe, Inc., 1952. A compilation of the author's lectures on social anthropology in which the history, assumptions, and concepts of the field are delineated. Covers the general scope of British social anthropology in terms of its theoretical orientations.

FIRTH, RAYMOND. "Contemporary British Social Anthropology," *American Anthropologist*, 53 (Oct.–Dec. 1951), pp. 474–89.

———. *Elements of Social Organization*. London: C. A. Watts & Co., Ltd., 1951. A theoretical perspective on the field of social anthropology, particularly with respect to concepts and values.

———. ed. *Two Studies of Kinship in London*. London: The Athlone Press, 1956.

FORTES, MEYER, ed. *Marriage in Tribal Societies*. London: Cambridge University Press, 1962.

———. "The Structure of Unilineal Descent Groups," *American Anthropologist*, 55 (Jan.–March 1953), pp. 17–41.

———, and EVANS-PRITCHARD, E. E., eds. *African Political Systems*. London: Published for the International African Institute by the Oxford University Press, 1940.

GILLIN, JOHN, ed. *For a Science of Social Man.* New York: The Macmillan Company, 1954. Several informative essays which treat the relationship between anthropology and other related disciplines.

GOLDSCHMIDT, WALTER. "Values and the Field of Comparative Sociology," *American Sociological Review,* 18 (June 1953), pp. 287–93.

GOODE, WILLIAM J. "Illegitimacy in the Caribbean Social Structure," *American Sociological Review,* 24 (Feb. 1959), pp. 21–30.

———. "The Sociology of the Family," in Robert K. Merton, *et al. Sociology Today.* New York: Basic Books, Inc., Publishers, 1959, pp. 178–96.

———. *World Revolution and Family Patterns.* New York: Free Press of Glencoe, Inc., 1963.

GOODY, JACK. "The Classification of Double Descent Systems," *Current Anthropology,* 2 (Feb. 1961), pp. 3–25.

———, ed. *The Developmental Cycle in Domestic Groups.* Cambridge Papers in Social Anthropology No. 1. London: Cambridge University Press, 1962.

GOULDNER, ALVIN W., and PETERSON, RICHARD A. *Technology and the Moral Order.* New York: The Bobbs-Merrill Company, Inc., 1962.

HERSKOVITS, MELVIN J. *Man and His Works: The Science of Cultural Anthropology.* New York: Alfred A. Knopf, Inc., 1949.

———. "Past Developments and Present Currents in Ethnology," *American Anthropologist,* 61 (July 1959), pp. 389–98.

HILL, REUBEN. "Interdisciplinary Workshop on Marriage and Family Research," *Marriage and Family Living,* 13 (winter 1951), pp. 13–28.

———, and HANSEN, DONALD A. "The Identification of Conceptual Frameworks Utilized in Family Study," *Marriage and Family Living,* 22 (Nov. 1960), pp. 299–311.

HOBHOUSE, L. T., WHEELER, G. S., and GINSBERG, M. *Material Culture and Social Institutions of the Simpler Peoples.* London: Chapman & Hall, Ltd., 1930. One of the earliest attempts to utilize statistical analyses of anthropological data as a method of comparison.

HOMANS, GEORGE C. *The Human Group.* New York: Harcourt, Brace & World, Inc., 1950. A sociological work exhibiting an admittedly heavy reliance on the field of social anthropology.

———, and SCHNEIDER, DAVID M. *Marriage, Authority and Final Causes.* New York: Free Press of Glencoe, Inc., 1955. A concentrated analysis of unilateral cross-cousin marriage.

HSU, FRANCIS L. K. "Structure, Function, Content, and Process," *American Anthropologist,* 61 (Oct. 1959), pp. 790–805.

INKELES, ALEX. "Some Sociological Observations on Culture-Personality Studies," in C. Kluckhohn and H. A. Murray, eds. *Personality in Na-*

ture, Society, and Culture. New York: Alfred A. Knopf, Inc., 1955, pp. 577–92.

JANOWITZ, MORRIS. "Anthropology and the Social Sciences," *Current Anthropology*, 4 (April 1963), pp. 139–54.

KARDINER, ABRAM. *The Psychological Frontiers of Society*. New York: Columbia University Press, 1945.

————, et al. *The Individual and His Society*. New York: Columbia University Press, 1939.

KLUCKHOHN, CLYDE, in R. Kluckhohn, ed. *Culture and Behavior: Collected Essays*. New York: Free Press of Glencoe, Inc., 1962.

————. *Mirror for Man*. Greenwich, Conn.: Fawcett Publications, Inc., 1951.

————. "Patterning as Exemplified in Navaho Culture," in L. Spier, A. I. Hallowell, and A. A. Newman, eds. *Language, Culture, and Personality*. Menasha, Wisc.: Sapit Memorial Publications Fund, 1941, pp. 109–30.

KROEBER, A. L. "Review of Benedict's 'Patterns of Culture,'" *American Anthropologist*, 37 (Oct.–Dec. 1935), pp. 689–90.

LEVI-STRAUSS, CLAUDE. *Structural Anthropology*. Trans. by Claire Jacobson and Brooke Grundfest Schoepf. New York: Basic Books, 1963.

LEVY, MARION J., JR. *The Family Revolution in Modern China*. Cambridge, Mass.: Harvard University Press, 1949.

————, and FALLERS, L. A. "The Family: Some Comparative Considerations," *American Anthropologist*, 61 (Aug. 1959), pp. 647–51. An examination of the utility of current anthropological conceptions of the family and their relevance for comparative analyses.

LEWIS, OSCAR. "An Anthropological Approach to Family Studies," *American Journal of Sociology*, 55 (March 1950), pp. 468–75. An outline of a suggested anthropological case-study approach to family-life research.

————. *The Children of Sanchez*. New York: Random House, Inc., 1961. See also the more recent *Pedro Martinez*, 1964.

————. *Five Families*. New York: Basic Books, Inc., Publishers, 1959.

LINDESMITH, ALFRED R., and STRAUSS, ANSELM L. "A Critique of Culture-Personality Writings," *American Sociological Review*, 15 (Oct. 1950), pp. 587–600.

LINTON, RALPH. "Age and Sex Categories," *American Sociological Review*, 17 (Oct. 1942), pp. 589–603.

————. "The Scope and Aims of Anthropology," in R. Linton, ed. *The Science of Man in the World Crisis*. New York: Columbia University Press, 1945, pp. 3–8.

————. *The Study of Man*. New York: Appleton-Century-Crofts, 1936.

LOWIE, ROBERT H. "Ethnography, Cultural and Social Anthropology," *American Anthropologist*, 55 (Oct. 1953), pp. 527–33.

――――. *Primitive Society*. New York: Liveright Publishing Corporation, 1947.

LYND, ROBERT S., and HELEN M. *Middletown: A Study of American Culture*. New York: Harcourt, Brace & World, Inc., 1929.

――――. *Middletown in Transition: A Study of Cultural Conflicts*. New York: Harcourt, Brace & World, Inc., 1937.

MAIR, LUCY. "Some Current Terms in Social Anthropology," *British Journal of Sociology*, 14 (March 1963), pp. 20–29.

MALINOWSKI, BRONISLAW. "Anthropology," *Encyclopaedia Britannica*, First Supplementary Volume. Chicago: Encyclopaedia Britannica, Inc., 1926, pp. 132–33.

――――. "Culture," *Encyclopedia of the Social Sciences*, 14 New York: The Macmillan Company, 1930.

――――. "The Group and the Individual in Functional Analysis," *American Sociological Review*, 44 (May 1939), pp. 938–64. The author's well-known statement on human needs, culture, and functionalism.

――――. *Sex, Culture, and Myth*. New York: Harcourt, Brace & World, Inc., 1962. Probably the best collection of essays by the author on the topics of marriage, the family, and kinship.

McEWEN, WILLIAM J. "Forms and Problems of Validation in Social Anthropology," *Current Anthropology*, 4 (April 1963), pp. 155–83.

MEAD, MARGARET. "The Contemporary American Family as an Anthropologist Sees It," *American Journal of Sociology*, 53 (May 1948), pp. 453–59.

――――. "Contrasts and Comparisons From Primitive Society," *The Annals*, 160 (March 1932), pp. 23–28.

――――. *Male and Female*. New York: The New American Library of World Literature, Inc., 1949.

――――. "Socialization and Enculturation," *Current Anthropology*, 4 (April 1963), pp. 184–88.

MERTON, ROBERT K. "Intermarriage and Social Structure: Fact and Theory," *Psychiatry*, 4 (Aug. 1941), pp. 361–74.

MITCHELL, J. *The Yao Village, A Study of the Social Structure of a Nyasaland Tribe*. Manchester, England: Manchester University Press, 1956.

MITCHELL, WILLIAM E. "Theoretical Problems in the Concept of Kindred," *American Anthropologist*, 65 (April 1963), pp. 343–54. See also George P. Murdock's reactions in "Kindred," *American Anthropologist*, 66 (Feb. 1964), pp. 129–32.

――――. "The Cross-Cultural Survey," *American Sociological Review*, 5 (June 1940), pp. 361–69.

――――. *Social Structure*. New York: The Macmillan Company, 1949.

MURDOCK, GEORGE P. "British Social Anthropology," *American Anthropologist*, 53 (Oct.–Dec. 1951), pp. 464–73. A discussion of the differences between American and British anthropology and a critique of the latter.

———. "Family Stability in Non-European Cultures," *The Annals*, 272 (Nov. 1950), pp. 195–201. A study of the stability of marriage in forty selected non-European societies. Information was gathered on the rights of the two sexes regarding divorce.

———, ed. *Social Structure in Southeast Asia*. Chicago: Quadrangle Books, Inc., 1960.

NADEL, S. F. *The Foundations of Social Anthropology*. New York: Free Press of Glencoe, Inc., 1951. A presentation that concentrates on the logical premises that underlie social anthropology and the prerequisites, conceptual and technical, of inquiries leading to social anthropological knowledge.

———. *The Theory of Social Structure*. New York: Free Press of Glencoe, Inc., 1957.

OLDEROGGE, D. A. "Several Problems in the Study of Kinship Systems," *Current Anthropology*, 2 (April 1961), pp. 103–07.

OPLER, MORRIS E. "Themes as Dynamic Forces in Culture," *American Journal of Sociology*, 51 (Nov. 1945), pp. 198–206.

PIDDINGTON, RALPH. *An Introduction to Social Anthropology*, 2 vols. Edinburgh: Oliver and Boyd, Ltd., 1950 and 1957.

RADCLIFFE-BROWN, A. R. "The Study of Kinship Systems," *Journal of the Royal Anthropological Institute*, 71 (1941), pp. 1–18.

———. *Structure and Function in Primitive Society*. New York: Free Press of Glencoe, Inc., 1952. A collection of the author's widely published theoretical essays over a twenty-five year span. A primary source for his view on functionalism, especially Chaps. 10 and 11.

———, and Forde, Daryll, eds. *African Systems of Kinship and Marriage*. New York: Oxford University Press, Inc., 1950. A volume devoted to studies of kinship and marriage in nine African societies. The eighty-five page introduction is an outstanding theoretical statement on kinship systems.

REDFIELD, ROBERT. "Relations of Anthropology to the Social Sciences and to the Humanities," in A. L. Kroeber, ed. *Anthropology Today: An Encyclopedic Inventory*. Chicago: University of Chicago Press, 1953, pp. 728–38.

RIVERS, WILLIAM H. R. *Kinship and Social Organization*. London: Constable Company, Ltd., 1914. A collection of three lectures by the author aimed at demonstrating the close relationship between methods of denoting kinship and forms of social organization, including those based on different varieties of the institution of marriage.

SAHLINS, MARSHALL D. *Social Stratification in Polynesia*. St. Louis: University of Washington Press, 1958.

SAHLINS, M. S., and SERVICE, E. T., eds. *Evolution and Culture*. Ann Arbor, Mich.: University of Michigan Press, 1960.

SCHAPERA, I. "Some Comments on Comparative Method in Social Anthropology," *American Anthropologist,* **55** (Aug. 1953), pp. 353–66.

SCHNEIDER, DAVID M., and GOUGH, KATHLEEN, eds. *Matrilineal Kinship.* Los Angeles: University of California Press, 1961.

SIRJAMAKI, JOHN. "Cultural Configurations in the American Family," *American Journal of Sociology,* **53** (1947–1948), pp. 464–70.

———. "The Institutional Approach," in Harold T. Christensen, ed. *Handbook of Marriage and the Family.* Chicago: Rand McNally & Company, 1964, pp. 33–50.

SMITH, M. B. "Anthropology and Psychology," in John Gillin, ed. *For a Science of Social Man.* New York: The Macmillan Company, 1954, pp. 32–66.

SMITH, RAYMOND T. *The Negro Family in British Guiana.* London: Routledge and Kegan Paul, Ltd., 1956.

SMITH, WILLIAM C. "The Ethnological Approach to the Family," *Journal of Applied Sociology,* **8** (Nov. 1923), pp. 102–07.

SPIRO, MELFORD E. "Is The Family Universal?" *American Anthropologist,* **56** (Oct. 1954), pp. 839–46.

STEWARD, JULIAN H. "Evolution and Process," in A. L. Kroeber, *et al. Anthropology Today.* Chicago: University of Chicago Press, 1953.

———. *Theory of Culture Change.* Urbana, Ill.: University of Illinois Press, 1953.

SUSSMAN, MARVIN B. "Unheralded Structures in Current Conceptualizations of Family Functioning," *Marriage and Family Living,* **24** (Aug. 1962), pp. 231–40.

TAX, SOL, *et al. An Appraisal of Anthropology Today.* Chicago: University of Chicago Press, 1953.

TIMASHEFF, NICHOLAS S. *Sociological Theory: Its Nature and Growth,* rev. ed. New York: Random House, Inc., 1957.

WARNER, W. LLOYD. *Black Civilization.* New York: Harper & Row, Publishers, 1937.

———, and Lunt, Paul S. *The Social Life of a Modern Community.* New Haven: Yale University Press, 1941.

WEST, JAMES (pseud.) *Plainville, U.S.A.* New York: Columbia University Press, 1945.

WHITE, LESLIE A. "The Definition and Prohibition of Incest," *American Anthropologist,* **50** (July–Sept. 1948), pp. 416–35.

———. *The Evolution of Culture.* New York: McGraw-Hill, Inc., 1959.

WHYTE, WILLIAM F. *Street Corner Society.* Chicago: University of Chicago Press, 1943.

ZELDITCH, MORRIS, JR. "Family, Marriage and Kinship," in Robert E. L. Faris, ed. *Handbook of Modern Sociology.* Chicago: Rand McNally & Company, 1964, pp. 680–733.

chapter 3

The Structure-Functional
Approach to Family Study*

Jennie McIntyre

Few terms are more common in the family literature than *structure* and *function*. They appear in the writings within almost any current frame of reference, but with a variety of meanings. Merton's discussion (1957) of the various uses of the term *function* helps to distinguish its meaning as used in the structure-functional approach from other uses found in the literature of the social sciences. One usage makes the term virtually equivalent to the term *occupation*. Merton points out this connotation of the word in Weber's work where he defines occupation as "the mode of specialization, specification and combination of the functions of an individual in so far as it constitutes for him the basis of a continual opportunity for income or for profit." (Weber, 1947.) In functional analysis by economists, too, the functions may refer to the distribution of occupations in the group being analyzed.

Another use of the word *function* is one which is more frequently used by sociologists. For example, Ogburn and Nimkoff, in their

* Grateful acknowledgment is made of the contribution of Norman W. Bell who served as editorial consultant for this framework and who read and critically reviewed the manuscript prior to its final revision. Many, although not all, of his suggestions have been incorporated into the final manuscript. Inadequacies and errors in the chapter as published, however, are entirely the responsibility of the author and the editors.

work on changes in the family, use the word to refer to activities. (p. 125.)

> Families have been either centers for, or have engaged as families in most of the activities common to mankind. These more or less universal activities of man may be classified broadly into such categories as working, loving, playing, governing, fighting, protecting and worshipping. It is possible then to summarize the functions of families into such a set of categories and to trace the changes from the family of self-sustaining farmers in the era of the household economy to that of the modern family.

In this passage the word is employed to refer to the activities engaged in by families. It is also used to refer to the activities assigned to a person of a particular social status. Although this is not the definition attached to the term *function* by writers using the structure-functional approach, a meaning very closely related to this seems to be implied when certain of these writers discuss functional prerequisites and functions of the family.

When used in its mathematical sense, the word *function* indicates a particular kind of relationship between two variables, namely, that the value of one depends on the value of the other. If a demographer states that birth rates are a function of economic status, he is implying that the birth rate varies in a specified manner as different economic strata are considered.

One of the early definitions of *structure* and *function* as they are used in structure-functional analysis was that set forth by Radcliffe-Brown in 1935. Using the analogy between social life and organic life, he says:

> As the terms are here used the organism is not itself the structure; it is a collection of units arranged in a structure, i.e., in a set of relations; the organism *has* a structure. . . . The structure is thus to be defined as a set of relations between the entities. . . . As long as it lives the organism preserves a certain continuity of structure although it does not preserve the complete identity of its constituent parts. . . . Over a period its constituent cells do not remain the same. But the structural arrangement of the constituent units does remain similar. The process by which this structural continuity of the organism

is maintained is called life. . . . As the word function is here being used the life of an organism is conceived as the *functioning* of its structure. . . . If we consider any recurrent part of the life-process, such as respiration, digestion, etc., its *function* is the part it plays in, the contribution it makes to, the life of the organism as a whole. (pp. 394–5.)

He then refers back to Durkheim's definition that the function of a social institution is the correspondence between it and the needs of the society.

In spite of the various usages to which this concept has been put in the years since Radcliffe-Brown and Malinowski defined it, there has been continuity in the core meaning of *function:* the contribution that an item makes to the maintenance of the whole. There has been, however, an increased emphasis on a need to specify which system is being served. (Merton, 1957, p. 52; Bell and Vogel, 1960, p. 6.) Emphasis may be on one or more of a range of systems: a total society, a social institution, an individual.

Ogburn's statement in 1933 concerning the loss of societal functions to the family and the relative increase of the "affectional" function for the family members focused the attention of sociologists on functions of the family. Winch suggests that there is a parallel between Ogburn's statement on the transfer of all familial functions except the affectional and Parsons' emphasis on the functions on behalf of personality rather than those directly supporting society. (Winch, 1963, pp. 5–6.) Parsons' concern is with the process of differentiation within society, the greater specialization of societal institutions. (Parsons, 1961; Parsons and Bales, 1955, pp. 26–31.) There does, nevertheless, seem to be a relationship between the two notions, as Winch suggests.

The family may be viewed as one of several subsystems in the society, with the relationships between family and society or family and other subsystems as the focus of investigation. The individual nuclear family may also be analyzed as a system in its own right— a boundary-maintaining system which is under various internal and external pressures toward boundary dissolution or maintenance. The first type of analysis has been referred to as *macrofunctionalism* and the latter as *microfunctionalism*. (Hill and Hansen, 1960.)

Previous delineations of the structure-functional framework in the study of the family include works by Hill and Hansen (1960),

Goode (1959), Winch (1963), Bell and Vogel (1960), Levy (1949), Pitts (1964), and Coser (1964). There are occasional apparent divergences and varying conceptualizations among these writers. This paper is an attempt to describe the core of the framework common to these authors and to those who have been making use of this framework in family studies.

FOCI OF STUDY

In the structure-functional approach to the study of the family, three major areas of functions have been particularly emphasized: the functions of the family for society, the functions of the subsystems within a family for the family or for each other, and the functions of the family for individual family members, including the development of personality. Another way of stating these three major areas is (1) the relationships between the family and broader social units, (2) the relationships between the family and subsystems, and (3) the relationships between the family and personality. In each case the relationship in either or both directions may be emphasized.

One of the major emphases concerning the relationships between the family and broader social units has been on the role that the family plays in the socialization of new members of society. Parsons and Bales indeed suggest that only a small kinship-structured unit, the family, may adequately carry out these responsibilities for very young children and hence the universality of the nuclear family. Both of these statements have been questioned by others. (Spiro, 1960; Levy, 1955; Levy and Fallers, 1959.) Such questions notwithstanding, the transmission of the values of the culture to new members of the family has been the focus of many studies, particularly, but not exclusively, in the work of Parsons and Bales. They single out this function and the stabilization of the adult personalities in the population as the two major functions of the family for society and see them as functions which are either fulfilled by parent-child interaction or become prescriptions for the parent-child relationship.

Other aspects of the relationship of the family to external social systems have been subsumed as relationships between the family and the economy, between the family and the polity, and between the family and the community. (Bell and Vogel, 1960.) Many studies of particular topics could, of course, come under more than one of these headings. A study of the means of transmitting the value of achieved, rather than ascribed status, through the use of particular kinship terms in the American kinship system, for example, is a study of the socialization process but also demonstrates how the family members are thereby equipped to take their places in the occupational system and to serve the function of supplying the labor for a particular type of economic system. (Schneider and Homans, 1955.) An important focus of research regarding the relationship between the family and external systems has been the congruence of family structure and industrialization-urbanization. Goode (1963), Levy (1949), and Smelser (1959) are concerned with the reciprocal influence of these two factors.

Much of the emphasis of studies of the internal relationships within a family has been on the division of labor between the sexes and on the functions of this division of labor for the maintenance of the family. The work of Parsons, Bales, Slater, and Zelditch, with emphasis on instrumental-expressive role differentiation, is particularly prominent here. (Parsons and Bales, 1955; Slater, 1961.) Instrumental-expressive role differentiation also appears as a subject of investigation in family research oriented primarily in other directions, as in Blake's study of the family and fertility in Jamaica. (Blake, 1961, pp. 72–76.) The functions of this division of labor for other systems, such as the occupational system, have also been discussed, as has the function of differential sex roles in the family of orientation for subsequent interaction in the family of procreation. The incest taboo too has been the focus of functional analyses of sex roles within the family. (Parsons, 1955.) Again, the tendency to investigate functions for more than one system is illustrated, as the functions of the incest taboo for the larger society are explored, as well as its functions for the balance of power within the nuclear family, and its functions for personality development.

In the introduction to his study of the postdivorce adjustment of divorcées, Goode includes a concise statement of what is and what is not of concern in his structure-functional study. His statement illustrates the emphasis on the family as a social system:

> The nuclear family is to be viewed as one type of boundary-maintaining social unit, under various internal and external pressures toward boundary dissolution and maintenance. Marital unhappiness is only a resultant of various factors that predispose

toward marital instability. . . . Within such a view, divorce is seen as one kind of mechanism for dealing with the pressures and problems inevitably caused by marriage. (1956, p. 9.)
It does not give advice on how to avoid divorce, or even how to avoid the problems that are caused by divorce. . . . It is concerned with the place of divorce and postdivorce adjustment in the kinship system. (1956, p. 3.)

This same study also considers the consequences of divorce for the individuals involved and might have studied the consequences for the larger society using this framework. An understanding of the place of the family in the society and of the individual family as a social system are the concerns of writers using this approach rather than the search for the correlates of marital happiness or information which might seem of immediate practical value to the marriage counselor.

The third major focus of study concerns the general area of the reciprocal relationships between the family and personality. The function of an emotional disturbance in a child for the family and the consequences for the personality development of the child are the subjects of a study of this nature. (Vogel and Bell, 1960.) Other examples are Strodtbeck (1958) and Parsons (1955). Spiegel and Bell (1959) present a review of studies concerning the development of pathology in a family setting. Some of these studies consider the family as a system, but the authors of this review report that most writers consider only particular relationships within the family, such as a mother-child relationship and its connection with disturbances. Ackerman points out the need to consider the relationships between the larger society, the family, and the individual in order to understand the development of personality. After listing the functions, or "social purposes," of the family he states:

Clearly the configuration of family determines the forms of behavior that are required in the roles of husband and wife, father, mother, and child. Mothering and fathering, and the role of the child, acquire specific meaning only within a defined family structure. Thus the family molds the kinds of persons it needs in order to carry out its functions, and in the process each member reconciles his past conditioning with present role expectations. (1958, p. 19.)

A point of view which can be found in the literature is that the family is a dependent variable when the relations between the family and other institutions are being studied. The explanation for observed structure and functions of the family in a given society is then assumed to lie outside the family. (For example, Winch, 1963.) The family is considered an independent variable only when personality development or socialization of the child is being considered. This point of view is not unanimous, however, and is not strictly consistent with structure-functional theory. For if a society is viewed as a social system characterized by an equilibrium tendency, the subsystems of which it is composed are all interrelated parts. Any factor which influences any one of these parts will necessarily have implications for any of the other parts as well as for the system as a whole. Bell and Vogel exemplify the tendency to consider the *reciprocal* functional interchanges between the family and societal subsystems. (1960, pp. 8–19.) Levy, too, sees the kinship structure as an independent variable influencing as well as being influenced by the rate of industrialization in China. (1949, Chap. 10.) A more recent work by Goode (1963) similarly considers the effects of the family as an independent factor in industrialization.

CONCEPTS

Society: "a social system which survives its original members, replaces them through biological reproduction, and is relatively self-sufficient." (Winch, 1963, p. 8.) The system is self-sufficient in that it meets the requisites for survival (see *Framework*) and apparently is territorially based insofar as discussion centers on the functions of, for example, the American family or the Chinese family. Because the basic societal functions must be fulfilled, society is a system of positions or roles related to these functions.

Social system: a system seen as two or more interdependent units which are at the same time actors and social objects to each other. The defining properties of social systems are differentiation, organization, boundary maintenance, and equilibrium tendency. That is, the actors occupy differentiated statuses or positions and perform differentiated roles; there is some organized pattern governing the relationships of the members and describing their rights and obligations with respect to one another, and some set of common norms and values, together with various types of shared cultural objects and symbols. A system is boundary-maintaining in that there tends to be a tighter, more integrated organization among its components than there is between components and elements outside the system. A social system is characterized by an equilibrium tendency in that the system has built-in mechanisms which operate to hold it in some sort of steady state, either a static or a moving stability, over a period of time. Concrete social systems are always components of larger systems and in turn are composed of smaller subsystems. The nuclear family is thus a component of the kinship structure of larger systems, including the society as a whole; on the other hand, it also consists of subsystems such as the mother-child subsystem. Functional subsystems are analytic systems rather than concrete groups, and are concerned with the functional problems which must be met if the society is to survive.

Equilibrium: "the concept of regularity under specific conditions as applied to the internal state of an empirical system relative to its environment. This regularity of course should always be treated as relative rather than absolute; indeed, it is generally subject to considerable ranges of tolerance, and of course its maintenance is by no means inevitable but, if the conditions on which it depends are changed beyond certain limits, it will disappear, again most probably giving way to other regularities than to sheer randomness. . . . It should be clearly understood that not only are equilibrating processes very frequently doubtful in their outcome so that breakdown of equilibrium is scientifically as important a phenomenon as its preservation, but also that equilibrium itself is neither attained nor maintained simply by the persistence of some 'static' factor." (Parsons, 1961, p. 338.)

Role differentiation: "the distribution of persons among the various positions and activities distinguished in the structure and hence the differential arrangement of the members of the structure." (Levy, 1949, p. 8.) The terms of role differentiation may be age, sex, generation, and, sometimes, economic and political positions. (Levy, 1949, p. 10.) Thus, to cite an obvious illustration, "the father is stronger than the son, (presumably young), so that he, rather than the son, is allocated to leadership roles in instrumental activities." (Zelditch, 1955, p. 313.)

Bales and Slater (1955) see role differentiation in the nuclear family as dependent not only on age and sex differences but also on factors which arise out of the interaction which occurs in any small decision-making group. The interaction processes result in specialization in two different kinds of activities: instrumental and expressive. They also include the expectations which members of a group develop regarding the activities of the various members. Differentiation then can be considered the "process of development by which such a constellation of roles come to be recognizable." (Bales and Slater, 1955, p. 259.)

Instrumental: primarily concerned with relations of the group to the external situation, including adaptations to external situations and establishment of satisfactory goal relations for the system vis-à-vis the situation. In the nuclear family the husband-father as bread-winner tends to specialize in the instrumental activities of his family.

Expressive: concerned primarily with integration or solidarity of the group, the internal relations of members to each other, and the emotional states of tension produced by performing their roles in the group. While the husband-father is away at work the mother may stay home, responsible for the emotional satisfactions of the family and symbolizing the integrative focus of the home.

An illustration of the characteristics of equilibrium tendency, boundary maintenance and role differentiation in the nuclear family viewed as a system is provided by Zelditch, although his subject is primarily role differentiation. (1955, pp. 310–12.) The members of the family typically disperse in the morning for job, school, shopping, and so on, that is, for instrumental activities. Typically, they are reunited some time later and the focus for a time is on expressive and integrative activities. Otherwise the system would tend to disappear and not be identifiable as a bounded system. In other words, the social system tends to *maintain its boundaries.* An overemphasis on instrumental activities would create a strain on the system if it were not counteracted by expressive and integrative activities. The converse would also be true. This tendency toward a balance of forces counteracting each other is an *equilibrium tendency. Role differentiation* is illustrated by the husband's primary responsibility for instrumental activities and the wife's primary responsibility for expressive activities.

Structure: the arrangement of the roles of which a social system is composed. Structure can, then, be divided into relational and unit categories. The most significant unit of social structure is not the person but the role; in more complex systems, however, the units may be smaller systems or subsystems. Relational components of structure are those comprising the stable elements in the relations between units. (Parsons, 1961; Parsons and Shils, 1951, p. 23.)

Position: a location in a social structure which is associated with a set of social norms. (Bates, 1956, p. 314.)

Status: "position plus the connotation of invidious evaluation, differential prestige, and hierarchy." (Winch, 1963, p. 10.) The term is sometimes used as a synonym of position without the evaluative connotations.

Role: "that organized sector of an actor's orientation which constitutes and defines his participation in an interactive process. It involves a set of complementary expectations concerning his own actions and those of others with whom he interacts." (Parsons and Shils, 1951, p. 23.) Role may be considered that "part of a social position consisting of a more or less integrated or related subset of social norms which are distinguishable from other subsets of norms forming the same position." (Bates, 1956, p. 314.) Some writers feel that the concepts *status* and *role* are best considered as a unity rather than separately, in which case the term *status-role* may then be used. (For example, Hill and Hansen, 1960.)

Function: usage that has evolved from the contribution that an activity or an item makes to the whole; the consequences of the activity or item for the system being considered. Function can also mean the activity by which the consequences referred to are attained. Thus, the reproductive function of the family results in the replacement of members of the society. The consequences of an activity are not ordinarily the same for the different levels of systems involved. The same activity may have utterly different consequences for the individual, his family, and for society as a whole or for some subsystem of the society.

Dysfunction: the negative consequences of an activity for a given system.

Manifest function: the recognized and intended consequences of an activity for a given system.

Latent function: the unrecognized and unintended consequences of an activity for a given system.

Functional prerequisites: the problems which must be solved or the activities which must be performed to insure the survival of a social system on a given level. "A given requirement can be termed a functional prerequisite of any social system if in its hypothesized absence the system would degenerate into the war of all against all

or if its members would simply cease to live, or if structural altera-
tion on the level concerned would take place." (Levy, 1949, p. 7.)

The use here of four more terms, *family, nuclear family, family
of orientation*, and *family of procreation*, does not differ in essence
from their usage elsewhere. Parsons, for example, suggests (1954)
that the criteria for the nuclear family are (1) a solidary relationship
between mother and child lasting over a period of years and tran-
scending physical care in its significance and (2) a special relationship of the woman to a man outside her own descent group who is
sociologically the father of the child, thereby securing the legitimacy
of the child's status in the larger kinship system.

Although most family functionalists accept Murdock's statement
of the universality of the nuclear family as a "distinct and strongly
functional group in every known society," a qualification of the
statement has been suggested. Levy indicates that in the traditional
Chinese family the nuclear family was not a significant unit in the
kinship structure. While it is undoubtedly true, he continues, that
in any society, including the traditional Chinese one, any individual
can identify his spouse and offspring, the aggregation of these individuals is not necessarily a system of action. Neither is it considered
a unit by the larger society nor is it the focus of primary loyalties in
the traditional Chinese system. Levy suggests that it is a Western
bias to assume that the nuclear family as defined by Murdock and
Parsons has primary significance. For comparative purposes, he suggests a definition of the family which he feels would more accurately
include those systems where that would not hold true. As a definition he suggests: "the smallest kinship unit on a membership basis in
a given society that is institutionally treated as a unit for generalized
purposes by other parts of the society and by other parts of the
kinship structure." (Levy, 1955; Levy and Fallers, 1959.)

BASIC ASSUMPTIONS

The assumptions basic to a conceptual framework are often merely
implicit in an investigator's work. Several family students using the
structure-functional approach, however, have explicitly stated their
own assumptions, facilitating the task of delineating them here. The
chief problem has been selecting those which are basic to the framework rather than to individual writers. The first three listed here are
necessary to all structure-functional studies of the family and con-

cern the place of the family in the larger society. Those assumptions concerned with the study of the family as a social system and the relationship between the family and the individual member are not always essential for every writer who concerns himself with these subjects. There is less similarity in the various studies of these subjects than in the former. This divergence notwithstanding, assumptions which are basic to some of the more comprehensive family studies are included here.

Another comment is perhaps in order before proceeding with the list. Hill and Hansen have compiled a quite different list of five underlying assumptions.[1] Without quarreling with their major points one might defend use of those assumptions named by other writers using the structure-functional approach. Hill and Hansen point out the foci of the framework and state as an assumption that this is the best way to study human behavior. Certainly researchers using this approach do seek a different kind of information than do investigators of the correlates of marital happiness, for example. The same might be said of writers of any school. The assumptions listed here appear to be those on which the framework is based.

1. Certain functional requirements must be satisfied if a society is to survive at a given level. (Bell and Vogel, 1960, p. 9; Winch, 1963, p. 15.)
2. There are functional subsystems to meet these requirements. (Bell and Vogel, 1960, p. 9; Winch, 1963, p. 20.)
3. In every society the family performs at least one of these basic functions. (Bell and Vogel, 1960, p. 8; Winch, 1963, p. 31.)
4. An individual family is a social system with functional requirements comparable to those of larger social systems. (Bell and Vogel, 1960, p. 19.)
5. An individual family is also a small group possessing certain generic characteristics in common with all small groups. (Parsons, 1954; Zelditch, 1955, p. 308.)

[1] "(1) Social conduct is best analyzed for its contribution to the maintenance of the social system, or for its nature under the structures of the system. (2) A social human is basically a reacting part of the social system; self-elicited (independent) action is rare and asocial. (3) The basic autonomous unit is the social system, which is composed of interdependent sub-systems (e.g., institutions, family systems, etc.). (4) It is possible to profitably study any sub-units of the basic system. (5) The social system tends to homeostasis." Hill and Hansen, (1960).

6. Social systems, including families, perform individual-serving functions as well as society-serving functions. (Winch, 1963, p. 20.)

PRODUCT

Of the large body of empirical research concerning the family apparently only a relatively small proportion has consciously used a structure-functional conceptual framework. Despite this apparent lack the framework has had an impact on research greater than its deliberate use would indicate. Many investigators, regardless of theoretical orientation, do make a point of indicating the functions of the item being studied, frequently for particular structural referents. Some writers consciously employing this framework have made use of the works of other investigators, synthesizing and fitting them into a structure-functional analysis of the family. The reader by Bell and Vogel (1960) is an example; another is Levy's study of the Chinese family (1949). Although Levy does add some new material, Parsons makes the point that this is not the important contribution of Levy's study. (In Levy, 1949, p. ix.)

> Much of its empirical subject matter will be familiar to students of the Western literature. The contribution of this study must not be sought primarily in the new facts it brings to light, but in two other directions—the perspective through which the material and its problems are seen, and the consistency and rigor with which the author's analysis is carried out. . . . This picture is considerably further systematized and placed in perspective by Dr. Levy's analysis, and is further illuminated by consideration of the relation between changes in the family structure and the industrialization of the economy.

As this example illustrates, the result is to make family study an integral part of the study of the larger society.

The impact of structure-functionalism on practice is more difficult to assess. There has undoubtedly been an influence on the teaching of family courses; nearly any textbook on the family, regardless of its orientation, includes at least some references to the functions of the family for the society. The result might be an increased emphasis on the part of teachers, and awareness on the part of students of the place of the family in the total society.

Conversations with marriage counselors suggest that structure-functionalism has had at most an indirect influence on counseling practice. The emphasis on the client as a part of a system rather than as an individual with an emotional problem may be in part the result of this influence. A marriage counselor names this emphasis in structure-functionalism as *inter*personality rather than *intra*personality analysis, and traces out the implications of system theory for counseling. She suggests that many counselors implicitly concern themselves with such system concepts as *role* and *role expectations*. She further suggests that counselors might profitably make these concerns explicit and orient the client to consideration of his problems in system terms. (Kargman, 1957.)

VALUES

Like most sociologists, writers using this frame of reference attempt to keep their work free of values, excluding the generally accepted values of science, of course. On the whole they have been as successful or more successful in this attempt than others in the social sciences. Critics of structure-functional work have considered the question of whether it places a value on the status quo through an emphasis on boundary maintenance and equilibrium. (Bock, 1963; Falding, 1963; Greenfield, 1961; Merton, 1957.) A more specific question is whether equilibrium and boundary maintenance are valued. The feeling that the term *equilibrium* implies valuation may be due to its usage in everyday language. *The American College Dictionary* gives "mental balance" as its third definition of the term. (1960, p. 406.) Equilibrium then must be better than disequilibrium. "A state of rest due to the action of forces that counteract each other," another definition in the same dictionary, is more akin to the term's usage in structure-functionalism, particularly if the idea of static or moving regularity is substituted for "state of rest." Not only is this meaning of the concept not intrinsically one of valuation, but neither should it be emphasized at the expense of disequilibrium. "Breakdown of equilibrium is scientifically as important as its preservation." (Parsons, 1961, p. 338.)

In spite of the inherent neutrality of the concept *equilibrium*, the idea that an item is functional if it contributes toward maintenance or preservation of a bounded system may lead to the feeling that a value is placed on the status quo. The authors who make greatest use of these concepts in works on the family do find the typical, contemporary urban middle class nuclear family with conventional role differentiation by sex functional for society and for the individuals concerned. (For example, Parsons and Bales, 1955.) Considering other functionalists, Greenfield notes that present scholars tend to view the small nuclear family as being in a state of functional inter-dependence with industry and Western civilization, and that the family is now functional in that it tends to maintain the new equilibrium (1961). If the contemporary family system is valued because it is functional for the present economic system, then by implication that economic system is also valued. Although not required by structure-functionalism, this evaluation is compatible with and perhaps even encouraged by this framework as it is used in family studies.

In contrast to an implicit evaluation of the contemporary family for its contribution to the larger society, Goode chooses to make explicit his own evaluation of the trend toward the modern nuclear family for its benefits for the individual:

> I welcome the great changes now taking place, and not because it might be a more efficient instrument of industrialization. . . . Rather, I see in it and in the industrial system that accompanies it the hope of greater freedom. . . . For me, then, the major and sufficing justification for the newly emerging family patterns is that they offer people at least the potentialities of greater fulfilment. (1963, p. 380.)

THE FRAMEWORK

A functional analysis of the family emphasizes the relationship between the family and the larger society, the internal relationships between the subsystems of the family, and/or the relationship between the family and the personality of the individual member. Hill has termed the former *macrofunctionalism* and the latter two *microfunctionalism*. (Hill and Hansen, 1960.) Although one or another of these aspects may be emphasized, each of the others is ordinarily at least implicitly recognized and all three are frequently given equal attention.

Macrofunctionalism ordinarily begins by positing a list of functional prerequisites of the society and a functional subsystem which arises to meet each of these prerequisites. Then the location of analytic subsystems in various concrete structures can be examined. The question of the functions performed by the family for other subsystems then is approached from the question of the extent to which these analytic subsystems are located in the family. The functional prerequisites named by various writers differ somewhat in number and in terminology but seem generally to fall into one of two categories. One of these might be considered a list of activities which must be performed if the society is to survive. A typical list is that suggested by Winch (1963):

1. Replacements for dying members of the society must be provided.
2. Goods and services must be produced and distributed for the support of the members of the society.
3. There must be provision for accommodating conflicts and maintaining order internally and externally.
4. Human replacements must be trained to become participating members of the society.
5. There must be procedures for dealing with emotional crises, for harmonizing the goals of individuals with the values of the society, and for maintaining a sense of purpose.

The analytic subsystems which he posits to correspond to these societal functions are, respectively, familial, economic, political, socializing-educational, and religious. In determining the extent to which these structures are located in a single concrete structure such as the family, the author is essentially regarding the extent to which families perform these activities for the society. By carrying his analysis further and viewing the individual-serving functions of a structure (basic assumption number six) as rewards to be dispensed to or withheld from the individual, this author arrives at the hypothesis that the power of a societal structure is positively correlated with the number of functions that it performs.

The second method of conceptualizing functional prerequisites is to consider the functions as consequences, rather than as activities. We then have a list of consequences, the activities which produce them, and the analytic subsystems responsible for their achievement:

1. Adaptation—the creation and distribution of valued goods and services; functional subsystem—the economy.
2. Goal gratification—the administration of the activities of the society to attain the system goals; functional subsystem—the polity.

3. Integration—integrating various parts and activities of the system by institutionalizing patterns of behavior and by using mechanisms of social control to motivate members to conform to these patterns; functional subsystem—community, or networks of diffuse affective relationships.
4. Pattern maintenance—the selection of certain general principles which can serve as reference points and guides for behavior; functional subsystem—value system. (Bell and Vogel, 1960.)

The relationship between the family and the larger society is then seen as a series of interchanges between the family and these functional subsystems. The nuclear family provides labor and family assets to the economy in exchange for wages and goods. It exchanges loyalty and compliance with the polity for leadership and decisions. To the community the nuclear family gives adherence and group participation and from it receives support and identity. Between the nuclear family and the value system the interchange is acceptance of standards and conformity for specifications of standards and approval. A functional subsystem, however, does not always have concrete structural referents. At other times its functions are said to be performed by a variety of concrete groups. In discussing the value system Bell and Vogel suggest that religion and the educational system fulfill part of its functions. (1960, p. 18.) The concept *value system*, as they use it, however, appears to include more than these or other concrete groups. They cite the Schneider-Homans study of kinship terminology as an example of how the value system of the society is reinforced while the patterns of the family are simultaneously maintained. In this example the value of achievement rather than ascription is transmitted along with the family patterns. There is no concrete referent for the subsystem in this instance. Again, the subject investigated is a societal function performed by the family. The functional interchanges between the family and the subsystems of society are reciprocal, however, and are assumed to balance out in the long run. When they do not balance, one expects change or indications of stress at some level—individual, familial, or societal. There is a recognition by these same authors (Bell and Vogel) that the functional substructures may be contained to a greater or lesser extent within the kinship structure. In some societies, for example, the economic substructure may exist largely within extended families. To say that functional substructures are contained to an extent within the kinship structure is to say that the family performs certain functions for the larger society. In the kind of society just mentioned, the family as family might be engaging in economic production.

Rather than explicitly defining a list of functional prerequisites for the society and investigating the extent to which the family is responsible for the achievement of those prerequisites, other writers take as their starting point the family itself and attempt to define a list of functions which the family performs for the society and for its members. Parsons has pointed out that a difficulty with this approach is that there is no agreement concerning the root or primary functions of the family. (1955, p. 8.) Such a list might include reproduction, placement, maintenance, socialization, and sexual controls. These functions are oriented toward the society by "producing an individual and keeping him in action." (Goode, 1959, p. 189.) Davis names the first four as core functions and states that other functions performed by the family, such as the economic, are by-products of its primary function, reproduction. (1948, pp. 394–96.)

A question raised by the macrofunctional approach is that of why functions are transferred from one concrete structure to another; since the family is the focus of attention, why are some functions tranferred from the family to other societal subsystems? One hypothesis is that the extent to which the societal functions are contained within the kinship structure in a given society depends upon the extent to which the society is structurally differentiated. (Bell and Vogel, 1960, p. 7; Parsons, 1955, pp. 8–10.) In the more complex society there will be a greater degree of differentiation, and the family will be a more specialized system and consequently responsible for few of the basic societal functions.

In treating the family as a social system and in investigating the relationships between the family and the subsystems which compose it, the general tendency is to consider the nuclear family as defined by Murdock (1949) as the system being studied. As a system, the nuclear family is faced with the problems common to all social systems: task performance, goal gratification, integration and solidarity, and pattern maintenance. The nuclear family, like other social systems, is characterized by differentiation, organization, boundary maintenance and equilibrium tendency. Although the family meets its own functional prerequisites, its activities do not necessarily result in the same function for the larger society or societal subsystem as for the nuclear family itself.

Because the nuclear family is a small group it may be viewed as a system with certain generic characteristics in common with all small groups. Parsons, indeed, maintains that its effectiveness in the performance of its functions as a family depends on its possession of these characteristics. Deriving their hypothesis from Bales's experimental work with small groups, he and his collaborators suggest that families as well as other small groups differentiate spontaneously on a hierarchical or power dimension and along the instrumental-expressive axis which cuts across the hierarchical dimension. (These terms have already been defined on p. 21.) Sex and age differences provide a natural basis for these differentiations. Parsons emphasizes role differentiation along the instrumental-expressive axis while others have used a somewhat different terminology to explain the categories into which roles are differentiated.

Regardless of the terminology used by the individual writer, however, the emphasis is on an allocation of responsibility for the tasks which must be performed if the family is to survive as a system. Levy states that there must be a distribution of individuals among the total number of positions in the structure and that

> failure to have a well-institutionalized method of handling this requirement, a structure of role differentiation, would result in the cessation of functioning of the larger structure of which it is a part, either because vital positions would not be filled, or because fighting would break out over who was to fill which position—or more likely a combination of both. In any case, the system could not persist. (1949, p. 9.)

Levy provides a variant list of the requisites of a kinship structure, but similar meanings can be detected. The fact that he uses the term *structural prerequisites* rather than *functional prerequisites* means only that he is describing the other side of the coin—the substructures necessary to fulfill the requirements of survival for the system. The structural prerequisites for a kinship structure as he names them are as follows:

Role differentiation, (as defined in section on concepts).

Allocation of solidarity: the distribution of relationships among the members according to the content, strength, and intensity of the relationship. *Content* refers to the type of relationship which is to exist and the members between whom it is to exist, for example, the emotional attachment between mother and child. *Strength* refers to the relative precedence of this relationship over others. The father-son relationship may take precedence over the husband-wife relationship, although not in the American kinship system. *Intensity* is the type of affect, love or fear, for example, and the degree of the affective involvement of the relationship.

Economic allocation: the distribution of goods and services making up the income of the structure and the distribution of the goods and efforts making up the output of the structure. There is differentiation regarding the division of labor in the production and distribution of goods and services, and in their consumption.

Political allocation: the distribution of power over and responsibility for the actions of the various members of the kinship unit. A substructure of political allocation is necessary because, if the family is to function as a unit, certain requirements must be met and someone must be responsible for their being met.

Allocation of integration and expression: the distribution of the methods and techniques of socialization, inculcation, and maintenance in the members of the values, attitudes, and procedures of that particular kinship structure. This category would seem to be more analogous to pattern maintenance, and Levy's allocation of solidarity would be analogous to integration and solidarity in the list of functional prerequisites mentioned previously.

CRITIQUE AND DISCUSSION

A problem of the macrofunctional approach is the difficulty of a clear definition of terms in the most general statements. Merton (1957) refers to the lack of a definitive formulation of a list of functional prerequisites in his paradigm for functional analysis. The problem is as apparent in functional studies of the family as in other functional works, especially when the emphasis is on the functions which the family performs for the larger society. It is especially difficult if by definition these functions must be performed for the survival of the society. The lack of cases of societies not surviving and of documentation of the determining factors in those cases where extinction may have occurred is only one difficulty. As Nagel points out, it is difficult to designate unambiguously the system which is to be investigated except in the case of primitive societies and, "in regard to the condition of survival by a society, there is nothing comparable in this domain to the generally acknowledged 'vital functions' of biology as defining attributes of living organisms. . . . It is therefore not easy to fix upon a criterion of social survival that can have fruitful uses and not be purely arbitrary." (1961, p. 527.) Homans (1964), also criticizes functionalism in part for the difficulty of clearly defining its key terms, such as *equilibrium* and *survival*. That is, unless it is possible to specify when a society is or is not in equilibrium or when it has or has not survived, it is not possible to deduce further propositions from a statement regarding equilibrium and survival. Beginning with the general propositions typical of structure-functionalism, one could not deduce statements about particular features of particular societies.

The concern for functional prerequisites may be at the root of another problem. If an item is considered not only functional but a functional necessity, then it is but a short step further to assume that it exists in order to fulfill that function. Writers using the structure-functional approach have at times seemed to assume that an explanation of the functions of an observed regularity is an explanation of its origin or its persistence. Levy points out the logical fallacy of "functional teleology" and several pages later explains the ubiquity of the incest taboo on the grounds that it is a functional prerequisite of kinship systems. Thus he writes, "It is not, however, permissible to observe that the existence of a given phenomenon is the result of its being a functional prerequisite of the phenomenon of which it is a part." (1949, p. 3.) And later, "It may well be that the basic factor in explaining the existence of the incest taboo is the necessity of reducing rivalry between members of the family unit to a minimum." (1949, p. 21.) He goes on to suggest that this explanation is not by itself sufficient and then names other functions which supposedly help account for the existence of the taboo. Levy is not alone in this respect. Parsons, for example, in a similar manner explains the universality of the incest taboo by its functions. (1954, p. 115.)

Merton also poses the problem of specification of the system being served by a function. (1957, p. 52.) As pointed out above, many family writers do point to different functions of the same item for various system levels. The practice of specifying an analytic subsystem as the system being served, however, or of saying that an analytic substructure is partly contained within the family is subject to the same criticism as the use of society as a referent. There remains a vagueness regarding the system to which reference is being made; to use these concepts is not to be any more specific than to say that the family performs an economic or a religious function for society. Functional explanations thus present many logical difficulties. They can be so deceptively simple and sensible that it is easy to assume that more has been proved than really has been. Nevertheless, as a way of penetrating beyond the surface form of and accepted reasons for any phenomena, the functional approach has been very useful. The challenge persists, and must be faced, of being alert to the logic of functional statements and developing ways of subjecting such statements to empirical tests.

REFERENCES

ACKERMAN, NATHAN W. *The Psychodynamics of Family Life.* New York: Basic Books, Inc., Publishers, 1958.

American College Dictionary. New York: Random House, Inc., 1960.

BALES, ROBERT F., and SLATER, PHILLIP E. "Role Differentiation in Small Decision-Making Groups," in Talcott Parsons and Robert F. Bales. *Family Socialization and Interaction Process.* New York: Free Press of Glencoe, Inc., 1955, Chap. V.

BATES, FREDERICK L. "Position, Role and Status: A Reformulation of Concepts," *Social Forces,* 34 (May 1956), pp. 313–21. Cited by Robert F. Winch in *The Modern Family.* New York: Holt, Rinehart & Winston, Inc., 1963, pp. 8–9.

BELL, NORMAN W., and VOGEL, EZRA F. *A Modern Introduction to the Family.* New York: Free Press of Glencoe, Inc., 1960. A textbook including reprinted articles from a wide variety of authors, interpreted from a structure-functional point of view. The authors' version of this conceptual framework is included.

BLAKE, JUDITH. *Family Structure in Jamaica: The Social Context of Reproduction.* New York: Free Press of Glencoe, Inc., 1961. An investigation of whether consensual unions are the functional equivalent of legal marriage in the Jamaican lower class. The author surveys both men and women involved and arrives at a negative answer.

BOCK, KENNETH E. "Evolution, Function and Change," *American Sociological Review,* 28 (April 1963), pp. 229–37.

BRAITHWAITE, LLOYD. "Social Stratification in Trinidad," *Social and Economic Studies,* 2 (Oct. 1953). A discussion of the societal functions of the lower-class family.

COSER, ROSE LAUB, ed. *The Family: Its Structure and Functions.* New York: St. Martin's Press, Inc., 1964.

Davis, Kingsley. "Marriage and the Family," in his *Human Society*. New York: The Macmillan Company, 1948, Chap. 15.

———. "Myth of Functional Analysis as a Special Method in Sociology and Anthropology," *American Sociological Review*, 24 (Dec. 1959), pp. 757–72.

Devereux, Edward C. "Parsons' Sociological Theory," in Max Black, ed. *The Social Theories of Talcott Parsons*. Englewood Cliffs, N.J.: Prentice-Hall, Inc., 1961.

Dore, R. P. "Function and Cause," *American Sociological Review*, 26 (Dec. 1961), pp. 843–53.

Falding, Harold. "Functional Analysis in Sociology," *American Sociological Review*, 28 (Feb. 1963), pp. 5–13.

Goldberg, David. "Some Recent Developments in Fertility Research," *Demographic and Economic Change in Developed Countries: A Conference of the Universities National Bureau Committee for Economic Research*. Princeton, N.J.: Princeton University Press, 1960, pp. 137–51. Not a structure-functional study, but the author suggests that fertility might profitably be studied within this framework.

Goode, William J. *After Divorce*. New York: Free Press of Glencoe, Inc., 1956. A functional analysis of post-divorce adjustment.

———. "The Sociology of the Family," in Robert K. Merton, Leonard Broom, and Leonard S. Cottrell, Jr., eds. *Sociology Today*. New York: Basic Books, Inc., Publishers, 1959, pp. 178–96. Includes the author's model for structure-functional analysis.

———. *World Revolution and Family Patterns*. New York: Free Press of Glencoe, Inc., 1963.

Greenfield, S. M. "Industrialization and the Family in Sociological Theory," *American Journal of Sociology*, 67 (Nov. 1961), pp. 312–22. A refutation of the arguments that the American nuclear family is a functional consequence of industrialization.

Hill, Reuben, and Hansen, Donald A. "The Identification of Conceptual Frameworks Employed in Family Study," *Marriage and Family Living*, 22 (Nov. 1960), pp. 299–311.

Homans, George C. "Bringing Men Back In," *American Sociological Review*, 29 (Dec. 1964), pp. 809–18.

———. *The Human Group*. New York: Harcourt, Brace & World, Inc., 1950, pp. 268–72.

Kargman, Marie W. "The Clinical Use of Social System Theory in Marriage Counseling," *Marriage and Family Living*, 19 (Aug. 1957), pp. 263–69.

Komarovsky, Mirra. "Functional Analysis of Sex Roles," *American Sociological Review*, 15 (Aug. 1950), pp. 508–16.

Levy, Marion J. *The Family Revolution in Modern China*. Cambridge Mass.: Harvard University Press, 1949.

————. "Some Questions About Parsons' Treatment of the Incest Problem," *British Journal of Sociology*, 6 (Sept. 1955), pp. 277–85.

————. *The Structure of Society*. Princeton, N.J.: Princeton University Press, 1952.

————, and FALLERS, L. A. "Family: Some Comparative Considerations," *American Anthropologist*, 61 (Aug. 1959), pp. 647–51.

MALINOWSKI, BRONISLAW. "The Group and the Individual in Functional Analysis," *American Journal of Sociology*, 44 (May 1939), pp. 938–64. Of historical interest in the application of functional analysis to the family.

MERTON, ROBERT K. "Manifest and Latent Functions," in his *Social Theory and Social Structure*. New York: Free Press of Glencoe, Inc., 1957, pp. 19–82.

MURDOCK, GEORGE PETER. *Social Structure*. New York: The Macmillan Company, 1949.

NAGEL, ERNEST. "A Formalization of Functionalism," in his *Logic Without Metaphysics*. New York: Free Press of Glencoe, Inc. 1956, pp. 247–83

————. *The Structure of Science Problems in the Logic of Scientific Explanation*. New York: Harcourt, Brace & World, Inc., 1961, pp. 520–35.

OGBURN, W. F. "The Family and Its Functions," *Recent Social Trends in the United States*, Report of the President's Research Committee on Social Trends, 1933.

————, and NIMKOFF, M. F. *Technology and the Changing Family*. Boston: Houghton Mifflin Company, 1955.

PARSONS, TALCOTT. "The Incest Taboo in Relation to Social Structure and the Socialization of the Child," *British Journal of Sociology*, 5 (June 1954), pp. 101–17.

————, and BALES, ROBERT F. *Family, Socialization and Interaction Process*. New York: Free Press of Glencoe, Inc., 1955.

————. "The Kinship System of the Contemporary United States," *American Anthropologist*, 45 (Jan.-Mar. 1943), pp. 22–38.

————. "The Point of View of the Author," in Max Black, ed. *The Social Theories of Talcott Parsons*. Englewood Cliffs, N.J.: Prentice-Hall, Inc., 1961, pp. 311–63.

————. "Some Considerations on the Theory of Social Change," *Rural Sociology*, 26 (Sept. 1961), pp. 219–39.

————. "The Social Structures of the Family," in Ruth Anshen, ed. *The Family: Its Function and Destiny*. New York: Harper & Row, Publishers, 1959, pp. 263 ff.

————, PARSONS, TALCOTT, and SHILS, E. A. *Toward a General Theory of Action*. Cambridge: Harvard University Press, 1951.

PITTS, JESSE R. "The Structural-Functional Approach," in Harold T. Christenson, ed. *Handbook of Marriage and the Family*. Chicago: Rand McNally and Company, 1964, pp. 51–124.

QUARANTELLI, E. L. "A Note on the Protective Function of the Family in Disasters," *Marriage and Family Living*, **22** (Aug. 1960), pp. 263–64. A study in which the author finds the extended family in the United States performing the protective functions to a greater extent than believed by some.

RADCLIFFE-BROWN, A. R. "On the Concept of Function in Social Science," *American Anthropologist*, **37** (July–Sept. 1935), pp. 394–402. An early statement of functionalism.

SCHNEIDER, DAVID M., and HOMANS, GEORGE C. "Kinship Terminology and the American Kinship System," *American Anthropologist*, **57** (Dec. 1955), pp. 1194–1208. An examination of the functions of kinship terminology for the kinship system and for the value system of the larger society.

SCOTT, F. G. "Family Group Structure and Patterns of Social Interaction," *American Journal of Sociology*, **68** (Sept. 1962), pp. 214–28. A paper in which the author considers the family as a small group. The author studies interaction processes in relation to a family member's position within the family structure. Uses a seven-category adaptation of Bales' twelve-category recording method.

SLATER, PHILLIP E. "Parental Role Differentiation," *American Journal of Sociology*, **67** (Nov. 1961), pp. 296–308. A refutation of the hypothesis of universal role differentiation along an instrumental-expressive axis. Such differentiation is not only optional in the nuclear family but may even be dysfunctional at times.

SMELSER, NEIL J. *Social Change in the Industrial Revolution*. Chicago: University of Chicago Press. 1959.

SPIEGEL, JOHN P., and BELL, NORMAN W. "The Family of the Psychiatric Patient," in Silvano Arieti, ed. *American Handbook of Psychiatry*. New York: Basic Books, Inc., Publishers, 1959, Chap. 5.

SPIRO, MELFORD E. "Is the Family Universal? The Israeli Case," in Norman W. Bell and Ezra F. Vogel, eds. *A Modern Introduction to the Family*. New York: Free Press of Glencoe, Inc., 1960, pp. 64–75.

STRODTBECK, FRED L. "Family Interaction, Values and Achievement," in David C. McClelland *et al. Talent and Society*. Princeton, N. J.: Van Nostrand Company, Inc., 1958, Chap. 4.

———. "The Family as a Three-Person Group," *American Sociological Review*, **19** (Feb. 1954), pp. 23–29. An empirical study attempting to contribute to the understanding of the extent to which propositions concerning *ad hoc* three-person groups may be extended to family groups.

Sussman, M. B., and Burchinal, L. "Kin Family Network: Unheralded Structure in Current Conceptualizations of Family Functioning," *Marriage and Family Living*, 24 (Aug. 1962), pp. 231–40. The conclusion that only by rejecting the concept of the isolated nuclear family can the family be understood as a functioning social system interrelated with other systems in society.

———, and ———. "Parental Aid to Married Children: Implications for Family Functioning," *Marriage and Family Living*, 24 (Nov. 1962), pp. 320–32. Further considerations of the functions of parental aid for status maintenance, occupational placement, and so on.

Vogel, Ezra F. Review of William J. Goode's *The Structure of the Family* in *American Journal of Sociology*, 66 (Jan. 1961), pp. 418–19.

———, and Bell, Norman W. "The Emotionally Disturbed Child as the Family Scapegoat," in Vogel and Bell, *A Modern Introduction to the Family*. New York: Free Press of Glencoe, Inc., 1960, pp. 382–97.

Weber, Max. *The Theory of Social and Economic Organization*, trans. by A. M. Henderson and Talcott Parsons. London: Oxford University Press, Inc., 1947.

Winch, Robert F. *The Modern Family*. New York: Holt, Rinehart & Winston, Inc., 1963.

Zelditch, Morris, Jr. "Role Differentiation in the Nuclear Family: A Comparative Study," in Talcott Parsons and Robert F. Bales. *Family, Socialization and Interaction Process*. New York: Free Press of Glencoe, Inc., 1955, Chap. 6.

chapter 4

The Institutional Frame of Reference in Family Study*

Daniel J. Koenig

and

Alan E. Bayer

The institutional framework was one of the earliest approaches employed in the study of the family. The approach originated with anthropologists in the eighteenth century, and in the nineteenth century was adopted by the early sociologists who were identified with organicism or evolutionism. During this period family analysis was principally evoluntionary analysis in which changes in the family were observed over time and the family was viewed in a broad institutional and historical perspective as lineally progressing toward a more perfect form. Also incorporated into the interpretation of family phenomena was the organismic analogy. Institutions were viewed as established practices, similar in origin and development to organisms, fulfilling necessary functions in society.

* Grateful acknowledgment is made of the contribution of John Sirjamaki who served as editorial consultant for this framework and who read and critically reviewed the manuscript prior to its final revision. Many, although not all, of his suggestions have been incorporated into the final manuscript. Inadequacies and errors in the chapter as published, however, are entirely the responsibility of the authors and the editors.

Later, the value conception of change as progress was generally abandoned by the institutionalists since the family does not necessarily improve with physical changes nor is there a linear regularity of change in the universal family. In contrast to the evolutionary school's conception of the family the contemporary institutional school's conception is more in agreement with empirical reality. Family evolution has not paralleled the evolution of organisms. (Zimmerman, 1947, pp. 62–64.)

Essentially, the current institutional approach is comparative, either historical or cross-cultural. Calhoun, for example, views American family institutions as a resultant of (1) medieval tradition based on ancient civilization, (2) the economic transition from feudalism to modern capitalism, and (3) the influence of the frontier environment. (1945, p. 13.) Queen and Adams also exemplify this historical approach in their treatment of the features of the family institutions in various cultures when they note that "some of them [aspects of family life] clearly have their roots in the past . . . [while] . . . other traits are relatively new." (1952, p. 21.)

Illustrative of other contemporary family theorists who view the family in its historical-institutional setting are Groves and Groves, who assert that European culture has exerted a great impact upon the American family institutions (1947, p. 115); Burgess and Locke, who describe the family as a constantly changing phenomenon throughout history (1953, p. vii); and Ogburn and Nimkoff (1955). The latter trace several changes in the family through a series of causes and effects all the way back to the invention of the steam engine and claim that many family changes are caused by factors wholly external to the family. Nimkoff has made this viewpoint more explicit in an earlier work in which he stated that "contemporary social institutions emerge as the end product of a long evolutionary process, and they cannot be adequately understood without some knowledge of their historical antecedents." (1947, p. 22.)

The family is often regarded by the institutionalists as but one of several institutions existing in society to satisfy personal and societal needs. (Kenkel, 1960, p. vii.) Institutionalists deal with entire societies, recognizing the fact that societies possess several or many institutions which fulfill specialized functions for both the society and the individual. The family, as an institution, is focused about reproduction and socialization. All the institutions are integrated into the social order and both influence and are influenced by the other institutions. (Truxal and Merrill, 1953, pp. 312–55.) Although the institution remains the unit of analysis, contemporary institutionalists emphasize the entire society. The resulting institutions are viewed as solutions to society or community problems such as social control or economic sustenance.

The institutional approach is distinguished from the structure-functional approach, nevertheless, since the unit of analysis in the former is the institution, while in the latter it is the social system. (Mogey, 1962.) Moreover, in the institutional approach behavior is seen as a manifestation of human needs and values, whereas structure-functionalists view behavior as the expected responses to positions in a system of mutually interrelated positions or roles.

Previous Attempts at Delineation

There have been several efforts to delineate the institutional framework. Notable among these are Hill and Hansen (1960), Sirjamaki (in Christensen, 1964, Chap. 2), and Kenkel (1960, Chap. 9). Hill and Hansen note that because of the continued connection with historical analyses, the institutional framework is not highly developed and studies utilizing this approach are often purely descriptive. The pure descriptions are useful in themselves for an over-all view, but the data do not permit a detailed analysis. Hill and Hansen also point out that institutions are often studied as social and cultural patterns of recurrent behavior or structure. Sirjamaki agrees that the approach is largely historical and cross-cultural, but feels that pure description is being replaced with a greater emphasis on testing propositions.

FOCI OF STUDY

Study from the institutional frame of reference has been largely comparative and descriptive. As a result, universal generalizations regarding the family have been possible and a historical perspective on family organization attainable.

Aside from its use in completely descriptive comparative analyses, the chief use of this frame of reference has been in the study of family functions. Principal concern has been with the loss of old functions, the maintenance of and change in traditional functions, and the acquisition of new functions not possessed by the family in former times, together with the causes of these institutional transformations.[1] In analyses, the family is viewed as a multifunctional institution with the reproductive, affectional, protective, socializing, religious, recreational, and status-giving functions in flux.

From an extension of the latter approach the study of changing relations within the family has also been made, particularly the changing roles of the husband-father and wife-mother—changing relations which are occurring in virtually all but preliterate or isolated societies. The trend is viewed as a move toward equality, with the female assuming a less submissive and a greater economic role, while the male assumes a less authoritarian and a greater affectional role. (Ogburn and Nimkoff, 1955, pp. 144–91.)

Another concern of those employing this frame of reference has been family change, or social change in general which involves families in society. Some, such as Westermarck (1922, Vol. III) and Sorokin (1937, Vol. IV, p. 776), predict a gradual breakdown of the family institution and its attendant values, while others merely forecast a continuation of the institution with some changes. Ogburn and Nimkoff, for example, predict a further decline in male authority and suggest a strengthened matriarchate. (1955, p. 285.)

The approach has traditionally viewed the family as an open system and generally as a dependent variable. Thus the influence of the family on other societal institutions is typically ignored, and the emphasis is upon determining the impact of societal influences and the other institutions upon the family. However, the family may be fruitfully viewed in analysis as an independent variable also, as was recognized several years ago by Zimmerman. Nevertheless little work has been undertaken from this perspective.[2] Zimmerman states the following:

> The family as an organization is extraordinarily stable over long periods of time, but for short periods, particularly during upheavals and revolutions, it can change remarkably, at least in its external aspects. Since it is closely related to social conditions, it does change slowly in time as these conditions change. However, since the family is a part of society with limits or

[1] See, for example, Ogburn and Tibbitts (1933); Ogburn and Nimkoff (1955); Kenkel (1960), pp. 187–318; Truxal and Merrill (1953), pp. 312–55; Groves and Groves (1947), pp. 285–313; and Sirjamaki (1953), pp. 28–54.

[2] Some students of the family, such as Goode and Nimkoff, have recently been concerned with analyzing the family as an independent variable. See, for example, Nimkoff (1965).

laws of its own, it often sets up such resistant conditions that the society appears to adapt itself to the family and the family becomes the *cause*, whereas in other periods it may seem to have been the *result* of social conditions. (1947, p. 41.)

This frame of reference is not restricted to the study of the family; it is, in fact, much used in the larger bodies of sociological and anthropological theory. Durkheim (1951), for example, made use of historical-institutional analysis to understand suicide. Similarly, the anthropologists Malinowski (1945) and Bohannan (1963) see the study of institutions as being necessary to the thorough investigation of man's social life.

In summary, the approach has been widely utilized in sociological analysis. As regards work in the family, the foci of study from the institutional frame of reference have been principally on (1) descriptive comparative studies of various family systems, (2) study of old, current, changing, and new functions of the family, (3) causes of changes in the family institution, (4) analysis of the internal workings and changing relations within the family, and (5) predictions as to the future state of the family institution based on the analysis of trends and contemporary societal changes.

CONCEPTS

The institutional approach lacks a body of "private" concepts, drawing heavily on concepts employed in general sociology and, to a lesser extent, in anthropology. The most basic concept is that of *institution*. However, there is lack of consensus among institutionalists as to the definition of even this most basic concept. Sirjamaki (1953, p. 8) and Queen and Adams (1952, pp. 5–17), for example, define institutions in terms of groups, whereas Kenkel (1960, p. 189) and Truxal and Merrill (1947, p. 225) consider the concept in the abstract as a system of practices and patterns. It is generally the latter definition, however, to which most institutionalists subscribe. In this respect, an institution can be defined as "an organized system of practices and roles, developed about a value or a cluster of values, and the machinery designed to regulate and control the affected areas of behavior." (Kenkel, 1960, p. 189.)

The following is a list of other central concepts, with definitions, employed by this school:

Society: an interdependent set of institutions applying to a group of people and providing a framework for social life. (Zimmerman, 1935, pp. 3–6.)

Cultural patterns (culture configurations): standardized behavioral forms, practices, rules, and sentiments existent in a society. (Sirjamaki, 1948, pp. 464–65; Sirjamaki, 1953, pp. 3–4.)

Social change: the differences found in an institution or in society as a whole at a later period when compared with an earlier one— differences which result from adaptation or adjustment to societal or institutional variations. (Zimmerman, 1935, pp. 93–94; Ogburn and Nimkoff, 1955, pp. 3–17.) Early institutionalists equated social change with linear progress, although this notion has been largely abandoned in recent works. (Zimmerman, 1935, p. 128.)

Cultural variation: the differences appearing cross-culturally or historically due to the diversity in institutional behavioral patterns in world societies as a result of different cultures and value systems. (Burgess and Locke, 1953, p. 25.)

Cultural inconsistency: the discrepancies and contradictions which often exist between the various aspects of culture. There are two types: (1) *cultural lag*, in which some aspects of a culture have changed less dynamically than others, thereby producing a discrepancy in the culture, and (2) *cultural conflict*, in which there is inconsistency as a result of the juxtaposition of incompatible cultures. (Kirkpatrick, 1955, p. 137; pp. 141–58.)

Stages of development (institutional evolution): the stages through which an institution evolves from the simple to the complex with each stage dependent upon the preceding ones. (Described in Nimkoff, 1947, pp. 50–51.) This notion of stages of development was used by the early institutionalists, but has been generally abandoned in present writings.

Environmental conditions: limitations and determinants imposed upon an institution by the natural environment (for example, weather, topography, natural resources) as contrasted to those imposed by social or biological conditions. (Queen and Adams, 1952, p. 23.)

Social conditions: limitations and determinants imposed upon institutions by the cultural patterns of a given society. (Sirjamaki, 1952, p. 4.)

Biological conditions: limitations and determinants imposed upon institutions as a consequence of the biological characteristics of man. (Ogburn and Nimkoff, 1955, p. 180.)

Structure: the social apparatus or framework created to fulfill institutional ends or objectives. (Truxal and Merrill, 1953, p. 272.)

Function: the activity performed by an institution in order to maintain social order. (Sirjamaki, 1953, p. 5.)

Family: "an enduring association of parent (or parents) and off-spring whose primary functions are the socialization of the child and the satisfaction of the members' desires for recognition and response." (Truxal and Merrill, 1953, pp. 14–15.) There are various types of families, classified as to various characteristics; however, these classifications vary considerably among different authors.[3]

Marriage: "a socially sanctioned sex relationship involving two or more persons of the opposite sex whose relationship is expected to endure beyond the time required for gestation and birth of children." (Kirkpatrick, 1963, p. 15.)

Status: the position in society conferred upon the individual by his identification with a particular group and which locates the individual in relation to other individuals and groups. (Truxal and Merrill, 1953, p. 249.)

Roles: generally institutionalized social expectations (obligations and rights) imposed upon the individual and arising from the status accorded to him. (Truxal and Merrill, 1953, p. 189.)

The preceding are the more basic concepts utilized by those employing the institutional frame of reference. Although most are by definition nonfamilial concepts, they may be more specifically defined in the family context and readily employed in the analysis of the family as an institution.

ASSUMPTIONS

Underlying the concepts are a number of assumptions made by those who employ this approach. In most general terms, the following are taken to be true by most institutionalists:

1. Institutions have developed in response to basic individual and social needs and change their form through continued group behavior and changing needs. (Sirjamaki, 1953, pp. 4–5, p. 7; Truxal and Merrill, 1953, p. 273.)

2. Institutions are necessary for social control. (Zimmerman, 1935, p. 28; Sirjamaki, 1953, p. 7; Truxal and Merrill, 1953, p. 312.)

---

[3] Kirkpatrick (1955), pp. 80–84 briefly considers a number of these classifications of family types, including those of Murdock, Zimmerman, and Burgess and Locke.

3. Institutions overlap, are interrelated, and undergo change as a result of changes in one or more of the other institutions. (Sirjamaki, 1953, p. 192; Zimmerman, 1947, p. 667.)

4. The forms which institutions take vary among different societies and are largely culturally determined, being relative to the social life of a given time and place. (Queen and Adams, 1952, p. 21; Sirjamaki, 1953, pp. 3–5.)[4]

5. For a thorough understanding of the etiology of, the changes in, and the present position of, an institution, the institution must be examined in terms of its historical antecedents. (Queen and Adams, 1952, p. 272; Zimmerman, 1947, p. ix.) Following as a corollary of this is the assumption that certain aspects of the future of an institution can be predicted from present and past trends. (Ogburn and Nimkoff, 1955, p. 267 ff; Zimmerman, 1947, p. 806.)

Two additional assumptions specifically related to the family can be found in the writings of many of those who employ this approach to study the family. These are the following:

1. The family is the most basic institution in society. (Queen and Adams, 1952, p. 274; Truxal and Merrill, 1953, p. 275.)

2. Family functions exist primarily for offspring. (Truxal and Merrill, 1953, pp. 271–72.) Sirjamaki makes this assumption explicit when he states: "the major functions of the family . . . exist to satisfy *not* [italics ours] the need of spouses but rather those of offspring." (1953, p. 6.)

PRODUCT

The impact of the institutional approach upon sociology in general, and the family in particular, can best be analyzed in terms of the origins and early development of sociology and, subsequently, in terms of the approach's impact upon recent sociological and family theory.

Originally, the institutional frame of reference was the only approach employed in sociology as well as in subfields such as the family. The founders and early adherents of sociology were virtually exclusively institutional in their study of human behavior. Examples of early works of this nature are William Graham Sumner's

---

[4] Zimmerman's *Family and Civilization* (1947) is largely a description of the various forms the institution of the family has taken throughout history and a description of the influence of societal and cultural factors upon the family.

Folkways (1907), Herbert Spencer's *Principles of Sociology* (1900), Lester Ward's *Pure Sociology* (1903), and F. Stuart Chapin's *Contemporary American Institutions* (1935).

Similarly, for many years institutional analysis was the dominant approach employed by students of the family, as is evidenced by Willystine Goodsell's *A History of the Family as a Social and Educational Institution* (1930), Robert Briffault's *The Mothers* (1927), Edward A. Westermarck's *The History of Human Marriage* (1922) and *The Future of Marriage in Western Civilization* (1937), and E. Franklin Frazier's *The Negro Family in the United States* (1939).

Gradually this approach began to be replaced by others, particularly by structure-functionalism or by studies utilizing a social-psychological approach. Today it is less widely utilized than it was a generation ago, although it is frequently used as a descriptive approach which places the family in a historical-cultural perspective, often in conjunction with one or more other approaches. The works of Goode, the Groves, Burgess and Locke, Kenkel, Kirkpatrick, Truxal and Merrill, Nimkoff, and especially Sirjamaki exemplify the use of this framework to supplement one or more other approaches. Indeed, it is a rarity for a treatise on the family not to employ this approach in part for the purpose of acquiring an overview of the family as a social institution.

Probably the major theoretical contribution in recent times made by a student of the family utilizing this approach in entirety is that of Zimmerman (1947). Although not much has been done either in extending or testing his theory of familism related to the trichotomous typology of atomistic, domestic, and trustee families, the theory represents a plausible contribution—one apparently worthy of further examination—and demonstrates that the approach is capable of enabling an individual to make important sociological contributions in the study of the family.

The decline of the approach is not the result of inherent shortcomings of institutional studies, but rather the consequence of a trend among sociologists to functionalism and behaviorism to deal specifically with problems which engage their interest such as personality formation, family roles, family life cycles, and so on. However, as sociologists become more interested in families in various world societies; as more comparisons between them are made; and as more writers test sociological generalizations about the family among two or more societies, sociologists are again becoming interested in institutional analyses of families.

Undoubtedly, structure-functionalism (today probably the dominant approach in sociology) has been influenced to a great extent by the institutional approach and has gained in popularity at the latter's expense, since structure-functionalism is a more comprehensive framework and is used to study the entire social system.

There is also considerable overlap with anthropology with regard to the concepts employed. It is difficult to assess the direction of influence in this case, but the probable explanation is that there has been a mutual exchange of concepts between the two approaches as a consequence of interdisciplinary development. Chinoy (1954, p. 42) notes the early concern of anthropologists with social evolution, and Timasheff (1961, pp. 134–35) refers to early anthropologists who searched for the origins of institutions.

The institutional approach has apparently contributed little to the practice of sociology in recent times. It is probable, however, that in the past its impact upon the teaching of sociology was profound. This would seem to follow as a result of its theoretical importance in the early stages of sociology. Similarly, we can assume that the influence of the institutional approach upon the teaching of courses in marriage and the family was significant in earlier times, judging from the number of treatises which were written from the institutional frame of reference.

In research, the impact of this approach has been somewhat more forceful. There have been numerous studies utilizing the institutional approach, but most have been of a descriptive, rather than analytical, nature.

Thomas's "Family Values in a Pluralistic Society" (1962) is an example of such a study. The article is concerned with specific Roman Catholic values relating to the family institution and a description of how the values of non-Catholics are influencing and altering the value system of the Roman Catholic family institution. The following passage is illustrative of the framework employed in this, and other, institutional studies:

> Granting the distinctiveness of the normative aspects of the Catholic family system briefly outlined above, an adequate analysis of the special problems that a Catholic minority will encounter in attempting to maintain their family system intact

in a pluralistic society necessarily involves certain assumptions concerning the functioning of society and its basic institutions. (pp. 34–35.)

In the recent past, these descriptive works had been waning, but apparently there has been a resurgence of this approach inasmuch as such works appear to be increasing along with the number of analytical studies employing this framework.[5]

Illustrative of the use of the institutional approach in analytical research is the work of Vincent (1960). In a study of the alleged mates of unwed mothers, he attempts to clarify the normative content of the designation "sexual exploiter." In conclusion, the author states:

> The significance of this interpretation is . . . a clarification of the mores from which the label ["sexual exploiter"] is derived.
> . . . Within the larger normative setting, this ex post facto label serves humane values by modifying the blame or censure of unwed mothers who lend support to the traditional role of motherhood by bringing their pregnancies to fruition. This label also serves to sanction the traditional protective role of the male . . . and serves to support cherished family values by censuring any father who leaves a mother in an unwed status whereby she overtly threatens the traditional family system. (p. 46.)

VALUES

Few, if any, values are explicitly stated by those utilizing this approach. However, several implicit values relative to the family are reflected in the writings of many of the adherents of this approach.

One of these values is that family life is superior to life as a single person. Familism and childbearing are viewed as the primary social duties of the individual. (Zimmerman, 1947, p. 810.) From this, a second value follows: children are desirable and are the major *raison d'être* of the family institution. (Queen and Adams, 1952, pp. 8–10; Truxal and Merrill, 1953, pp. 278–79.)

Another value implicit in many of the writings from the institutional frame of reference is that family stability is more important than happiness. Related to this is a fourth value that, while the

[5] Reuben Hill (1962) suggests that in a sense family research has come full circle and that the trend is toward more cross-cultural studies.

individual is of some importance, the society as a whole, and social institutions specifically, are of greater importance. Thus, although happiness is recognized as one of the goals of the present family (Zimmerman, 1947, p. 35), in institutional analysis it is the stability of the family and the smooth functioning of the social institutions in general which are more important. (Kephart, 1961, pp. 19–21.) For example, individual cases of illegitimacy, while they may be extremely unhappy, are relatively unimportant. (Truxal and Merrill, 1953, p. 275.) What is of importance is the continuation of the reproductive functions of the family. Nor are those few individuals who remain single of particular concern, for they are numerically few, since the vast majority of the people in society eventually marry. (Sirjamaki, 1953, p. 71.)

A few institutionalists also view the incidence of divorce from this perspective. It is apparently of minor concern if a divorced couple experiences unhappiness, provided they later remarry. What is of importance is that a high divorce rate be accompanied by a high remarriage rate, thereby stabilizing society and perpetuating the institution of marriage. (Ogburn and Nimkoff, 1955, p. 227.) Furthermore, the adjustment of individual children of divorced couples is often overlooked; at best, it is considered of little consequence if the children of divorced couples are somewhat unhappy or if they are forced to make painful adjustments to new fathers or mothers.

In summary, although none are explicitly stated, at least four interrelated family values are implied in much of the writing from this framework. These are (1) family life is better than the life of a single person, (2) children are desirable in marriage, (3) family stability is more important than happiness, and (4) the perpetuation of society and societal institutions is more important than the individual.

THE FRAMEWORK

Although most of the concepts used by institutionalists are also used by those employing other frames of reference, when institutionalist concepts are employed in conjunction with the assumptions which are unique to this frame of reference the resultant framework becomes somewhat different from others. The unit of analysis is an institution rather than an individual, a group, a social system, or a culture.

An institution is an organized system of norms and values, statuses and roles, and rights and obligations centered around certain important activities within a society. It develops in response to basic human and social needs and changes its form as a result of the changing effect of social, environmental, and biological conditions, as well as from the effect of its historical antecedents. The most basic of these organized systems is the institution of the family, which is not only altered over time but also varies from one society or subculture to another. This variation results in a number of different family types.

The family is an instrument of social control, with its functions primarily centered around reproduction and the socialization of offspring. That the family institution and its functions are basic to the existence of society does not preclude the existence of numerous other institutions, however. These other institutions influence, and are influenced by, the family. It is this interaction between institutions which leads to a dynamic society, although, for analytical purposes, institutionalists may view the family as a closed system independent of other institutions, and may study it as but one of several institutions within the total society.

In summary, the concepts of this framework are employed in a unique manner when integrated with the assumptions. However, analysis at one point begins to overlap with the structure-functional framework when the interrelationship of institutions is discussed; at a second point the institutional framework overlaps with comparative analyses of family institutions and of family development and change using both historical and cross-cultural data. The pure type of institutional analysis originally was evolutionary analysis, but more recently it has been comparative analysis of family institutions, family development, and family change using both historical and cross-cultural data. The "pure" approach is seldom the exclusive approach used in present writing. Contemporary writers often use this framework for only a section of their works, or utilize the institutional approach to some degree in comparative analysis and in the study of the interrelationship of institutions.

CRITIQUE AND DISCUSSION

In recent decades the impact of this approach on sociology in general, and on family study in particular, has been considerably less than at the turn of the century. Today few writers employ this approach exclusively, with most using it in conjunction with other frames of reference. As Hill (1962) notes, however, it appears that family sociologists have been returning to this approach, and he cites an extensive bibliography utilizing this frame of reference.

As with many of the other approaches described in this volume, the institutional approach overlaps with other frames of reference, particularly the structure-functional and the anthropological. But the institutional approach remains exceptional in several respects, and it is this uniqueness which makes it invaluable and essential for a complete understanding of family phenomena. One may effectively isolate the family for study by means of this approach, thereby more intensively and analytically investigating family structures, functions, and value systems than can be done when a large number of actors within the system must be considered, or when account of the total social system must be made. It is probably for this reason that many authors find it fruitful, indeed, necessary, to incorporate this approach in at least a section of their works. The complete exclusion of the view of the family as an institution in an analysis of the total family would almost certainly be viewed as a shortcoming. Moreover, the approach is particularly relevant for cross-cultural tests of theoretical propositions.

One of the major attributes of the institutional frame of reference, the view of the family *in toto*, is also the cause of its two primary shortcomings. First, the individual is of minimal concern to those employing this frame of reference. The study of the individual is incidental to the institutional approach and the individual is considered by the institutionalists only insofar as he is a part of the family institution.

The other major shortcoming of the institutional approach is that it deals with the modal family. Kenkel notes that the institutional framework largely ignores relationships in specific families as well as the behavior of individual family members, focusing on the family itself rather than on the internal workings of particular family groups. (1960, p. 187.)

This is a limitation inherent in the approach. It is true that the institutionalist may study minority family systems within the society, yet the limitation must remain, for it is manifestly impossible to analyze every family group that would result by breaking down socio-demographic variables. The institutional approach at times is used in study of the Catholic family, the Negro family, the rural family, or the middle-class family, but what of the Negro, Catholic, rural, middle-class family? Clearly, then, although modal family systems may be analyzed, the approach does not permit intensive study of unique families within a given society or of the interpersonal relationships within these families.

The family type studied is admittedly more numerous in the society than is any other family type, yet it excludes a great number—in some cases, the majority—of families in any given society. Truxal and Merrill (1953, p. 291), for example, confine themselves to the "middle-class, urban, white, native-born family" in American society.

A final shortcoming, probably common to all approaches, is the fact that the framework, in itself, is not adequate for a complete understanding of the family. On the other hand, the utilization of the institutional frame of reference is indispensable to a balanced and realistic analysis of the family.

REFERENCES

BLITSTEN, DOROTHY R. *The World of the Family.* New York: Random House, Inc., 1963. A cross-cultural analysis of major types of family organization in China, Europe, Scandinavia, Israel, Russia, and the Moslem countries.

BOHANNAN, PAUL. *Social Anthropology.* New York: Holt, Rinehart & Winston, Inc., 1963.

BRIFFAULT, ROBERT. *The Mothers,* 3 vols. New York: The Macmillan Company, 1927. A work centered about a discussion of whether males or females have been the more important and predominant force in human history, the author's thesis being a matriarchal theory of social evolution.

BURGESS, ERNEST W., and LOCKE, HARVEY J. *The Family: From Institution to Companionship.* New York: American Book Company, 1953. A tracing of the changes which are transforming the American family, in the authors' judgment, from an institution to a companionship relationship.

———, and WALLIN, PAUL. *Engagement and Marriage.* Philadelphia: J. B. Lippincott Company, 1953. A compilation of extensive research on courtship and the early years of marriage with an interpretation of the findings.

CALHOUN, ARTHUR W. *A Social History of the American Family: From Colonial Times to Present.* New York: Barnes & Noble, Inc., 1945. A discussion of the impact of societal influences on the family in an attempt to understand the forces relevant in the evolution of American family institutions.

CHAPIN, F. STUART. *Contemporary American Institutions*. New York: Random House, Inc., 1954.

———. *Cultural Change*. New York: Appleton-Century-Crofts, 1928.

CHINOY, ELY. *Sociological Perspective*. New York: Random House, Inc., 1954.

CHRISTENSEN, HAROLD T. "Cultural Relativism and Premarital Sex Norms," *American Sociological Review*, 25 (Feb. 1960), pp. 31–39. A cross-cultural examination of sexual norms and their relationship to marriage.

———, ed. *Handbook on Marriage and the Family*. Chicago: Rand McNally & Company, 1964. Various discussions. The institutional approach is briefly mentioned in the first chapter. In the second chapter ("The Institutional Approach," pp. 33–50), the institutional approach is discussed by John Sirjamaki. William Kephart's chapter ("Legal and Procedural Aspects of Marriage and Divorce," pp. 944–68), presents an excellent discussion, institutional in nature, of the family as a legal entity.

———, and CARPENTER, GEORGE R. "Value-Behavior Discrepancies Regarding Premarital Coitus in Three Western Cultures," *American Sociological Review*, 27 (Feb. 1962), pp. 66–74. An extension of Christensen's earlier study of the Mormon, Midwestern, and Danish cultures and an analysis of the deviancy in practice from the institutionalized norms.

DURKHEIM, EMILE. *Suicide*, trans. by John A. Spaulding and George Simpson. New York: Free Press of Glencoe, Inc., 1951.

FRAZIER, E. FRANKLIN. *The Negro Family in the United States*. Chicago: University of Chicago Press, 1939. A historical-institutional analysis examining the influences acting upon the Negro family from slavery to the present.

GOODE, WILLIAM J. *World Revolution and Family Patterns*. New York: Free Press of Glencoe, Inc., 1963. An analysis and interpretation of the major changes in family patterns of the Arab countries, China, India, Japan, Sub-Sahara Africa, and the Western cultures.

GOODSELL, WILLYSTINE. *A History of the Family as a Social and Educational Institution*. New York: The Macmillan Company, 1930.

———. *A History of Marriage and the Family*, rev. ed. New York: The Macmillan Company, 1934. An interpretation of the family beginning with the Greek, Roman, and Christian influences and culminating with the total societal impact on the contemporary American family.

GROVES, ERNEST R., and GROVES, GLADYS H. *The Contemporary American Family*. Philadelphia: J. B. Lippincott Company, 1947. Another discussion of the historical-institutional influences acting upon the family to give it its present form. See especially, "The European Background of the American Family," pp. 115–39.

HILL, REUBEN. "Cross-National Family Research: Attempts and Prospects," *International Social Science Journal*, 14 (Oct. 1962), pp. 425–51. A suggestion that family research has come full circle, returning to cross-cultural and comparative studies. Included is an extensive cross-cultural bibliography that can be considered as a list of works from the contemporary institutional frame of reference.

——, BACK, KURT W., and STYCOS, J. MAYONE. *The Family and Population Control*. Chapel Hill, N. C.: University of North Carolina Press, 1959. A socio-demographic analysis of possibilities of population control in Puerto Rico.

——, and HANSEN, DONALD A. "The Identification of Conceptual Frameworks Utilized in Family Study," *Marriage and Family Living*, 22 (Nov. 1960), pp. 299–311. A delineation of five conceptual frameworks, one of which is the institutional approach. Concepts, a few assumptions, and a brief development of the approach is included.

"INTERNATIONAL ISSUE ON THE FAMILY," *Marriage and Family Living*, 16 (Nov. 1954). An entire journal of individual articles describing and analyzing the family in specific societies and subcultures.

JAMES, E. O. *Marriage and Society*. London: Hutchinson & Co. (Publishers), Ltd., 1952.

KENKEL, WILLIAM F. *The Family in Perspective*, 2nd ed. New York: Appleton-Century-Crofts, 1961. A delineation, in the second part of this book, of the institutional approach and an analysis of the American family from this frame of reference.

KEPHART, WILLIAM M. *The Family, Society, and the Individual*. Boston· Houghton Mifflin Company, 1961. Discussion, early in the book, of minority family systems and experimental family systems, followed by an analysis of the contemporary American marriage patterns and family organization. The book is institutional throughout with constant attention given to the well-being of society as a whole.

KIRKPATRICK, CLIFFORD. *The Family: As Process and Institution*, 2nd ed. New York: The Ronald Press Company, 1963. Utilizes the institutional approach interwoven with other approaches.

MACE, DAVID, and MACE, VERA. *Marriage East and West*. New York: Doubleday & Company, Inc., 1960. A comparison and contrast of Asian patterns of courtship, love, and marriage with Western customs.

MALINOWSKI, BRONISLAW. *The Dynamics of Culture Change*. New Haven: Yale University Press, 1945.

MOGEY, JOHN. "Introduction," *International Social Science Journal*, 14 (Oct. 1962), pp. 411–24.

MORGAN, E. S. *The Puritan Family*. Boston: Boston Public Library, 1944. An analysis of the Puritan family in terms of their norms and practices regarding love, marriage, parenthood, children's education, and so on.

MURDOCK, GEORGE P. *Social Structure*. New Haven: Yale University Press, 1949. A cross-cultural analysis of many aspects of marriage and the family in 250 societies.

NIMKOFF, MEYER F., ed. *Comparative Family Systems*. Boston: Houghton Mifflin Company, 1965. A presentation of case studies of twelve different family types and a consideration by the editor of the family as an independent variable causing societal changes as well as a dependent variable, influenced by other social institutions.

———. *Marriage and the Family*, 2nd ed. Boston: Houghton Mifflin Company, 1947. An intermingling of several approaches with heavy reliance on the institutional-historical approach in discussing the influences which acted upon the family to bring it to its present form.

OGBURN, WILLIAM F., and NIMKOFF, MEYER F. *Technology and the Changing Family*. Cambridge, Mass.: Riverside Press, 1955. A listing of what family scholars consider to be the ten most significant changes in the American family from 1900 until the present. They explain these changes largely in terms of historical factors brought about by technological innovations.

———, and TIBBITTS, CLARK. "Social Trends in the Family" in *Recent Social Trends in the United States: Report of the President's Research Committee on Social Trends*. Wesley C. Mitchell, Chairman. McGraw-Hill Book Company, Inc., Vol. 2, 1933. A classic analysis of family functions: past, present, and transitional.

QUEEN, STUART A., and ADAMS, JOHN B. *The Family in Various Cultures*. Philadelphia: J. B. Lippincott Company, 1952. A historical-institutional analysis of the family systems in eleven cultures.

———, HABENSTEIN, ROBERT W., and ADAMS, JOHN B. *The Family in Various Cultures*, 2nd ed. Philadelphia: J. B. Lippincott Company, 1961.

SIRJAMAKI, JOHN. *The American Family in the Twentieth Century*. Cambridge, Mass.: Harvard University Press, 1953. An analysis of the American family, placed in an institutional setting, from its European origins to its contemporary form.

———. "Cultural Configurations in the American Family," *American Journal of Sociology*, 53 (May 1948), pp. 464–70. The suggestion that eight cultural configurations, the approved rules or sentiments which motivate behavior, give the American family institution its distinctive character.

SOROKIN, PITIRIM A. *Social and Cultural Dynamics*, 4 vols. New York: American Book Company, 1937.

SPENCER, HERBERT. *Principles of Sociology*. New York: Appleton-Century-Crofts, 1900.

STERN, BERNHARD J., ed. *The Family: Past and Present.* New York: Appleton-Century-Crofts, 1938.

SUMNER, WILLIAM G. *Folkways.* Boston: Ginn and Company, 1907.

THOMAS JOHN L. *The American Catholic Family.* Englewood Cliffs, N.J.: Prentice-Hall, Inc., 1956. A description and analysis from the institutional perspective of the special problems encountered by American Catholics, as a minority group, in maintaining their marriage and family ideals.

———. "Family Values in a Pluralistic Society," *American Catholic Sociological Review,* **23** (Spring 1962), pp. 30–40.

TIMASHEFF, NICHOLAS S. *Sociological Theory,* 2nd rev. ed. New York: Random House, Inc., 1961.

TRUXAL, ANDREW G., and MERRILL, FRANCIS E. *Marriage and the Family in American Culture,* 2nd ed. Englewood Cliffs, N.J.: Prentice-Hall, Inc., 1953. Attributes family instability to individualistic institutional patterns in the process of developing new social norms.

VINCENT, CLARK E. "Unmarried Fathers and the Mores: 'Sexual Exploiter' as an Ex Post Facto Label," *American Sociological Review,* **25** (Feb. 1960), pp. 40–46.

WARD, LESTER. *Pure Sociology.* New York: The Macmillan Company, 1903.

WESTERMARCK, EDWARD A. *The Future of Marriage in Western Civilization.* New York: The Macmillan Company, 1936. An institutional treatment of marriage in which the author projects what he feels to be the future of marriage on the basis of his study of the past. See especially Chapter 1, "The Meaning and Origin of Marriage," and Chapter 7, "The Predicted Disappearance of Marriage."

———. *The History of Human Marriage,* 3 vols. New York: Allerton Book Company, 1922.

ZIMMERMAN, CARLE C. "American Roots in an Italian Village," *Genus,* **11** (1955), pp. 78–139.

———. *The Family of Tomorrow.* New York: Harper & Row, Publishers, 1949. An extension of the author's earlier work (*Family and Civilization*), attempting to explain the constant movements of the Western family system from one type to another.

———. *Family and Civilization.* New York: Harper & Row, Publishers, 1947. An analysis of the entire family since recorded history began. The author specifies three family types—trustee, domestic, and atomistic—and relates them to the concept of familism or family cohesiveness.

———, and FRAMPTON, M. E. *Family and Society: A Study of the Sociology of Reconstruction.* Princeton, N.J.: D. Van Nostrand Company, Inc., 1935.

chapter 5

The Interactional Framework
in the Study of the Family*

Jay D. Schvaneveldt

The interactional framework is a system for viewing the personal relationships between husband and wife and parents and children. The family is conceived as a *unity of interacting personalities.*[1] By this is meant a living, changing, growing thing. The framework views the family not in the legal conception, not in any family contract, but rather in the interaction of its members. (Burgess, 1926.)

Within the family each member occupies a position or positions to which a number of roles are assigned. The individual perceives norms or role expectations held individually or collectively by other family members for his attributes and behaviors. The response of the others in the family serves to reinforce or to challenge this conception. Stone states: "It is this tendency to shape the phenomenal world into roles which is the key to role-taking as a core process in interaction." (1959, p. 22.) An individual defines his role expectations in a given situation in terms of a reference group and by his own self-

* Grateful acknowledgment is made of the contribution of Sheldon Stryker, who served as editorial consultant for this framework and who read and critically reviewed the manuscript prior to its final revision. Many, although not all, of his suggestions have been incorporated into the final manuscript. Inadequacies and errors in the chapter as published, however, are entirely the responsibility of the author and the editors.

[1] Burgess uses the term *unity* in contrast to *unit* to distinguish between the view of the family as a mere collection of interacting individuals and a unity of interacting persons (1926), pp. 3–9.

conception. The individual family member role-plays. The family and its individual members are thus studied through an analysis of overt interacts. (Hill and Hansen, 1960.) Each family is not only supported but also limited by the pattern of family life which has evolved in its interaction in society at large. Through this limitation and support each family in the interactional process achieves its own tempos and rhythms of family living.

Komarovsky and Waller (1945) state that the interactional approach furnishes a framework into which all kinds of contributions which have to do with the human-nature aspects of the family may be fitted. Much of the attention has been on the formation of personality in the parental family. "The literature on this subject is rich, but all of it may be regarded as part of the study of the family as a unity of interacting personalities." (Komarovsky and Waller, 1945, p. 448.)

Mowrer and Mowrer (1951) define the unique unit of study in the interactional framework as the dynamic relationship between husband and wife. This approach views the processes of interaction through an analysis of the dynamic relationships between the interactive patterns of family members in terms of needs, behavior patterns, and adjustment processes. These characteristics have covered a wide range illustrated by studies dealing with romantic attitudes, personal adaptability, insight, frustrations, economic standards, and desire for response. From marriage comes interaction within the relationship. The two individuals have to adjust themselves to each other as well as to many other new people and situations. They have to be able and willing to give up much of the personal freedom they have achieved in order to make a satisfactory adjustment to the new relationship.

Kirkpatrick (1955) describes the interactionist framework as one in which the child observes the roles played by family members and incorporates these roles or "me's" into his own personality structure. In the dynamic process of family members living together there is interaction of roles. The concept of the family as a unity is a bridge between the family institution (seen from societal frame) and the individual actor as a member of a family. Each family member is required to integrate himself into multiple roles within the family roles and also the extrafamilial roles.

The unique, differentiating characteristic of the interactional approach is that it is based on the action of the family resulting from the communication processes. It views family behavior as an adjustive process where cues are given and individual members respond to these stimuli. The primary focus of the framework has not been with external or environmental factors as such, but with the *action* of the family members in constant flux. It is true however, that the framework is (or can be) useful in viewing the relationship between the larger system of action and the family system. Members in the family are viewed as gauging their own behavior by assessing and judging the actions of others. Personality is not a static entity but a dynamic concept as the members live in day-to-day interaction in the family. Shibutani elaborates this concept:

> If the motivation of behavior, the formation of personality, and the evolution of group structure all occur in social interaction, it follows logically that attention should be focused upon the interchanges that go on among human beings as they come into contact with one another. (1961, p. 23.)

The interactionist is interested in the family as a unity of persons acting in habits and sentiments. As Waller and Hill state: "The family is a number of human lives not only mixed together but compounded with one another." (1951, p. 5.) This approach is helpful in understanding the relationship between the family and society. It concerns itself with processes of interaction within the family group and in relating these in turn to social interaction taking place within the social structure of society. Interaction in each stage of family development determines and gives direction to interaction in the subsequent stages of family action. (Waller and Hill, 1951.)

In summary it may be said that the interactional approach strives to interpret family phenomena in terms of *internal* processes. These processes consist of role-playing, status relations, communication problems, decision-making, stress reactions, and socialization processes. Little attempt is made to view the over-all institutional or cross-cultural relationships of family structure and function.

Previous Attempts to Delineate the Framework

The symbolic interactionist theory was most comprehensively subjected to systematic treatment by Mead (1934). Rose (1962) is the most recent scholar to analyze and consolidate the approach in the social psychological realm. In the family field specifically we note four attempts at delineating some aspects of the framework.

The first was undertaken by Waller (1938). Waller used the now classic statement by Burgess of viewing the family as a unity of interacting personalities, but in addition added the statement by Dollard: "each with a history." (1935, p. 110.) Waller outlined many of the concepts and assumptions that are still being employed by the interactionists in their study of the family.

Hill (1951) revised the original Waller book on the family and in so doing refined many of the concepts and assumptions of the earlier publication. Among other things, Hill expanded the treatment of the process of personality development as it is influenced by family interaction. Hill also changed the view of the family from a *unity* of interacting personalities to that of an *arena* of interacting personalities. The focus on the family as an *arena* provides for the emergence of conflict, for children to grow at different rates, and parents to reconcile their own inner desires, in the family in a way that *unity* does not. Stryker's articles (1959, 1964) have done much to spell out the concepts, assumptions, foci, and limitations of the interactional framework as specifically applied to family study. Hill and Hansen (1960) have the most detailed delineation of the framework to date. They have given the approach not only a historical perspective but also a graphic description including the basic concepts and assumptions, and have also attempted to tie it in with time and social-space dimensions.

Brief History of the Framework

Early formulations of the framework have been expressed by many writers. Stryker (1964) indicates that the origin of the framework goes back at least to Hegel, and that more recent treatment has been provided by Baldwin, Dewey, Cooley, and Mead. Waller, Burgess, Hill, and Foote as well as others have viewed the family from the perspective of the interactional framework. Empirical research guided by the framework was conducted by these and many others. "Perhaps half the sociologists of the United States were nurtured, directly or indirectly, on its conceptions and approaches to research work." (Rose, 1962, p. vii.)

Contemporary writers have also drawn upon the writings of Simmel, Weber, and Sorokin, who wrote much concerning the concept of *interaction* in society. According to Simmel, society is much more than the individuals composing it; in fact, society's true significance is revealed in its contrast with the sum of individuals. The social sciences, Simmel argued, have so far studied only a few types of reciprocal relations, chiefly economic and political. Others which he felt worthy of study in the interactional process included such everyday phenomena as looking at one another, dining together, exchanging letters, helping others, and being grateful for help. (Wolff, 1950, pp. 9–11.)

In common with many sociologists going back to Simmel, Sorokin (1947) chooses interaction as the unit into which social phenomena should be analyzed. He explains: "In its developed forms, the superorganic is found exclusively in the realm of interacting human beings and in the products of their interaction." (Sorokin, 1947, p. 4.) The subjects of interaction are either human individuals or organized human groups.

Christensen (1964) states that, considered substantively, the interactionist framework is the most pronounced characteristic of twentieth-century family study. Hill and Hansen (1960) similarly conclude that interactional theory has been the framework most frequently used in the past twenty years in American family sociology.

It was Ernest W. Burgess who first suggested that the family be viewed within the scope of the interactional framework. In a 1926 article Burgess spoke of the family as a unity of interacting personalities. Dollard later expanded that with: "each with a history in a given cultural milieu." (1935, p. 110.) In broad generalization the interactionist approach has developed from the fields of sociology and social psychology. The family, as a substantive focus, received its real momentum in about the middle of the 1920's with the classic statement by Burgess.

The name of the framework as it appears in the literature is not entirely clear.[2] The term *interactional* has been conceptualized in more recent writings. Some writers have referred to the approach as *action theory*, following the terminology of Weber. Those with a psychological adherence have addressed it as *role theory*. "Others refer to the framework as the 'Chicago tradition' after the fact that most of the early contributors to the framework were associated with the University of Chicago." (Rose, 1962, p. viii.) Still another

[2] *Interaction* and *symbolic interaction* are often used interchangeably in the research literature. Usually, symbolic interaction refers to processes in socialization. Interaction is more often sociological in focus whereas symbolic interaction is characterized by a social-psychological emphasis.

writer, Kirkpatrick (1955) refers to the framework as the *role-process approach.*

The framework is thus richly endowed with study by some of the great pioneers in sociology and, specifically, in the area of family sociology. Researchers, theorists, and teachers have called heavily upon this conceptual scheme for viewing the family.

FOCI OF STUDY

Broadly speaking, the interest has been on the internal workings of the family. Within the internal workings of the family the areas receiving considerable attention have been dating, mate selection, marital adjustment, parent-child relationships, and personality formation within the family context. Symbolic interaction, cradled in social-psychological theory, concerns itself with the processes of socialization of the child and development of personality. (Stryker, 1959.) Adults define for the child the meaning of events, values, and norms. This process is illustrated by Waller and Hill: "The child comes into the world to find an interactive system already established in the interweaving, intermeshing habit systems of the adults of his society." (1951, p. 39.) The personality in the child develops slowly over time. A certain type of personality emerges or becomes stabilized to a degree by the interactive process of defining acts of others and thus becoming aware of one's own actions. This results in a persistent or stable pattern of behavior.

Marital accord, marital discord, family accord, and family discord have been the focus of much study within this framework. These areas of study might be called the dynamic relationships between husband and wife. The interplay of personality with regard to wishes, attitudes, and sentiments is also considered. Burgess and Wallin (1953) stated that certain interpersonal relations of husband and wife are important factors making for development, equilibrium, or frustration in marriage. Some of these relationships which they submitted and which have been the concern of this framework in subsequent investigations are love and affection, sex, emotional interaction, compatibility, interaction of cultural backgrounds, common interests, expectations, decision-making, and adaptability.

Definitions and concepts of roles form the core of the framework and as such have received considerable attention. Social intercourse in marriage, patterns of expectancy and dependency, and sexual interaction leading to sexual adjustment are examples of the type of problems considered from the vantage point of this framework.

Interpersonal relations as affected by the expansion or contraction of the family due to death or birth have been sources of much study from the interactional frame of reference. Role-taking and role performance, communication, and role-playing have been studied in considerable detail. Sussman (1963) points out that differences by social class of stability of interpersonal relationships and differences of decisions concerning expenditures are also problems fitting into this framework. Problem-solving has also been studied and, in this same area, recent research has been applied to performance and attitudes of couples while under certain types of modification due to counseling processes. The function of family relationships in the use of leisure time and adjustment of older people in the home have been studied. Neurotic interaction in the family and in the marital relationship have received considerable attention.

CONCEPTS

Because of the wide application of this framework it has necessarily used concepts which are also used by other frameworks. Social psychology and sociology as well as psychology have used many of the concepts which are employed in the interactionist family framework. The genesis of the approach is accredited to social psychology. Many of the concepts used by social psychologists in the interactional school have not been used to any great extent by students of the family. Concepts falling into this classification will not be presented in this family interactionist framework. The major criteria for selection was their use and frequency of appearance in the literature related to the study of the family.

CONCEPT	DEFINITION AND/OR ILLUSTRATION
Interaction	Interaction is the generic name for a whole set of processes taking place between individuals. The behavior of one individual is the cause and effect in relation to the behavior of others. Interaction denotes the social behaviors involved when two or more persons interstimulate each other by any means of communication, and hence modify each other's behavior. In interaction persons define each other's actions as they interact one with another.

CONCEPT	DEFINITION AND/OR ILLUSTRATION
Act	An act refers to purposive behavior which begins in an impulse requiring some adjustment to appropriate objects in the external world. (Stryker, 1959, p. 113.) Shibutani defines the act as: "a unit which begins with a condition of disequilibrium within the organism and ends with the restoration of equilibrium." (1961, p. 64.)
Social act	"A *social act* is one in which the appropriate object is another individual. . . . Every social act implicates at least two individuals, each of whom takes the other into account in the processes of satisfying impulses." (Stryker, 1959, p. 113.)
Symbolic environment	The environment as it is mediated through significant symbols is the symbolic environment. It is based on learned meanings and values. The person must define the situation before he can act, that is, as he represents it to himself in symbolic terms. Only man has a symbolic environment. (Stryker, 1959, p. 114.)
Definition of the situation	Definition of the situation is the social act whereby an actor interprets stimuli in a setting. Each actor perceives, makes judgments, and initiates action based upon his definition of the stimuli in the setting. "The situation is the set of values and attitudes with which the individual or the group has to deal in a process of activity and with regard to which this activity is planned and its results appreciated." (Thomas and Znaniecki, 1927, p. 68.) The definition is the representation of a situation to oneself in symbolic terms.
Reference group	According to Shibutani, the reference group is "that group, real or imaginary, whose standpoint is being used as the frame of reference by the actor." (1961, p. 257.)
Identification	One's identity is formulated when others place him as a social object by assigning

CONCEPT	DEFINITION AND/OR ILLUSTRATION
	him the same status that he himself calls forth. Foote states: "We mean by identification appropriation of and commitment to a particular identity or series of identities." (1951, p. 17.)
Interpersonal relationship	A relationship based on personal interaction rather than any legal or structural basis is an interpersonal relationship. The term refers to the system of the interaction between two or more persons. The parts of the systems are interrelated in such a manner that change in one part brings about change in the other parts. The term refers to the persons acting and reacting to one another in a social situation. The system involves appearance, verbal communication, and overt gestures.
Stimulus	Stimulus may be viewed as any action or agent which causes or changes an activity in an organism. Coutu states that: "anything which will induce action is called a stimulus." (1949, p. 211.)
Status	Status is the position one maintains in groups because of the way in which one is evaluated as a person. *Personal* status is usually associated with primary groups and rests upon intimate interaction processes. *Social* status refers to relative rank in the community and is determined primarily by norms which govern one's social class.
Position	"Positions are socially recognized categories of actors, any general category serving to classify persons." (Stryker, 1964, p. 137.)
Role	Turner (1962) defines a role as a pattern of consistent behavior of a single actor. The pattern of consistent behavior refers to clusters of values and interpretations that guide an individual's behavior in a specific social setting.

CONCEPT	DEFINITION AND/OR ILLUSTRATION
Role-taking	Role-taking is the anticipation of the responses of others involved with one in a social act, and the subsequent modification of one's behavior in the light of such anticipations. (Mead, 1934.) This process involves selective perception of the actions of others and imagining how one looks from another person's standpoint.
Role-playing	Role-playing involves taking the responses of another and organizing them into a pattern of behavior. Role-playing refers to the organization of conduct in accordance with group norms. It involves living up to obligations because of certain commitments.
Role-making	Roles exist in varying degrees of consistency. The individual has to form his behavior as if they had some clarity. The result of this formation is role-making: the creation and modification of existing roles. (Turner, 1962.)
Significant other	The significant other refers to the specification of certain individuals in the interaction process who occupy certain rank on the "significance" continuum. Persons awarded high status on this continuum are given greater weight or priority. Persons who are regarded in this manner are significant others. (Mead, 1934, pp. 144–64; Stryker, 1959, p. 115.)
Group	A group is any number of human beings in reciprocal communication. It is not a collection of individuals but a *set* in which relationships are involved.
Primary group	Primary–group relationships involve a high degree of intimacy and extensive communication. A group is primary to the extent that it is based upon and maintains primary relations. Broom and Selznick specify Cooley's original definition of the primary group: "Some groups, like the family, arise

CONCEPTS	DEFINITION AND/OR ILLUSTRATIONS
	from primary relations and are especially capable of sustaining them" (1963, p. 139).
Habit	A habit is an action we have acquired as a result of experience: an attitude or tendency to act in a specific way.
Gesture	A gesture is "any part of the act which stands for, or comes to be a sign of those parts of the act yet to occur." (Stryker, 1959, p. 113.) It may be presented vocally as well as by physical movement or expression.
Family	A family consists of one or more men living with one or more women in a socially-sanctioned and more or less enduring sexual relationship, with socially recognized rights and obligations, together with their offspring. Burgess (1926) states the family is a unity of interacting personalities. It does not consist or exist on a legal or a contractual basis, but in the interaction of its members. The family in this conception lives as long as interaction is taking place and only dies when interaction ceases.
Family integration	Family integration means the bonds of coherence and unity running through family life, of which common interests, affection, and economic interdependence are of great importance.
Self	The self is "that which is an object to itself." (Mead, 1934, p. 140.) "One's self is the way one describes to himself his relationships to others in a social process." (Stryker, 1959, p. 115.) Lindesmith and Strauss (1956) define the self as (1) a set of stable responses at the conceptual level, which (2) exercise regulation over other responses at a lower level.
Task behavior	Task behavior is interaction directed toward the completion of group or individual tasks.

CONCEPTS	DEFINITION AND/OR ILLUSTRATIONS
Communication	Communication is the exchange of meaningful symbols, both words and gestures. Shibutani refers to communication as "that interchange of gestures through which consensus is developed, sustained, or broken." (1961, p. 141.)
Adaptation	Adaptation is family and individual survival or integration in a given cultural milieu. It refers to the process of adjusting to new or different conditions. It may also be used to indicate cultural modification to suit a particular human environment. Adaptation is the process of acquiring fitness to live in a given environment.
Dyadic relation	The dyadic relation is the interaction which occurs between the two partners in a social-stimulus situation. It refers to a pair in sociation, usually but not always of associative character. It is the relationship between a *pair* of units or actors.
Socialized person	The socialized person is one who has learned to participate effectively in social groups. It is the person who has learned the requirements for behavior found in a given culture and conforms to them most of the time. The individual receives most of his socialization from interaction in the family.
Non-socialized person	The non-socialized person is one who does not present the performance that is called for in a given social situation. It is a person who has not internalized norms and values of group interaction to a degree sufficient for him to act and react in socially described manners.
Thinking	Thinking is the internalized manipulation of symbols. It is the process by which possible solutions are arrived at by use of words, anticipations, and past experience.
Volition	Volition is "the process of selecting among alternatives symbolically present in the ex-

CONCEPTS	DEFINITION AND/OR ILLUSTRATIONS
	periences of the individual." (Stryker, 1959, p. 115.)
Self-consciousness	Mead defines self-consciousness as "the ability to call out in ourselves a set of definite responses which belong to the others of the group." (1934, p. 163.)

Nearly all of the concepts in the interactionist approach refer to action and/or interaction in relation to the internal processes in the family. The concepts for the most part refer to *communication* processes and levels of role *performance* by family members. Such concepts depict the behavior of others. The concepts illustrate that interaction at the family level takes place in a cultural medium which is itself the product of past interaction. Very few of the concepts have any relation to institutions outside of the family but instead focus primarily on the roles of family members in a dynamic pattern of interaction.

BASIC ASSUMPTIONS

The basic assumptions of the interactional approach were presented, albeit not systematically, by Mead (1934). It remained for Rose (1962) to systematize the work of Mead. As pertains to the family, Stryker (1959, 1964) and Hill and Hansen (1960), have formally presented assumptions that have been used in the interactional approach to family study. Waller (1938) and Waller and Hill (1951) have presented important contributions to a formation of assumptions. Waller and Hill state that "the family is a number of human lives not only mixed together but compounded with one another." (1951, p. 5.) This general type of assumption has not been formally outlined by the writer in the delineation of assumptions in the framework; rather the properties of such general assumptions are incorporated in more basic assumptions which have already been presented. The discussion here of assumptions is based primarily on the works of Stryker (1959, 1964) and Rose (1962).

1. Man lives in a symbolic as well as physical environment and is stimulated in social situations to act by symbols as well as by physical stimuli. (Rose, 1962.) One learns nearly all symbols through interaction with other people, specifically members of the family,

and therefore most symbols can be thought of as common or shared meanings and values.

2. Through symbols, a man has the capacity to stimulate others in ways other than those in which he himself is stimulated. Role-taking is involved in all communications by means of significant symbols. The individual can imagine, that is, evoke within himself, how the recipient of his communication interprets that which has been transmitted. Man communicates to others in order to evoke meanings and values that he intends to evoke. (Rose, 1962.)

3. Man has the capacity to learn huge numbers of meanings and values through symbolic communication. He learns these by inter-acting with other persons. This is the process of socialization in which the individual learns the cultural and subcultural values and roles which he is to follow. (Rose, 1962.)

4. Symbols appear in social-stimulus situations both as isolated entities and as clusters. The role of the person at a given time is guided and directed by the related meanings stemming from the cluster of symbols. Thus a person is likely to play many roles in the course of a day.[3] (Rose, 1962.)

5. "Thinking is the process by which possible symbolic solutions and other future courses of action are examined, assessed for their relative advantages and disadvantages in terms of the values of the individual, and one of them chosen for action." (Rose, 1962, p. 12.) Thinking is a symbolic process because the alternatives the thinker assesses have certain relevant meanings, and the assessment is made in terms of the individual's values. The individual in thinking manip-ulates his own role in imagining himself in possible situations.

6. Interaction cannot be fully understood by means of external observation. It must be viewed in the context of how the participants define one another in the social-stimulus situation. (Hess and Handel, 1959.) Foote (1951) states, "Definitions of the situation account for attitudes, not the reverse." Any particular action is formed in the light of the situation in which it takes place.

7. It is assumed that the human being is an actor as well as reactor. That is, the human being does not simply respond to stimuli occur-

---

[3] The term *structure* has also been used with *role*. It refers to a cluster of related meanings and values that govern a social setting. A structure and the roles that are related in it are two aspects of the same thing. One is seen from the view of the individual and the other from that of the social setting. See Arnold M. Rose, (1962), p. 10.

ring outside himself. (Stryker, 1959.) What is a stimulus depends on the activity in which the organism is engaged.

8. "man must be studied on his own level. The position of symbolic interactionism is anti-reductionist; it argues that valid principles of human social-psychological behavior cannot be derived from . . . the study of non-human forms." (Stryker, 1959, p. 112.)

9. The basic unit of observation is interaction. From the process of interaction both the individual and society are derived. (Stryker, 1959.) The acting individual is the basic autonomous unit in the social setting.

10. The human infant is neither social nor antisocial, but rather asocial. The child possesses potentialities for social development. (Stryker, 1959.)

11. "Social conduct is most immediately a function of the social milieu." (Hill and Hansen, 1960, p. 309.) Individuals act toward social-stimulus situations as they define the situation. Social organizations enter into action only to the extent to which they shape social situations.

12. A final assumption has to do with interrelationships of the parts and the whole.

(a) The relationship represents more than the sum of the personalities that make it up.

(b) The dynamics of the two units, individual and group, are therefore not interchangeable, and the integrative processes appropriate to the one level of organization cannot be imposed upon the other.

(c) An effect on the one partner in the relationship will always influence the behavior of the other. (Ackerman, 1954.)

Thus it can be stated that a marital relationship is something beyond the sum of the personalities that make it up. The relationship itself influences and changes each partner and this in turn influences the relationship anew.

PRODUCT

Theory

The interactional framework in sociology and social psychology applied to family study is a framework that has grown crescively. Mead set forth the framework in 1934 and very few attempts have been made at extending or refining his outline. Waller (1938), Waller and Hill (1951), Stryker (1959, 1964), and Hill and Hansen

(1960) represent steps in the conceptualization of the approach as applied to the family. For the most part the framework has had a partial formulation in one area and some development in another, but very little by way of a systematic and logical evolution of a centralized system of theory. The influence from the framework has been extensive, but the lack of systematic formulation and unification renders the theoretical contributions and extensions of the theory somewhat disparate. At the present time one could safely say that there is no adequate cumulation of theory applied to the family. From a theoretical view, then, it appears that the interactional framework as originally suggested by Burgess has been followed more than it has been formulated.

Burgess (1926) drew from the theoretical formulations of Mead, Cooley, Park, and others in making his classical statement in regard to a theoretical conception of family study. Mead (1934) up to the present time has not been surpassed by any theorist in more completely expanding and delineating the theory of the interactional framework. Burgess (1926, 1947) and Burgess and Locke (1945) have applied the interactionist theory to family study and have been instrumental in shifting the theoretical focus of the family scholar from the institutional approach toward family study to the interactional approach of viewing the family as a companionable relationship of interacting personalities.

Waller (1938) and Waller and Hill (1951) have done extensive work in their attempts to relate theoretical implications of the interactional framework to the study and understanding of the family. These two works have been instrumental in shifting the view of the family as a static social unit to that of a living, functioning unity. Stryker (1959, 1964) illustrates the utility of the theory as it now stands and as it may be used in the study of the family. Rose (1962) has the most extensive accumulation of the results of the interactional framework in the social-psychological study of human behavior. Although few attempts are made in his volume of essays to develop new theory, he does attempt to systematize the impact of the school and show the present status of the approach.

In summary it may be stated that the greatest impact of the interactionist approach on theory has been that of shifting the focus of family study from a broad institutional approach to that of a direct focus on the internal workings of families as individual family members interact.

Research

Interactionist theory has had considerable impact on family research and thought. Hill and Hansen state, "The interactional approach . . . has been the most frequently used in the past twenty years in American family sociology." (1960, p. 302.) Because of its small size the family facilitates intensive and extensive research into the basic processes of interaction.

The framework has contributed much by way of methodological procedures. It has focused on influences, structures, and variables for study on the level of common family experiences. Empirical research has thus tended to use observations from a selected portion of day-to-day interaction. The methods of observation are manifold, ranging from unstructured observation to highly structured measurement. Thus the impact of the framework has been to shift family study from library research and historical reconstruction to actual field observations and case-history studies. Angell (1936), Cavan (1938), Koos (1946), and Hill (1949) all employed the interactional framework to the study of the family under crisis situations. They employed the techniques of observation, interview, statistical samples, and case histories as they assessed family stability while the family was attempting to function under adverse conditions. A similar type of study of the family was *The Unemployed Man and His Family*, (1940) by Komarovsky, in which she depicted family interaction under the stress of economic threats.

Lemasters (1957), Eliot (1958), and Dyer (1963) attempt to study the relationship of interacting units in the family and the process of adjustment when a family member is eliminated by death or when one is added by birth. Bossard (1945) has developed a law of family interaction which can be applied to a group to determine the number of interpersonal relationships when the size of the group is increased or decreased.[4]

The research by Ingersoll (1937) and Bronson *et al.* (1959) illustrates how authority patterns and affectional ties from one generation of family members to the next can be studied by the

[4] The basic meaning of the law is that every increase in the number of members of a primary group results in more than a corresponding increase in the number of sets of interrelationships. The larger the group becomes, the more disproportionate the increase becomes. The number of persons increase in simply arithmetical progression while the number of personal interrelationships within the group increases in the order of triangular numbers.

interactionist framework. Stryker (1956) has also contributed research study in this area. Buerkle and Badgley (1959), Hobart and Klausner (1959), and Udry, Nelson, and Nelson (1961) exemplify the utility of the interactional approach to the study of marital roles, marital adjustment, and marital role-taking. In this same vein but somewhat distinctive are the works of Middleton and Putney (1960), Vidich (1956), Kenkel and Hoffman (1956), and Folkman (1956), representative of the interactional framework in the assessment of husband and wife, reaction, and interaction, with some illustrations of parent-child interaction. Nye (1957) illustrates the effects of parent-child interaction in broken homes and in unhappy unbroken homes. Using employment of the mother as the independent variable, Nye (1959) assessed adjustment of adolescent children in the family. These types of study illustrate the range of problems to which this framework can be applied in assessing family interactional patterns.

Ernest Mowrer's work of 1939 is an example of the framework applied to understanding the family from a standpoint of disruption. Mowrer and Mowrer (1951) adequately use the framework to discuss the social psychology of marriage and family living in the American culture. Hess and Handel (1959) relate concepts and assumptions to their interactional study of five families. They successfully exploit the case-study method in the study of interaction of family members. Hill, Stycos, and Back (1959) show that the approach can be used in diverse areas of family interaction and that cross-culturally it meets the need for a frame of reference which lends itself to wide diversity.

Stryker (1959, 1964) spells out the concepts and assumptions of the interactional approach for family study and suggests fruitful areas of further investigation. Along with this Hill and Hansen (1960) have assessed research possibilities from the interactional approach. Strodtbeck (1951, 1958) and Blood (1958) provide examples of new research techniques by which a researcher can study the family while using the interactional approach.

In summary the research projects stemming from this framework have been voluminous. We could say with little hesitation that the interactional approach has been one of the most widely used approaches to family study. Referring once again to Rose (1962), who states that half of all sociologists were nurtured on the interactional approach, perhaps we could go one step further and state that within the family field at least three-fourths of the researchers have employed this approach at some time.

Practice

Christensen (1964) states that Burgess' suggestion (1926)—that we study the family as a unity of interacting personalities—has been a key factor in the shift from viewing the family broadly as a social institution to that of an internal association. This naturally has had a great effect upon teaching, counseling, and casework by considering such topics as dating, mate selection, marriage adjustment, parent-child relationships, and personality formation within the family context.

With this approach to the family a practitioner can get inside the family group and analyze its functions as far as they involve interaction between and among members. Each family member can thus be viewed as a developing member in a changing group. This approach is useful to the helping professions not only because it provides a practical way of inspecting the family, but also because it allows them to isolate and specify the potential sources of difficulty as family members relate to one another and to their society.

Sullivan (1953) has utilized this approach and relates the concepts to the therapeutic setting. He focuses heavily upon the interpersonal and symbolic nature of personality as formulated in the socialization of the family members. These concepts and insights which he used in psychiatry and, specifically, with persons suffering from schizophrenia have influenced all types of counseling and therapy.

Ackerman (1954, 1958) and Eisenstein (1956) provide examples of how the interactional framework has been employed in the field of psychoanalytic therapy.[5] Their works also illustrate the dynamics of family interaction with special emphasis on the neurotic element in marital and family interaction. Their systems have had a great impact upon welfare agencies and especially on theory and practice in the case–work approach.

Fibush (1957) describes a process of evaluation of marital interaction in the treatment of one partner. Skidmore and Garrett (1955) tactfully used the joint–interview technique in the counseling re-

[5] Many of the concepts of the interactional approach are compatible with the psychoanalytical approach. It is not suggested that the assumptions are the same, but it is to be pointed out that such scholars as Ackerman and Eisenstein, as well as scholars in the sociological framework, see the family as a dynamic unity.

lationship in order to observe the interaction of the marital partners. They felt the technique to be very fruitful, with the counselor acting as a third party in helping the couple to interpret each other's feelings in the interactional setting.

Beatman (1957) and Weise and Monroe (1959) show the utility of the interactional approach not only in its actual treatment of family members but also as a theoretical framework to be used in social case work. By using some of the concepts and assumptions from the interactional framework these practitioners outline a scheme of treatment and a framework for understanding family dynamics. Gomberg (1958), in his plea that case workers treat the family as a unity and not as discrete family members, recommends this framework because only by focusing on the whole family can one help people to live more productive lives within the internal structure of the family.

Kuhn (1962) analyzes the interview from the interactional frame of reference and shows that all types of interviews are really social acts. His analysis suggests the utility of the symbolic interactional reference for the practicing professions in which the counselor-client interaction is the major therapeutic instrument. Freidson (1962) shows how the frame of reference is used and applied in the medical profession with the patients.

In summary it appears that no other approach to the study of the family lends itself to such a diversity of functional practices. The framework has had a great influence on teaching concerning marriage and the family, on all types of therapy which use verbal interaction, on case work, and on medical and family centers which treat marriage and family problems.[6]

VALUES

Perhaps the most easily identifiable value in the interactional frame of reference is the view that marital happiness is something to be achieved and nurtured—even above marital stability. Kolb (1948, 1950) is critical of works such as those of Burgess and Cot-

---

[6] Some suggested research problems under this framework:
  1. Values of families living in intergenerational settings as opposed to values of families living in isolated settings.
  2. A comparison of husbands and wives in regard to role-taking. Who is the most accurate and versatile? Who is the most rational?
  3. A comparison of the socialization process of children in homes where husband and wife share the same value framework and where they do not.

trell (1939) and Locke (1951) which place their emphasis on adjustment and conformity. The welfare and happiness of marital partners and family members are held above the belief that the marital union or family union should stay intact. The happiness of individual family members appears to be the dominant value.

Along with the above value but distinct in many respects is the value placed on sex. Perhaps this should be labeled as an instrumental value rather than one of ultimate concern. This is the view that sex is something in marriage beyond creative function. Sex is something to be cultivated for the mutual enjoyment of both partners. It is an art rather than a function to be used for procreation or merely for the pleasure of the male involved.

THE FRAMEWORK

The term *interaction*, as has been pointed out, refers to the peculiar and distinctive character of relationships which occur between human beings and, in our case, members of the family. The peculiarity consists in the fact that human beings *interpret or define* each other's actions instead of merely reacting to them. The wife's response, for example, is made not merely to the actions of the husband but also to the meaning which both partners attach to such actions. Thus one recognizes that the family members act and react by the use of symbols. The key concept involved in the use of symbols is *communication*. Interpersonal relations among family members based on communication is one of the major distinguishing aspects of this approach. The symbols are interpreted by family members, and interaction takes place by ascertaining the meaning of one another's actions. "This mediation is equivalent to inserting a process of interpretation between stimulus and response in the case of human behavior." (Rose, 1962, p. 180.)

Foote and Cottrell (1955) comment that emphasis in this framework is on the development of competence in interpersonal relations. As Burgess (1953) states, the study of intimate relations of married life is facilitated with the interactionist framework. Interaction does not describe a state, but a process.

Burgess and Locke (1953) refer to the source of social control for the family unit as one of the major distinctions between the institutional and interactionist frameworks. In the institutional approach, the control of behavior is derived from the social structure outside of the family. In contrast, social control in the interactionist approach is viewed as stemming from mutual affection and compatibility of the family members. It may be said that the institutional approach is more community oriented while the interactionist approach is based on interpersonal relationships among family members.

It should be pointed out that the framework also differs from the structure-functional approach in sociology. Under the perspective of interaction, social action comes from acting individuals who fit their respective types of action to one another through a process of interpretation. Family interaction is the collective actions of such individuals. As opposed to this view, structure-functional conceptions generally lodge social action in the action of society or in some unit of society.

Family life or family interaction consists of acting units developing acts to meet the situation in which they are placed. The interactionist would state that most of the situations encountered by a family member as he goes through the socialization process are defined or structured for him in some way. Through previous interactions family members have developed and acquired common understandings or definitions of how to act in a particular situation. These common understandings are the forces which enable family members to act alike. The interactionist focuses on the definitions of situations by family members, but, unlike the situationist, he does not emphasize the social situation but, rather, the interaction. The interactionists would consider Thomas as fitting into their framework rather than into the situational approach because he placed the stress on the definition of the situation as defined by acting members and not on the situation itself. In contrast to this approach the situationist states that the situation merits study without any reference to the way in which organisms react to it.

The interactionist is concerned with the behavior of the acting members of the family. It is the goal of the framework to catch or freeze the process of interpretation through which family members view the role of the member whose behavior is under study. From the standpoint of the interactionist approach, the family is the framework inside of which social action takes place, and is not the determinant of that action. Secondly, the organization and changes in the family unit are the products of the activity of acting units and not of forces which leave such acting units out of account.

The interactionist seeks to discover the symbolic meaning or interpretation which precedes the overt act. The interactionist assumes that the actors (family members) respond symbolically, that is, in terms of definitions of the situation. They do not respond to uniformly objective stimuli. The interactional framework may be thought of as process, composed of *mutually interrelated* behaviors on the part of two or more individuals or groups in which each step rises meaningfully out of the preceding steps.

The interactionist framework is distinctive as an approach used among social psychologists. Unlike other approaches in social psychology, the interactionist focuses upon naturalistic observations, interviews, or questionnaires as techniques rather than upon experimentation under artificially controlled settings. A second characteristic rests on the assumption that family relationships are continually in flux. Social life in the family is assumed to be in process rather than in equilibrium. This emphasis on process distinguishes the approach from that of the functional theory in sociology. The interactionist approach to family study also differs from psychoanalytic theory in that it has not and does not focus or give thought to the unconscious process in family interaction. The interactionist states that adult behavior is derived from interaction and communication processes, whereas the psychoanalyst states that it is derived from ontogenetic deductions. Thus, behavior is traced back to acquired reactions, with the emphasis on early childhood.

A third distinctive characteristic of the interactionist approach is the assumption that all social objects are interpreted by the individual family member and have special meaning. Thus social objects are never viewed as physical stimuli but as definitions of the situation. This aspect of the framework is largely what distinguishes it from that of the positivist or behaviorist theories in sociology and psychology. (Rose, 1962.)

Role-taking is the central process in the interactional approach. In this process, every role is a way of relating to other roles in the situation. A role cannot exist without some counter roles toward which it is oriented. Interaction is always a dynamic process, that is, a process of continuously testing the concept one has of the role of the other. "In the socialization of the children in a family and also continuously in family interaction the product of the testing process is the stabilization or the modification of one's own role." (Turner, 1962, p. 2.) As part of the same process, one acquires expectations of how others in the family will behave. The knowledge of others is needed by the individual in order that he may be able to predict what others will expect of him. Such knowledge enables him to know how they will react to him. With this understanding he is able to guide his own role performance successfully.

CRITIQUE AND DISCUSSION

Contributions

The interactionist framework has been so widely used because, among other factors, it is able to focus successfully on the family as a small group. The institutional approach has too wide a sweep to catch the single family unit. Thus the interactional framework has been instrumental in the shift from institutional analysis of the family to analysis of the internal workings of the family. As a result, the framework has been instrumental in the development and establishment of family-life education at both the secondary and college level.

The interactional framework has enabled students of the family to exploit Thomas' concept of the *definition of the situation*. Hess and Handel (1959) and Stryker (1959), along with others, state that this definition is the very thing that causes attitudes toward others in relationships and is not the thing that is caused. The framework has been responsible for producing hundreds of research projects and articles on the family since the early work was outlined by Mead. Burgess (1926) set the stage for using this framework in family research and for viewing the family as a unity of interacting personalities. Dollard (1935) added that we should also include the history of each family. Thus we have the impact of the case-history approach coupled with the interactional framework, a combination that has been significant not only in research and teaching but also in counseling theory and case work. The merit of the interactionist conception of the family is that it furnishes an inclusive framework into which may be fitted all kinds of contributions having to do with the human-nature aspects of the family.

In summary, the contributions of the framework are manifold, but particularly important are the contributions to teaching on a functional level; an understanding of family dynamics which is useful for practicing groups; and a research model which presents itself for use at all phases of family functioning. The interactional approach has probably done more than any other framework to remove family study from the realm of speculation to the field of scientific study and analysis.

Inadequacies and Contradictions

As a research framework the interactional approach addresses itself primarily to a study of the internal workings of the family. It may be used in the study of the family as an entity in relationship to the community, but such a study is more difficult to carry out. As a model for family study it also lacks a universally understood name to guide and promote it. The term *interactionist* is not a universal title used by all students who approach the family from this vantage point. In the study of the internal processes of family life there seems to be a scarcity of studies which view all of the family members. More often the focus has been on husband-wife relationships or mother-child interaction. For a framework which sees the family as a unity of interacting personalities this appears to be an obvious gap.

Some critics feel that the approach fails to recognize the biogenic and psychogenic influences on family behavior. It remains to be seen what will become of this accusation, but at present the interactionist would state that these influences set limits but are not the determining factors in regard to family interaction. The focus is on the family in process and not on a static entity.

Another area of contradictions and inadequacies deals with concepts and assumptions. Because of its diversified origins, the writers who use the interactional framework cannot claim complete agreement in concepts and assumptions. A review of the literature also reveals that there is no single view of the interactional framework. Because of the wide application of the approach, there is an undue lack of unification of theoretical findings and of methods. This wide application of the approach to action-oriented or problem-oriented research has left the framework devoid of new formulations and refinements of previous delineations. It appears that users of the interactionist approach are unusually prone to study the family without systematic concepts, assumptions, or theory.

Thus it must be noted once again that the original formulations of Mead (1934) and, specifically in the family field, Burgess (1926) have been widely used and extensively followed, but extended very little. There is need for a unification of agreement on concepts and assumptions in order that the interactional approach may more adequately function as a frame of reference for the study of the family and eventually mesh with other frameworks into what could be called a general family theory.

REFERENCES

ACKERMAN, NATHAN W. "The Diagnosis of Neurotic Marital Inter-action," *Social Casework*, 35 (April 1954), pp. 139–47. A discussion of types of interaction and presentation of an outline as to how one is distinguished from another.

————. *The Psychodynamics of Family Life*. New York: Basic Books, Inc., Publishers, 1958. An interactionist point of view for family life. It places great emphasis on the dynamic aspects of marriage and the family and is especially useful to the practicing groups.

ANGELL, ROBERT O. *The Family Encounters the Depression*. New York: Charles Scribner's Sons, 1936. A description of the problems en-countered by families during the depression and their struggle to cope with such problems. Angell uses the interactional framework.

BEATMAN, FRANCES L. "Family Interaction: Its Significance for Diagnosis and Treatment," *Social Casework*, 38 (March 1957), pp. 111–18. A study that points out the importance of seeing the family as a process in diagnosis and for treatment.

BLOOD, ROBERT O. "The Use of Observational Methods in Family Re-search," *Marriage and Family Living*, 20 (Feb. 1958), pp. 47–52.

BOSSARD, J. H. L. "The Law of Family Interaction," *American Journal of Sociology*, 50 (Jan. 1945), pp. 292–94. A presentation of the formula and the theory behind a law describing how the number of interpersonal relationships varies with the number of people in a group.

BRONSON, W. C., KATTEN, E. S., and LIVSON, N. "Patterns of Authority and Affection in Two Generations," *Journal of Abnormal and Social Psychology*, 58 (March 1959), pp. 143–52. A discussion of types of affection as related to types of family structure and how these are passed from one to the next generation.

BROOM, LEONARD, and SELZNICK, PHILIP. *Sociology: A Text with Adapted Readings*, 3rd ed. New York: Harper & Row, Publishers, 1963.

BURGESS, E. W. "The Family and Sociological Research," *Social Forces*, 26 (Oct. 1947), pp. 1–6. A partial delineation of the theory of inter-action for family study and description of some of the processes evolving from an interacting unity.

————. "The Family as a Unity of Interacting Personalities," *The Family*, 7 (1926), pp. 3–9. The classic reference where Burgess first suggested the interactional approach. He describes the process and presents case histories to illustrate what he means by a unity of inter-acting persons.

————, and WALLIN, P. *Engagement and Marriage*. Philadelphia: J. B. Lippincott Company, 1953. Extensive research on courtship and the early years of marriage. The focus is on those factors which make for success or failure in marriage.

————, and LOCKE, H. J. *The Family from Institution to Companionship*. New York: American Book Company, 1945. An illustration of how the family over time has changed from an institution to a companion-ship association. The authors employ the interactional framework throughout.

————, and COTTRELL, L. S. *Predicting Success or Failure in Marriage*. Englewood Cliffs, N.J.: Prentice-Hall, Inc. 1939.

CAVAN, R. S. *The American Family*. New York: Thomas Y. Crowell Company, 1953. A text written for the college level within the inter-actional framework. Cavan does not delineate the framework but em-ploys it as a mold in which she presents a series of chapters on the family process.

————, and RANCK, K. R. *The Family and the Depression*. Chicago: University of Chicago Press, 1938. An example of the interactional ap-proach used to study the family under adverse conditions.

COOLEY, C. H. *Human Nature and the Social Order*. New York: Free Press of Glencoe, Inc., 1956.

CHRISTENSEN, H. T. *Handbook on Marriage and the Family*. Chicago: Rand McNally & Company, 1964. History and some of the impact of the interactional approach in Chapter 1. Other frameworks are con-tained in the volume.

COTTRELL, L. S. "The Present Status and Future Orientation of Research on the Family," *American Sociological Review*, **13** (April 1948), pp. 123–36.

————. "Analysis of Situational Fields in Social Psychology," *American Sociological Review*, **7** (June 1942), pp. 370–87. An illustration using the interactional approach that, among other things, the definition of the situation is a key concept in the framework.

COUTU, WALTER. *Emergent Human Nature: A Symbolic Field Interpre-tation*. New York: Alfred A. Knopf, Inc., 1949.

DOLLARD, JOHN. "The Family: Needed Viewpoints in Family Research," *Social Forces*, **35** (Oct. 1935), pp. 109–13.

DYER, E. D. "Parenthood as Crisis: A Re-Study," *Marriage and Family Living*, **25** (May 1963), pp. 196–201. The results of a re-study of the LeMasters' study of 1957. Illustrates the interactional framework in the study of the family under impact of a new member.

EISENSTEIN, VICTOR W. *Neurotic Interaction in Marriage*. Philadelphia: J. B. Lippincott Company, 1953.

ELIOT, T. D. "Adjusting to the Death of a Loved One." Paper presented at the Annual Meeting of the Groves Conference on Marriage and the Family, 1958. A discussion of the reactions and adjustments of families to the death of a family member. He also suggests some facts to consider in treatment.

ELKIN, FREDERICK. "Socialization and Presentation of Self," *Marriage and Family Living*, 20 (Nov. 1958), pp. 320–25.

FIBUSH, ESTHER W. "Evaluation of Marital Interaction in the Treatment of One Partner," *Social Casework*, 38 (June 1957), pp. 303–07

FOLKMAN, J. D. "Stressful and Supportive Familial Interaction," *Marriage and Family Living*, 18 (May 1956), pp. 102–06. A discussion of life experiences and types of family organization which are most likely to be related to mental breakdown. A comparison of the two groups is presented.

FOOTE, N. N. "Identification as the Basis for a Theory of Motivation," *American Sociological Review* 16 (Feb. 1951), pp. 14–21.

———, and COTTRELL, L. S. *Identity and Interpersonal Competence.* Chicago: University of Chicago Press, 1955. A very good review of the literature and past work in the family field. The authors point to new areas of family research stressing identity and personal competence which they say includes six factors: judgment, autonomy, creativity, health, intelligence, and empathy.

FRIEDSON, ELIOT. "Dilemmas in the Doctor-Patient Relationship," in Arnold M. Rose, ed. *Human Behavior and Social Processes.* Boston: Houghton Mifflin Company, pp. 207–25. An outline of the frictions between patient and doctor as they engage each other in the interactional process. It illustrates the utility of the approach.

GOMBERG, ROBERT. "Family Diagnosis, Trends in Theory and Practice," *Social Casework*, 39 (Feb.-March 1958), pp. 73–83. An illustration of the importance of seeing the family in process and treating the family as a whole and not as separate members of a family unit.

HESS, ROBERT D., and HANDEL, GERALD. *Family Worlds: A Psychological Approach to Family Life.* Chicago: The University of Chicago Press, 1959. A study of five families from the interactional framework. Many of the concepts and assumptions are presented by the writers.

HILL, REUBEN. "Social Stresses on the Family," *Social Casework*, 39 (Feb.-March 1958), pp. 139–50. An article which makes available much of the insight from the crisis studies of the family and points out how this may be helpful to caseworkers.

———. "A Critique of Contemporary Marriage and Family Research," *Social Forces*, 33 (March 1955), pp. 268–77. An attempt to assess the status of several frameworks to family study including the interactional approach.

———. "Review of Current Research on Marriage and the Family,"

American Sociological Review, **16** (Oct. 1951), pp. 694–701. A brief history of the interactional school. Tells some of the work that has been done.

————. *Families Under Stress.* New York: Harper & Row, Publishers, 1949.

————, and HANSEN, DONALD. "The Identification of Conceptual Frameworks Utilized in Family Study," *Marriage and Family Living* (Nov. 1960), pp. 299–311. A presentation of the current status of several frameworks including the background and major adherents of each.

————, STYCOS, J. M., and BACK, K. W. *The Family and Population Control: A Puerto Rican Experiment in Social Change.* Chapel Hill, N.C., The University of North Carolina Press, 1959. A research project viewing population control as a phenomenon of family planning and action. Gives the report of a seven-year project illustrating the problems of teaching birth control to a 90 per cent Catholic nation.

HOBART, C. W. and KLAUSNER, J. "Some Social Interactional Correlates of Marital Role Disagreement and Marital Adjustment," *Marriage and Family Living,* **21** (Aug. 1959), pp. 256–63. A report that gives many of the concepts and assumptions of the interactional approach and reports, among other things, the part effective communication plays in marital adjustment.

HUNTINGTON, ROBERT M. "The Personality Interaction Approach to Study of the Marital Relationship," *Marriage and Family Living,* **20** (Feb. 1958), pp. 43–46. One of the better research articles in which the concepts and some of the assumptions of the framework are made explicit.

INGERSOLL, H. "Study of Transmission of Authority Patterns in the Family," *Genetic Psychology Monograph,* **38** (March 1948), pp. 225–99. Very detailed research illustrating that parents pass on to their children the basic power structure that they themselves have used.

KENKEL, W. F. *The Family in Perspective: A Fourfold Analysis.* New York: Appleton-Century-Crofts, 1960.

————, and HOFFMAN, D. K. "Real and Conceived Roles in Family Decision Making," *Marriage and Family Living,* **18** (Nov. 1956), pp. 311–16. A study which points out processes by which spouses function in their ability to recognize their roles in the decision-making process.

KING, MORTON B. "Some Comments on Concepts," *Social Forces,* **34** (Oct. 1955), pp. 1–4. A clearly presented discussion of concepts for social research, many of them pertaining to the interactional approach.

KIRKPATRICK, CLIFFORD. *The Family: As Process and Institution.* New York: The Ronald Press Company, 1955. A volume presenting the impact of the interactional framework as presented in form and content of a textbook on the family. As the title indicates, Kirkpatrick interprets the family not only as an institution, but as a fluid social group.

KOLB, WILLIAM L. "Family Sociology, Marriage Education, and the Romantic Complex: A Critique," *Social Forces*, 29 (Oct. 1950), pp. 65–72. A study in which Kolb refers to the values in the literature by family researchers and points out that the romantic complex is being replaced by a conformity complex.

———. "Sociologically Established Family Norms and Democratic Values," *Social Forces*, 26 (May 1948), pp. 451–56. A study of the value judgments which family scholars use in their research and which Kolb feels are not justified in scientific research.

KOMAROVSKY, MIRRA. *The Unemployed Man and His Family*. New York: The Dryden Press, Inc., 1940. An illustration of the adjustment problems of families under adverse conditions and the consequent problems for family stability.

———, and WALLER, WILLARD. "Studies of the Family," *American Journal of Sociology*, 50 (May 1945), pp. 443–51. A depiction of the stages of family studies and classification of them. One of the classifications deals with the interactional framework and development.

KOOS, EARL L. *Marriage*. New York: Holt, Rinehart & Winston, Inc., 1958. An example of an introductory textbook written within the interactional framework.

———. *Families in Trouble*. New York: King's Crown Press, 1946. Koos uses a series of interviews, histories, and insights. A volume depicting family interaction under adverse living conditions. He illustrates traits of stable and unstable families.

KUHN, MANFORD H. "The Interview and the Professional Relationship," in Arnold M. Rose. *Human Behavior and Social Processes*. Boston: Houghton Mifflin Company, 1962, pp. 193–206. A study which suggests the potentialities of symbolic interactional theory for the practicing professions in which counselor-patient verbal interaction is the chief tool.

LEMASTERS, E. E. "Parenthood as Crisis," *Marriage and Family Living*, 19 (Nov. 1957), pp. 352–55. An illustration of how the birth of the baby upsets established interactional patterns in family living to the degree that families experience crisis situations.

LINDESMITH, ALFRED R., and STRAUSS, A. L. *Social Psychology*. New York: The Dryden Press, Inc., 1949. An integrated view of more significant effects of group membership upon individual behavior. One of the best sources for a synthesis of many of the concepts related to the interactional approach.

LOCKE, HARVEY J. *Predicting Adjustment in Marriage: A Comparison of a Divorced and a Happily Married Group*. New York: Holt, Rinehart & Winston, Inc., 1951.

MEAD, GEORGE H. *Mind, Self, Society*. Chicago: University of Chicago Press, 1934. The most comprehensive formulation, even today, of the interactional theory. The book is rich with concepts and assumptions, many of which have been used in the study of the family.

MIDDLETON, RUSSEL, and PUTNEY, SNELL. "Effect of Husband-Wife Interaction on the Strictness of Attitudes Toward Child Rearing," *Marriage and Family Living*, **22** (May 1960), pp. 171–73. A presentation of how interaction differs according to race and social class and the consequences of such interaction in relationship to the child.

MIYAMOTO, FRANK S., and DORNBUSCH, SANFORD M. "A Test of Interactionist Hypotheses of Self-Conception," *American Journal of Sociology*, **61** (March 1956), pp. 399–403. Results of a study which give support to the symbolic interactionist view of self-conception. The attitude of others is related to self-conception.

MOWRER, ERNEST R. *Family Disorganization: An Introduction to a Sociological Analysis*. Chicago: University of Chicago Press, 1939. An illustration of how the approach lends itself to family breakdown. Shows some of the causes and trends in family disorganization.

———, and MOWRER, HARRIET. "The Social Psychology of Marriage," *American Sociological Review*, **16** (Feb. 1957), pp. 27–36. An article which shows the utility of this approach in viewing the marriage and the interaction of husband and wife.

MOWRER, HARRIET. "Getting Along in Marriage," in Howard Becker and Reuben Hill, eds. *Family, Marriage, and Parenthood*. Boston: D. C. Heath and Company, 1948, Chap. 11. One of the best treatments of marital accord and marital discord from the interactional point of view.

NYE, F. IVAN. "Employment Status of Mothers and Adjustment of Adolescent Children," *Marriage and Family Living*, **21** (Aug. 1959), pp. 240–44. A study in which the author treats the employment of the mother as the independent variable and illustrates the effect of this type of interaction on adolescent development. This study is an example of the framework's utility of showing relationships between the family and agencies outside the family.

———. "Child Adjustment in Broken and in Unhappy Unbroken Homes," *Marriage and Family Living*, **19** (Nov. 1957), pp. 356–61. An illustration of the consequences of certain types of family interaction upon the growth and development of children.

PARK, R. E., and BURGESS, E. W. *Introduction to the Science of Sociology*. Chicago: University of Chicago Press, 1924.

ROSE, ARNOLD M. *Human Behavior and Social Processes: An Interactional Approach*. Boston: Houghton Mifflin Company, 1962. One of the most comprehensive attempts to systematize the work of Mead and draw together in one volume the current interactional work.

SHERIF, MUZAFER. "A Glance at Group Relations at the Crossroads: Introduction," in Muzafer Sherif and M. O. Wilson. *Group Relation at the Crossroads.* New York: Harper & Row, Publishers, 1953, pp. 1–32.

SHERMAN, S. N. *et al.* "Concepts of Family Striving and Family Distress: The Contributions of M. Robert Gomberg," *Social Casework*, 39 (July 1958), pp. 383–91. An illustration that Gomberg's main emphasis was on treating the family as a whole and in the context of the social situation.

SHIBUTANI, TAMOTSU. *Society and Personality: An Interactionist Approach to Social Psychology.* Englewood Cliffs, N.J.: Prentice-Hall, Inc., 1961. A helpful source in showing the unique focus of the interactional framework. Concepts and assumptions are set forth with clarity.

SIMMEL, G. *The Sociology of Georg Simmel*, Kurt H. Wolff, trans. and ed. New York: Free Press of Glencoe, Inc., 1950, pp. 9–11.

SKIDMORE, REX A., and GARRETT, HILDA V. S. "The Joint Interview in Marriage Counseling," *Marriage and Family Living*, 17 (Nov. 1955), pp. 349–54. An illustration of the utility of husband-wife interaction in the counseling session.

SOROKIN, PITIRIM A. *Society, Culture, and Personality.* New York: Harper & Row, Publishers, 1947.

STRYKER, SHELDON. "The Interactional and Situational Approaches," in Harold T. Christensen, ed. *Handbook of Marriage and the Family.* Chicago: Rand McNally & Company, 1964, pp. 125–70. An expansion of the piece that appeared in the *Journal of Marriage and Family Living.* This chapter represents a systematic tracing of the evolution of the framework from social psychology and shows how this framework has been utilized by writers such as Burgess, Waller, Hill, and Foote. Contains a detailed bibliography.

———. "Symbolic Interaction as an Approach to Family Research," *Marriage and Family Living*, 21 (May 1959), pp. 111–19. One of the best summarizations of the interactional approach to family study. The article illustrates concepts and assumptions and points to fruitful areas of research within the interactional approach.

———. "Role-Taking Accuracy and Adjustment," *Sociometry*, 20 (Dec. 1957), pp. 286–96. Stryker tests the idea that role-taking is adjustive in the static sense and finds that idea wanting.

———. "Relationship of Married Offspring and Parents: A Test of Mead's Theory," *American Journal of Sociology*, 52 (Nov. 1956), pp. 308–19. A study which shows the testing of hypotheses concerning accurate role-taking which were tested on married offspring relationships. The tests supported Mead's theory.

SULLIVAN, HARRY S. *Interpersonal Theory of Psychiatry.* New York: W. W. Norton & Company, 1953. A discussion of interpersonal interaction in the family as this affects the child's socialization. Sullivan formulates many new concepts and insights toward family relationships.

SUSSMAN, MARVIN. *Sourcebook in Marriage and the Family*, 2nd ed. Boston: Houghton Mifflin Company, 1963. A source containing a number of studies having their focus in the interactional approach.

THOMAS, W. I., and ZNANIECKI, FLORIAN. *The Polish Peasant in Europe and America*, Vol. 1. New York: Alfred A. Knopf, Inc., 1927, p. 68. A formulation of the concept *definition of the situation* and the importance of the attitude of the actor in the social stimulus situation.

TIMASHEFF, NICHOLAS S. *Sociological Theory: Its Nature and Growth*. New York: Random House, Inc., 1957, Chaps. 8 and 14.

TURNER, RALPH H. "Role-Taking: Process Versus Conformity," in Arnold M. Rose. *Human Behavior and Social Processes*. Boston: Houghton Mifflin Company, 1962, pp. 20–40. A vivid illustration of the use and utility of role-taking and role-making in the interactionist approach.

UDRY, J. R., NELSON, H. A. and NELSON, R. "An Empirical Investigation of Some Widely Held Beliefs About Marital Interaction," *Marriage and Family Living*, 23 (Nov. 1961), pp. 388–90. A test of the assumption that interaction in the marital union is the same as in any type of dyad.

VIDICH, ARTHUR J. "Methodological Problems in the Observation of Husband-Wife Interaction," *Marriage and Family Living*, 18 (Aug. 1956), pp. 234–39. An illustration of the technical and social problems connected with the study of husband-wife interaction.

WALLER, WILLARD. *The Family: A Dynamic Interpretation*. New York: The Cordon Co., 1938. One of the first family texts written within the interactional framework. The interactional framework is outlined in Chapter 1. Waller presents many of the concepts and assumptions of the approach.

———, and HILL, REUBEN. *The Family: A Dynamic Interpretation*, rev. ed. New York: The Dryden Press, Inc., 1951. An expansion as well as a refinement of the original Waller volume. Hill brings the data up to date and more minutely conceptualizes family living patterns and habits into the interactionist approach.

WEISS, V. W. and MONROE, R. R. "A Framework for Understanding Family Dynamics," *Social Casework* 40 (Jan.–Feb. 1959), pp. 3–9. Many of the concepts and assumptions of family interaction pulled together in an attempt to develop a framework for family study and treatment.

chapter 6

A Conceptual Framework for Studying the Family: The Situational Approach*

E. M. Rallings

One approach to behavior problems is through the study of the situations to which behavior is a response. Building upon the earlier work of physiologists and behavioristic psychologists, some sociologists have found this a particularly significant avenue for studying man's behavior.

These sociologists see the situational approach as a separate and distinct one, commensurate in importance with the study of the individual and his traits, and worthy of being set forth as a separate field of scientific investigation. In other words, situations need to be studied inductively, without any reference to the way in which organisms react to them. It is felt that this will require interdisciplinary cooperation of physiologists, psychologists, cultural anthropologists, and the like, in order to understand as accurately as possible the nature of the elements which have combined to form the situation under study. The situational approach, with its present assumptions

* Grateful acknowledgment is made of the contribution of Eleanor S. Boll, who served as editorial consultant for this framework and who read and critically reviewed the manuscript prior to its final revision. Many, although not all, of her suggestions have been incorporated into the final manuscript. Inadequacies and errors in the chapter as published, however, are entirely the responsibility of the author and the editors.

and conclusions, is a sociological approach, but one which draws upon work done in the related fields of child study, psychiatry, education, and social work. (Bossard and Boll, 1943, pp. 30–35.)

Previous Attempts to Delineate the Framework

William I. and Dorothy S. Thomas recognized the importance of the situational approach in child study, although not delineating it fully. This quotation seems to be a fair statement of their appraisal: "We regard this approach as the only one capable of giving a rational basis for the control of behavior which may be a substitute for the common sense, perceptual, ordering-and-forbidding type of control which has been traditional and which, to the degree that it had efficiency in the past, has now broken down." (1928a, p. 501.) They recognized the contributions of the behavioristic school in psychology, but considered the main objective of the situational approach to be sociological.

Carr has made extensive application of the situational approach to the study of sociological problems in general. He sees the purposes of situational analysis as being: "(1) To break down any situation into its component elements and processes. (2) To determine and ultimately to measure the relationships among the problem phenomena, the situation, and its conditioning variables. (3) To discover laws, i.e., (a) invariant uniformities of coexisting relationships, and (b) invariant uniformities of succession, or phases and trends." (1948, p. 10.) He further states that sociological observers are always concerned with *situational* and not merely *personal* behavior. (1948, p. 20.)

Hill and Boulding used the situational approach in a study of families under the stress of separation during World War II. They adopted the Bossard-Boll theoretical framework in its entirety, except that they included the traditional patterns of culture under family structure.[1] According to Boulding, this change allows the use of cultural content to describe the external realities of the situation which the family as an organization must meet and to which it must react. (1949, p. 51n.)

Hill and his associates have delineated the situational approach in two articles (1957, 1960). They find a close similarity between the psychological habitat-ecological approach of psychology—developed

[1] Bossard had used cultural content to expound the traditional patterns and cultural heritage of family life.

by Barker and Wright (1955)—and the situational approach based on the theoretical work of Lowell Carr and W. I. Thomas and used as an approach for family research by Bossard and his students at the University of Pennsylvania.

However, the psychological habitat-ecological approach is not one of the conceptual frameworks listed and analyzed in the recent Hill article (1960). The reason given for this is "not because it fails to yield information pertinent to family study, but because it does not cope with the family as an entity or with its possible sub-groupings." (Hill, 1960, p. 305n.)

An important distinction noted between the two is that situational analysis studies the situation itself, or the individual's overt behavior in response to the situation. On the other hand, psychological habitat-ecological analysis centers attention on the individual's psychological milieu—the uniqueness of each individual's habitat and his perception of appropriate behavior.

In summarizing the situational approach, Hill and Hansen used quotations from the writings of Bossard and Boll to set forth these important facts about this fame of reference: Situationalists agree with the interactionists that the family is a unity of interacting persons but emphasize the study of the family as a social situation for behavior. A *social situation* is made up of stimuli which are external to the organism, which have a special relatedness to each other, and which operate as a unit. Not all behavior is rational but all behavior is purposive in relation to the situation which calls it forth. The family is considered relatively open to outside stimuli, but the work done in this area to date has been centered upon individual behavior as influenced by family situations. (1960, pp. 305–06.)

As editor of the *Handbook of Marriage and the Family*, Christensen sketches the various theoretical approaches to studying the family, including the situational approach. (1964, pp. 19–22.) However, he leaves the definitive exposition of the situational approach to Stryker, who argues that the things which unite situationalism and symbolic interactionism are more important than the things which make them different. (1964, pp. 163–66.)

Historical Development

The role of the environment as a causative factor in human behavior has long been recognized. Bossard and Boll illustrate this:

Among the first students of crime to employ positive methods was Tarde, who championed the view that the criminal was entirely a social product. Among the psychologists was Watson ... with an almost complete disregard for inborn or constitutional traits. White, among the psychiatrists, is clear in his relative emphasis upon environmental factors in the causation of mental disorders. Adler, of the psychoanalytic group, reveals a similarly high estimate of the importance of environmental conditioning. (1943, pp. 9–10.)

Continuing their historical summary, Bossard and Boll point out that the scientific study of behavior from the standpoint of environment came in time to be referred to as the situational approach. (1943, pp. 3 ff.) Thus conceived, the term *situation* was used to refer to the stimuli which impinge upon the organism from conditions exterior to the organism.

The procedure of studying behavior in relation to situations was begun by physiologists such as Loeb and Jennings who worked with tropisms, that is, reactions of organisms to light, heat, electricity, acids, and so on. Next, this kind of study was applied by psychologists such as Thorndike, Yerkes, Watson, and Kohler in experiments with rats, dogs, monkeys, and babies.

Much of the emphasis in recent years has proceeded to the next logical step, and now this technique has been applied to the study of human behavior. Based on Pavlov's classic experiment, comparative physiologists and psychologists did extensive work with the conditioned reflex—showing the extreme modifiability of human behavior. Taking their cue from Freud, psychiatrists emphasized the importance of the situations prevailing during the first few years of a child's life in personality development.

Finally, sociologists became aware of the possibilities of the situational approach—largely by way of the striking concepts of Cooley (1902). He introduced his concepts of "the self as a social product," "the looking-glass self," and "the individual and society as two aspects of the same thing" in 1902, but a decade passed before their implication began to be recognized.

The publication of Thomas and Znaniecki's monumental work on the Polish peasant in 1927 was the next step in this developmental chain, according to Bossard and Boll. They suggest that Thomas and Znaniecki have used what is essentially a situational approach, for throughout the entire work runs the fundamental theme of the relationship between personality and the environing culture. (1942, p. 12.) Timasheff does not agree, holding that "*The Polish Peasant* can be considered the first major work in modern sociology written in the functional spirit." (1955, p. 223.)

More important than this disagreement is the direct link which Rose sees between Thomas and Znaniecki's work and the symbolic interactionist's position in current social psychology. (Rose, 1962, pp. 3–18.)

Somewhat later Thomas himself drew the line between the constitutional and the situational studies of personality development, and defined the sociological approach. Studies which concern themselves with the stimuli to which persons react are situational studies. In these, the main objective is to discover how the behavior of the individual is determined by his relations to other individuals in a society. This, Thomas says, is sociological. (1928a, p. 506.)

What Thomas describes as sociological would today more appropriately be called *social psychological*. For confirmation of this, note the similarity between the statement of Thomas and the explanation of social psychology given by Lindesmith and Strauss: "It is focused . . . upon explaining the behavior of individuals as it is controlled, influenced, or limited by the social environment." (1956, p. 2.) Adding further support to this point of view is the work done in social psychology in the thirties by the Murphys (1935), Plant (1937), Dashiell (1935), and others.

In 1943 Bossard and Boll made a special plea that sociologists leave the study of the individual's behavior to biologists, psychologists, and others, and concentrate on the social situations to which individuals react. They characterize the situational approach as "the sociological approach becoming specific." (1943, pp. 227–30.)

Thus, at the outset, the writer was faced with a choice between the Thomas approach and the Bossard-Boll approach to the situational study of the family. The definition of the concept *social situation* was crucial, for the acceptance of the Bossard-Boll definition would lead in one direction and the acceptance of Thomas' definition would lead in another direction.

The selection of the Bossard-Boll definition of the social situation as the most appropriate one for the situational frame of reference was made after much consideration and with a certain amount of hesitation. The choice was necessary because Thomas did not specifically exclude internal stimuli, as did Bossard and Boll. (1943, p. 21.) Thomas said:

> The situation involves three kinds of data: (1) The objective conditions under which the individual or society has to act, i.e., the totality of values—economic, social, religious, intellectual, etc.—which at the given moment affect directly or indirectly the conscious status of the individual or the group. (2) The pre-existing attitudes of the individual or the group which at the given moment have an actual influence upon his behavior. (3) The definition of the situation, i.e., the more or less clear conception of the conditions and consciousness of the attitudes. (Volkart, 1951, p. 57.)

His concept of the situation seems to parallel Mead's concept of environment as "all the factors to which a responding unit responds." (1934, p. 246.) On the other hand, the Bossard-Boll definition of the situation seems to more closely parallel Reuter's definition of environment, as it is commonly used and understood: "The conditions and influences external to the person, group, or other entity, that affect its life and development." (1941, p. 115.) The difference is a basic one. Reuter's definition of the environment does not include any reciprocal relationships among the stimuli nor the emergent nature of the situation.

The choice of the Bossard-Boll definition of the social situation as the appropriate one for this approach to the study of the family in no way implies that Thomas' position concerning the "definition of the situation" is inaccurate or unimportant. It simply means that the writer is attempting to keep the situational approach in the area of sociology, where it seems to belong. To use Thomas' definition would necessitate a definite veering toward the area of social psychology and an attempt to assess the contributions of men who combine the situational and interactionist approaches, as, for example, Coutu. His definition is, "A situation is the total configuration of relevant behaviors and stimuli involved in an adjustment problem. For any one person the situation is for him those components of the configuration to which he is at the moment sensitive." (1949, p. 14.)

Bossard's emphatic rejection of any interest in the way individuals define situations (1948, p. 46) leaves no alternative. A choice must be made between the Thomas approach and the Bossard approach.

The latter has been chosen for the reasons stated—with the sure knowledge that the interactionists' approach will give full credit to the great contributions of W. I. Thomas. Despite this choice, a brief outline of some important theoretical contributions of Thomas will be given later.

FOCI OF STUDY

Child Development

W. I. and Dorothy Thomas were primarily interested in the practical effects of various situations on the development and behavior of American children. Their ultimate aim was to discover what situations were conducive to the production of mentally healthy children and adults, that is, who abstained from delinquent or criminal behavior. While recognizing the complexities of situations as the chief problem involved in studying their effects, the Thomases gave illustrations—chiefly from studies conducted in schools—of how the effect of situations on behavior can be studied (1928a).

However, as Bossard (1948, p. 45) points out, the Thomases' approach is only slightly more situationally oriented than those of the many other researchers of that era who explicitly recognized the situational factors in their research, but who emphasized the personality development of the child. Some more recent examples (1961) of the latter group can be found in Kluckhohn, Murray, and Schnieder.

In his *Sociology of Child Development*, Bossard claims chief emphasis on "the social situations in which children live and grow from infancy to maturity." (1948, p. ix.) He is interested in the personality development of the child, but even more interested in the situations in which the personality is evolving.

Internal Operation of the Family

Bossard and Boll focused on the inner workings of the family in their books, *The Large Family System* (1956) and *Ritual in Family Living* (1950). In the former, a study of the effect of family size on family relations and child development was attempted. This involved not only the form and organization of the situation, but also the interaction of the elements of the situation. In the latter, the family culture, as shown by the rituals engaged in, was analyzed by the use of the family life cycle. Also, there was an intergenerational analysis.

Family Crises

Hill and Boulding used this frame of reference in an attempt to understand the meaning of war separation for individual families. The focal point was the departure of the husband-father for military service. The family situation was analyzed in terms of structure, social interaction, and cultural content. (1949, pp. 50–51.)

Situational Contexts as Related to Family Norms

Blood investigated the relationships between such situational variables as "the vulnerability of the living room to damage" and permissiveness on the part of the parents. (1953, pp. 84–87.)

Bonilla studied the various social situations encountered by mobile Puerto Rican families as they relate to the sexual norms for husbands and wives. (1958, p. 1886.)

Perhaps also of interest is the Bossard-Boll classification of the family studies they reviewed into three main types of family situations: (1) those involving intra-family relationships, for example, the possessive home, (2) those involving family patterns, for example, the one-child family, and (3) those involving external factors, for example, the inadequately financed home. (1943, pp. 111–12.) However, the studies they reviewed were not consciously set up and promulgated as being studies within the situational frame of reference.

Rallings made use of the Bossard-Boll classificatory system in a comparative study of the family situations of married and never-married males. It was explicitly stated, however, that the situations studied were the respondent's definition of the family situations in his childhood home. (1964, p. 11.)

CONCEPTS

An effort has been made to arrange these concepts in descending order of cruciality for this framework, and also with the most closely interrelated concepts grouped together. Only those non-familial concepts are listed which are needed for an understanding of the familial concepts. However, some of the familial concepts defined here are often generalized by definition to nonfamilial areas. The recorded familial concepts are most often used as independent variables, although this is not invariably true.

Social situation: "a number of stimuli, external to the organism but acting upon it, organized as a unit and with a special relatedness to each other as stimuli of the specific organism involved." (Bossard and Boll, 1943, p. 25.) Lundberg has called this "a field of force—a segment of life to which the organism reacts as a whole." (1939, pp. 217 ff.)

Family situation: "a unit of stimuli, operating within the confines of the family circle, and organized in relation to the person or object which serves as the focal point of the particular case being considered." (Bossard and Boll, 1943, pp. 39–40.) No one family situation is a pure type—the result of the influence of one special factor—but each has to be classified as such for purposes of analysis. They are regarded, then, as they stand out in time—a sort of stereoscopic picture. As an illustration, consider the home of the unwanted child. The child can be considered the focal point, and the situation analyzed in terms of all the stimuli which impinge upon him from all material objects, lower animals, and persons in the situation, all acting as interrelated parts of the whole.

Situation structure: "the form and organization of the situation." (Bossard and Boll, 1943, p. 27.) This is a still-life picture of the situation—the situation in repose. In a scientific study of the structure of a situation, we take it apart, examine each part as to its nature, and inquire into the way these parts are organized into a unit.

Situation process: "the interaction of the elements of the situation." (Bossard and Boll, 1943, p. 27.) *Interaction* is used here as a category of analysis to identify the reciprocal or interdependent relationship between the elements of a situation. In contrast to situation structure, we have here a moving picture of the situation.

Situation content: "the ideas, attitudes, words, etc., which we speak of as culture." (Bossard and Boll, 1943, p. 28.) Both structure and process are vehicles or channels for content, that is, culture.

Constituent elements of a situation (also called *polar points*): "the animate and inanimate objects present in a situation, e.g., persons, animals, and material objects—such as the thin floor in an apartment house." (Bossard and Boll, 1943, p. 46.) A situation can be analyzed from the position of any relevant constituent element, and in each case the results would be different.

Emergent: that segment of the process in a given situation which can be perceived by any observer. This suggests more than supersummation and is intended to communicate the idea of function as distinguished from structure. (Coutu, 1949, pp. 51–57.)

Family subculture: the entire complex of family habits, attitudes, and relationships which aid the child (or other family member) in the selection, interpretation, and evaluation of the various cultural patterns to which he is exposed. (Bossard and Boll, 1943, pp. 57–68.)

Family pattern: the one outstanding fact or feature which gives tone or meaning to the entire complex of attitudes, habits, and relationships which cluster around the situation. Bossard and Boll, in summarizing the various studies of family situations during the period from 1926 to 1940, found that the studies could be grouped into four categories according to these patterns: (1) size, (2) the way in which the home life is organized as in, for example, the cooperative family, (3) the prevailing activity of the family as in, for example, the nomadic family, and (4) some outstanding value or goal as in, for example, the social-climbing family. (Bossard and Boll, 1943, pp. 154 ff.)

Family values: objects of family desire and appreciation. This is the way Bossard and Boll employ the term (1943, pp. 172 ff.), although they do not define it.

Family goals: the ends to which the family is directed by its values. Again, Bossard and Boll do not define this concept, but evidence of this usage is seen in their work. (1943, pp. 65–68.)

Family ritual: "a prescribed procedure, arising out of family interaction, involving a pattern of defined behavior, which is directed toward some specific end or purpose, and acquires rigidity and a sense of rightness as a result of its continuing history." (Bossard and Boll, 1950, p. 29.) An example of a family ritual is "the night before Christmas ritual" described by Bossard and Boll. (1950, p. 18.)

Expressed culture: "that part of the cultural content of family situations which operates on the surface, with activities and words to be taken relatively at their face value." (Bossard and Boll, 1943, p. 240.)

Repressed culture:[2] "that part of the cultural content of family situations which exists and operates beneath the level of awareness, in the mental hinterland of the persons involved." An example of this would be the gangster's son who becomes a priest—the result of the subtle but persistent pressures in family situations to force the child into lines of activity that are compensatory for what was left

[2] This concept is seldom used, nor does it fit with the generally accepted definitions of culture. However, it is a part of the Bossard-Boll schema and needs to be included among the concepts.

unfulfilled in the lives of the parents. (Bossard and Boll, 1943, p. 240.)

Behavior: "the entire response or adjustment pattern of the individual." (Bossard and Boll, 1943, p. 5.)

Space-time segment: "a particular phase during a specific period of time." (Carr, 1948, p. 104.)

BASIC ASSUMPTIONS

1. A social situation exists as an objective, separate reality and may be studied as such. (Bossard and Boll, 1943, p. 33.)
2. The basic unit of focus in a social situation is a specific human organism. A change in the basic unit of focus changes the entire situation. (Bossard and Boll, 1943, pp. 40, 46.)[3]
3. Each social situation is the result of the interaction of social, physical, and cultural elements.[4]
4. Each social situation exhibits a reality beyond its component parts, that is, an emergent.[5]
5. Social situations are not only constantly changing, but they are also being modified as they change. (Bossard and Boll, 1943, p. 35.)
6. Behavior is a function of the situation, and though not completely rational, is adjustive with regard to the eliciting situation.[6]
7. The family is a miniature society, with a culture all its own. (Bossard and Boll, 1943, pp. 51, 101.)

[3] A restatement of the Hill-Hansen assumption: "The basic autonomous unit is the individual in a situation." (1960), p. 309. The use of the word *autonomous* seems questionable in the Bossard-Boll framework. Also, the fact that the basic unit of focus is ordinarily a specific human organism does not rule out the possibility of focusing on some inanimate object or some non-human organism.

[4] The stated assumption of Hill and Hansen which most nearly parallels this is: "Social conduct is a function of the situation (social, cultural, physical milieu)." (1960), p. 309. The writer chose to discard *social conduct* as did Bossard and Boll (1943), p. 5, and used the three adjectives to describe the elements of the social situation.

[5] This only represents a simplification of the Hill-Hansen assumption: "Situations and human groupings, as unities of organization, have emergent realities (i.e., have a reality beyond that of its component parts)." (1960), p. 309.

[6] This assumption takes a part of the Hill-Hansen assumption listed in footnote 5 and joins it to a paraphrase of this assumption: "Behavior is purposive (i.e., problem solving, though not completely rational) in relation to the situation which elicits it." (1960), p. 309.

8. The child sees his cultural heritage through the eyes of his family. (Bossard and Boll, 1943, p. 57.)

9. The individual must adjust all through his life to forces and persons greater than he. (Bossard and Boll, 1943, p. 54.)

PRODUCT

In trying to evaluate the theoretical contributions made by the situational approach, we again encounter the diverging pathways of Thomas versus Bossard and Boll.

Thomas chose behavior, especially adjustive behavior, in his later years as the central concern of his sociological theory. He felt that action in a social situation is the social fact to be explained. While owing a debt to the behaviorists, Thomas never accepted their main contention that human action is scientifically explicable without reference to the minds of the actors on the social scene. (Timasheff, 1955, p. 149.) It is in this area—definition of the situation[7]—that Thomas made his greatest impact. It is interesting to note that those who have made the most use of the definition of the situation have been social psychologists. As a case in point, see Cottrell. (1942, pp. 370–87.)

Thomas did not write a final synthesis presenting his ideas in a systematic manner, but the essential features of his position have been given by Volkart. (1951, p. 2.)

Blumer did an exhaustive critique of the *Polish Peasant in Europe and America*, but unfortunately for this paper the emphasis was on the methodology employed. Blumer did go into a considerable discussion of concepts, in which he strongly criticized the author's use of attitudes and values in his effort to arrive at laws of becoming, that is, laws of social change. However, he lauds Thomas and Znaniecki's efforts to draw attention to the subjective factor in human experience—at the same time not neglecting its interaction with objective factors. (1939, p. 71.)

Bossard and Boll faced a two-pronged difficulty in that they had to divorce themselves from the behaviorist school and at the same

---

[7] Thomas and Znaniecki postulate that the process of defining a situation entails two phases; the first is characterized by vagueness, but in the second the situation becomes definite and the individual begins to control his new experience. (1927), Vol. II, p. 1847. As he is defining a situation, an individual has to take social meanings into account and interpret his experience in terms of "his own needs and wishes, but also in terms of the traditions, customs, beliefs, aspirations of his social milieu." (1927), Vol. II, p. 1852.

time champion the intensive inductive study of the situation. By considering only external stimuli they automatically eliminated the subjective side of the situation which was so important to Thomas and to almost all modern sociologists. Possibly this step was necessary to delineate a pure situational approach, but the lack of significance attributed to a study of only the objective side of the situation is perhaps shown by the miniscule amount of research engendered by this approach.

Despite a dearth of family research in this area, we can point to some significant studies. One of the earliest of these was Buhler's study of the living situations in different homes. She classified five distinct kinds of family organization according to a central interest, for example, the family in which the household was the center of interest. (1939, pp. 108–10.)

The work of Bossard and Boll has been outlined earlier in the section of this paper dealing with the foci of study. Their efforts have been primarily descriptive in nature and this is not unexpected, since their approach emphasizes objective observation of natural situations. The heuristic value of their work seems very limited.

Blood's rather recent research is more nearly what Hyman (1955, p. 81) calls an "explanatory survey." He studied permissiveness within the context of the whole family living in its physical setting, the family residence. There were two measures of permissiveness used: (1) amount of time children were allowed to play indoors, and (2) the parents' "pick-up policy" (that is, rules concerning children's putting away of their toys). The dependent variables were (1) children's interference with the parents' life, and (2) behavior problems with the children. The ingredients of the situation considered important were (1) the philosophy of the parents concerning child rearing, (2) age of the children, and (3) vulnerability of the living-room furnishings to damage.

Blood focused on the effect of permissiveness on the *parents* rather than on the children. This is not a peculiarity of this frame of reference, but is presumably a reaction against the pervasive emphasis in many studies on the effects of permissiveness on the personality development of the child.

Bossard and Boll (1943, pp. 233, 237) suggest that the situational approach can be used to make distinctive contributions to the developing understanding of human behavior by studying prestige and culture lag in family situations.

With regard to the pragmatic application of the situational approach we find considerable activity outside the field of the family,[8] but little real application directly to family problems. One of the most direct interests has been evidenced in the area of social casework. (Sheffield, 1930–1931, 1937; Queen, 1930.) The concern here is with the client's powers of adequate and appropriate response to the shifting demands of specific situations.

Closely related to this, Pollak (1956) describes the use of the situational approach in diagnosis and therapy involving ten cases in a test project at the Child Guidance Institute of the Jewish Board of Guardians. In evaluating the test project, Hershel Alt, executive director of the Board of Guardians, felt that it had been of positive value to the agency. It was particularly helpful in turning the clinicians from treatment focused on the child alone to treatment of all the family members involved.

Another practical application, in an institutional setting, is the "total push" or milieu therapy, which is one type being used in some mental institutions today. It is an attempt to integrate all of the patients' daily activities with the therapeutic process. (Coville, Costello, and Rouke, 1960, p. 262.)

More directly related to the family is the placing of mental patients in foster homes under the careful observation of trained therapists. If the situation is not conducive to growth, the patient is moved to a different foster home. (Kronhausen and Kronhausen, 1959, pp. 29–35.)

In a recent journal article, Alexander describes "conjoint family therapy." (1963, pp. 146–54.) This, too, seems to be an application of the situational approach, though, like the others, not strictly following the Bossard-Boll formula.

VALUES

It seems to the writer that the ultimate value of the situationalist is seen in his implicit belief that the most important human behavior occurs in family situations, and that these situations offer the best opportunities for understanding—and eventually directing—human behavior on a societal scale. (Bossard and Boll, 1943, pp. 40–41.)

---

[8] Some of the general applications of the situational approach may be seen in the following articles: Carr (1945), Eliot (1943), Freidson (1953), Raush, Dittmann, and Taylor (1959).

THE FRAMEWORK

The situational approach to the study of the family is an observational, descriptive effort to record some part of the infinite variety of family situations. In this recording all observable behavior is considered—with the realization that it is the result of physical, cultural, and social elements, but with no effort made to include the family members' definition of the particular situation. However, each situation can be analyzed with each element of the situation in turn providing the focal point. In practice, an individual is the most common focal point.

Since family situations are constantly changing and being modified as they change, the observer must delimit the situation with regard to time, space, and constituent elements. Having done this, he is able to recognize an emergent from each situation—something that is more than a summation of all the constituent elements.[9]

What, then, is the intent of this intensive inductive study of the family situation as an objective, separate reality? We begin with the assumption that behavior is adjustive—a function of the situation—hence behavior in the family is a function of the family situation. By observing and analyzing this behavior in many situations, even though no two situations are alike, the situationalist believes that he will eventually be able to understand—and so predict—human behavior. This does not mean absolute predictions, universally applicable, but probability predictions with a substantial potential for generalization.

Of considerable importance in working toward this goal are the evident regularities in family behavior called *family patterns*. These patterns are largely determined by the values and goals of the family members. These in turn are principally a product of the various subcultures to which they have been exposed, especially the family subcultures.

CRITIQUE AND DISCUSSION

Throughout the attempt to understand and delineate this frame of reference, the writer has felt a growing conviction that to call W. I.

---

[9] For example, consider a family breakfast. You, as the observer, have recorded all the pertinent data concerning the structure of the situation. You record the details of process as breakfast is eaten, yet beyond these two things there is an emergent which is apparent to you. It is the tone of the whole family complex which shows up in this particular situation.

Thomas the father of the situational approach in sociology is a mistake: that he is an interactionist with leanings toward the structure-functional approach.[10] Also, the impression of the writer is that Thomas made his greatest contribution not through the promulgation of a situational frame of reference but by sensitizing behavioral scientists to the importance of the subjective factor in making social analyses. Von Wiese (1941, pp. 48–58) could more properly be called the father of the situational approach in sociology, and Bossard and Boll certainly its leading exponents in the area of the family. However, their attempt to delineate the approach in their book, *Family Situations*, though careful and orderly, is not entirely clear. In his research and writing, Bossard followed rather faithfully his idea of the situational approach, but due to a misunderstanding of his position, or a conviction that the subjective side of the situation was too important to ignore, his rather limited and pure situational approach has rarely, if ever, been used.[11]

There are several rather significant disadvantages to the Bossard-Boll approach outlined in this paper. First of all, tremendous amounts of time and effort would have to be expended in order to collect enough data to even consider limited prediction of behavior. Secondly, many trained observers would be needed, since responses from the actors are ruled out. It is treacherously easy to slide from description of a situation to the describer's definition of the situation, as Bossard and Boll point out. (1943, p. 231.) In the third place, the collected material does not lend itself readily to the statistical approach.

More important than any of these, perhaps, is the uneasiness with which sociologists—and even more, social psychologists—regard an attempt to leave out, even for purposes, of analysis the meaning imputed to the situation by the actors in the situation. In this regard Carr's situational approach seems more acceptable, but unfortunately it has never been consciously applied to the family, although Blood (1953) combined elements of Carr with Bossard and Boll.

The contributions from this approach have been meager indeed,

[10] The close tie with the interactionist school has already been documented, also Timasheff's evaluation of the *Polish Peasant* as done in the "functional spirit." To pursue this a bit further, it seems to the writer that Thomas' concern with social disorganization and social control indicates his structure-functional leanings—with the accent on function.

[11] Some of the problems attendant to the situational approach are discussed by Queen (1930), Smith (1944), and Cottrell (1950).

and with both Bossard and Carr dead, the future does not look bright. The very multidimensionality of a situation, considered holistically, is enough to give pause to most researchers. One might ask, "Why not let the structure-functionalist study the structure of family situations, the interactionist study the process of family situations, and the cultural anthropologist study the family culture?" Bossard and Boll found it necessary to look at family situations in this manner. Certainly no sociologist would argue against the position that all behavior occurs in a contextual framework and can be understood only within this framework. Only insofar as he takes cognizance of this fact in his theory and research will his contributions make possible significant advances in the behavioral sciences.

Even if the family is studied from the conceptual frameworks as previously delineated, there still remains the need for a synthesis and a facing up to the reality of situational emergents which these approaches do not seem capable of handling.

Perhaps a merging of the interactional and situational frames of reference within sociology is indicated. We might call this framework the "intersitual" conceptual framework. If this were done, a willingness to work closely with the social psychologists in delineating and using this hybrid conceptual framework would be needed. In this era of increasing interdisciplinary cooperation, perhaps even this is not too far-fetched.

REFERENCES

ALEXANDER, IRVING. "Family Therapy," *Marriage and Family Living,* **25** (May 1963), pp. 146–54.

BARKER, R. G., and WRIGHT, H. F. *Midwest and its Children.* New York: Harper & Row, Publishers, 1955.

BLOOD, ROBERT O., JR. "A Situational Approach to the Study of Permissiveness in Child Rearing." *American Sociological Review,* 18 (Feb. 1953), pp. 84–87. A paper presenting the data from the author's doctoral dissertation at the University of North Carolina entitled *Developmental and Traditional Child-Rearing Philosophies and Their Family Situational Consequences,* 1952.

BLUMER, HERBERT. *Critiques of Research in the Social Sciences.* Vol. 1: *An Appraisal of Thomas and Znaniecki's "The Polish Peasant in Europe and America."* New York: Social Science Research Council. 1939.

BONILLA, E. S. "The Normative Patterns of the Puerto Rican Family in

Various Situational Contexts," *Dissertation Abstracts*, 18 (1958), pp. 18–86. An effort to analyze the cultural norms that differentiate, legitimize, and sanction the structure of statuses and roles of the Puerto Rican family and to analyze the stability and change of these cultural norms in the context of various life situations.

BOSSARD, JAMES H. S., and BOLL, ELEANOR S. *Family Situations*. Philadelphia: University of Pennsylvania Press, 1943. A full development of the situational approach, as applied to the study of family, with a summary and synthesis of specific studies of family situations. The authors declare this approach to be the ideal framework for sociologists. Contains a bibliography of over 300 items.

———, and ———. *The Large Family System*. Philadelphia: University of Pennsylvania Press, 1956. An original study of one hundred large families (with six or more children) based on the case histories given by family members. It is not a statistical study, but rather an analysis which seeks to suggest some features of large family living and its possible meaning for child development.

———, and ———. *Ritual in Family Living*. Philadelphia: University of Pennsylvania Press, 1950. A pioneer study of ritual in family living, involving data from more than four hundred families. A three-generational study of family ritual using the life cycle as a conceptual tool is also presented. Family rituals are considered the "hard core" in a cultural approach to the study of the family.

BOSSARD, JAMES H. S. *The Sociology of Child Development*. New York: Harper & Row, Publishers, 1948. An emphasis upon the social situations in which children live and grow from infancy to maturity. Contains a bibliography with more than 600 items.

BUHLER, CHARLOTTE. *The Child and his Family*. New York: Harper & Row, Publishers, 1939.

CARR, L. J. *Situational Analysis: An Observational Approach to Introductory Sociology*. New York: Harper & Row, Publishers, 1948. An outline of how to apply the situational approach to the study of sociology in general. The author states that the exclusive problem phenomena of the sociologist are the "composition, forms, structure, functions, and changes of human groups as such."

———. "A Situational Approach to Conflict and War," *Social Forces*, 24 (March 1946), pp. 300–03. A presentation of situations seen as a species of problem phenomena in themselves. They are considered the center of scientific interest as an attempt is made to study social process in observable units.

CHRISTENSEN, HAROLD T., ed. *Handbook on Marriage and the Family*. Chicago: Rand McNally & Company, 1964.

COOLEY, CHARLES H. *Human Nature and the Social Order*. New York: Charles Scribner's Sons, 1902.

COTTRELL, L. S., JR. "Some Neglected Problems in Social Psychology," *American Sociological Review*, 15 (Dec. 1950), pp. 705–12. A presentation which includes "the situation" as one of the neglected problems and comments on the vagueness in which the term is used and the difficulties encountered in identifying precisely and describing the situations to be studied.

―――. "The Analysis of Situational Fields in Social Psychology," *American Sociological Review*, 7 (June 1942), pp. 370–87. A set of assumptions and concepts with which to interpret human social interaction within the social-psychological framework.

COUTU, WALTER. *Emergent Human Nature*. New York: Alfred A. Knopf, Inc., 1949. In the words of the author: "purports to be an integrated conceptual formulation for social psychology in a form which synthesizes the situational or field approach with the symbolic interactionist approach."

COVILLE, W. J., COSTELLO, T. W., and ROUKE, F. L. *Abnormal Psychology*. New York: Barnes & Noble, Inc., 1960.

DASHIELL, J. F. "Experimental Studies of the Influence of Social Situations on the Behavior of Individual Human Adults," in Carl Murchison, ed. *A Handbook in Social Psychology*. Worcester, Mass.: Clark University Press, 1935, Chap. 23.

ELIOT, THOMAS D. "Human Controls as Situation-Processes," *American Sociological Review*, 8 (Aug. 1943), pp. 380–88. An advocation of the term *situation-process* so that the time dimension is included with the static-spatial concept. The applicability of the situational approach, using the concept *situation-process* to personal and societal problems is expanded.

FREIDSON, ELIOT. "The Relation of the Social Situation of Contact to the Media in Mass Communication," *Public Opinion Quarterly*, 17 (Summer 1953–54), pp. 230–38.

HILL, REUBEN, and BOULDING, ELISE. *Families under Stress*. New York: Harper & Row, Publishers, 1949. "A search for the characteristics and processes which set off successful from unsuccessful families in the face of two war-born crises." The teaming of statistical and case-study methods is the procedure used.

―――, and HANSEN, D. A. "The Identification of Conceptual Frameworks Utilized in Family Study," *Marriage and Family Living*, (Nov. 1960), pp. 299–311. A comprehensive and significant effort to identify and analyze five of the approaches to the study of the family in America, with the emphasis on the abstract concepts and assumptions of these approaches.

―――, KATZ, A. L., and SIMPSON, R. L. "An Inventory or Research in Marriage and Family Behavior: A Statement of Objectives and Progress," *Marriage and Family Living*, 19 (Feb. 1957), pp. 89–92.

HYMAN, HERBERT. *Survey Design and Analysis.* New York: Free Press of Glencoe, Inc., 1955.

KLUCKHOHN, C., MURRAY, H. A., and SCHNEIDER, D. M. *Personality in Nature, Society, and Culture.* New York: Alfred A. Knopf, Inc., 1961.

KRONHAUSEN, E., and KRONHAUSEN, PHYLLIS. "The Therapeutic Family— the Family's Role in Emotional Disturbance and Rehabilitation. *Marriage and Family Living,* 21 (Feb. 1959), pp. 29–35.

LINDESMITH, A. R., and STRAUSS, A. L. *Social Psychology.* New York: Holt, Rinehart & Winston, Inc., 1956.

LUNDBERG, GEORGE A. *Foundations of Sociology.* New York: The Macmillan Company, 1939.

MEAD, G. H. *Mind, Self, and Society.* Chicago: University of Chicago Press, 1934.

MURPHY, LOIS B., and MURPHY, GARDNER. "The Influence of Social Situations upon the Behavior of Children," in Carl Murchison, ed. *A Handbook in Social Psychology.* Worcester, Mass.: Clark University Press, 1935, Chap. 22.

PLANT, JAMES S. *Personality and the Cultural Pattern.* New York: The Commonwealth Fund, 1937.

POLLAK, OTTO. *Integrating Sociological and Psychoanalytic Concepts.* New York: Russell Sage Foundation, 1956.

QUEEN, S. A. "A Study of Conflict Situations," *Publication of the American Society,* 24 (1930), pp. 57-64. An analysis of sixty families served by the Kansas City Provident Association. The analysis was conducted on the basis of the clients' problems, attitudes, and habit-attitudes. All analyses were productive, but an analysis of the client and social worker using the situational approach was even more productive. The situation is not every activity of the parties and all the elements in their environment, but the relationships between persons at some particular time and place—but not discounting prior experiences.

———. "Some Problems of the Situational Approach," *Social Forces,* 9 (June 1931), pp. 480–81. A study in which the concept *situation* is viewed as an intellectual tool similar to the anthropologists' concept *culture complex.* The problems of this approach are summed up in this question: "How can anything as complex as a 'situation' be made manageable for purposes of research?"

RALLINGS, E. M. *A Comparative Study of the Family Situations of Married and Never-Married Males.* Unpublished Ph.D. dissertation, Florida State University, 1964.

RAUSH, H. L., DITTMAN, A. T., and TAYLOR, T. J. "Person, Setting, and Change in Social Interaction," *Human Relations,* 12 (Nov. 1959), pp. 361–77.

RAUSH, HAROLD L., FARBMAN, IRWIN, and LLEWELLYN, LYNN G. "Person Setting, and Change in Social Interaction," *Human Relations* 13 (Nov. 1960), pp. 305–32.

REUTER, E. B. *Handbook of Sociology.* New York: The Dryden Press, Inc., 1941.

ROSE, A. M., ed. *Human Behavior and Social Processes.* Boston: Houghton Mifflin Company, 1962.

SHEFFIELD, ADA E. *Social Insight in Case Situations.* New York: Appleton-Century-Crofts, 1937. A further exposition of earlier journal articles in which the author sees the situation as the unit of attention in social work. The client's situation is seen as a definite web of elements, current and past, that reveal and explain his present need in its wider bearings. Application of this approach is made in "The Case of Herbert," described in some detail.

———. "The 'Situation' as the Unit of Family Case Study," *Social Forces,* 9 (June 1930), pp. 465–74. The author sees a growing interest among social workers in the assessment of their clients as a unit in a "total situation." She feels this is intelligent and necessary for thoroughness in treatment of the client. The concern then is with the client's powers to respond adequately and appropriately to the shifting demands of specific situations.

SMITH, MAPHEUS. "Psychological Foundations of Situational Sociology," *Sociology and Social Research,* 29 (Nov. 1944), pp. 123–35. A social situation is defined as a set of circumstances in which two or more related organisms exist or engage in activity. Social situations may be explained by a combination of satisfactory spatial, temporal, and psychological conditions. The first two are particularly important for static and potential situations. Some of the psychological conditions are also important for potential social situations. This is particularly true of the general ability to receive and interpret sensory stimulation.

STRYKER, SHELDON. "The Interactional and Situational Approaches," in Harold T. Christensen, *The Handbook of Marriage and the Family.* Chicago: Rand McNally and Company, 1964.

THOMAS, W. I. "The Behavior Pattern and the Situation," *Publications of the American Sociological Society,* 22 (1928), pp. 1–13b. A presentation of four areas of study which may be used in studying behavior problems: (1) attitudes, (2) values, (3) forms of adaptation, and (4) the total situation. The latter is emphasized and illustrated in the fields of child study, psychology, psychiatry, delinquency, education, and mass psychology.

———, and THOMAS, DOROTHY S. *The Child in America.* New York: Alfred A. Knopf, Inc., 1928 (a). An incisive critique of the practical programs and scientific techniques used in studying and working with American children. In a chapter on methodology of behavior study, the authors recommend the use of control groups and the situational approach.

————, and ZNANIECKI, F. *The Polish Peasant in Europe and America,* two vols. New York: Alfred A. Knopf, Inc., 1927.

TIMASHEFF, N. S. *Sociological Theory: Its Nature and Growth,* rev. ed. New York: Random House, Inc., 1955.

VOLKART, E. H., ed. *Social Behavior and Personality.* New York: Social Science Research Council, 1951. The most notable writings of W. I. Thomas, with prefatory remarks for each section which forms a systematic analysis of Thomas' basic theory. Contains complete bibliography of W. I. Thomas.

VON WIESE, LEOPOLD. *Sociology,* trans. by F. H. Mueller. New York: Oskar Piest, 1941. A presentation of the *theory of social relations* based on the thesis that men (as social beings) and social structures (as groupings of men) come into being through the social processes which string them together continuously. A social process is made up of attitude, which is partly innate and partly the result of experience, and situation, which is partly the result of nonhuman environment and the attitude of other men participating in the social process.

chapter 7

The Psychoanalytic Frame of Reference in Family Study*

Alan E. Bayer

For the past seventy-five years there has been developing a new frame of reference for viewing human behavior. This system of theory, originally developed by Sigmund Freud with the aid of devoted colleagues, and since then by three generations of followers, is called *psychoanalysis*. The term, *psychoanalysis*, is used in the following ways (Freud, 1949–1950, Vol. V, p. 107):

1. To describe a special technique for the study and treatment of personality malfunction.
2. To designate observations of human personality and behavior which are not disclosed by the investigation of solely rational thinking and action.
3. To signify that theoretical system of psychology which consists of the abstraction of the observations of unconscious mental events and the inductive inferences made from these observations.

In this chapter, the emphasis will be placed upon the second and third uses of the term.

* Grateful acknowledgment is made of the contribution of George Simpson who served as editorial consultant for this framework and who read and critically reviewed the manuscript prior to its final revision. Many, although not all, of his suggestions have been incorporated into the final manuscript. Inadequacies and errors in the chapter as published, however, are entirely the responsibility of the author and the editors.

In essence, psychoanalysis is the study of the unconscious and of the relations of the unconscious to the human mind and to the human body. It may be summarized briefly as follows:

Man is a complicated energy system with innate needs which are constantly trying to achieve pleasurable fulfillment. These innate needs are generally in conflict with cultural norms and social institutions. This antisocial aspect of human mind and personality—the id—is rooted in the unconscious and combines with the two other major aspects of the mind: the ego, which aids in the consideration of reality, and the superego, which deals with morality. These three aspects interdevelop in early childhood, are based largely on sexual factors, and establish the core of personality. If their interdevelopment is unified and balanced the individual is able to carry on normatively efficient and satisfying transactions with his environment.

In the process of growth, the individual passes through various stages of psychosexual development, each of which is assimilated into the preceding stages and each of which involves new adaptations which must be achieved if one is to be adequately prepared for the later sequential stages. The core personality structure (that is, the emotional foundations and the pervasive behavior patterns) is laid down in the early years of life, and subsequent behavior may be traced back and explained with reference to the earliest stages. These earliest emotional experiences are stored in the unconscious and become the basis for consciousness and later adaptation to the social environment.

Historical Development[1]

These basic formulations in psychoanalysis were first framed by Sigmund Freud, whose writings extend from the 1890's through the 1930's. Freud's early interest was in organic neurology and functional neurosis. In attempting to discover a treatment for neurosis, he studied hypnosis in 1885–1886 under Jean Charcot, the outstanding hypnotist of the time, but he became dissatisfied with hypnosis because he felt its effects were only temporary and did not get at the root of the trouble. Similar disappointing results were subsequently experienced with electrotherapy. He then turned to Josef Breuer's method of free association, the delivery and recall of ideas and experiences as they come to mind as a result of verbal stimuli.

---

[1] A thorough history of the psychoanalytic movement through 1914 is presented by Freud in *Collected Papers* (1949–1950), Vol. I, pp. 287–359.

In his work with patients he continually employed this method and, from the results, became interested in the sexual life of the child. Gradually, the idea began to take shape that there were dynamic forces at work in the mind, based on the individual's early experiences, which were responsible for much, if not all, of human behavior.

Freud's writings and treatment of neurotic patients brought his name to the attention of a number of individuals who became his followers. By 1910, however, several of these followers were obviously disagreeing with him, primarily as a result of his strong emphasis on sexuality. Among these were Carl Jung, Otto Rank, and Alfred Adler, all of whom developed rival schools. But there were important followers who stayed with Freud and helped to establish psychoanalysis as an international movement. One of the most important of these followers was his daughter, Anna. Other Freudians who have made significant contributions to psychoanalysis include Ernest Jones, Karl Abraham, John Flugel, Heinz Hartman, George Simpson, and Erik Erikson. Today, the psychoanalytic school is still basically Freudian, with several extensions of the theory and occasional attempts at a theoretical integration of new principles with Freud's original position.

For the purpose of this chapter, the psychoanalytic frame of reference is viewed primarily in terms of the Freudian school, with its basic tenets and extensions. Non-Freudians may indeed be considered as non-psychoanalytical. In fact, their psychologies have been given different names, such as *individual psychology* (Adler), *analytical psychology* (Jung), and *will therapy* (Rank). No consideration will be given here to these non-Freudian schools or the schools identified as neo-Freudian, which involve major revisions of Freudian theory (such as those of Erich Fromm, Karen Horney, and Harry Stack Sullivan).

Previous Attempts at Delineation

The psychoanalytic frame of reference has been described by a number of writers, although not solely because it is a method and focus for the study of marriage and the family. Some do not, in fact, consider it a valid approach to family analysis. Hill and Hansen (1960), for example, reject psychoanalysis as a frame of reference for family study, claiming "it does not cope with the family as an entity or with its possible subgroupings." Christensen dismisses psychoanalysis as "peripheral," contending that it does not deal with "larger pluralities" or the social system at large. (1964, pp. 20–21.) Other noted family sociologists are intensely hostile toward the approach, but still other prominent ones, among them Komarovsky and Waller (1945), identify psychoanalysis as an important frame of reference for family study. The latter authors, for example, have stated that:

> Freudian psychology has contributed heavily to our knowledge of this [the family] field. Freudianism may, in fact, be thought of as a sort of familistic social psychology which tends always to explain the behavior of the adult in terms of his previous experience in the parental family and possibly tends to minimize nonfamily and later influences. . . . Nearly all the Freudian literature pertains in some way to the life of the child in the parental family. (p. 448.)

Thus, although some family sociologists do not recognize psychoanalysis as a frame of reference for family study because it does not emphasize the family as a group, others see psychoanalysis as a significant frame of reference for viewing the family. The latter often see psychoanalysis not merely as a way of looking at certain aspects of the family but as a (or in some cases *the*) frame of reference for looking deeply at all aspects of the family. Indeed psychoanalytic theory is to no small extent inherently family theory and must therefore be considered in this context.

Many volumes have been written in an attempt to describe the psychoanalytic approach.[2] Most offer a discussion of the basic concepts in the approach, but practically all fall short in delineating one or more of the following areas of the psychoanalytic frame of reference: the basic assumptions underlying the frame of reference,

---

[2] Among the more industrious and relatively complete attempts at delineation of the framework are A. A. Brill, *Fundamental Conceptions of Psychoanalysis* (1921); Calvin S. Hall, *A Primer of Freudian Psychology* (1954); Calvin S. Hall and Gardner Lindzey, *Theories of Personality* (1957), pp. 29–75; Ives Hendrick, *Facts and Theories of Psychoanalysis* (1958); and Herman Nunberg, *Principles of Psychoanalysis* (1955).

Freud's own delineation of psychoanalytic theory is to be found in several of his books for the general public. Especially helpful in crystallizing the psychoanalytic approach as he formulated it are *The Psychopathology of Everyday Life* (1904), *A General Introduction to Psychoanalysis* (1917), *New Introductory Lectures on Psychoanalysis* (1933), and *An Outline of Psychoanalysis* (1949).

the extent of impact of this school on research and practice, the types of problems the framework deals with, the values inherent in the frame of reference, and/or the imperfections of the system.

FOCI OF STUDY

In addition to being a treatment technique for personality disturbances and a theoretical system concerning human motivation and its unconscious foundations, the psychoanalytic frame of reference has been notably employed in studying the individual within the family and in studying the family as an institution. Other major areas of focus include (1) mental disorders, (2) the nature of society and culture, and (3) group life in general. However, even in these three areas it has been found that early family and childhood experiences are causal antecedents. Thus, from the psychoanalytic frame of reference (1) much of psychopathology is seen as the result of early traumatic family experiences, (2) cultural norms and social institutions are viewed as the derivatives of deep psychobiological drives channeled into approved familial or societal interaction, and (3) group identification and participation is seen as dependent upon earlier emotional relations of the child with his parents and siblings.

No area of marriage and family life is outside the boundaries of the psychoanalytic approach. The principal concerns of this frame of reference relative to the family arena are (1) personality development and child-rearing practices, (2) the influence of early familial experience on the individual (socialization in the family), (3) dating, courtship, and mate selection, (4) sexual adjustment in marriage, and (5) deviant familial behavior—desertion, divorce, homosexuality, out-of-wedlock motherhood, and prostitution.

CONCEPTS

Within the psychoanalytic frame of reference there has developed a myriad of concepts and constructs.[3] Perhaps more than in most other frames of reference considered in this volume, psychoanalysis has developed its own terminology. The following is a list of the more central and important concepts, with definitions, employed by this school.

Psychic states: the various levels of awareness. There are three

---

[3] Freud gives an excellent concise statement as to how scientific concepts are constructed, modified, and made logically consistent in *Collected Papers* (1949–1950), Vol. IV, pp. 60–61.

principal levels: (1) conscious—those psychic processes or events of which the individual is aware; (2) preconscious—psychic material which, though one is not aware of it at the moment, is available and can be recalled; (3) unconscious—those psychic processes or events of which the individual is generally unaware and of which he is incapable of becoming conscious without insight, even though these processes are basic to what is overtly understood and expressed. (Freud, 1933, pp. 99–101.)

Elements of personality: the various aspects of the mind which intertwine to make up the total individual. There are three interlocking elements: (1) id—the primitive and instinctual nature of man. It is entirely unconscious and is the source of all the psychic energy of the individual; (2) ego—an individual's experience of himself; the representation of reality as given by the senses; (3) superego—the moral aspect of the personality, built up mainly by early experiences of the child with his parents. There are two subsystems of the superego: (*a*) conscience—internalized parental prohibitions and (*b*) ego ideal—an internalized picture of the individual as he would like himself to be, based on parental approvals and ambitions. (Hall and Lindzey, 1957, pp. 32–36.)

Instinct: a general term for a natural or congenital impulse or drive; a stimulus from within. There are assumed to be two basic instincts: (1) eros (also referred to as *life instinct* or *sex instinct*)— the self-preservation and reproductive impulses; the impulse to live and love; (2) destructive instinct (also referred to as *death instinct* or *aggressive instinct*)—the impulses aiming at destruction of objects, persons, and things. (Freud, 1950, pp. 54–67.)

Drive reduction: the decrease in stimulation from a given instinct. (Hall, 1954, pp. 57–61.)

Tension: a feeling of strain; an inability to find satisfactory outlets for instincts. In strain there are two forces: (1) cathexes—urging forces; (2) anticathexes—checking forces; internal frustration as a result of the ego and superego checking imprudent actions. (Hall, 1954, pp. 46–51.)

Libido: energy, particularly mental or psychic energy which stems from the life instinct. In particular connections it refers only to sexual desire.[4] (Freud, 1949, pp. 22–23.)

Pleasure principle: the tendency inherent in all instinctual impulses

[4] There is no term analogous to *libido* to designate the energy of the death instinct.

or wishes to seek satisfaction independent of all other considerations. (Hall and Lindzey, 1957, p. 33.)

Reality principle: the tendency to do what is demanded by the external world rather than by instinctual impulse or wishes. (Hall and Lindzey, 1957, p. 34.)

Stages of development: the unfolding of personality through various levels of experience; a series of dynamically differentiated but cumulatively determinative periods in life. Human development is divided into three principal periods: (1) the infantile period—the time from birth to age five or six. This period has three stages: (*a*) the oral stage, in which satisfaction is obtained chiefly from the mouth through incorporation; (*b*) the anal stage, in which the eliminative functions and organs become centers of satisfaction; (*c*) the phallic stage, in which pleasure is associated with the genital organs; (2) the latent period—the years from age five or six to the beginning of adolescence; (3) the adolescent period (also referred to as the beginning of the genital stage)—the years from puberty to about age eighteen or twenty.[5] (Freud, 1949, pp. 25–32.)

Fixation: the attachment of energy onto an object; the instinctual attachment to an early stage of development, or an object from such a stage, so that there is difficulty in forming new attachments, developing new interests, or establishing new adaptations. (Hall, 1954, pp. 93–95.)

Ambivalence: the directing of antithetical feelings toward the same object or person, particularly feelings of both affection and hostility. (Freud, 1935, p. 370.)

Compulsion: a need which cannot easily be controlled by the will to undertake a futile and rationally purposeless act or ritual. (Hendrick, 1958, p. 368.)

Obsession: a generally inconsequential or irrelevant idea, not under the control of the will, upon which conscious attention is focused. (Hendrick, 1958, p. 377.)

Oedipus complex: The male child's innate unconscious desire for incestuous sexual union with his mother, coupled with hostile wishes toward his father. (Freud, 1949, pp. 29–30.)

Electra Complex: The female child's counterpart of the Oedipus complex, involving a renouncement of mother love and an uncon-

---

[5] Stages of development are generally traced only through adolescence. Stages beyond this level are posed by some of those using this approach, however. See, for example, Erikson (1950), pp. 219–34.

scious desire to bear the father a child.[6] (Hendrick, 1958, pp. 49–50.)

Erogenous zone (also called *erotogenic zone*): sensitive regions of the body where stimulation evokes a feeling of pleasure, particularly sexual pleasure. (Freud, 1949, p. 24.)

Mental mechanisms (also called *dynamisms* or *defense mechanisms*): semi-automatic reaction patterns which distort reality and operate unconsciously. The principal mechanisms are the following: (1) repression—prevention of painful or rejected instinctual desires and ideas from appearing in consciousness, although they still remain unconsciously active and determine behavior and experience; (2) displacement (transference)—transfer of energy from one object to another that does not arouse as much unconscious conflict; (3) projection—interpretation of situations and events by reading into them one's own experiences and feelings; the unconscious attribution of one's own feelings to others; (4) regression—retreat to an earlier developmental level involving less mature responses; (5) reaction formation—the attempt to negate repressed wishes by exaggerating opposed attitudes and behavior; (6) identification—increasing one's feelings of worth by identifying himself with illustrious institutions or persons who stand as parental surrogates and approximate the ego ideal or relieve superego guilt; (7) compensation—covering up of a weakness or defect by emphasizing to the point of exaggeration the manifestations of a relatively less defective or more desirable characteristic; (8) fantasy—gratification of frustrated desires in imaginary achievements. (Nunberg, 1955, pp. 211–50.)

BASIC ASSUMPTIONS

At the root of psychoanalytic theory are some assumptions also common to the social sciences in general. But there are other basic assumptions and theoretical foundations in psychoanalysis which are specific to it. Freud, writing in 1922, summarized these under the heading of "The Corner-Stones of Psycho-analytic Theory" as follows (1949–1950, Vol. V, p. 122):

> The assumption that there are unconscious mental processes, the recognition of the theory of resistance and repression, the appreciation of the importance of sexuality and the Oedipus complex—these constitute the principal subject-matter of psy-

[6] Although this concept was deemed unnecessary by Freud (1949–1950), Vol. II, p. 211*n*, it may still be found in many of the volumes utilizing this frame of reference.

cho-analysis and the foundations of its theory. No one who cannot accept them all should count himself a psychoanalyst.

Thus implied is that the one basic assumption underlying all psychoanalytic concepts and theory is the functioning of the unconscious.[7] Subsidiary assumptions derivative from this basic one are the following:

1. No behavior is purely accidental and all behavior stems from energy arising from the id. Furthermore, (*a*) behavior is geared toward gratification of instincts and the vicissitudes the instincts have endured (that is, tension reduction) and (*b*) behavior is a function of the quantitative distribution of energy in the personality elements.
2. Man is basically antisocial and the world into which he is born is basically hostile to his instinctual desires.
3. Repression is man's lot and is also basic to the existence of society.
4. Personality is not inborn but is a product of the individual's earliest life experiences in the family. These experiences are sexual—using *sexual* as a term which involves orality, anality, genitality, and the Oedipus complex.

These assumptions—the existence of the unconscious, the instinctual nature of behavior, the antisocial disposition of man, repression as basic to society and culture, and the experiential development of personality through infantile sexuality—form the basic soil in which psychoanalytic concepts are rooted and from which the psychoanalytic frame of reference flowers.[8]

PRODUCT

The psychoanalytic frame of reference has had profound effects throughout the social sciences and the humanities in addition to its therapeutic place in medicine. Among its pre-eminent effects are

[7] Although Brown (1959), p. 3, makes the case that psychoanalysis is singularly grounded on the theory of repression, it is apparent that basic to the theory of repression is the theory of the unconscious. Also, in some sources Freud (1949), pp. 13–14, 105, and (1950), p. 9, has stated that the division of mental life into the conscious and the unconscious is *the* fundamental premise on which psychoanalysis is based.

[8] These underlying assumptions have been the focus of especial confusion in the past, particularly because many writers, in attempting to delineate the psychoanalytic frame of reference, have confused the basic assumptions with concepts and with hypotheses.

also those it has had on the study of family life. The impact of this approach on research, theory, and practice in marriage and family living has been so great as to make it impossible for students and practitioners in this field to ignore it.

Research

Nevertheless, there are those who claim that it is well-nigh insuperably difficult to conduct sociological research through the psychoanalytic frame of reference. The principal research problems, which stem largely from the assumption of the unconscious, are (1) the concepts of the psychoanalytic frame of reference are difficult to define operationally, (2) the frame of reference largely excludes social factors, and (3) it is basically a closed system with circular arguments and conclusions. Yet the impact of psychoanalysis on the study of the family has been so inexorable as to produce many studies designed to test hypotheses derived from psychoanalytic theory.[9] But many of these studies have taken over only superficial aspects of family theory and psychoanalytic theory, leaving many of the deeper implications scarcely touched. (Hilgard, 1952, p. 43.)

A great deal of the research has been of the case-study method, dealing with abnormal behavior. More recently, however, an increasing amount of empirical research has been undertaken with normal samples. Sears (1943) and Orlansky (1949), for example, have reviewed several hundred empirical studies which have been formulated through the psychoanalytic frame of reference and which are largely based on normal subjects. Many of these studies have been concerned either with investigating mental mechanisms of defense or with establishing a definite answer to the question of the relation of infant discipline and rearing patterns to character development. The results, however, have been contradictory. For example, in Sewell's (1952) study of 162 children he found no relationship between the nature of infant training and personality development. Ribble (1944) and Goldman-Eisler (1962), on the other hand, have shown a definite relationship between early infantile experience and subsequent personality.

It has been held that because of the nature of the psychoanalytic frame of reference research findings which are based merely on

[9] Several of these studies may be found in, among other sources, the three major journals—*International Journal of Psychoanalysis, The Psychoanalytic Quarterly,* and *The Psychoanalytic Review.*

sociological methodology have little validity. Thus, research findings by non-Freudians which are contrary to psychoanalytic theory are generally ignored by psychoanalysts. For example, Simpson (1957) criticizes adversely Sewell's findings on the ground that orthodox sociological methodology is inappropriate to the investigation of problems posed by psychoanalysis. To Simpson, sociological empiricism does not come to terms with the peculiar character of the data unearthed by psychoanalysis, and the methodology used by researchers in this area needs to be based on this peculiarity.

In conclusion, much of the empirical family research undertaken, purportedly based on the psychoanalytic frame of reference, has been of a questionable and contradictory nature. It has also been challenged as inadequate and lacking in familiarity with the foundations of psychoanalysis. For the future, it appears that more sophisticated research designs and tools need to be developed which will more adequately and objectively examine hypotheses derived from psychoanalytic theory.

Anthropological research has also been carried out through the psychoanalytic frame of reference. (See Chapter 2) Among anthropologists who have used this frame of reference are Ralph Linton, Abram Kardiner, Cora Dubois, and Ruth Benedict. But, as with Sewell's work in sociology, anthropological findings which have sought to dispute psychoanalytic theory have been challenged. For example, Malinowski (1927) in his study of the Trobriand Islanders concluded that there are no repressed instinctual hostile feelings of the boy child toward the father (the Oedipus complex). Rather, says Malinowski, the forces of repression are due to authority and discipline by the maternal uncle (the social father) and hostility is therefore posited upon him. Jones (1925), a psychoanalyst and later Freud's biographer, disputes Malinowski's interpretation, which had been stated in articles by Malinowski as early as 1916. Jones reinterprets Malinowski's findings so as to substantiate the psychoanalytic deductions. To Jones, Malinowski misinterpreted his observations because of his lack of a grounding in psychoanalysis. To Jones, the hatred of the father is still present among Trobriand Islanders but is merely displaced to a safer, more distant object (the uncle). Furthermore, says Jones, the child in Trobriand society unconsciously views his uncle as the lover of his mother and therefore envisages the uncle as his father in his internalized imagery. Therefore, the child hates him. The Oedipus complex cannot be avoided but its object can be displaced. Here are illustrated the arguments concerning the adequacy of the concepts to be used for several different interpretations; the closed and circular nature of the theoretical system; and again, as in sociology, the clash between the orthodox anthropological field worker and the psychoanalytic interpreter.

Theory

A good deal of psychoanalytic theory or applied theory focuses on marriage and family living. One of the earliest definitive works using this frame of reference is Flugel's *The Psycho-Analytic Study of the Family* (1921). Among other more recent works which have employed this frame of reference in marriage and family theory are Ackerman, *The Psychodynamics of the Family* (1958); Eisenstein, *Neurotic Interaction in Marriage* (1956); Kenkel, *The Family in Perspective* (1960), Chaps. 18–20; and Simpson, *People in Families* (1960). Parsons and Bales, in *Family, Socialization and Interaction Process* (1955), have also sought to employ some aspects of the psychoanalytic frame of reference (in combination with other frames of reference, particularly the structure-functional) in their development of family theory, although to a lesser extent than the other writers mentioned in this list.

The psychoanalytic frame of reference has been used to deal with practically every aspect of marriage and the family. The following are illustrative of some of the uses to which this frame of reference has been put in family theory:

1. Mate selection. Psychoanalytic theory is applied to mate selection on the personal level, with particular emphasis on the unconscious. For example, mate selection is seen as a function of:
   a. Displacement of love from the parent of the opposite sex to others of the opposite sex. (Flugel, 1921, pp. 200–16.)
   b. Attachment to a person because of his partial fulfillment of the ego ideal. (Winch, 1952, pp. 322–33.)
   c. One's Oedipal attachment which compels him to fall in love with and marry someone who resembles the parent. (Kenkel, 1960, p. 443.)
2. Parent-infant relationships. The psychoanalytic frame of reference is applied to parent-child relationships particularly with reference to the effect of the parent upon the child's development, but it also takes into account the influence of the child

upon the parents. For example, not only may the child resent the presence of the parent of the same sex, but parental jealousy may also arise toward the child because of competition for the same love object, though in this case the hostile feelings will frequently be confined to the unconscious. (Simpson, 1960, pp. 45–46.)

3. Step-parent and step-child relationships. For example, the child's feelings of love and hate towards his real parents are often barred from expression, but substitution of a step-parent removes these barriers so that the new parent may often receive the full force of the love or hate which had hitherto been pent up. (Flugel, 1921, p. 101.)

4. Sibling relationships. In childhood, brothers and sisters struggle for the attention and affection of the parent with deep rivalry and competitiveness. Jealousy and hostility are thus inherent in sibling relationships. On the other hand, there may also be affection between siblings, especially when there is a considerable difference in ages or maturity, so that an elder sister, for example, takes on some of the attributes of the mother as regards the younger children, thereby establishing an affectionate relationship. (Flugel, 1921, pp. 19–20.)

5. Husband-wife relationships. From the psychoanalytic frame of reference the quality of the husband-wife relationship may be viewed as a function of the love or hate originally held for a parent transferred to the spouse, as the spouse is unconsciously identified with the parent of the opposite sex. (Kenkel, 1960, pp. 443–45.)

6. In-law difficulties. Problems in the in-law relationship have been dealt with in psychoanalysis also. Difficulties may arise, for example, in the following situations. (Flugel, 1921, pp. 92–94.)

   a. Because of the original infantile attachments toward parents, one marriage partner may continue to look to his parents as the source of ideals and aspirations rather than to the spouse, thereby leading to difficulty between one partner and the parents of the other.

   b. The individual may transfer the feelings of hatred which he originally directed toward his own parents onto his parents-in-law.

   c. There may be a transference of affection or hostility which the parent originally experienced toward his own children onto his son-in-law or daughter-in-law.

7. Atypical or abnormal situations.

   a. Celibacy. From this frame of reference celibacy is seen as a function of the fixation of the love impulse onto the mother, to the virtual exclusion of all others. (Flugel, 1921, pp. 49–51.)

   b. Impotence or frigidity. This may be the function of anxiety associated with unconscious incestuous fears which have been generalized to all members of the opposite sex. Or infantile castration anxieties, exaggerated narcissistic tendencies, hostilities, the unconscious equation of ejaculation with soiling or urinating, and similar infantile attitudes may lead to failure to maintain an erection or penetrate the vagina. (Eisenstein, 1956, pp. 105–12.)

These are but a few illustrations of the use of the psychoanalytic frame of reference in family analysis and are by no means exhaustive of the psychoanalytic interpretations that have been made of the specific phenomena. These examples do, however, serve to show how the psychoanalytic frame of reference has been employed to develop theory on typical, atypical, and abnormal components of marriage and the family.

Practice

The psychoanalytic school has had pervasive influence on religion, education (especially progressive education), medicine, criminology, and, indeed, upon practically every area of life. Within the area of marriage and the family, it has completely altered the field of family social work. Psychoanalysis has had a very profound impact on attitudes toward and practices in premarital sexual behavior, family-life education, child-rearing, child placement in adoption, and marriage counseling.

Burgess and Wallin (1954, p. 162) have attributed the increase in premarital sexual relations in recent decades to the works and influence of psychoanalysis. Ogburn and Nimkoff (1955, pp. 55, 186–87) also attribute today's more "naturalistic" approach to sex as stemming from the "new psychology" and cite this "new psychology" as one of the causes of women take a more active role in sexual relations.

Ogburn and Nimkoff (1955, pp. 198–203) also attribute the change from corporal punishment to permissiveness in child-rearing practices as a result of the "new psychology." This influence of psychoanalysis may be found stressed in a number of books which are written as guides to parents. For example, Thomson (1953, p. 104) recognizes the Oedipus complex and cautions parents to expect the child to express love of the parent of the opposite sex and jealousy of the other parent who is viewed as a rival. Others, including Erikson (1950) and Josselyn (1955), present their works on child care from a psychoanalytic frame of reference also.

In marriage counseling a great deal of emphasis is put upon psychoanalysis, and many counselors are calling for even more training in this area. Albert (1963, p. 183), for example, states that "it . . . appears highly worthwhile to urge that universities and other training centers require that marriage counselors-in-training receive a thorough grounding in motivation, personality development, abnormal psychology, and diagnostics, as well as a working knowledge of psychoanalytic theory." Regensburg (1954) and Green (1954) also support this view. To Green, successful marital casework is virtually impossible without knowledge of (1) ego structure and function, (2) defense mechanisms, and (3) significant conflicts in the client's conscious and preconscious psychic life.

These latter examples are but a few of the possible illustrations of the influence of the psychoanalytic frame of reference on practice in the area of marriage and family living.

VALUES

Rieff (1959, p. 301) has stated that psychoanalysis may be treated as a philosophy. As a philosophy, the whole frame of reference may be viewed as a system of values and, indeed, Rieff attempts to interpret some of the basic assumptions underlying psychoanalysis as propositions of values (pp. 197–99). Interpretation of a science (or "protoscience") as a philosophy, however, leaves large areas of all theory, regardless of its content, in the realm of valuations by those who promulgate it (particularly when viewed by those who hold alternative or contradictory hypotheses). From this perspective it may be said that the frame of reference includes a large number of value judgments.

When establishing the presence of values in theoretical scientific systems from an analysis of theoretical statements as to what is "good" and what is "bad," on the other hand, the area of psychoanalysis appears to have few, if any, implicit or explicit value judgments or value objectives, aside from the values inherent in any of the social sciences (such as that knowledge *per se* is good).[10]

This is not to say, however, that no values have arisen as a result of the utilization of this framework. The framework has fostered a number of value judgments which are closely linked to the theoretical system, such as (1) good mental health is better than anything else, and (2) a lasting marriage is better than one that is dissolved (particularly in reference to child adjustment). Ogburn and Nimkoff (1955, pp. 187, 198–203) point out that psychoanalysis has led to the values that (1) the individual child is more important than the individual adult, (2) an understanding attitude toward the child is better than physical punishment, (3) knowledge of sex is good, and (4) women should enjoy sex and should have freedom of expression equal to that of men (that is, females need not be passive).

LaPiere (1959) stresses the view that psychoanalytic social reformers value security and adaptability over conflict and competition, permissiveness over punishment and control (particularly as it pertains to child-rearing, crime prevention, and education), and adjustment to the environment over active manipulation of the environment.

THE FRAMEWORK

Psychoanalytic theory forms an intergrated framework. There is a definite interrelationship and interdependence among concepts and assumptions, the underlying and unifying assumption being that of the unconscious. The notion of the unconscious permeates psychoanalytic theory.

The basis of personality is the id, which is entirely unconscious and which is the repository of the instincts. The infant enters the world as wholly id. His instinct-impetus orients all behavior toward pleasure (tension reduction). Aboriginal infantile pleasure is oral-incorporation. By about the first year of life the child enters the anal stage of the infantile period in which a great deal of conflict

[10] The case for psychoanalysis as a science, or at least a "protoscience," is concisely and effectively made by Demos (1959), pp. 329–31.

is experienced between instinctual wishes and external restraints
or reality (particularly as regards toilet training). Anal-sadism becomes weaponry; anal-retentiveness, property; and anal-preoccupa-
tion, productivity. Which of these becomes predominant depends
on the training agent—the mother or mother-surrogate. During
basic anality the individual begins to develop his ego.

In the third stage of the infantile period (the phallic stage), from
about age three to age five or six, the child's interests are centered
on pleasurable experiences derived from the sex organs. The pleasure derived from the genital regions is associated with the parent
of the opposite sex, and the child becomes involved in the Oedipus
complex. It is a complex rather than a "simple" because it is filled
with ambivalence (love and hate, activity and passivity, even hetero-
sexuality and homosexuality). The resolution (or irresolution) of the
conflicts in this complex culminates in the development of the superego (ego ideal and conscience). The child passes into the period of
latency, in which sexual desires have undergone repression. The child
thereafter experiences little sexual desire or stimulation, unless severe
traumatic infantile experiences have been suffered and are reinforced during this period. At puberty, however, genital changes
arouse these repressed sexual feelings and the individual enters the
genital stage. Adolescence re-creates the earlier parental cathexes
and is thus a time of revolt, struggle for independence, and the
beginning of the search for new love objects onto which may be
displaced the sexual feelings originally directed toward the parent
of the opposite sex.

Each stage of development is built upon previous stages. Provided
that the individual has the capacity to resolve the problems and
conflicts in each stage, he will develop normally; to the extent that
he has not, he will be maladjusted. All premarital, marital, and
parental behavior to follow is determined by infantile experiences
stored as internalized, generally unconscious imagery.

The latter paragraphs illustrate the close integration and interrelation of the concepts and the assumptions of this frame of reference. The basic compatibility of the concepts of psychoanalysis
with each other and with its basic assumptions may be shown in
yet another way. Psychoanalytic theory involves many complementary terms or dualisms (pairs of antagonistic but interlocking
entities). For example:

1. Life instinct against death instinct.
2. Id (antisocial orientation) against superego (altruistic orientation).
3. Pleasure principle (immediate gratification) against reality principle (postponement of pleasure).
4. Cathexes (urging forces) against anticathexes (checking forces).
5. The conscious against the unconscious.
6. Sadism against masochism.
7. Fixation against transference or displacement.

Such pairs of concepts yield a well-integrated model capable of explaining phenomena which by merely superficial study might otherwise appear to be contradictory.

CRITIQUE AND DISCUSSION

The psychoanalytic frame of reference is an interrelated and highly complex system with few contradictions (although the concepts and theories from this frame of reference allow the explanation of apparently contradictory phenomena). Its implications range widely and its ability to yield interpretations is still untapped to an unknown degree. With this potential the frame of reference will undoubtedly continue to be, as it has been in the past, a widely used perspective on the family.

The psychoanalytic frame of reference has had an impact not only on various aspects of family study but also on anthropological surveys that deal with the family. Very recently it has been introduced even into the structure-functional study of the family as in the work by Parson and Bales (1955). Several books and a large number of articles on the family have employed the psychoanalytic frame of reference, and few are the introductory texts on marriage and the family which do not at least make reference to psychoanalysis.

It must also be pointed out, however, that psychoanalytic theory has become a thorn in the side of orthodox empirical validation in sociology because its conceptual basis is the unconscious, its complementary concepts allow contradictory interpretations, and its nature is relatively impervious to operational definitions. Nevertheless, a great deal of research has been attempted in recent years to test hypotheses derived from psychoanalytic theory. Yet much of this work has been on the more superficial aspects of the theory, and the results have been highly contradictory, causing some heated controversy between Freudians and non-Freudians. Sears (1943), after reviewing a number of psychoanalytic studies, recognized this problem and reaches this conclusion:

> Psychoanalysis relies upon techniques that do not admit of the repetition of observation, that have no self-evident or denotative validity, and that are tinctured to an unknown degree with the observer's own suggestions. These difficulties may not seriously interfere with therapy, but when the method is used for uncovering psychological facts that are required to have objective validity it simply fails. (p. 133.)

Kubie (1959) makes a similar point. He also notes that psychoanalysis is unique in that the theory is developed and revised almost exclusively upon the basis of auditory data, which is distorted even during the process of perception. Further, he points out that analysis of these types of data seldom can prove that an interpretation using the psychoanalytic frame of reference (the hypothesis) is adequate, unique, and necessary (that is, the data rarely meet the ultimate criterion of validity).

Criticisms of psychoanalytic research have been summarized as follows (Colby, 1960, pp. 52–57):

1. Uncontrolled observations.
2. Unrecorded observations.
3. Lack of quantification.
4. Lack of experiment.
5. Lack of control.
6. Lack of follow-up.
7. Lack of confirmation.
8. Lack of consensus upon operational definitions.
9. Lack of consensus upon interpretation.
10. Obscurantist language.

In conclusion, many of the difficulties with the psychoanalytic frame of reference are due to its resistance to positivism. Brown (1959) states the reason for this problem:

> Empirical verification, the positivist test of science, can apply only to that which is fully in consciousness; but psychoanalysis

is a mode of contacting the unconscious under conditions of general repression, when the unconscious remains in some sense repressed. (p. 320.)

However, because psychoanalytic theory has lacked a large amount of what is claimed to be objective validation and because the theory does not yield easily derivable or testable hypotheses for investigation does not necessarily mean that the theory is bad. Indeed, psychoanalytic theory has been widely used with no small success in family therapy and has been accepted by a number of professionals in the marriage and family area as worth a great deal of consideration. With this basis, psychoanalytic theory will continue as a dynamic force affecting much of every-day life in the family and it will remain as a major influence in a vast amount of marriage and family research and family theory for some time to come.

REFERENCES

ACKERMAN, NATHAN W. *The Psychodynamics of Family Life*. New York: Basic Books, Inc., Publishers, 1958. An attempt to correlate the psychological and psychoanalytic process of individual behavior with family behavior in order to be able to place individual clinical diagnosis and therapy within the broader framework of family diagnosis and therapy.

ALBERT, GERALD. "Advanced Psychological Training for Marriage Counselors—Luxury or Necessity?" *Marriage and Family Living*, 25 (May 1963), pp. 181–83.

BRILL, A. A. *Fundamental Conceptions of Psychoanalysis*. New York: Harcourt, Brace & World, Inc. 1921.

BROWN, NORMAN O. *Life Against Death: The Psychoanalytical Meaning of History*. Middletown, Conn.: Wesleyan University Press, 1959.

BURGESS, ERNEST W., and WALLIN, PAUL. *Courtship, Engagement and Marriage*. Philadelphia: J. B. Lippincott Company, 1954.

CHRISTENSEN, HAROLD T., ed. *Handbook on Marriage and the Family*. Chicago: Rand McNally & Company, 1964.

COLBY, KENNETH M. *An Introduction to Psychoanalytic Research*. New York: Basic Books, Inc., Publishers, 1960. A discussion of the application, problems, and methods appropriate to psychoanalytic research.

DEMOS, RAPHAEL. "Psychoanalysis: Science and Philosophy," in Sidney Hook, ed. *Psychoanalysis, Scientific Method, and Philosophy*. New York: New York University Press, 1959, pp. 329–35.

EISENSTEIN, VICTOR W. *Neurotic Interaction in Marriage.* New York: Basic Books, Inc., Publishers, 1956. A partial psychoanalytic approach to marital tension, stressing unconscious emotional needs. Marital relationships are discussed in terms of diagnosis, prognosis and treatment.

ERIKSON, ERIK H. *Childhood and Society.* New York: W. W. Norton & Company, Inc., 1950. A cross-cultural psychoanalytic study of child personality and problems.

FLUGEL, JOHN C. *The Psycho-Analytic Study of the Family.* London: Hogarth Press and The Institute of Psycho-Analysis, 1921. One of the earliest definitive works which employs an orthodox psychoanalytic approach to family analysis. Included is a psychoanalytic discussion of family influence upon individual growth and personality, love and hate, abnormal personality, parent-child and quasi-parent-child relationships, and marital interaction.

FREUD, SIGMUND. *Collected Papers,* five vols. trans. by Joan Riviere. London: Hogarth Press and The Institute of Psycho-Analysis, 1949–1950. A series of a large number of technical papers written by Freud since 1893, most of which had not previously been translated into English.

———. *The Ego and the Id,* trans. by Joan Riviere. London: Hogarth Press and The Institute of Psycho-Analysis, 1950. First published in German in 1927. This volume yields a concise discussion of the psychic states, the elements of personality, and the two classes of instincts.

———. *A General Introduction to Psychoanalysis,* trans. by Joan Riviere. New York: Liveright Publishing Corporation, 1935. A course of twenty-eight lectures delivered by Freud, dealing with the psychology of errors, dreams, and a general theory of the neuroses.

———. *New Introductory Lectures on Psycho-Analysis,* trans. by W. J. H. Sprott. New York: W. W. Norton & Company Inc., 1933.

———. *An Outline of Psychoanalysis,* trans. and ed. by James Strachey. New York: W. W. Norton & Company Inc., 1949. One of the last and unfinished works of Freud, first published in German in 1940. A concise introduction to the basic assumptions and concepts of Freudian psychoanalytic theory.

———. *The Basic Writings of Sigmund Freud,* trans. and ed. by A. A. Brill. New York: The Modern Library, Inc., 1938.

GOLDMAN-EISLER, FRIEDA. "Breastfeeding and Character Formation," in Clyde Kluckhohn and Henry A. Murray, eds. *Personality in Nature, Society, and Culture,* 2nd ed. New York: Alfred A. Knopf, Inc., 1962, pp. 146–84.

GREEN, SIDNEY L. "Psychoanalytic Contributions to Casework Treatment of Marital Problems," *Social Casework,* 35 (Dec. 1954), pp. 419–23. Advocation and review of the psychoanalytic frame of reference in the treatment of marital problems.

GRINKER, ROY R. *Mid-Century Psychiatry: An Overview.* Springfield, Ill.: Charles C. Thomas, Publisher, 1953.

HALL, CALVIN S. *A Primer of Freudian Psychology.* New York: The New American Library of World Literature, Inc., 1954. A comprehensive and highly systematized presentation of Freud's principal theories. Includes a lucid discussion of the organization of personality, the dynamics of personality, and the development of personality as defined by Freud.

——, and LINDZEY, GARDNER. *Theories of Personality.* New York: John Wiley & Sons, Inc., 1957, Chap. 2. A brief introduction to basic Freudian psychoanalytic theory; includes an extensive bibliography of some sixty works.

HENDRICK, IVES. *Facts and Theories of Psychoanalysis,* 3rd ed. New York: Alfred A. Knopf, Inc., 1958. A thorough treatment of psychoanalytic concepts, theories, and therapy. Also included is a section on the psychoanalytic movement and its principal areas of application.

HILGARD, ERNEST R. "Experimental Approaches to Psychoanalysis," in E. Pumpian-Mindlin, ed. *Psychoanalysis as Science.* Stanford: Stanford University Press, 1952.

HILL, REUBEN, and HANSEN, DONALD A. "The Identification of Conceptual Frameworks Utilized in Family Study," *Marriage and Family Living,* 22 (Nov. 1960), pp. 299–311.

JONES, ERNEST. "Mother-Right and the Sexual Ignorance of Savages," *International Journal of Psychoanalysis,* 6 (April 1925), pp. 109–30. A cross-cultural psychoanalytic appraisal of inheritance and succession, authority, mother-right, and residence patterns, with an attempt to refute Malinowski's conclusions through the use of psychoanalytic interpretations.

JOSSELYN, IRENE M. *The Happy Child.* New York: Random House, Inc., 1955. A book on child care employing, to some extent, the psychoanalytic frame of reference, especially in Chapters 4 through 8, which focus on the psychoanalytic stages of development.

KENKEL, WILLIAM F. *The Family in Perspective.* New York: Appleton-Century-Crofts, 1960, Chaps. 18, 19, 20. An elementary introduction to basic psychoanalytic concepts and tenets; a review of psychosexual development; and a brief psychoanalytic discussion of adolescence, mate selection, and sexual adjustment in marriage.

KOMAROVSKY, MIRRA and WALLER, WILLARD. "Studies of the Family," *American Journal of Sociology,* 50 (May 1945), pp. 443–51.

KUBIE, LAWRENCE S. "Psychoanalysis and Scientific Method," in Sidney Hook, ed. *Psychoanalysis, Scientific Method, and Philosophy.* New York: New York University Press, 1959, pp. 57–77.

LAPIERE, RICHARD T. *The Freudian Ethic.* New York: Duell, Sloan & Pearce, 1959. A discussion of the effect of psychoanalytic theory upon various aspects of life, particularly child training, education, crime, business, and government. The Adjustment and mediocrity are seen as the result of psychoanalytic teachings and as replacing the Protestant ethic which has so dynamically advanced American society.

MALINOWSKI, BRONISLAW. *Sex and Repression in Savage Society.* New York: Harcourt, Brace & World, Inc., 1927.

MENNINGER, KARL. *Theory of Psychoanalytic Technique.* New York: Basic Books, Inc., Publishers, 1958.

NUNBERG, HERMAN. *Principles of Psychoanalysis.* New York: International Universities Press, Inc., 1955. A thorough introduction to psychoanalytic concepts and theory.

OGBURN, W. F., and NIMKOFF, M. F. *Technology and the Changing Family.* Boston: Houghton Mifflin Company, 1955.

ORLANSKY, HAROLD. "Infant Care and Personality," *Psychological Bulletin,* 46 (Jan. 1949), pp. 1–48. A review of approximately 150 studies which have attempted to relate infant care (breast feeding, "mothering," sphincter training, restraint of motion, and infant frustration and aggression) to subsequent personality.

PARSONS, TALCOTT, and BALES, ROBERT F. *Family, Socialization and Interaction Process.* New York: Free Press of Glencoe, Inc., 1955.

REGENSBURG, JEANNETTE. "Application of Psychoanalytic Concepts to Casework Treatment of Marital Problems," *Social Casework,* 35 (Dec. 1954), pp. 424–32.

RIBBLE, MARGARET, A. "Infantile Experience in Relation to Personality Development," in J. McV. Hunt, ed. *Personality and the Behavior Disorders,* Vol. 2. New York: The Ronald Press Company, 1944, pp. 621–51.

RIEFF, PHILIP. *Freud: The Mind of the Moralist.* New York: The Viking Press, Inc., 1959.

RUITENBEEK, HENDRIK M., ed. *Psychoanalysis and Existential Philosophy.* New York: E. P. Dutton & Co., Inc., 1962.

SEARS, ROBERT R. "Survey of Objective Studies of Psychoanalytic Concepts," *Social Science Research Bulletin,* 51 (1943). A review of over 160 articles and books whose writers have investigated various psychoanalytic theories and concepts.

SEWELL, WILLIAM H. "Infant Training and the Personality of the Child," *American Journal of Sociology,* 58 (Sept. 1952), pp. 150–59. A study of 162 farm children in an unsuccessful attempt to relate infant training experiences to personality adjustment and personality traits.

SHAFFER, LAURANCE F., and SHOBEN, EDWARD J. *The Psychology of Adjustment,* 2nd ed. Boston: Houghton Mifflin Company, 1956, Chap. 14. A brief introduction to levels of consciousness, forces and energies, personality systems, stages of development, mechanisms, and the Oedipus and castration complexes. Also includes an overview of other major variants of psychoanalysis and an appraisal of psychoanalysis.

SIMPSON, GEORGE. "Empiricism and Psychoanalysis in the Sociology of the Family," *Marriage and Family Living*, 19 (Nov. 1957), pp. 382–84. A criticism of the use of sociological methodology to investigate psychoanalytic theory, with particular reference to the work of Sewell.

———. *People in Families*. New York: Thomas Y. Crowell Company, 1960. A highly successful and wide-ranging attempt to relate the sociological research of the family with psychoanalytic principles of interpretation of marriage and family life, with a strong psychoanalytic emphasis throughout.

SNYDER, WILLIAM U., and SNYDER, B. JUNE. *The Psychotherapy Relationship*. New York: The Macmillan Company, 1961.

STEPHENS, WILLIAM N. *The Oedipus Complex*. New York: Free Press of Glencoe, Inc., 1962. A discussion of the Oedipus complex and cross-cultural correlation analyses which tend to support the theory.

THOMPSON, CLARA, et al., eds. *An Outline of Psychoanalysis*. New York: The Modern Library, Inc., 1955.

THOMSON, MARY M. *Talk It Out With Your Child*. New York: McGraw-Hill, Inc., 1953. A book written as a child guide for parents, with psychoanalytic concepts and theory interspersed throughout.

WINCH, ROBERT F. *The Modern Family*, 1st ed. New York: Holt, Rinehart & Winston, Inc., 1952. A study of the forms and functions of the family, together with an emphasis on the parent-child relationship and needs as they may affect marriage and the family.

chapter 8

A Social-Psychological Conceptual Framework of the Family[*]

William D. Brown

Social psychology is a broad term applied to the study of interpersonal and intergroup stimulation and response. It is a relatively new field, having come into existence during the twentieth
century with the publications of E. A. Ross, *Social Psychology*
(1908) and William McDougall, *The Group Mind* (1908). The
former stressed the basic sociological orientation of social psychology, while McDougall regarded social psychology as an entity of
the field of psychology. Other scholars (Krech and Crutchfield,
Newcomb, and Dennis) have argued as to whether social psychology is to be seen as a facet of another discipline or as a discipline
in its own right. General consensus in this area is still inconclusive.
Throughout the field of social psychology are found many references to psychoanalytic theory, due to the earlier conceptualizations
formulated by the psychoanalytic school in the area of psychology.
In addition, we find a certain amount of overlapping between the
two fields due to the fact that many of the neo-Freudians, once they
ceased to embrace the psychoanalytic approach *in toto,* turned

[*] Grateful acknowledgment is made of the contribution of John T. Greene
who served as editorial consultant for this framework and who read and
critically reviewed the manuscript prior to its final revision. Many, although
not all, of his suggestions have been incorporated into the final manuscript.
Inadequacies and errors in the chapter as published, however, are entirely the
responsibility of the author and the editors.

their attention to problems which later were included in the area known as social psychology.

The main concern of social psychology has been twofold: (1) a study of individual behavior, and (2) the behavior of groups of individuals in a social environment. In actuality sociologists have utilized the social-psychological conceptual framework to study the family more often than have psychologists. This is readily apparent when we examine the contributions of Waller, Hill, Hess and Handel, Ackerman, and Parsons and Bales, to mention a few. Therefore it is notable that both disciplines apply something of a holistic view within this framework in that the individual and the group are studied not as independent variables but rather as interdependent variables.[1] The consensus within the field is that the individual cannot be separated from his environment if we are seeking to understand and analyze his behavior, because both the individual and the environment are interdependent. For the purpose of a given study, the independent and dependent variable might be temporarily isolated for examination, but in the final analysis, the isolation method must be discarded in order that a meaningful study of the socialization process may result.

Attempts to delineate the social-psychological frame of reference have been quite numerous. However, attempts to delineate a social-psychological conceptual framework of the family per se have not been undertaken. This does not mean that the social psychological framework is limited in relation to the study of the family. (See bibliography.) Actually, the family has been treated quite extensively as the basic group of orientation for the individual. The end result has been that while the family has been treated extensively in social psychology, the approach by most writers has been to treat the family as a dependent variable. The one noteworthy exception is Zimmerman, who, in *Family and Civilization* (1947), sought to treat the family as the independent variable. Therein he stressed familism as a causal factor in the development or decay of civilizations.

[1] While this is the case in general, the reader should be cognizant of Newcomb's concept of the intervening variable. Newcomb (1950), p. 31. In the case of delinquency, the independent variable consists of social influences; the intervening variable is the motives or attitudes, the individual's desire to be a gang leader; and the dependent variable is the actual social behavior, that is, the delinquent's actions.

A listing of previous attempts at specifying this frame of reference could be done at some length, if we consider as a valid criterion the fact that scholars in this field have utilized the family as a basic concept and therefore worked with it extensively as a dependent variable in approaching generally held concepts in the area. The dilemma here is that we would broaden the horizons of an area which already needs delimiting. Conversely, our attempt could be quite limited if we were to include only those works in the area of social psychology which treated the family as an independent variable. In order that we might avoid the former dilemma, we have restricted our study to three areas within the field of social psychology. These include: (1) the self-concept, (2) personality interaction, and (3) need theory. Each of these areas contains many concepts which are distinctly relevant to the family. Our task, then, has evolved around a process of sorting out concepts and assumptions from these areas which have been developed with a more direct bearing on the family.

These concepts have been developed by various scholars within the three areas stated above. Although other family theorists have been concerned with the self-concept, Rogers has been most outstanding in his work on the relationship of the self-concept to the family. This is due perhaps to his extensive therapy with individuals and to the self-concepts of these individuals in their associations with members of their families.

In the area of personality interaction, Sullivan and Mead have appeared as the major proponents of concepts relating to the family. Murray (1938), in his study of personology, also contributed heavily in this area. In addition, Adler (1930) stressed personality interaction in a study of what he termed "individual psychology." It is also noteworthy that Horney (1945) and Fromm (1941) have contributed to this area of social psychology.

Concepts concerning the family have been expounded at length by certain scholars who write in a social-psychological vein but who have given much attention to need theory. Eminent authorities in this area have included Murstein and Winch (1954), who conducted studies on need theory and Terman (1938), who conceptualized the psychological needs as they relate to marriage and the family.

It is to be recognized from the start that none of these individuals could be called family theorists in the strict sense of the term, for the family has not been their chief concern; rather, the family has been viewed as only one variable affecting the individual. Yet, each has theorized and conceptualized certain terms which are directly related to the family, employing these terms in their respective works. Our task, then, is to move from a macroscopic to a microscopic view of pertinent concepts concerning the family within the social-psychological framework.

FOCI OF STUDY

The principal concern of these scholars laboring within the framework of social psychology as they have studied the family has centered (1) on the concept of the self and its relationship to the family and (2) on the interpersonal relationships between individuals and members of their families. Rogers (1961) stresses the self-concept as a focal point, while Huntington (1958) concerns himself with personality interaction as related to marital relations. The self as a concept is closely interwoven with personality interaction, and the overlapping of the two is readily apparent.

The self-concept approach has been mainly concerned with the individual and the way he views himself, that is, the manner in which he perceived himself as a person. It is important that we recognize this fact with respect to the individual and his relation to his family of orientation, because self-perception is seen as having a definite effect in regard to the individual's interaction with groups. This is especially true where the family is concerned, because the family is the primary group from which one structures his roles. The chief objective within this particular framework has been to describe the individual as he relates his personal behavior to the family, and, conversely, as the family relates its behavior to the individual.

Interpersonal theory—that is, personology and individual psychology as exemplified in the works of Adler, Murray, and others—has been mainly confined to personality interaction. However, the social determinants of the individual's behavior have been brought into play as an integral part of the individual's interaction with the family, thus warranting our studying this area of social psychology as it relates conceptually to the family. Sullivan (1953) believes that interpersonal relations are important in the development of the individual far beyond the early years. The family, in this connection, is seen as one of the many institutions which will have a direct effect on personality formation of the individual. Interpersonal theory is seen as being directly related to the self-concept approach.

Needs theory has been viewed from the perspective of the needs of the individual as he relates to other individuals, especially within the confines of marriage.[2] Terman (1938) confines the list of needs in the main to general needs such as happiness and gratification. Winch (1954) is more concerned with direct needs, for example, abasement, achievement, approach, autonomy, deference, dominance, hostility, nurturance, recognition, succorance, status aspiration, and status striving. Complementary needs within marriage, such as love, are seen by Murstein (1961) as needs which are variable, varying according to the individual's surroundings. These needs are met in a direct or an indirect fashion, and although interaction is important in many of these needs, in some instances self-perception is to be viewed as the dominant factor in fulfilling needs.

Many of the studies in the area of need theory have been confined to neurotic needs and to the neurotic interaction which results in the family from the neurotic needs of individual family members. Eisenstein (1956) traces this neurotic interaction which fulfills neurotic needs within a marriage. Since this work is viewed mainly from the psychoanalytic viewpoint, we will not be concerned with it further within this approach. However, we should be aware of the fact that recent developments have placed emphasis on the complementary effects of neurotic needs as they relate to neurotic behavior within the family setting. (Eisenstein, 1956.)

The chief concern of the social-psychological approach is to use the family as only one variable within a larger group of variables.[3] Studies in this area are not confined to the family per se; rather, the family is seen as the basic group for the role orientation of the individual.

[2] Needs theory is here confined to "psycho-socio" needs of the individual rather than both the psycho-socio and the physiological needs of family members.

[3] Another approach within this general framework is that of "field theory." This approach views the family as a group in relation to other larger groups. Thus the family is viewed as a subgroup, but one which is influenced markedly by the mores of a larger group or groups. Lewin in Jung, (1940), p. 55 views the married pair as the basic group, composed of two partners, who in turn are members of a larger group, the family, which in turn belongs to society, a still larger group.

CONCEPTS

There are three general concepts basic to the approach herein, namely, personality, interaction, and needs. The personality of the individual is the most basic element with which we are to be concerned. In addition, when we talk in terms of the family, we are concerned with more than just the individual's personality; here we must remain cognizant of the individual and his interaction with other family members and eventually with society at large. Last, in order for an individual to be able to cope adequately with others, at least a minimum of needs must be fulfilled. Therefore we can see that a breakdown of such needs is most relevant to the task at hand.

Personality: a whole embodying all of the physiological, psychological, and social characteristics of an individual. There is no way to separate or treat as a controlled variable any single component of the personality; therefore the personality must be viewed as a whole. This is characteristic of the holistic view of social psychology.[4]

Interaction: reciprocal action between two or more individuals. Self-concepts are crystallized by the individual through his interaction with others, especially as he perceives the manner in which he is regarded by others through the process of interaction.

Needs: wants, lacks, or demands which must be filled for the individual. In this paper we are concerned with psychological needs which seek to be fulfilled through interaction with others, especially within the family. Needs must be met in one manner or another, directly or indirectly, in order for the individual to function most effectively. Here we must remain cognizant of the individual and his interaction with other family members and eventually with society at large. Last, in order for an individual to be able to cope adequately with others, at least a minimum of needs must be fulfilled. Therefore we can see that a breakdown of such needs is most relevant to the task at hand.

Self-Concepts

In the area of self-concepts, five are basic to the social-psychological framework.

Individual: qualities which, according to Rogers (1961, p. 108),

---

[4] See Coleman, *Abnormal Psychology and Modern Life,* for definition of the "holistic" concept.

make each person unique among all others. Individuals are like snowflakes in that no two are alike. However, the individual will not necessarily make use of his uniqueness; the early environment, for example, is shaped to a large extent by the individual's family. The family's influence is thus seen as an antithesis to the unique aspects of the individual's personality. The family modifies the uniqueness of the individual so that the latter loses certain distinctive personality qualities. The family members often have a tendency to want the individual members to become more like themselves.

Self: a pattern of perceptions relating to the individual which is consciously recognized by the individual. The self-concept or self-structure is defined (Rogers and Dymond, 1954, p. 55) as an organized, conceptual pattern of the characteristics of the way the individual perceives himself and the way he believes others perceive him. The values attached to these perceptions of the self by the individual are also a part of the self.

Real feelings: those feelings which exist in each individual but are often not allowed to surface due to what other members of the family expect. Every individual has real feelings but these are often ignored, particularly where the individual desires to view another family member in a particular light. A relationship can exist on the basis of the real feelings, or on the basis of a defensive pretense. Most individuals utilize a defensive pretense rather than their real feelings. Each family member has ambivalent feelings toward other family members. Through the process of inhibition negative feelings are not allowed expression. Therefore the basis of an intrafamily relationship is often a defensive pretense rather than real (or what we might term *true*) feelings. When a relationship exists on a real-feeling basis, individuals find that negative feelings are not the only feelings they have toward other family members, (Rogers, 1961, p. 318). The ambivalence within our own real feelings is allowed to come to the forefront of consciousness through the recognition and acceptance of our real feelings.

Expressive feelings: feelings permitting some expression of true feelings. The individual family member, providing he has insight, can express his real feelings to other family members. When real feelings are granted expression, parents and children cease to hide their true personal feelings from each other (Rogers, 1961, p. 315). Individuals can come close to expressing the true feelings which exist within them through expressive feelings. However, due to our socialization, real feelings are never expressed completely. Our defense mechanisms will not allow us complete freedom of expression due to our inhibitions.

Two-way communication: the complete process of understanding another's thoughts and feelings as well as understanding the implications involved in such thoughts and feelings. (Rogers, 1961.) Likewise, the individual must also be thoroughly understood by the other, with the same implications. Though individuals have the capacity for two-way communication, it is rarely utilized because of the lack of insight on the individual's part as to how to obtain it. While two-way communication is rarely found in marriages, it is seen as one of the experiences which tend to solidify the family into an effective group.

The self-concept, that is, the manner in which the individual perceives himself as a person, is of importance because the individual must perceive of himself as an individual before he can perceive of himself as a family member. This—perception of one's self as an individual—involves the concept of a separate person, and other concepts such as the self, real feelings, expressive feelings, and two-way communication. Only through the utilization of these does the individual come to have a self-concept.

Interpersonal Concepts

Self-system: that part of the personality of the individual which serves as the anti-anxiety system. (Perry and Gawel, 1953, pp. 108–9.) This system is involved in a constant process of maintaining interpersonal security for the individual as he is involved in interpersonal acts. The self system thus becomes the "protector" of the individual, guarding the self from criticism or embarrassment. Because of its role as the personality's guardian from anxiety, the self system tends to become isolated from the rest of the personality. It is thus necessary for the individual to hold the self in high esteem, protecting it from criticism. It is this system that is transmitted originally from the mother to the infant. The self system may interfere with one's ability to live constructively with others.

Social relationship: (1) that interaction which occurs between two partners in a relationship and (2) those portions of each of the partner's personalities which are in any respect oriented to, or affected by, the personality of the other partner. (Huntington, 1958, p. 45.) The interaction of the personalities of both the husband and wife establish the social relationship within the marriage. It is the social relationship that is of primary concern within the marital relationship, because this relationship is composed of the interaction which takes place between the two married partners.

Personifications: those images which one individual holds of himself or of another person. Obviously these personifications may be positive or negative (Hall and Lindzey, 1957, p. 138), and commence with the infant as he perceives his own mother and later his father. This concept is directly related to the foregoing in that one's personifications are, in the marital union, derived from the social relationship.

"I": the response which the organism makes to the attitudes of others. The *I* concept has been greatly expounded by Mead. (Strauss, 1956, p. 242.) As far as action on the part of the individual is concerned, both the I as well as the me are involved. (Young, 1952, p. 164.) In the process of interaction the active I is affected by the various me's which the personality has taken from others. The I is essentially an actor and is perceived only in historical retrospect.

"Me": attitudes of others, as they are perceived by the individual. In overt or covert activity the attitudes of other persons which one assumes as factors influencing his own behavior will constitute the immediate me. (Young, 1952, p. 165.) After the I has acted, it immediately becomes part of the me.

The interpersonal area embraces concepts which extend the individual's personality beyond himself. This is the point of interaction between the individual and others in society, including the family members. Thus the self system, with its social relationships and personifications, aids the individual in understanding himself and others. The concepts *I* and *me* aid the individual not only in seeing himself as an individual but also in seeing himself as he feels others expect him to be.

Socialization process: the process which forces the individual to compromise between his own personal whims and impulses and the desires of the group. A given individual is a compromise between (1) the individual's own impulses and (2) the demands and interests of other people. These outside influences are brought to bear in a collective manner through the various institutions found within a society. Through the socialization process the individual takes on characteristics of the group. The family is perhaps the most important institution involved in the socialization process of the individual. This is due to the early associations with the family and their direct effect on the process of socialization within the individual.

Sociocultural determinants: this concept is derived from the interdependence between the individual and others. As such, it is directly related to the concept of socialization process. Society exerts a marked influence upon the individual, and the importance of this influence is such that the individual becomes an interdependent part of a system of human interaction rather than a completely unique individual. (Kluckhohn and Murray, 1953, p. 6:) The process of socialization is thus not left to the individual alone; rather, it is arrived at through sociocultural determinants. Again the family is most important in that it is one of the greatest influences on the individual.

Personology has a direct bearing on this framework in that it points out the major contribution of environmental factors as opposed to psychoanalytic theory, which largely ignores the environment of the individual. This contribution can be attributed, in the main, to Murray.

Style of life: that system by which the individual personality functions: the whole (of the personality) that commands the parts. (Adler, 1927.) Although everyone has a style of life, no two people have the same, as the style for an individual compensates for his particular inferiorities. The style of life is formulated by the age of four or five, according to Adler, who emphasizes the importance of the family because it influences the individual as he is formulating his particular style of life.

Social context: a complex of interpersonal relationships which help shape the personality for life. From the day of birth, the individual is engulfed in a social context. In order for his needs to be met, the individual soon finds that he must react in an acceptable manner. The first person with whom the individual finds himself in a social context is the mother. (Adler, 1929.) As the individual grows, his social context comes to include more and more people. It is through the influence of all these contacts that the individual comes to recognize the social context in which he must operate.

Social interest: interest for the welfare of the group. From the cooperation between the infant and the mother at the start of life, the individual becomes involved in a network of interpersonal relations which shape his personality. Adler further believed that social interest is inborn, that is, that it is a natural aptitude on the part of the individual. Although the basic ingredient is innate, it must be brought to fruition, at which time it replaces the selfish interest in favor of social interest. (Adler, 1929.) Through this process the individual becomes other-oriented and finds interest' and meaning in life beyond his own personality. This concept is more important to family solidarity.

Order of birth: the order in which the individual and his siblings are born. Adler believed that order of birth directly influenced the personalities of the individual children, with the oldest abhorring the idea of a rival, the middle child being ambitious, and the youngest spoiled. The youngest and oldest are more likely than the middle child to become problem children.

Basically, these concepts concerned with the individual establish him as one who can turn in and interact as a part of a larger entity, that is, society. Yet we must first come to terms with those concepts which establish one as an individual. Only then can we extend our understanding to the larger group such as the family, or, ultimately, to society.

Needs

Rather than be concerned with the basic needs as defined by such scholars as W. I. Thomas, we will be concerned with needs as a matter of intensity. The strength of a need is not always present in the same intensity nor is it an unvarying characteristic within an individual. (Murstein, 1961, p. 196.) Rather, any need will vary according to (1) where the individual is and (2) who is present in addition to the individual. Thus, while the following needs are generally found in all people, the degree to which they are present will depend in the main upon several factors, including the socialization of the individual and his method of interaction with others.

Love: the experience of deriving gratification for important psychic needs from a person of one's peer group of the opposite sex. The experience may be replaced by an expectation of deriving such gratification from another person other than a peer. (Winch and Ktsanes, 1954, p. 241.)

Need gratification: fulfillment of one's needs. All individuals have needs but all needs in individuals are seldom gratified. Every person seeks someone who will provide him with maximum need gratification. Since the needs between individuals are variable, various types of mates are needed in order to fulfill or gratify individual needs in any group. (Winch and Ktsanes, 1954, p. 242.)

Onlies: a concept developed by Terman to refer to children who were reared as only children, that is, those who have no siblings. (1938, p. 209.) Onlies have not been used to sharing with others in the home and have often been the center of attention. Marriage, which involves considerable sharing, can thus be a threatening experience for onlies, as Terman discovered. In this particular study, he found that marriages of two onlies, that is, where both the husband and wife were only children, are decidely worse than those marriages where only one partner is an only, as measured by the criterion of marital happiness.

Firm discipline: discipline which is firm but not harsh. Firm discipline allows the child to become cognizant of what he can expect in the interrelationship within the family. Firm and consistent discipline tends to be associated with marital happiness. (Terman, 1938, p. 299.) Permissive or overly harsh discipline appears to correlate negatively with marital happiness.

Achievement: approval-seeking behavior which originates in this earlier setting. The need for achievement is present in children but the means of achievement are quite different. The child needs to feel that there is one thing or one area in which he is unique. First-born children have a very high need for achievement. (Sampson, 1962, p. 157.) The source of this strong need for achievement in the oldest child is the intense dependent relationship which existed prior to the arrival of siblings.

Belonging: the feeling that one is a member of a group. When he feels that he is one of the group, then his need to belong has been met. The acceptance of others or the simple fact of being allowed to belong fulfill the need to avoid isolation and insecurity. (Winch, 1952, p. 174.)

Hostility: those feelings of anger within the individual which are laden with emotional overtones. These feelings lead to negative reaction on the individual's part and it is only a matter of how this negative reaction is to be discharged. The level of one's need to express hostility is relevant to the process of selecting a mate.

(Winch, 1958.) This touches on the complementary needs theory where a hostile person would be likely to marry one who would enjoy receiving expressions of hostility.

Orgasm: a sexual climax which relieves the emotional and physic energy stored in the individual. In Western culture marriage is the accepted outlet for the fulfillment of the need for orgasm in sexual relations. Wallin (1960, p. 194) found in females that the orgasm is associated with completeness of relief of the sexual needs. A lack of orgasm is seen as possibly but not necessarily frustrating. The preferred rate of intercourse was associated with the completeness of relief rather than with frequency of orgasm.

These needs are chosen because they are considered basic to the social-psychological framework where the family as an institution is concerned. Ultimately these needs must be fulfilled in a satisfactory manner in order for the individual to become other-oriented rather than remaining self-oriented.

BASIC ASSUMPTIONS

Basic assumptions underlying the social-psychological frame of reference as it concerns the family will be divided into (1) the self-concept, (2) personality interaction, and (3) needs theory. This seems necessary because, although each of these areas is a part of social psychology, each area utilizes a different approach to the family.

Self-Concept

1. All experiences cumulate within the life of the individual, affecting his total personality.
2. The individual calls on this totality of experience whenever he makes a decision or takes action in any manner.
3. Others play an important role in developing the inner perception one has concerning his own personality.
4. Each individual has the capacity of uniqueness.
5. Parents can retard or stimulate uniqueness in the child.
6. Family members as a group have a direct bearing on the individual's becoming a separate and distinct person.
7. The individual tends to be less of an individual and more of a family member due to pressures of the family group.
8. Two-way communication fulfills basic needs of the self.

Personality Interaction

1. Social determinants shape the personality.
2. The self system is innate, and no two self systems are identical.
3. Personifications, at least initially, depend on the parent-child relationship.
4. Outside influences are brought to bear in a collective manner through various institutions, chief of which is the family.
5. Individuals must compromise personal desires in order to become socially accepted.
6. Everyone has a unique style of life.
7. All of a person's behavior springs from his style of life.
8. The formative years in the life of an individual are the earliest years.
9. Social interest, while innate, is brought to full fruition only through guidance on the part of the family in early life.

Needs Theory

1. Children who have been raised with siblings have fewer adjustments to make in marriage than do only children.
2. Sibling attitudes will influence the degree of marital adjustment on the part of the individual.
3. Parents have a great deal to do with the child's childhood happiness.
4. The child's early associations, particularly in the family, have a direct bearing on the child's family of procreation.
5. Discipline within the home has an effect on the personality development of the child.
6. There is a basic psychological need for belonging.
7. This sense of belonging is often fulfilled through marriage.
8. Needs of the marriage partners are expressed in their interaction with each other. (Huntington, 1958, p. 45.)

Each of these three sets of assumptions is ordered from the most general to the most specific. Where it has been possible, the interrelatedness of one assumption with another has been indicated.

PRODUCT

The self-concept in social psychology has made significant contributions to the area of counseling. Although there has been little research on the self-concept and only a limited amount of theory formulated, much of the client-centered therapy in marriage counseling owes its existence to the self-concept framework. Professional counselors in the area of marriage and the family have been affected by this, although its impact has been felt more keenly in the area of pastoral counseling. Allport (1943), Hilgard (1953), and Rogers (1961), make broad use of the self-concept theory in allowing the individual family member to develop his own pattern of uniqueness through the counseling process.

Interpersonal theory has stressed chiefly the relationships between the individual and his social world. This theory is based on a Freudian tenet that the individual's formative years are the earliest years. Thus the importance of the family as the individual interacts with various family members has led to research in this area. Huntington (1958), Chance (1959), and Erikson (1950) have based much of their writing on this point, with the individual depicted as one of the characters in a drama which stars many people. The individual is thus one of the spokes, as are all other individuals within his social world, in the wheel which is society. The important product of this theory is that the individual cannot be understood, nor can he be studied outside of, or divorced from, his culture.

Needs theory has resulted in several pieces of research in the area of marriage and family living. Winch (1958), Winch and Ktsanes (1954), and Blazer (1963) have been but a few of those employing this frame of reference in studying the family. Complementary needs have been stressed, for example, where people marry mates who will fulfill certain needs in their own personalities. (Murstein, 1961.) One of the latest bodies of knowledge contributed from this field has been that of neurotic need-fulfillment within marriage. (Eisenstein, 1956.) Need-fulfillment in marriage is not necessarily viewed as positive *per se*, because the needs may be so seriously neurotic that a mate would have no realistic hope of ever fulfilling the neurotic requirements. This is a new approach to needs theory, and more research is needed in this field.

VALUES

The values of the social-psychological framework as it applies to the family have been gleaned from each of the three areas referred to above. In some instances the values will not be applicable to all areas under study.

1. The individual should be viewed within the framework of his

culture rather than separate from it for study purposes. Mead and Cooley, among others, expound this view. They feel that one's personality is intimately bound with one's culture. Therefore this school holds that it is better to view the individual within the framework of his culture.

2. Sociologists and social psychologists agree that the family is the most important social unit. Adler sees the individual as maturing through his contacts with others. Since this process commences with the relationships within the family, the family has more influence on the formative years of the personality than any other group. Thus great value is attached to the family in the shaping of the personality.

3. Counseling and/or therapy is the best approach in helping the individual to become less defensive and less concerned with protecting the self. Rogers (1961, p. 325) places great value on this because he feels that the individual can thus be aided in achieving a better adjustment within his environment, primarily with other members of his family.

4. Novel experience is desirable in human behavior. Individuals tend to become group-minded rather than individual in their thinking and acting. The different behavior patterns are desirable because individuals are thus encouraged to develop individually rather than as a part of a larger unit, that is, the group.

5. Compromise is the best manner in which to develop as a member of a larger group. Because man is civilized, individualistic behavior cannot always be given full freedom. Some sort of check seems desirable and this comes about through compromise as the individual adapts himself to the group.

6. Making use of guidance clinics is to be preferred to waiting for spontaneous developing of social interest in the individual. These guidance clinics are thus means of aiding the individual in adjusting. Adler (1929) spent much of his time developing guidance centers which, in addition to personal help they provided, served to educate the public to the validity of this approach in promoting personality development and healthy social functioning.

7. Marriage is to be preferred to remaining single because marriage meets certain basic needs in man that no other institution can fulfill. Basic studies which tend to uphold this view include those of Winch (1957), Winch and Ktsanes (1954), and Blazer (1963).

8. Membership in a group is to be valued above maintaining complete individuality. Group membership aids one in developing

socially acceptable roles. Interpersonal relationships which are very important to society are refined and learned only through contact with other members of a group.

9. A happy home is to be preferred over an unhappy one. Studies have shown that the happy home, if experienced in childhood, is positively correlated with successful marriage. (Terman, 1938, p. 237.) The impression gained from one's childhood home is lasting and apparently influences to no small degree the success one will achieve when one marries.

THE FRAMEWORK

The basic tenet of the family theorists who use the social-psychological framework is the importance of the role of social variables in shaping the personality. (Hall and Lindzey, 1957, p. 151.) Freud emphasized biological dimensions in the development of personality, which are important to the family, but social psychologists have added social factors. There is a certain amount of overlapping between the Freudian approach and this approach of the social psychologists. Indeed, the social psychologists built on Freud's theories, adding the social dimension to the importance of personality development.

Individuals and societies are also seen as flexible because they are capable of growing and expanding to include new and different stimuli. The family is thus seen not as a static institution, but rather as one that is malleable. It is those families and groups which allow for the individual growth within their confines that are most successful in serving both the individual and society.

The view that all individuals are unique is another belief of the social psychologists. Each person is seen as having unique drives, needs, and so on. Thus it is necessary that the family allow within its structure room for the development of those unique attributes discernible in each individual.

The family is, in addition, viewed as an interdependent unit composed of several individuals. The family does not exist as a group because of its comradeship, but rather because of the degree of interdependence among the family members. The family is thus solidified by the interdependence of the roles played by all family members.

Social psychologists assume that it is impossible to study the family apart from its immediate environment. This same logic applies to the individual. It is felt that culture and personality are connected in such a manner that we are destroying the true perspective of the picture when we attempt to isolate either from the other for purposes of study. The family, because of its interdependence on the separate members of the unit and also because of its interdependence on the culture in which it exists, can only be seen in its true perspective when it is studied in its interrelationship to other individuals and groups.

Man is viewed by the social psychologist as innately a social being, and it is only through the process of learning that he acquires anxiety and fear. This principle is opposite that which was expounded by Freud, that is, that man is innately destructive. If we could meet all of man's needs when they arise, according to the social psychologists, there would be no reason for frustration and man would become basically social.

CRITIQUE AND DISCUSSION

The position of the social psychologists in the area of family theory has been not to disclaim Freudian theory *per se*, but to build on it by adding the social dimension. The family has been studied as a social unit rather than as a sum of purely biological individuals. The social determinants are thus seen to be important in shaping the family as a unit, in that these social determinants are chief among those approaches which lead to an understanding of interpersonal behavior.

One of the most important contributions of this approach has been the stressing of the social-psychological needs as they are met within marriage and the family. The meeting of these needs is seen as a prerequisite to the continuation of the family as a unit.[5] That all needs are not healthy needs has also been stressed (Eisenstein, 1956); however, the point emphasized here is that the marriage and/or the family should meet the needs as they arise within the individual. More research seems indicated in this area because only meager empirical data have been accumulated thus far. It would seem that larger samples are necessary and that more objective means are needed in order to discover and measure needs and their intensity within a given marriage or family setting.

Critics have stated that the social-psychological approach has added nothing to Freudian theory and that by dwelling upon the social character of the personality it has tended to alienate man from

[5] See Merton's concept of *functional prerequisites*.

his biological heritage. (Hall and Lindzey, 1957, p. 154.) Such criticism is perhaps justified in some respects, yet, conversely, Freudian psychology can be criticized for not sufficiently stressing the importance of social determinants in shaping the personality and the personality's importance in interaction between persons and other institutions. In this respect we might say that both theories are lacking because neither embraces enough of what the other has to offer. A synthesis of the two theories is therefore indicated and, if accomplished, would obviate the need for such criticisms.

In the area of marriage and the family, social psychology as delineated here has not been responsible for a large amount of research to verify its theories. Research in this area has been sparse and there is a great need for more research before this field can make any dramatic new steps in regard to personality, marriage, and the family.

Because so many different areas of interest have mushroomed forth within social psychology, it is impossible for us to interrelate all of them in a paper such as this. Our selection has been limited to four—interpersonal psychology, individual psychology, needs, and self-concept—but there is a need for more extensive work in connecting the many individual theories into one cohesive theory. That there is great value in the social-psychological approach is not to be denied, but some sort of clarification of the individual approaches into broad areas is definitely needed in order to make more complete use of the social-psychological approach as it relates to concepts and theories concerning the family.

REFERENCES

ACKERMAN, NATHANIEL. *The Psychodynamics of Family Living: Diagnosis and Treatment of Family Relationships.* New York: Basic Books, Inc., Publishers, 1958.
ADLER, ALFRED. "Individual Psychology," in C. Murchison, ed. *Psychologies of 1930.* Worcester, Mass.: Clark University Press, 1930, pp. 395–405.
———. *Problems of Neurosis.* London: Kegan, Paul Trench & Co., 1929.
———. *The Practice and Theory of Individual Psychology.* New York: Harcourt, Brace & World, Inc., 1927.
ALLPORT, GORDON W. "The Ego in Contemporary Psychology," *Psychological Review,* 50 (Sept. 1943), pp. 451–78.
BLAZER, JOHN A. "Complementary Needs and Marital Happiness," *Mar-*

riage and Family Living, **25** (Feb. 1963), pp. 89–95. A study relating the fulfillment of needs as this fulfillment leads to greater marital happiness.

CHANCE, ERIKA. *Families in Treatment*. New York: Basic Books, Inc., Publishers, 1959. A thorough approach to family growth as a product of treatment received with the aid of professional help.

CHRISTENSEN, HAROLD T., ed. *Handbook of Marriage and the Family*. Chicago: Rand McNally & Company, 1964. A particularly notable discussion is the chapter by Edward Z. Dager, "Socialization and Personality Development in the Child," pp. 740–81.

COLEMAN, JAMES C. *Abnormal Psychology and Modern Life*. Chicago: Scott, Foresman and Company, 1956.

DENNIS, WAYNE, ed. *Current Trends in Social Psychology*. Pittsburgh: The University of Pittsburgh Press, 1947.

EISENSTEIN, VICTOR W., ed. *Neurotic Interaction in Marriage*. New York: Basic Books, Inc., Publisher, 1956. A study of neurotic needs as they are met or denied in the marital relationship.

ERIKSON, ERIK H. *Childhood and Society*. New York: W. W. Norton & Company, Inc., 1950.

FROMM, E. *Escape from Freedom*. New York: Holt, Rinehart and Winston, Inc., 1941.

HALL, CALVIN S., and LINDZEY, GARDNER. *Theories of Personality*. New York: John Wiley & Sons, Inc., 1957. A study of the contributions and inadequacies of the major contributors to personality theory.

HESS, R. D., and HANDEL, G. *Family Worlds: A Psychosocial Approach to Family Life*. Chicago: The University of Chicago Press, 1959.

HILGARD, ERNEST R. *Introduction to Psychology*. New York: Harcourt, Brace & World, Inc., 1953. An introductory psychology text which describes the various psychological approaches and schools by defining the problems with which they are chiefly concerned.

HORNEY, KAREN. *Our Inner Conflicts*. New York: W. W. Norton & Company, Inc., 1945.

HUNTINGTON, ROBERT M. "New Approaches in Family Research: A Symposium; the Personality-Interaction Approach to Study of the Marital Relationship," *Marriage and Family Living*, **20** (Feb. 1958), pp. 43–46. A study of the interaction of personalities within the confines of marriage and the manner in which this interaction affects the marriage.

JUNG, MOSES, ed. *Modern Marriage*. New York: Appleton-Century-Crofts, 1940. Contains a chapter by Kurt Lewin of special interest for its description of the basic tenets of "field theory" as applied to marriage in a comprehensive manner.

KLUCKHOHN, CLYDE, and MURRAY, HENRY A., eds. *Personality in Nature, Society and Culture*. New York: Alfred A. Knopf, Inc., 1953.

KRECH, DAVID, and CRUTCHFIELD, R. S. *Theory and Problems of Social Psychology.* New York: McGraw-Hill, Inc., 1948.

LINDZEY, GARDNER, ed. *Handbook of Social Psychology,* Vol. 1. Reading, Mass.: Addison-Wesley Publishing Company, Inc., 1954.

MCDOUGALL, WILLIAM. *The Group Mind.* New York: G. P. Putnam's Sons, 1908. One of the earliest works to treat social psychology from the psychological viewpoint.

MURSTEIN, BERNARD I. "The Complementary Need Hypothesis in Newly-weds and Middle-Aged Married Couples," *Journal of Abnormal and Social Psychology,* **63** (July 1961), pp. 194–97. Another one of the few studies on need theory as it relates to the family, especially to marriage.

MURRAY, H. A., *et al. Explorations in Personality.* New York: Oxford University Press, Inc., 1938.

NEWCOMB, T. M. *Social Psychology.* New York: The Dryden Press, Inc., 1950.

PARSONS, TALCOTT, and BALES, ROBERT F. *Family, Socialization and Interaction Process.* New York: Free Press of Glencoe, Inc., 1955.

PERRY, HELEN S., and GAWEL, MARY L., eds. *The Interpersonal Theory of Psychiatry.* New York: W. W. Norton & Company, Inc., 1953.

ROGERS, CARL R. *On Becoming A Person: A Therapist's View of Psychotherapy.* Boston: Houghton Mifflin Company, 1961. A clear picture of how Rogers views the value of therapy in bringing about change in family members in their inter-relationships.

———, and DYMOND, ROSALIND F., eds. *Psychotherapy and Personality Change.* Chicago: The University of Chicago Press, 1954.

ROSS, E. A. *Social Psychology.* New York: The Macmillan Company, 1914. One of the earliest works to treat social psychology from the viewpoint of the discipline of sociology.

SAMPSON, EDWARD E. "Birth Order, Need Achievement, and Conformity," *Journal of Abnormal and Social Psychology,* **64** (Feb. 1962), pp. 155–59. A discussion of the different needs that are associated with the birth order of the individual and the manner in which they are met.

STRAUSS, ANSELM, ed. *The Social Psychology of George Herbert Mead.* Chicago: The University of Chicago Press, 1956. A thorough study of Mead's approach to social psychology, his concepts, and basic theories.

SULLIVAN, HARRY S. *The Interpersonal Theory of Psychiatry.* New York: W. W. Norton & Company, Inc., 1953.

TERMAN, LEWIS M. *Psychological Factors in Marital Happiness.* New York: McGraw-Hill, Inc., 1938. One of the first studies to stress the family of orientation as a crucial variable in the development of the family of procreation as a compatible unit.

WALLER, WILLARD, and HILL, REUBEN. *The Family: A Dynamic Interpretation.* New York: The Dryden Press, Inc., 1938.

Wallin, Paul. "A Study of Orgasm as a Condition of Women's Enjoyment of Intercourse," *Journal of Social Psychology*, 51 (Feb. 1960), pp. 191–98.

Winch, Robert F. *Mate Selection: A Study of Complementary Needs.* New York: Harper & Row, Publishers, 1958.

———. *The Modern Family.* New York: Holt, Rinehart & Winston, Inc., 1952.

———, and Ktsanes, Thomas and Virginia. "The Theory of Complementary Needs in Mate-Selection: An Analytic and Descriptive Study," *American Sociological Review*, 19 (June 1954), pp. 241–49.

———, and McGinnis, Robert, eds. *Selected Studies in Marriage and the Family.* New York: Holt, Rinehart & Winston, Inc., 1953.

Young, Kimball. *Personality and Problems of Adjustment.* New York: Appleton-Century-Crofts, 1952. A complete, detailed book on personality theory: how it is organized and the concepts utilized by social psychologists in working from this frame of reference.

Zimmerman, Carle C. *Family and Civilization.* New York: Harper & Row, Publishers, 1947.

chapter 9

The Developmental Conceptual Framework to the Study of the Family*

George P. Rowe

The developmental framework for the study of the family has been the only approach consciously formulated by students of the family in advance of research it seeks to organize. Hill and Hansen (1960) suggested that although this new approach is not precisely unique, it has attempted to transcend the boundaries of several approaches through the incorporation of their compatible sections into one unified scheme.

This framework joins the social-system approach with the closely related ideas of structure-function and the social-psychological recognition that we are dealing with dynamic persons who are both family members and individuals at the same time. Through the efforts of Hill and his students, a synthesis of these concepts has emerged into a view of the family as a "semi-closed system of interacting personalities." (Hill and Rodgers, 1964, p. 178.) To unfreeze

* Grateful acknowledgment is made of the contribution of Roy H. Rodgers who served as editorial consultant for this framework and who read and critically reviewed the manuscript prior to its final revision. Many, although not all, of his suggestions have been incorporated into the final manuscript. Inadequacies and errors in the chapter as published, however, are entirely the responsibility of the author and the editors.

these interactional processes, the social time dimension was added to focus attention on the longitudinal career of the family system— the family life cycle. The family member and the family as a unit as they advance through the various stages of the family life cycle confront certain role expectations which have been called *developmental tasks*. The better equipped a family is for each of its members to meet his developmental tasks and the more closely the family accomplishes its group tasks, the more successful is the development of the family.

To describe the origins of this interdisciplinary approach, it is necessary to acknowledge the source of the theoretical concepts that have contributed to its inception. Rural sociologists first utilized the concept of the family life cycle. As early as 1931 Sorokin, Zimmerman, and Galpin constructed a four-stage family life cycle. Kirkpatrick, Tough, and Cowles (1934) treated the family cycle from the standpoint of the age and growth of children. Home economists have applied this concept for some time in the stress of long-time planning in the use of both human and material resources to meet anticipated requirements in the course of family history.

The concept of developmental tasks had its roots in Freudian psychology. Drawing heavily on the earlier works of Freud, Sullivan, and Erikson but keeping within the framework of human development, Havighurst (1948) was the first to formulate developmental tasks for each stage in the life cycle of the individual from birth to old age. Developmental tasks for both parents and children were first specified for each stage of the family life cycle by the Committee on the Dynamics of Family Interaction at the 1948 National Conference on Family Life. (Duvall and Hill, 1948.) Developmental tasks for the family as a whole were introduced in the First Interdisciplinary Workshop on Marriage and Family Research held at the University of Chicago in 1950. (Duvall, 1957, p. 521.)

From structure-functional theory in sociology and anthropology arose the concept that families must fulfill functional prerequisites for survival, continuation, and growth. (Parsons, 1949, pp. 6–7.) The family as a social system is organized to meet these functions, and some of the functional prerequisites were later incorporated into family developmental tasks.

Symbolic interaction theory has been applied to the study of the family largely as a result of the early work of Burgess (1926) who pictured the family as a "unity of interacting personalities." His emphasis on personality in symbolic interaction has been extended to encompass the individual and family careers. The concepts of *role* and *position* have been given a longitudinal dimension to explain the dynamics of internal family behavior.

Duvall (1957) was the first person to put together these interrelated concepts and compatible research into a textbook, *Family Development*. Taking advantage of her personal involvement in earlier workshops and conferences, she tried to consolidate rather than to extend the conceptual framework. Rodgers (1962) in his Ph.D. dissertation under Hill stated that his first objective was to "bring together into a more consistent body a set of concepts which may be utilized to analyze the family developmentally." He accomplished this by making use of role theory to delineate family change in detail. Furthermore, he went to considerable effort to devise a new set of *family–life–cycle categories* (his term for *stages*) to test his conceptual framework. More recently Hill joined with Rodgers to write a chapter in Christensen's handbook (1964) entitled "The Developmental Approach." This attempt without a doubt is the most comprehensive treatment to date.

FOCI OF STUDY

Although no comprehensive empirical test has been made of the family-development approach, as Hill and Rodgers have reminded us (1964), the major focus appears to be on the change in the process of internal family development viewed microanalytically with the dimension of time being central. The family is first seen as a semiclosed system engaged in interactive behavior within the system.

In the research literature most studies focus on only a particular segment of the family life cycle, attempting to describe specific characteristics of a stage with reference to past stages and implications for those yet ahead. Representative studies reflecting the analysis of a particular phase of the family life cycle will be briefly outlined.

Burgess and Wallin (1953) studied young married couples three to five years after the start of marriage. They found very little evidence of disillusionment since the couples' first interviews during engagement. On the other hand, both LeMasters (1957) and Dyer (1963) found that intrafamily crises resulted with the addition of the first child. LeMasters concluded, however, that all but a few couples eventually made a successful adjustment to parenthood, sug·

gesting a developmental process in this transition into the child-centered triad family system.

Changing relationships of parents and children at successive stages of the cycle of family development often result in conflict between the generations. (Rockwood, 1952.) McArthur (1962) reported that a parent-youth conflict sometimes arises from difficulties both encounter in accomplishing their respective developmental tasks simultaneously.

Husband-wife relationships likewise change with time. When child–rearing pressures have diminished the husband-wife dyad takes on increased significance. Deutscher (1962) listed the kinds of socialization experiences that prepared couples for postparental life. Foote (1963) stated that if either a husband or wife lags in his personality development relative to the other, serious mismatching could occur, particularly when the children are launched. Streib (1958) and Thompson (1958) demonstrated the relationship between preretirement anticipation and adjustment to the family patterns in retirement.

Other studies have tried to embody the entire family life span in analysis. Blood and Wolfe (1960) have constructed longitudinal family change by means of cross-sectional data. That is, they sampled families at various stages of the family life cycle and presented their findings to give a picture of change throughout the family career. They used family life cycle stages to explain variation in the values of parenthood, satisfaction with companionship and love of spouse, and the tenor of husband-wife interaction. Rodgers (1962), employing the method of historical retrospect, presented longitudinal design by comparing three generations of the same extended family system from their formation to the time of the study. Grandparent families furnished data for over forty years. Feldman (1963) through cross-sectional investigation found three points in the family life cycle requiring the greatest amount of reorganization: when the first child is born, when the last child enters school, and when the last child leaves home. Treating the husband–wife relationship as the dependent variable, he is presently investigating the transition into parenthood by interviewing both marital partners at three time intervals: the second trimester of pregnancy, the end of the neonatal period, and during the child's fifth month of life.

The focus of family–development research reviewed up to this point has been on internal family dynamics as a consequence of interactional situations within the family system. A second kind of family dynamics results from transactional situations external to the family system. Although Bell and Vogel (1960) suggested that much research employs the family life cycle as an independent demographic variable without considering dynamic developmental processes, the interrelatedness of the family system with other social systems has, nevertheless, been found to be significant.

Kirkpatrick, *et al.* (1934) explained the standard of living by particular stages of the family life cycle. Lansing and Kish (1957) accounted for spending patterns by treating the family life cycle as the independent variable. Agan (1950), Bigelow (1950), and Foote, *et al.* (1960) considered the family life cycle as independent in transactional behavior, but they also attempted to capture internal family dynamics.

In order to compare secular changes in family practice from one generation to another and between different segments of the population, norms have been established for the various stages of the family life cycle. Lively (1932) compared secular trends of older and younger farm families in Ohio. By the use of census figures, Glick (1957) depicted modal families at various stages since 1890. Glick, Heer, and Beresford (1963) have used such information as age at marriage, the rate of new household formation, the number of children, and other demographic data to predict family composition and age to 1980.

CONCEPTS

Development

The concept of *development* will first be treated as it applies to the family as we define and illustrate the interrelated concepts that compose the developmental approach. Although *development* is used in many scientific disciplines, the most abstract definition, according to Harris (1957, p. 10), is that it is a process which occurs in an organism or a living structure over an extension of time.

In human development much is known about the functioning of the organism as it moves forward through life. Changes occur by processes within and by interaction with the environment. The organism both responds to and evokes what it needs from the environment. (Frank, 1955.)

Just as an individual family member grows, develops, matures, and ages while undergoing the successive changes and readjustments from conception to senescence, so the family has a sequence from formation through expansion and contraction to dissolution. The successful development of the family is contingent upon the satisfactory accomplishments of biological requirements, cultural imperatives, and personal aspirations and values if the family is to continue to develop as a unit. (Hill, 1951.) Family development is inherently bound up in the satisfaction of the needs and desires of members to make it possible for them to grow to maturity. To progress as a unit the family develops to the extent that reciprocal interaction patterns emerge to fulfill the individual's continuously changing needs and desires.

The Family as a Unity of Interacting Personalities

To account for family process Burgess' concept of visualizing the family as a unity of interacting personalities is an indispensible element of the developmental framework. Bossard (1945, p. 293) mathematically defined the family interaction pattern as a "law of family interaction."[1] Frank (in Duvall and Hill, 1948) stated that the number of interacting processes can be separately named and discussed, but they are difficult to dissociate in the study of family living.

The Family as a Semi-closed System

Rodgers (1964, p. 264) advanced the definition of the family as a semi-closed system which he believes reflects Hill's thinking and is representative of the family development literature:

1. The family is not entirely independent of other social systems, neither is it wholly dependent, thus it is a semi-closed system.
2. The family as a small group system is interrelated in such a manner that change does not occur in one part without a series of resultant changes in other parts.
3. The family is composed of dynamic persons who are both

[1] The law of family interaction states that $X = \dfrac{Y^2 - Y}{2}$ with X equal to the number of interpersonal relationships and Y equal to the number of persons (positions) in the family structure. The formula demonstrates that with the addition of a person to the family, the number of relationships increases in the order of triangular numbers and declines inversely when a family member departs.

group members and individuals, and, therefore, changes in both group relationships and individual personality factors must be taken into account.

Position, Role, and Norm

The well-known concepts of position, role, and norm will be defined in the context of the family–development framework as formulated by Hill and Rodgers (1964). *Position* refers to the location of the family member in the family structure. In the American nuclear family these positions could be husband-father, wife-mother, son-brother, and daughter-sister. A *role* is the dynamic part of a position defined by the norms of the culture. Each position contains a number of dominant and recessive roles related reciprocally to at least one role in each of the other family–member positions. Typical roles for adults in the family are mothering, expressing affection, disciplining, homemaking, and providing financial resources. Children's roles include, among many others, sharing household responsibilities, studying, consuming, and taking part in recreation. A *norm* is a behavioral expectation commonly shared by family members. An almost universal norm in American middle-class society is for the husband-father to be a breadwinner.

The concepts of *position* and *role* have been given longitudinal dimensions to trace family change through time. Rodgers (1962, p. 44) defined *role sequence* as the longitudinal character of a single role and he defined *positional career* as the longitudinal history of an individual family position composed of an ever–changing cluster of roles. The *family career* is viewed as the longitudinal expression of the role complex of the family structure as it develops.

Developmental Tasks

The family role pattern constantly changes with the addition and departure of members and with the emergence of new norms (role expectations) called *developmental tasks*.

A developmental task has been conceptualized as midway between a human need on the one hand and cultural demands on the other, taking into consideration physiological maturation and readiness for learning. (Havighurst, 1956.) Using the development foundation laid by Erikson (1950), Havighurst was the first to present a published definition: "A developmental task is a task which arises at or about a certain period in the life of an individual, successful achievement of which leads to his happiness and success with later tasks while failure leads to unhappiness in the individual, disapproval by society and difficulty with later tasks." (1948, p. 6.)

Tryon and Lilienthal (1950) specified ten ever-changing individual developmental tasks from birth to late adolescence.[2] Duvall (1957) carried these tasks into old age. Pikunas and Albrecht (1961) have constructed a rather detailed outline of tasks at the different life stages. Utilizing concepts from role theory, Rodgers offered this definition:

A developmental task is a set of norms (role expectations) arising at a particular point in the career of a position in a social system, which, if incorporated by the occupant of the position as a role or part of a role cluster, brings about integration and temporary equilibrium in the system with regard to a role complex or set of role complexes; failure to incorporate the norms leads to lack of integration, application of additional normative pressures in the form of sanctions, and difficulty in incorporating later norms into the role cluster of the position. (1962, p. 55.)

The importance of this concept for family development is the realization that developmental tasks are faced by family members who are simultaneously at different stages of human development. Adults, moreover, who are fulfilling the role of parents will have additional developmental tasks relating specifically to parent-child relationships that are not present in the family without children. Changing developmental tasks for both children and parents were carefully worked out for each stage of the family cycle at the National Conference on Family Life (Duvall and Hill, 1948) and have subsequently been presented in more detail by Duvall (1957, 1962).

[2] Ten ever-changing developmental tasks:
1. Achieving an appropriate dependence-independence pattern.
2. Achieving an appropriate giving-receiving pattern of affection.
3. Relating to changing social groups.
4. Developing a conscience.
5. Learning one's psycho-socio-biological sex role.
6. Accepting and adjusting to a changing body.
7. Managing a changing body and learning new motor patterns.
8. Learning to understand and control the physical world.
9. Developing an appropriate symbol system and conceptual abilities.
10. Relating one's self to the cosmos.

Not only do family members undertake individual tasks, but the family as a whole is confronted with certain responsibilities that are necessary for continuous growth and development. Duvall defined *family developmental tasks* as "growth responsibilities that arise at a certain stage in the life of a family, successful achievement of which leads to satisfaction and success with later tasks, while failure leads to unhappiness in the family, disapproval by society, and difficulty with later family developmental tasks." (1962, p. 45.)

Duvall listed nine ever-changing family developmental tasks that span the family life cycle. (1958, p. 336.) They are to establish and maintain:

1. An independent home.
2. Satisfactory ways of getting and spending money.
3. Mutually acceptable patterns in the division of labor.
4. Continuity of mutually satisfying sex relationships.
5. Open system of intellectual and emotional communication.
6. Workable relationships with relatives.
7. Ways of interacting with associates and community organizations.
8. Competency in bearing and rearing children.
9. A workable philosophy of life.

Family Life Cycle

According to Christensen (1964, p. 22) the point of departure in the developmental framework is the concept of the *family life cycle* which has been termed *family career* by Rodgers (1962) and Farber (1962). In this cycle of family development, stages or categories have been conveniently delineated for purposes of study. The demarcation of one stage from the next is determined by the amount of transition which is required in the family by a particular event. Just as the individual passes through certain stages in the human life cycle the family progresses through critical transitional phases based on changes in plurality patterns, the age of the oldest child, the school placement of the oldest child, and the functions and status of the family before children arrive and after they depart from the home. (Duvall and Hill, 1948.)

Numerous attempts have been made to delineate the stages of the family life cycle but in general there have been two broad divisions —expansion and contraction. During the expansion period children are born and reared. As children become emancipated the complexion of family life changes by a gradual diminishing of attention toward children with the emphasis turning to the married pair itself. As they advance through the middle years to retirement and finally senescence, one of the original pair will die, causing readjustment for the remaining partner. The cycle of family life terminates on the death of the surviving spouse.

Table I traces the trend in definitions of the stages of the family life cycle since 1931. The first systematic attempt in recent years was undertaken by the Committee on the Dynamics of Family Interaction preparatory to the National Conference on Family Life, with Duvall and Hill serving as cochairmen. The age and role of the oldest child was used as the criteria in the expansion phase through Stage V. Then in Stage VI the crucial family members become those remaining at home, generally the youngest children. During Stage VII emphasis again returns to the married couple as it was in Stage I. Duvall (1957, p. 8), recognizing the increased life expectancy, added Stage VIII to depict aging couples from the retirement of the breadwinner(s) to the death of one or both spouses. Duvall explained the obvious overlapping of stages in multi-child families: "A family grows through a stage with its oldest child and in a sense repeats as subsequent children come along." (1957, p. 9.)

Feldman (1961) followed somewhat the eight stages formulated by Duvall but added three stages for childless couples to correspond to the stages of families in the childbearing, child–rearing, and old age stages respectively. Unsatisfied with Duvall's classification, Rodgers (1962) devised a twenty-four category family-life cycle giving attention not only to the oldest child but also accounting for changes in the position of the youngest family member. Trying to provide for important role-complex changes he inserted a category for the young adult before the stage of the launching family and added at the end of the cycle the category of widowhood.

Of course, there have been other convenient ways to differentiate the stages in the family life cycle. Nelson presented variations in the family life cycle schema that have developed within the discipline of rural sociology. (1955, pp. 307–12.) Cavan (1953) has extended the family life cycle forward to encompass the premarital period of the couple. Whatever schema is used for defining the stages, however, it is merely a classification for purposes of analysis. According to Duvall, "the genius of the concept is the explicit awareness that each

TABLE I
Delineations of Stages in the Family Life Cycle

FAMILY CYCLE STAGE	SOROKIN, ZIMMERMAN, AND GILPIN (1931)	NATIONAL CONFERENCE ON FAMILY LIFE (1948)	DUVALL (1957, p. 8)	FELDMAN* (1961, p. 6)	RODGERS (1962, pp. 64-65)
I	Starting married couple	Couple without children	Couple without children	Early marriage (childless)	Childless couple
II	Couple with one or more children	Oldest child less than 30 months	Oldest child less than 30 months	Oldest child an infant	All children less than 36 months
III		Oldest child from 2½ to 5	Oldest child from 2½ to 6	Oldest child at preschool age	Preschool family with (a) oldest 3-6 and youngest under 3; (b) all children 3-6
IV		Oldest child from 5 to 12	Oldest child from 6 to 13	All children school age	School-age family with (a) infants, (b) preschoolers, (c) all children 6-13
V		Oldest child from 13 to 19	Oldest child from 13 to 20	Oldest child a teenager, all others in school	Teenage family with (a) infants, (b) preschoolers, (c) school-agers, (d) all children 13-20
VI	(III) One or more self - supporting children	When first child leaves till last is gone	When first child leaves till last is gone	One or more children at home and one or more out of the home	Young adult family with (a) infants, (b) preschoolers, (c) school-agers, (d) teenagers, (e) all children over 20

FAMILY CYCLE STAGE	SOROKIN, ZIMMERMAN, AND GILPIN (1931)	NATIONAL CONFERENCE ON FAMILY LIFE (1948)	DUVAL (1957, p. 8)	FELDMAN* (1961, p. 6)	RODGERS (1962, pp. 64–65)
VII	(IV) Couple getting old with all children out	Later years	Empty nest to retirement	All children out of home	Launching family with (a) infants, (b) preschoolers, (c) schoolagers, (d) teenagers, (e) youngest child over 20
VIII				Elderly couple	When all children have been launched until retirement
IX			Retirement to death of one or both spouses		Retirement until death of one spouse
X					Death of first spouse to death of the survivor

* Feldman enumerates Stages IX, X, and XI to classify childless families to correspond to families with children in the stages of childbearing, childrearing, empty nest, and old age (Stages II to VIII).

stage has its beginnings in the phases that are past and its fruition in development yet to come." (1957, p. 7.)

BASIC ASSUMPTIONS

There are a number of underlying assumptions that need to be made explicit for an understanding of family development.

1. First of all, the family is defined as a nuclear or conjugal unit, a family of procreation from the wedding until the last spouse is deceased. It has generally been assumed that the family will have children either through actual birth or adoption to parallel the modal family in the United States.

2. Families and individuals change and develop in different ways according to the living process from within and stimulation by the social milieu. (Hill and Hansen, 1960.) There are certain individual and family developmental tasks that must be completed to facilitate mastery of other tasks currently being attempted, and they create readiness for succeeding tasks.

3. Developmental tasks are looked upon as strivings for a goal rather than specific jobs to be completed at once. The accomplishment of developmental tasks is "not looked upon as an all-or-none proposition. Seldom in the family cycle are all its members 'caught up' with themselves and with what is required of them." (Kenkel, 1960.)

4. The basic focus is on the individual actor within the family setting. Although the family system as a whole is important with the impingement of normative pressures, it is dependent on the actions and reactions of its members. (Hill and Hansen, 1960.)

5. Each individual family member and each family is unique in its complex of age–role expectations in reciprocity. (Hill and Rodgers, 1964.) Families vary widely as to the number of positions, age composition, and occupational status of the breadwinner(s). For example, a man currently around thirty with a wife still in her twenties could have been married long enough to be in the teen–age stage of the family life cycle. On the other hand, a man of forty may marry a woman somewhat younger. The couple will be in their fifties before they reach the teen–age stage (provided they have children).

6. Human conduct is best seen as the function of the preceeding as well as the current social milieu. (Hill and Hansen, 1960.) The family as a social system is affected by its relationship with external

social systems which require different kinds of transactive behavior at different stages of the family life cycle.

PRODUCT

The developmental frame of reference has been applied to an orientation of child–rearing. Duvall (1946) has drawn a distinction between developmental and traditional conceptions of parenthood. *Developmental* parenthood includes respect for individual family members, satisfactions in personal interaction, pride in the growth and development of children, and the provision of a permissive, growth-promoting type of guidance. In contrast, the *traditional* conception attempts to make children conform to patterns of being neat, clean, obedient, respectful, polite, and socially acceptable. Duvall has stated that developmentalism, the concern for wholesome development of the human personality, has increased in recent years. (1962, p. 116.) "Developmentalism does not imply unrestrained permissiveness, but rather the kind of setting that is conducive to optimal development with the freedom and controls that are good to grow in, both as parents and as children."

Elder (1949) applied this dichotomy to the study of fatherhood; Connor, Green, and Walters (1958) extended the framework to investigate conceptions of mother, father, and children as held by each family member respectively.

The biggest implication of the developmental framework is the growing recognition in research that the measurement of family development precludes longitudinal design. To overcome the practical difficulties of following the same group of families through their entire life cycle of fifty years or so, Hill and Rodgers (1964) enumerated five alternatives that have been tried.

First of all they indicated that a synthetic pattern of development constructed from cross-sectional data has been the most frequent but least defensible of the compromises in current use. Recent studies employing the cross-sectional method have been reported by Lansing and Kish (1957), Foote, *et al.* (1960), Blood and Wolfe (1960), and Feldman (1961).

The second alternative has been termed *retrospective history-taking* to reconstruct family history through the device of recall. Cowles (1953) secured data through a good part of the family cycle by interviewing farm couples in completed families (that is, in which the wife was past the child-bearing age). More recently Rodgers

(1962) used this technique in his intergenerational study in the Minneapolis-St. Paul area.

There have been a number of segmented longitudinal studies to test hypotheses about family change at selected developmental stages in the family life cycle. LeMasters (1957), Streib (1958), Thompson (1958), Deutscher (1962), and Dyer (1963) have employed the principles of longitudinal design over short periods moving forward in time.

Hill and Rodgers (1964) stated that a most promising compromise to the true longitudinal study is the use of segmented longitudinal panels with controls as exemplified by the work of Feldman (1963). Feldman tried to capture family change in the transition to parenthood by interviewing couples before and after the birth of their child using comparable families without children as his control group. Finally, Hill and associates at the University of Minnesota Family Study Center combined Feldman's panel approach with retrospective history-taking to study changing patterns of family planning and decision-making.

In family-life education there is evidence of the application of the developmental framework. High-school and college courses in marriage and family living have been organized around a framework of family development. Some of the textbooks reflecting the impact of developmentalism have been written by Foster (1950), Waller and Hill (1950), Cavan (1953), Kirkpatrick (1955), Duvall (1957, 1962), and Kenkel (1960). Pope stated that in the Cooperative Extension Service "the family cycle approach has great appeal, as is evidenced by the large numbers of requests for programs based on that concept." (1958, p. 272.)

Social case work and family counseling have adopted approaches oriented to the developmental rationale. Scherz (1962) suggested that family therapy should be directed toward solving the particular problems that interfere with the accomplishment of individual and family developmental tasks. Rapoport (1963) stressed that the disequilibrium provoked by intrafamily crises at critical periods in the family life cycle can be made amenable by the skilled intervention of a family therapist.

VALUES

It is difficult to pick out any particular value in this approach that is not generally held by contemporary American families. Of course, the approach is somewhat provincial as illustrated by the fact that practically all recent studies have dealt with middle-class urban American families and to date no cross-cultural verification study has been attempted to test the universal applicability of this framework.

There appears to be undue emphasis on child welfare in the developmental framework. For example, Duvall stated that families grow and develop to the extent that their oldest child progresses in the expansion period. (1962, p. 10.) Foote (1963) questioned the preoccupation with child development at the expense of healthy personality development of the married couple.

The choice of having children rather than remaining childless appears to be an implicit value in this framework due to the fact that stages of the family life cycle are organized around the birth and departure of children from the home. Blood and Wolfe (1960) and Feldman (1961) have constructed childless stages but they have been used primarily as control groups.

Finally, it could be deducted that family–member welfare is a value above welfare of the family as a social system. Duvall's developmental-traditional dichotomy is concerned with the wholesome development of the human personality as opposed to making family members conform to socially acceptable patterns.

THE FRAMEWORK

The developmental framework encompasses the internal dynamic processes in the life cycle of the nuclear family of procreation from the wedding to the death of a surviving spouse. The family structure is pictured as a semi-closed system neither entirely independent of nor dependent on other social systems. Each family member occupies a position in the structure with each position characterized by roles related reciprocally to at least one role in each of the other family–member positions. Likewise, each position may contain roles involved with reciprocal roles external to the family system. The family as a unity of interacting personalities is interrelated in such a way that a change does not occur in one position or role without a resultant change in another. Culture defines in large measure the interrelated roles and positions which are unique to a particular family system.

The family system changes through time due to changes in age composition, plurality patterns, school placement, and the functions and status of the family within the larger society. Stages or categories of the family life cycle have been delineated for purposes of study largely on the basis of the transition or adjustment required by particular situations in the family career. Family development is inherently related to the degree that each position and the family role complex as a collectivity complete their individual and family developmental tasks respectively. These tasks or role expectations arise due to biological requirements, cultural imperatives, and personal aspirations and values. The achievement of family developmental tasks at each family life-cycle stage is interrelated with the accomplishment of individual developmental tasks which are encountered simultaneously by each family position. The sequential linking of the family role complexes over the cycle of the family life becomes the family developmental career.

Illustration I depicts the longitudinal view necessary to describe the processes of family development over a long period of time. Each stage of the family life cycle is related to previous events and has implications for future stages as the family matures. Of course, this developmental schema only presents a skeleton outline, but when developmental tasks of each family member are incorporated and the family developmental tasks are specified, the changing developmental pattern is discernable.[3]

The developmental framework, which has gleaned much from other conceptual frameworks, has specifically been formulated with the conceptual demands of family research uppermost in mind. The result has been the emergence of a kind of theoretical eclecticism equipped to systematically study the family.

This approach differs from the psychoanalytic frame of reference in that human personality is considered to be more than the consequence of early childhood experiences. Although recognizing the importance of pre-adolescent training, this system views human development as a dynamic process continuing until death. Developmentalism owes a debt to symbolic interaction theory as it has been applied to the family, but it attempts to unfreeze the family at one point in time during the family career. Functional prerequisites are embodied in the developmental framework but very little attention is given to macrofunctional analysis of the relationships between the

[3] Hill and Rodgers (1964), p. 188, have depicted an expository schema of family development illustrating stages of family life assuming a couple with two male and two female children. Eight stages of the family–life cycle are summarized listing changes in age composition, size of family, number of interpersonal relations, positions, age and relatedness–positional–developmental tasks, and major family goals.

U.S. Modal Nuclear Family with Positional Careers and the
Family Career Traced by Stages of the Family Life Cycle

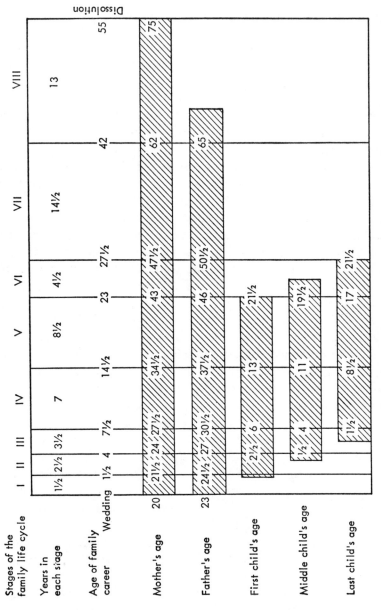

This illustration is based on data supplied by Glick (1957, pp. 53–70) and Duvall (1962, pp. 14–18). It has been adjusted to fit a modal first marriage from the wedding to the death of the remaining spouse with years rounded to one half to facilitate comprehension. The age in which each child leaves home has been arbitrarily established at 21½ in accord with the average age at first marriage. An eight-stage family life cycle follows. (Duvall 1962.)

215

family system and other social systems. The developmental framework narrows down the institutional approach by accounting for family change through a series of microanalytic studies of family interaction over a period of time rather than explaining change macroanalytically in terms of broad institutional variables.

CRITIQUE AND DISCUSSION

This framework has been found to deal effectively with internal family change. Unfortunately it has never been completely tested empirically although it appears to offer operational definitions for use in the longitudinal type of research. Hill (1964) has reported, however, that methodologically we still face problems in operationalizing the framework. We need to continue to perfect and operationalize the abstract and complex concepts embodied in the framework.

The next step would be to describe more fully the processes which are captured in the family development conceptual model. It will be some time, I believe, before we reach the point of predicting family development on the basis of a given set of circumstances.

Due to the time-consuming and costly aspects of investigating a particular group of families through their entire life history, workable research alternatives will have to suffice. Stott (1951, 1954) seriously questioned the assumption that process and change can legitimately be inferred from mean differences between families in different stages of the family life cycle studied concurrently in cross-sectional analysis. The method of retrospective-history taking offers possibilities, but how much validity can be attached to the memory of individual subjects? It is possible, however, to reconstruct family life careers in terms of membership composition by this method. It is encouraging to note the recent attempts to capture family change by means of segmented longitudinal panels with controls. Certainly this is a start in the right direction but it will take time to pull together the bits and pieces.

In order to have a true theory the hypotheses derived from the study of segmented parts of the family life cycle will have to somehow be cemented together into a more internally consistent arrangement. It seems that the time is ripe for a comprehensive test of the developmental framework utilizing the best theoretical contributions advanced to date. It is surprising that no one has designed a combination longitudinal and cross-sectional analysis. Families could be pinpointed and sampled prior to entering critical transitional stages in the family life cycle and then restudied at six-month intervals or so up to two or more years until they are established in a new developmental stage. This could be particularly profitable in the early stages when the time period from one stage to the next is usually not so long. By the end of several years a developmental pattern can be fitted together for a considerable portion of the family life cycle.

Until the more complete job is achieved more limited systematic middle-range theory-building needs to be accomplished. For example Duvall's hypothesis that families progress to the extent that their oldest child develops needs to be subjected to rigorous examination. Is the proposition advanced by Rodgers that families develop as a result of the role complex determined by the development of the oldest and youngest child in combination any better?

In addition to these, there are other limits to the existing body of knowledge relative to family development. Even with Rodgers' more complex twenty-four-category-family-life cycle, no provisions are made to study the variations in sex composition of the children and his framework handles the changing role complex of only two-child families. These questions and others must be answered before a true theory of family development will emerge.

REFERENCES

AGAN, TESSIE. "Housing and the Family Life Cycle," *Journal of Home Economics*, 42 (May 1950), pp. 351–54. Makes recommendations for housing requirements at each stage of the family life cycle.

BELL, NORMAN W., and VOGEL, EZRA F., eds. *A Modern Introduction to the Family*. New York: Free Press of Glencoe, Inc., 1960. In the introduction, "Toward a Framework for Functional Analysis of Family Behavior," (pp. 1–33), a discussion of the functions of the modern nuclear family.

BIGELOW, HOWARD F., and BOND, RUTH L. "Financial Plans in the Family Life Cycle. What are Usual Family Patterns?" *Journal of Home Economics*, 42 (Jan. 1950), pp. 27–29.

BLOOD, ROBERT O., JR., and WOLFE, D. M. *Husbands and Wives*. New York: Free Press of Glencoe, Inc., 1960. Stages in family life cycle used as independent variables to explain variation in husband-wife relationships.

BOSSARD, J. H. "The Law of Family Interaction," *American Journal of Sociology*, 50 (Jan. 1945), pp. 292–94.

BURGESS, ERNEST W. "The Family as a Unity of Interacting Personalities," *The Family*, 7 (March 1926), pp. 3–9.

———, and WALLIN, PAUL. *Engagement and Marriage*. Chicago: J. B. Lippincott Company, 1953. Research study which began with 1,000 engaged couples and was followed up with a study of 666 couples after they had been married three to five years. Robert A. Dentler and Peter Pineo have published a study of these same couples ten years later in the areas of "Sexual Adjustment, Marital Adjustment and Personal Growth of Husbands: A Panel Analysis." *Marriage and Family Living*, 22 (Feb. 1960), pp. 45–48.

CAVAN, RUTH. *The American Family*, 2nd ed. New York: Thomas Y. Crowell Company, 1953. The first three stages of the family cycle put into the premarital period.

CHRISTENSEN, HAROLD T. ed. *Handbook of Marriage and the Family*. Chicago: Rand McNally & Company, 1964, Chap. 1.

CONNOR, RUTH, GREENE, HELEN F., and WALTERS, JAMES. "Agreement of Family Member Conceptions of 'Good' Parent and Child Roles," *Social Forces*, 36 (May 1958), pp. 353–58.

COWLES, MAY. "Changes in Family Personnel, Occupational Status, and Housing Occurring over the Farm Family's Life Cycle," *Rural Sociology*, 18 (Mar. 1953), pp. 35–44.

DEUTSCHER, IRWIN. "Socialization for Post-parental Life," in A. M. Rose, ed. *Human Behavior and Social Processes*. Boston: Houghton Mifflin Company, 1962. Outline of the change from family with children to launched family.

DUVALL, EVELYN M. "Implications for Education Through the Family Life Cycle," *Marriage and Family Living*, 20 (Nov. 1958), pp. 334–42. Individual and family developmental tasks.

———. "Conceptions of Parenthood," *American Journal of Sociology*, 52 (March 1946), pp. 193–203. A report of implications from her Ph.D. dissertation on parenthood using the dichotomy between the traditional and developmental approaches.

———. *Family Development*, 2nd ed. Philadelphia: J. B. Lippincott Company, 1962. A bringing up to date of her first textbook, utilizing the latest research.

———. *Family Development*. Philadelphia: J. B. Lippincott Company, 1957. The first textbook to bring into one place the developmental concepts relative to the family.

———, and HILL, REUBEN. *Dynamics of Family Interaction*. From National Conference on Family Life (also called First White House Conference on Family Life). Conference held in Washington D.C., Spring 1948. Duvall and Hill co-chairmen. Mimeographed material on file in Home and Family Life Department of Florida State University and other institutions concerned with the Committee on the Dynamics of Family Interaction.

DYER, E. D. "Parenthood as Crises; a Re-study," *Marriage and Family Living*, 25 (May 1963), pp. 196–201. A validation of earlier study by LeMasters (1957) that intrafamily crises result from the addition of an unprepared-for child.

ELDER, RACHEL ANN. "Traditional and Developmental Conceptions of Fatherhood," *Marriage and Family Living*, 11 (Aug. 1949), pp. 98–106. Uses Duvall's dichotomy for fathers.

ERIKSON, ERIK H. *Childhood and Society*. New York: W. W. Norton & Company, Inc., 1950, Chap. 7. A work that derives early stages from Freudian psychology.

FARBER, BERNARD. "Types of Family Organization: Child-oriented, Home-oriented, and Parent-oriented," in A. M. Rose, ed. *Human Behavior and Social Processes*. Boston: Houghton Mifflin Company, 1962. The concept *career* used to denote the progression by an individual through a series of roles within the family.

FELDMAN, HAROLD A. *Development of Husband-Wife Relationship*. Renewal proposal for United States Public Health Service research grant M-2931 from the National Institute of Mental Health. Mimeographed, Ithaca, N.Y.: Cornell University, 1963.

———. *A Report of Research in Progress in the Development of Husband-Wife Relationships*. Mimeographed, Ithaca, N.Y.: Cornell University, Jan. 30, 1961.

FOOTE, NELSON. "Matching of Husband and Wife in Phases of Development," in Marvin Sussman, ed. *Sourcebook in Marriage and the Family*, 2nd ed. Boston: Houghton Mifflin Company, 1963, pp. 14–20. A report on studies of friendship and sociability in marriage conducted at the University of Chicago.

———, et al. *Housing Choices and Housing Constraints*. New York: McGraw-Hill, Inc., 1960. A projection of housing needs by stages of the family life cycle.

FOSTER, ROBERT G. *Marriage and Family Relationships*, rev. ed. New York: The Macmillan Company, 1950, pp. 207–09. Phases of the family life cycle divided into establishment, child-rearing, recovery, and active retirement.

FRANK, LAWRENCE K. *Individual Development*. Garden City, N.Y.: Doubleday & Company, Inc., 1955. Establishment of a frame of reference appropriate for the study of development.

GLICK, PAUL C. *American Families*. New York: John Wiley & Sons, Inc., 1957. A study using United States Census data to describe norms in the family life cycle.

———, HEER, DAVID, and BERESFORD, JOHN. "Family Formation and Family Composition: Trends and Prospects," in Marvin Sussman, ed.

Sourcebook in Marriage and the Family, 2nd ed. Boston: Houghton Mifflin Company, 1963, pp. 30–40. A projection of family development norms into the future.

HARRIS, DALE B., ed. *The Concept of Development.* Minneapolis: University of Minnesota Press, 1957. Papers considering the concept of development and its usefulness in various disciplines studying human affairs. Papers were given in Dec. 1955 at the University of Minnesota.

HAVIGHURST, ROBERT J. "Research on the Development Task Concept," *School Review,* **64** (May 1956), pp. 215–23.

————. *Developmental Tasks and Education.* Chicago: University of Chicago Press, 1948. The first definitive outline of individual developmental tasks for each stage of human development.

HILL, REUBEN. "A Critique of Contemporary Marriage and Family Research," *Social Forces,* **33** (March 1955), pp. 268–77. The developmental framework and its utility for longitudinal research.

————. "Interdisciplinary Workshop on Marriage and Family Research," *Marriage and Family Living,* **13** (Feb. 1951), pp. 13–28. A report on the first Interdisciplinary Workshop on Marriage and the Family, co-sponsored by the National Council on Family Relations and the University of Chicago, 1950.

————. "Methodological Issues in Family Development Research," *Family Process,* **3** (March 1964), pp. 186–206.

————, and RODGERS, ROY H. "The Developmental Approach," in H. T. Christensen, ed. *Handbook of Marriage and the Family.* Chicago: Rand McNally & Company, 1964, Chap. 5. The best conceptualization of the developmental approach to date.

————, and Hansen, Donald A. "The Identification of Conceptual Frameworks Utilized in Family Study," *Marriage and Family Living,* **22** (Nov. 1960), pp. 299–311. Analysis of the developmental framework from the standpoint of basic assumptions, structural concepts, bridges, observable overt behavior, social space, and social time.

KENKEL, WILLIAM F. *The Family in Perspective.* New York: Appleton-Century-Crofts, 1960, Part III. An incorporation of the concepts of developmental tasks and a four-stage family life cycle.

KIRKPATRICK, CLIFFORD. *The Family as Process and Institution.* New York: The Ronald Press Company, 1955, Part III.

KIRKPATRICK, E. L., TOUGH, ROSALIND, and COWLES, MAY. *The Life Cycle of the Farm Family in Relation to its Standards of Living and Ability to Provide.* Research Bulletin 121. Madison, Wis.: University of Wisconsin Agricultural Experiment Station, 1934. A delineation of four stages of the family based on age and school placement of first child, with pre-child and post-child families too infrequent in number to classify.

LANSING, JOHN B., and KISH, LESLIE. "Family Life Cycle as an Independent Variable. *American Sociological Review*, **22** (Oct. 1957), pp. 512–19. A study in which the authors find the family life cycle a better explanatory variable than individual age through use of multi-stage stratified, clustered probability samples using cross-sectional method.

LeMasters, E. E. "Parenthood as Crises." *Marriage and Family Living*, **19** (Nov. 1957), pp. 353–55. A report that the birth of the first child reached crisis proportions in the vast majority of college-educated middle-class urban families.

Lively, C. E. *The Growth Cycle of the Farm Family*. Mimeographed Bulletin No. 51, Ohio Agricultural Experiment Station, Columbus, Ohio: Oct. 1932. A comparison of secular trends of older and younger farm families.

McArthur, Arthur. "Developmental Tasks and Parent-Adolescent Conflict. *Marriage and Family Living*, **24** (May 1962), pp. 189–91. An illustration of three developmental tasks of adults and adolescents that often come into conflict.

Morgan, Mildred I. "The Contributions and Needs of Home Economics Research in the Area of Family Relations," *Journal of Home Economics*, **51** (May 1959), pp. 358–61. A list of areas of research needed within the framework of the family life cycle.

Nelson, Lowry. *Rural Sociology*, 2nd ed. New York: American Book Company, 1955.

Parsons, Talcott. *Essays in Sociological Theory: Pure and Applied*. New York: Free Press of Glencoe, Inc., 1949, pp. 6–7. A definition of functional prerequisites for providing minimum biological and psychological needs, maintaining order, and giving adequate motivation.

Pikunas, Justin, and Albrecht, Eugene J. *Psychology of Human Development*. New York: McGraw-Hill, Inc., 1961, pp. 320–23. Presentation of a chart of human development through senescence by approximate age with physiological growth, dynamics, motivation, developmental tasks, major hazards, and personality, self and character.

Pope, Edward V. "Extension Service Programs Affecting American Families," *Marriage and Family Living*, **20** (Aug. 1958), pp. 270–77. An illustration of how extension family-life educational programs utilize the concept of the family life cycle.

Rapoport, Rhona. "Normal Crises, Family Structure, and Mental Health," *Family Process*, **2** (March 1963), pp. 68–80. A study which postulates developmental tasks at first stage of family development and measures performance to determine how this related to outcome of a year's marriage.

Rodgers, Roy H. "Toward a Theory of Family Development," *Journal of Marriage and Family*, **26** (Aug. 1964), pp. 262–70. A good follow-up of his dissertation. He again diagrams the longitudinal dimensions of position and role to constitute the family career.

————. *Improvements in the Construction and Analysis of Family Life Cycle Categories.* Kalamazoo, Mich.: Western Michigan University, 1962. A Ph.D. dissertation from the University of Minnesota that tries to extend the developmental framework through the incorporation of role theory and a twenty-four-category classification of the family life cycle.

Scherz, Frances, H. "Multiple-Client Interviewing Treatment Implications," *Social Casework,* 43 (March 1962), pp. 120–25. A statement that social case work should be directed to solving problems interfering with the accomplishment of family developmental tasks.

Sorokin, Pitirim, Zimmerman, Carle C., and Galpin, C. J. *A Systematic Source Book in Rural Sociology,* Vol. II. Minneapolis: University of Minnesota Press, 1931, p. 31. Presentation of a four-stage family life cycle: married couple, family with one or more children, family with one or more self-supporting children, and couples growing old.

Stott, Leland H. "The Longitudinal Approach to the Study of Family Life." *Journal of Home Economics,* 46 (Feb. 1954), pp. 79–82. A study which questions cross-sectional methods to infer longitudinal changes in the family.

————. "The Problem of Evaluating Family Success," *Marriage and Family Living,* 13 (Nov. 1951), pp. 149–53. Developmental tasks and functional prerequisites used interchangeable to judge family success at various stages of the family life cycle.

Streib, Gordon F. "Family Patterns in Retirement," *Journal of Social Issues,* 14 (March 1958), pp. 46–60. A report on Cornell University research of families in retirement.

Thompson, Wayne E. "Pre-Retirement Anticipation and Adjustment in Retirement," *Journal of Social Issues,* 14 (March 1958), pp. 35–45. A report on Cornell University research of the relationship between anticipating retirement and the adjustment to retirement.

Tryon, Caroline, Lilienthal, Jesse W., Jr. "Child Growth and Development." *NEA Journal,* 39 (March 1950), pp. 188–99. Abstract from 1950 Yearbook of the Association for Supervision and Curriculum Development, *Fostering Mental Health in our Schools,* of which Tryon was editor. Uses chart of behavior categories and enumerates developmental tasks through late adolescence.

Waller, Willard, and Hill, Reuben. *The Family: A Dynamic Interpretation.* New York: The Dryden Press, Inc., 1951. A revision by Hill of Waller's earlier book to reflect later concepts of family development.

chapter 10

An Economic Framework for Viewing the Family*

Ann Smith Rice

"Throughout human history," wrote Linton, "the family has been an economic unit. . . . Romantic love, or even congeniality between partners, is even now less important in most societies than economic need to keep the family clothed, fed and sheltered." (1952, pp. 67–82.) Although the economic history of the family in the Western world may be said to have begun with Xenophon's *Oeconomicus* in 411 B.C., Kyrk deplored the fact that, "No one has yet gathered the material that will give the complete history of the family as an economic unit. . . . There are economic histories of nations ancient and modern," she said. "There are histories of industry and commerce and of particular economic institutions. But no one as yet has consistently traced the changes that came to the family as such through the historic developments in industrial technique and in economic arrangements." (1933, p. 18.) Sorokin (1928, p. 597) recognized the existence of an economic school in sociological theories, calling it "one of the oldest" and "one of the most important [schools] in the social sciences," and yet Hill

* Grateful acknowledgment is made of the contribution of Frederica Carleton, who served as editorial consultant for this framework and who read and critically reviewed the manuscript prior to its final revision. Many, although not all, of her suggestions have been incorporated into the final manuscript. Inadequacies and errors in the chapter as published, however, are entirely the responsibility of the author and the editors.

and Hansen in 1960 failed to include an economic framework in their marshalling of existing conceptual frameworks for family research.

The use of economic concepts began early in history as a means of identifying causal effects of economic factors on social institutions. Economic laws were formulated to explain such phenomena as rent and wages, propensity to consume, value and utility, and even population and social order. Income and wealth were treated as concepts interrelated with those of over-all standards of living and economic status by Le Play as early as 1829, by Engel (1857), Rowntree (1902), and, more recently, by Morgan, David, Cohen, and Brazer (1962).

The economic or materialistic interpretation of history depicted by Karl Marx and Frederic Engels in the late 1850's led to a multitude of sociological, political, philosophical, and economic studies in an attempt either to validate or to repudiate such a theory. In the process, the relationship between economic and non-economic phenomena was found to be a much more complex one than the causal interpretation of society suggested by Marx.

In more recent years, emphasis has turned to measures of size and distribution of income, consumption, and standards of living—measures of family welfare. Contemporary studies of correlations between economic conditions and family life—not as principal causes or primary factors, but as a framework for analysis of interacting variables—are growing more numerous in sociology and home economics as well as in economic research. Psychologists have entered the field through their interest in the process and motivations of decision-making; historians, through their interest in the shift of production from the home to industry.

The mutual interdependence of economic and non-economic factors has led to efforts to isolate economic variables or concepts useful in the study of marriage and the family. The effects of consumer behavior and consumption on family life were analyzed by Kyrk (1923, 1933), Zimmerman (1936), Hoyt (1938), Reid (1938), and again by Kyrk (1953). In 1962 Sussman and Burchinal conceptualized *parental aid* in an attempt to link the family network to a modified extended family system in Western industrialized society. Brady (1958) recognized the interdependence of family status, personal income, and size of consumer unit. Rice (1964), examined the effect of childlessness upon the economic life cycle of American families. Magrabi (1963) conceptualized *choice*, proposing a model for preferences and constraints in consumption. Seldom has an economic concept received as much interest as the working-wife concept has commanded in recent years. These are but a few of the concepts which have been formulated for specific purposes but which, viewed collectively, begin to form a conceptual framework.

The present attempt to identify and define an economic conceptual approach has resulted in a framework of economic concepts based on analysis of family welfare. This framework is a network of interwoven concepts relating to the well-being of the family. A triad of basic concepts serves as the foundation of the economic conceptual framework:

1. Standards of living and their dependence upon custom, habit, emulation, tastes, and the means for financing consumption: income and occupation.
2. Socio-economic status and its numerous indices of rank: occupation; source of income; education; housing; and material goods and services, that is, the products of consumption.
3. Consumer behavior and the motivating forces behind consumption: wants and needs, utility and value.

Because of the relativity of family welfare to the civilization in which it exists, a fourth major concept emerges: the economic conditions of the society.

The economic framework is still in the stage of formulation, and it may be that the changing economic factors—particularly in Western industrialized countries—will continue to develop and change the framework along with the society to which the framework relates. It is clear, however, that an economic framework for viewing the family does exist and that it has arrived at the point of maturity that allows it to be classed as a conceptual framework.

Previous Attempts to Delineate the Framework

Apparently no previous attempt has been made to conceptualize a general economic framework for the study of the family. However, several attempts have been made to delineate frameworks similar to this economic framework: the home-economics approach, the combined household-economics and home-management approach, and the home-management conceptual framework. In the area of economics, a conceptual framework to explain family income has been devised by Morgan, *et al.* (1962)—a framework which comes close to the economic framework presented in this chapter, although Morgan's major emphasis is upon analysis of the economic phenomena and not specifically upon family analysis.

In an attempt to locate a home-economics approach, Hill stated that:

> The traditional home economists have applied the technology of management which deals with resources of time, money, and energy, but until recently have skirted family values and family relationships in their research. (1955, p. 275)

Later, Hill, Katz, and Simpson (1957) and Hill (1960), dropped the combined household-economics and home-management approach because "of its apparent failure to generate a full-fledged conceptual framework." It is not surprising that they found no single home-economics approach for study of the family which could be formulated into a conceptual framework. In the opinion of this writer, there would not be found a single approach used by home economists in the study of the family any more than there is a single approach that can be attributed to sociologists, psychologists, or economists. Home economists, like specialists in each of the other fields concerned with family life, use a variety of approaches. Knoll (1963) proposed a conceptual framework for home management alone, naming *decision-making* and *organization* as basic concepts and proposing the addition of *process* to the list of concepts.

The economic-conceptual framework described in this chapter differs from related frameworks reviewed here, principally in the broader coverage which it allows and in the focus of interest upon the welfare or well-being of the family.

History of the Development

Economic factors have played an important role in human behavior and social organization since the beginning of civilization. Confucius, Mencius, and the Hindu thinkers stressed the importance of economic conditions when they taught that poverty calls forth dissatisfactions of both people and social orders and that a satisfactory economic situation of the people is a necessity for social order. These early philosophers believed that economic factors conditioned religious and political phenomena, and they considered the securing of food and other economic necessities a primary task of good government.

The ancient Greek historians and philosophers, Thucydides, Plato, and Aristotle, used economic factors for explaining numerous social processes, pointing to the effects of poverty and wealth on human psychology and behavior and naming poverty and wealth as the causes of social and class struggle.

Explanation of the course of human behavior and social process is common in early writings of classical economists such as Adam Smith, John Stewart Mill, and Adelung, who all expounded theories directly related to family and social life. Smith considered making a living the chief economic function of the family but recognized the importance of consumption in determining the levels of living.

Two mining engineers, Ernst Engel and Frederic Le Play, are credited with founding the study of social economics. They proposed, in the early 1800's, that the material welfare of society could be understood and promoted by studying family living. Engel emphasized the material conditions of life whereas Le Play believed that the social organization was primary because it was the family and its society which produced the material possessions.

Le Play organized the school which has been active since 1829, publishing monographs and conducting family–living studies almost continuously. He analyzed the family in operation through the family budget and standard of living, using the case–study method almost exclusively. Le Play formulated and tested the hypothesis that if one knew the entire family budget, he could describe the kind of family; if one knew the type of family, he could understand the total social structure of which it was a part.

Engel, a student of Le Play, founded the statistical school of social economics. While director of the Saxon Statistical Bureau in the 1850's, he analyzed the distribution of income and proportionate expenditures in the budgetary studies of Ducepetiaux and Le Play, and formulated a theory of the relationship between income and proportional expenditures for food and other necessities. Engel compared increases in his quet unit (a unit of consumption) with size of family, using a curve of growth, and concluded that costs of living are influenced by occupation and by social class. Engel counted as one of the fundamental problems of man the provision for his economic welfare.

In 1875, Carroll Wright, first United States Commissioner of Labor, apparently on the basis of studies made by himself in Massachusetts, worked out percentage relationships between income and expenditures for housing, clothing, and savings, and erroneously attributed the whole to Engel. It is his restatement, he extended the law to cover all categories of expenditures, which is often cited as Engel's Law.

Karl Marx employed economic phenomena to determine or explain the course of human behavior and social processes, bringing to a head the economic interpretation of history in his theory of class struggle. In 1859 Marx summarized his theory with a statement which provoked great controversy:

> The mode of production in material life determines the general character of the social, political and spiritual process of life. (Sorokin, 1928, p. 524.)

This and other works of Marx and Frederick Engels set off a chain of theories, hypotheses, and research to prove or contradict such a causal relationship between existing institutions and production and other economic factors.

In 1872 Senior, following the classical school, maintained that the limits of economics were the production and distribution of wealth. He justified his slighting of consumption by relating the wealth of a country to productive or unproductive consumption. He classified consumption commodities as necessaries, decencies, and luxuries—concepts which are still in use today.

Statistical studies of family living continued in the nineteenth century with the anticipation of improved standards of living for the masses as a result of industrialization in Europe. Welfare studies of poverty were conducted by Charles Booth from 1886–1888 in London and by Rowntree in York, England in 1902. Rowntree's study is still considered a scientific and comprehensive measure of the amount of poverty that existed in the community. More recent studies by Rowntree and Lavers (1951) and by Zweig (1949) have followed Rowntree's early pattern of distinguishing primary from secondary poverty, and of using a scale based on the number, sex, and age of persons in the family for measuring the level of the family's welfare.

Faith in the possibility and desirability of improving living conditions in the United States after the Civil War stimulated statistical studies of living conditions in various states. Between 1870 and 1900 more than one hundred statistical economic studies of family living were conducted by state bureaus of labor. In 1888 the United States Bureau of Labor Statistics began a study to determine living conditions in the country as a whole. (Brady, 1948, p. 172.) Carroll Wright directed family living studies using as criteria for welfare the adequacy or inadequacy of annual income to provide the family necessities and have something left over for savings. If saving was possible with the average worker's income, the income was considered adequate. The first really elaborate study of consumer incomes and expenditures for all income groups in the entire United States, for urban as well as rural areas, was made through the cooperation of the Bureau of Labor Statistics (urban areas), the Bureau of Home Economics (rural areas), the National Resources Committee, and the Central Statistical Board, in 1935–1936. Although these data could not give as detailed a picture of exactly *how* families lived as Le Play's data had done, another study could: a study made in 1924–1925 by Robert and Helen Lynd—*Middletown*. This related to the total level or plane of living, although much attention was given to its material basis, to the range of consumption levels, and to the consumption process and the satisfactions derived from it.

The first family budgets in this country expressed in quantities of goods and services, to which prices were applied in determining the total cost, were made by order of Congress in 1907. The study investigated the earnings and living conditions of working women and children. A minimum standard of living and the cost of a fair standard were determined for cotton-mill communities. Later, budget studies were conducted in Seattle by Ogburn in 1917, by the State of California in 1921, and in New York City. Sydenstricker and King in 1921 analyzed the problem of comparing families as to adequacy of income by developing what they termed a *fammain scale* to measure the relative variation for food expenditures according to age and sex, and an *ammain scale* to represent the variation in the gross demand for articles of consumption.

Since development of the ammain scales, consumption scales measuring the relative income required by families of differing composition to maintain a particular level of material well-being have been recognized as important tools in studies of standards of living, and four such scales are in use today.[1] All such budget studies and scales

[1] The Works Progress Administration Maintenance Budget; the Original City Worker's Family Budget based on income level and adequacy of diet; a separate scale by the same source and based on income saved; and the fourth, the Scale of Equivalent Income currently in use by the Bureau of Labor Statistics. *Monthly Labor Review* (Nov. 1960), p. 1198.

were developed to measure a family's needs which in turn indicate the relative costs of maintaining families of different sizes and demographic characteristics in a specified community. Rather than adding to the conceptual framework, the major contributions of these economic studies were in methodology and in the means of gathering evidence of needs and desires and the satisfaction of wants.

Economic theory continued to develop during the late nineteenth and early twentieth centuries. Marshall in 1916 dealt with wants and their satisfaction and with agents of production and distribution of the national income. He equated consumption with demand and conceived of certain broad levels of consumption permeating the social structure. He used the concepts *standard of life* and *standard of comfort*. Marshall made further use of Senior's concepts—necessaries, decencies, and luxuries—in relation to wants and he viewed social class, place, and time as elements causing wants to vary.

In 1925 Weber introduced the factor of probability as a substitute for absolute law into economic thinking. He believed that economic activity may be the result of either need or desire for profit, and implied that, primarily, Western society has tended to seek gain or profit rather than to satisfy needs. From 1899 until late 1920's, Veblen attempted to give a longitudinal or evolutionary view to economic thought. He hypothesized that changes in human behavior result from changing institutional patterns. According to Veblen's theory of consumption, the leisure class initiates modes of consumption, and other classes imitate. The importance attached to wealth, through both instincts and institutions, furnishes the key point in Veblen's theory of the standard of living. His concept of a standard of living is fundamentally a pecuniary one. The minimum physical needs assume only a minor significance in the activity of living, and wealth arouses esteem only as others know it. Veblen further postulated that a public demonstration of wealth is possible only by the conspicuous consumption of time and goods. Leisure time is often absent from the standard for consumption of goods, as the psychological returns are greater if money is spent on goods than if divided between goods and leisure. Veblen added to the framework the concepts of *pecuniary emulation, invidious distinction,* and *conspicuous consumption.*

The class concept has continued to be given growing emphasis in the twentieth century. Socio-economic factors have emerged as the major indices of social class, although the social psychologists tend to lean toward self-awareness and ways of life as basic indices. Numerous attempts have been made to combine both approaches. There appears to be general agreement that research in the family area today is more meaningful and valid when social class is controlled. There is less agreement as to the criteria which are most useful in measuring social class or socio-economic status. Many different measurements have been used: income, source of income, occupation, education, type and size of home, area of residence, and status items such as material possessions and general manner of living. While Lawson (1960) and others have focused attention upon testing the correlation between existing indices, Hollingshead (1957) has sought to reduce the number of factors necessary in measuring social position, and the Bureau of the Census has added the concept of "consistency" of factors.

FOCI OF STUDY

Since the economic conceptual framework has not previously been delineated, there are few if any studies which have incorporated all of its underlying concepts and viewed the welfare of the family from within the complete economic framework. With a few exceptions, the studies employing economic concepts do so without regard to forming a systematic or related chain of findings upon which to build economic theory. Many studies focus upon the economic variable under consideration, stopping short of the ultimate goal of family economic studies—that of analyzing the effect of the economic variable upon the family. Hence, some studies are principally explanatory and remain descriptive. Among the studies which are considered within the framework of the economic approach, four major areas of focus have emerged:

1. Standards of living.
2. Socio-economic status.
3. Economic conditions of the society.
4. Consumer behavior and motivation.

For the purpose of clarity, the foci of recent economic studies will be discussed according to these four headings, with studies cited as examples of the types of problems being considered in the area by those concerned with family welfare.

Standard-of-Living Studies

Recent studies relating to the standard of living of a family or a society have concentrated upon analysis of custom, habit, emulation, tastes, and the means for financing consumption-income and occupation. Three additional areas have also emerged: studies comparing the standards of societies and cultures, studies relating birth rate and population to standards of living, and a multitude of studies examining the effect of a gainfully employed wife upon family phenomena.

Scientific analysis of the welfare of families almost always necessitates determination of income. Income and welfare studies conducted during the last fifteen years have made use of the survey technique of research, using probability samples. After World War I, representative samples of broad populations began to be used to provide evidence of the extent of unemployment, or to provide consumption habits as a basis for standard cost–of–living indices. Such surveys have progressed from measurement and description to empirical studies aimed at determining the causes of differences in consumption, possibilities for change, and interrelation of economic factors with social variables. According to Morgan:

> The most important difference in interest has been between an attempt at deductive explanation for differences in individual earnings on the one hand, and a focus on description and evaluation of the inequality in the distribution of total family incomes on the other. . . . To go from individual wage rates to family incomes one must deal with unemployment, moonlighting, extra earners, living with relatives, income from capital, and transfer income. (Morgan, *et al.*, 1962, p. 16.)

Recent interest has been directed toward family income as a dependent variable subject to human decisions.

The importance of the source of the family income, especially if a second gainfully employed member is the wife, is evident by the volumes of recent research relating working wives to family phenomena. Stolz (1960) reviewed fifty-two research studies relating to effects of maternal employment on children. Later (1963), Nye edited an entire book of research on the effects of the wife's working on the internal power structure and other family variables. Rice (1963), in an unpublished paper, examined the social consesequences of working wives. Gianopulos (1957), Dickins (1958),

Hoffman (1960), Glenn (1959), Nye (1959), Caudle (1964), and numerous others have added to the growing stream of knowledge regarding this recent change in the division of labor responsibilities within the family.

Family income, formation, consumption, and labor-force behavior are analyzed by Mincer (1960) as aspects of a simultaneous choice situation. Warren (1960) relates income to housing. Brady (1958) recognized the interdependence of family status, personal income, and size of consumer unit. The standard of living which is used to determine the adequacy of the family income is found to differ from community to community and from region to region. Recent research points to the size of the family as a determinant of its welfare. Age and other characteristics of family members have been examined in relation to the family's needs and wants. The establishment of a measuring stick by which the welfare of a family or individual can be determined is the focus of numerous contemporary research studies conducted by both sociologists and economists, as well as by home economists.

Wealth and its relevance to consumption and saving has received considerable attention. Wealth plays a central role in the permanent income hypothesis. In the Friedman formulation, the ratio of permanent consumption to permanent income is assumed to rise with increases in the ratio of wealth to income.

Numerous studies have been conducted in recent years by and for the International Labor Office in an effort to compare the standard of living of one country with that of another. Lamale (1963), Carroll (1962), and others of the United States Bureau of Labor Statistics have reported on workers' wealth and family living standards. Results of the 1960–1961 Survey of Consumer Expenditures and Income conducted by the Department of Labor and Department of Agriculture for purposes of revising the consumer price index are now available. Data collected by these sources serve as the basis for analytical research on the family and for corrective welfare measures throughout the nation.

Numerous economic theorists have developed variations of the Malthusian Theory of Populations to show interrelation between birth rate, population, and standard of living. Malthus' theory was that food and population increase at different rates: food by arithmetical progression, population by geometric progression. He divided into two groups the checks on population which had developed throughout history: the pressure of population upon natural resources, which he found to be vice and misery (war, famine, pestilence); and moral restraint, which included all of the social customs which men have used to keep down the growth of population and thus to avoid vice and misery.

Later economists have contributed to the population theories the concepts *plane of living* and *increasing and diminishing returns*. John Stuart Mill used the Malthusian Theory in relation to the law of diminishing returns from land; Marshall outlined the law of diminishing returns in relation to individual factors of production; and Pigou (1924) finally concluded that a national minimum standard of living should be set and that the attention of a country should be directed toward the prevention of any increase of population which would force the marginal families below this level.

In contemporary economic population literature, Kuznets' (1961) cycle of fertility of different population groups demonstrates that variations in the fertility of a given population are caused primarily by changes in two classes of factors: economic conditions and demographic composition. Economic conditions he takes to be employment and income experiences of the group. Kuznets' model appears frequently in current literature in contrast to Malthus' model and to historical periods of the United States or present-day underdeveloped countries. Hagen (1959) adds to the conventional concepts of population growth two elements: the effect of a modified standard of living and the effect of the desire to perpetuate the family.

Socio-economic Status

Recent studies of socio-economic status examine the numerous indices of rank—occupation, source of income, education, housing, and material goods and services (the products of consumption)— and show how these indices differentiate one family from another.

The development and acceptance of the democratic way of life and the technological advances that have come with it in Western societies have abetted social and economic mobility of the family and produced changes in the family functions themselves. As noted by Broom and Selznick (1958), the wider distribution of income and the availability of a greater percentage of staple and luxury goods and services at a reasonable cost have tended to narrow the differences between social classes. There is discussion in the current literature as to whether or not *class* is a general term which includes socio-economic status as well as a way of life; whether *class* is descriptive of the way of life and separate from socio-economic status. Warner (1949) and Reissman (1959), among others have taken the first view. Reissman believes that class can be translated as meaning:

1. The level of personal achievement (economic status).
2. The person's or family's social position in the community.
3. The style of life.

Even when socio-economic factors are not defined as part of social class, they serve as indices for determining social class.

There is general agreement that control of social class or socio-economic class is desirable in family research today. This is based on the prevailing assumption that differences in personal and collective behavior are related to class lines. There is less consensus, however, as to what criteria are appropriate in measuring social class. The factors most consistently used are income, source of income, occupation, education, type and size of home, area of residence, status items (material possessions), cultural tastes, the general manner of living, choice of religion, parental practices in child rearing, and ethnic origin; by far the majority of these are determined, or at least limited, by income and wealth—economic factors.

The mutual validation of indices and the translation of socio-economic status and social class into interchangeable terms was suggested by Warner, Meeker, and Eels (1949) as the next step in such research, much of which has now been done. Hollingshead (1957) reduced to two (occupation and education) the indices necessary to determine social position. Haer (1955) and Lawson and Boek (1960) have concentrated on comparison of the more frequently used instruments for measuring status.

Socio-economic factors are currently being used in descriptive studies of family form in this and other countries as well as serving as control of variables in a multitude of family studies. Abington (1958) related money–management experiences to subculture, sex, social status, and age. Friedman (1961) related socio-economic factors and religious differences in fertility. Through a Barbadian case study, Greenfield (1961) related socio-economic factors to family form. His was a descriptive study of the marriage customs and family life in Barbados as they relate to economic factors.

Numerous researchers have dealt with occupational differences relating this economic factor to family life. In 1950 Hall and Jones attempted the social grading of occupations. Kephart (1955) analyzed occupational level and marital disruption. In 1958 Atelsek investigated whether certain personal and social characteristics of older job-seekers were associated with their relative success or failure in maintaining themselves in the labor force. Matthews (1959) explored the relationship of job satisfaction to the leisure-time activity of professionals. In 1960 Inkeles described the "industrial man," relating status to experience, perception, and value.

So many economic studies focusing on income have been conducted in recent years that Morgan, David, Cohen, and Brazer were led to formulate in 1962 a framework around the income concept, and the *Monthly Labor Review* (1960) illustrated how income and budget costs could be estimated according to family type.

Economic Conditions of the Society

Studies in the area of economic conditions of the society relate family phenomena to changes in the economic conditions of the society. More than forty years ago the influence of national economic conditions determined by business cycles on marriages and divorces was studied by Ogburn and Thomas (1922). In 1959 Barry related child training to subsistence economy and in 1960 Middleton and Nimkoff showed that in primitive societies there is a rough relationship between the type of family system and economic factors.

Because of the depression of the 1930's, many studies of poverty were made. Other works of that time related the economic conditions of the 1930's to family phenomena such as postponement of marriage, small families, doubling up in housing, and power structure within the family. The relationship of prolonged unemployment to disorganization and disintegration of the family was stressed. Such studies include those of Angell (1936), Cavan and Ranck (1938), Cooley (1938), Winona Morgan (1939), Komarovsky (1940), Bakke (1940), Gilmore (1940), and Warner (1941). In 1959 Cavan organized the depression studies according to social class and analyzed the evidence from the composite studies for the various classes, relating the differences in conditions between the 1930's and 1950's.

Historical studies such as that of Oliver (1956) which traces technological changes through the years; sociological studies such as Ogburn and Nimkoff's *Technology and the Changing Family* (1955); and economic studies such as Kyrk's *Family in the American Economy* (1953) add to the knowledge of the effect of technological developments on family organization, on family function, and on family contribution to the society. Nimkoff further examined the relationship between a technological economy and the preferred family system. Feldman (1957) examined the family in a "money world."

Some controversy appears in recent literature between sociologists and economists over the relationship between economic conditions and family system, especially the extended family or kinship system. The concept *parental aid* is employed by Sussman and Burchinal (1962) to explain the extension of the nuclear family in modern industrialized society into a kin-family network composing a modified extended family. The major portion of research using parental aid as a concept has been done since 1950. Rogers (1958) analyzed parental aid to married college students; Christopherson (1960) did likewise. Cushing (1948), Kenkel (1950), and Clark (1962) focused on attitudes toward acceptance by married college couples toward parental aid. Sussman (1953) also used the parental-aid concept when he studied help patterns within the kinship matrix of isolated nuclear families in the working-class and middle-class households of Cleveland. Sussman and Burchinal (1962), in conceptualizing parental aid point out:

> In an affluent society, a considerable proportion of the family's income in the middle years of life can be devoted to a variety of ends which reflect the values and special interests of the parents rather than being dictated by requirements of biological necessity. (1962, p. 323.)

With the continual up-grading of income in the middle-class and working-class families and with the increase in the number of working wives, a larger and larger percentage of the family income is becoming available for discretionary use. Inheritance tax laws make the transfer of wealth to relatives at regular intervals during the parents' lifetime more prudent. This trend is referred to as a "downward diffusion of an upper class norm." (Sussman and Burchinal, 1962.)

Clark and Warren (1963) and others at Cornell University have converted the types of aid into dollar values to permit exact determinations of amount of all types of aid and the net balance of aid exchange patterns between parents and married children with a given time period. Whether the desire for independence (including financial autonomy) on the part of the young married children will outweigh the resultant consequences and relationships created by the acceptance of available parental aid is a question which will, in all likelihood, form the framework for numerous future studies.

Familism is used in an entirely different approach by Moore and Wolf, economists. The kinship system is used in explaining economic development of underdeveloped countries by Moore (1955). He and other development economists postulate that the kinship system in nonindustrial society is likely to provide a major barrier to the individual mobility necessary for industrialization because of the social security provided by the extended family system. This trend of analysis is continued by Wolf (1962) in his analysis of the influence which institutions exert upon economic behavior. He views the joint or extended family system as operating to deter economic growth in underdeveloped countries by creating discontinuities between production and distribution. Wolf assumes that the individual family member is less likely to contemplate a wealth-increasing investment in productive assets that will yield future returns for two reasons: (1) because the joint family system involves shared rights and obligations encompassing a large number of near and distant relatives and (2) because the individual family member receives the right of support and security from the group in return for the obligation to share his wealth and to provide support and security for other members of the group. He must bear all of the cost but must share the fruits of his venture.

Obviously empirical research is needed in this area as well as in the area of population studies. Recent population studies interrelate birth rate, population, and standards of living. Hagen's modified standard-of-living effect (1959), which he added to conventional conceptions about population, and Kuznets' cycle of fertility of different population groups (1961) are examples of the direction which population research is taking in relation to the welfare of societies. The concept of population control is focused at present on underdeveloped countries. Longitudinal research is essential in the case of underdeveloped countries, in order to validate, repudiate, or modify opposing theories.

Consumer Behavior and Motivation

Consumer behavior and the concept of consumption are inherent in any research on family welfare. The focus of research in this area has been to link family and personal phenomena (wants, needs, values, utility) and psychological factors (motivations and decision-making processes) with economic behavior. A wealth of material has been produced, most of which may be classified as (1) determination of specific expenditures or assets, (2) influence of variables other than income on spending, (3) decision processes, or (4) theories of spending or saving behavior. In a review of research on this topic, Ferber (1962) points to two approaches which have been used to ascertain the factors influencing the consumption of specific consumer products. One approach attempts to explain static differences in product purchases by different households in terms of household characteristics. This approach parallels the consumption function and is characterized by a search for so-called Engel curves between specific expenditures (or savings) and income level, holding other relevant variables constant. During the past twenty years, many such studies have been conducted.

The second approach has attempted to explain temporal differences in aggregate purchases in terms of market variables, usually disregarding household characteristics except for aggregate income. Examples of the two approaches are found in the work of Brady (1955), Honey (1956), and Houthakker (1957), Suits (1958), Ferber (1958), Reid (1952 and 1958), and Maisel and Winnick (1960), all of which indicate that consumer purchases are influenced by and in turn have influence on a wide variety of socio-economic characteristics. Evidence of the purchase of durables as substitutes for financial savings is shown by Klein (1954) and Maynes (1959).

The focus of the studies on asset ownership is centered on the investment decisions of the household and on explanation of differences in the total stock of assets and their distribution among households over long periods of time. (Katona, 1949 and 1960; Lydall, 1958.) Findings of these studies indicate that with income held constant, households headed by people with more education tend to have larger stocks of assets and lower debt, and that higher-income households have more in financial assets and less in durables. Occupational differences are pronounced. Liquid assets are directly related to wealth by numerous investigators including Guthrie (1960),

Kreinin (1957 and 1961), and others at the Survey Research Center of the University of Michigan.

In order to determine the influence of variables other than income on consumer behavior, recent investigators have used, primarily, three sets of variables: socio-economic characteristics of the household including age and life cycle; financial practices; and attitudes and expectations. The advent of the theory of relative income and introduction of permanent income hypotheses have created new interest in nonincome family variables. Katona (1949), Brady (1952), Klein (1954), and Fisher (1959 and 1962), have related variations in expenditures to differences in family size and vice versa.

The decision-making process has received greatest attention in the study of deliberation entering into consumer purchases. Juster (1957 and 1960), Ferber (1954), and Mueller (1958 and 1960) conclude that many purchases of durable goods are planned and thought out carefully in advance. Bilkey (1953 and 1957) has made use of consumer panels to explain the decision process in terms of accumulation of desires for and against making a purchase (psychic tensions). This study measures intensity of desires for and against an action in terms of positive and negative valences; the closer the household to action, the more the excess of positive valences over negative.

Clawson (1960) has extended Bilkey's theory into a general model of decisions to buy for the household. Mueller (1958) attempts to ascertain the role of innovation in household purchases, discovering that the innovators (the first to buy new types of appliances) are generally the young, well-educated married couples with children, and those who are financially optimistic. Whyte (1955) traces how people through interpersonal contact become interested in purchasing a particular product, finding neighborhood communication to be a deciding factor. His study stresses the importance of the group in motivating people to purchase new products, inferring that it is the group that determines when a luxury becomes a necessity. Husbands and wives are compared by Wolgast (1958) to determine who makes the purchasing decisions.

Bodkin (1960), Kreinin (1961) and Friedman (1960) examine the effect of windfall incomes on consumption. Foote (1960) published a symposium on household decision-making which reflects the current thinking on decision-making in an optimistic manner, and indicating that empirical work in this area is only just beginning. It is hoped that this type of research will turn more in the direction of its effect upon the family rather than upon the market.

It should be recognized that a large proportion of the consumer-behavior studies have related two economic factors (such as income or occupation to consumer behavior) rather than relating consumption to family phenomena. It is hoped that the future direction of research regarding consumer behavior will turn more toward relating economic behavior to family phenomena.

Economists are interested in changes—changes in choice patterns over time, changes in systems of living, and changes in behavior—rather than in behavior itself. Clark (1958) reminds us that "we need to find out more about what causes attitudes to change, how needs, incentives, and expected outcomes affect attitudes and behavior."

CONCEPTS

Because the scope of the economic approach is so broad that its concepts are interrelated in some manner or other with each of the institutions of society, delineation of the fundamental concepts of the approach is a tedious task. It is made even more complicated because the materialistic nature of its elements has led investigators to employ and define substance-bound rather than more general substance-free concepts. For these reasons, only the more crucial and more generally accepted concepts are defined below.

Welfare: well-being. Welfare is the state of prosperity of an individual or group in relation to the prosperity of the society. Hoyt (1954) conceives of welfare as being dependent upon the use made of resources to provide (1) physical necessities, (2) goods and services deemed necessary by the consensus of scientific opinion, and (3) psychic necessities which grow out of the relationship of an individual to the family or of the family to its society.

Dynamics: the persistence or change in levels of welfare of individuals within their lifetimes and from one generation to another. (Morgan, *et al.,* 1962.)

System of living: the total individual and group behavior as it is integrated about the efforts to satisfy desires. For example, an extreme emphasis upon fashionable clothing may lead to a relative decline in expenditures for food and other necessities. The dominant values implicit in systems of living are denoted by the phrase *manners of living.* Such values as frugality or luxury, asceticism or self-indulgence, and stability or flexibility of expenditures provide the centers around which the systems of living are integrated. It is the differences in these values which enable one to discriminate between various systems of living. (Zimmerman, 1936, pp. 3–4.)

Standard: a physical, written, graphic, or other kind of representation of a product or a procedure established by authority, custom, or general consent with which other products or procedures of a like nature are compared for identification or measurement or to which they are made to conform. (Coles, 1949; Gordon, 1961.) Two general uses of the concept are found in economic studies. One refers to standards in commodities; for example, butter is graded on the basis of flavor, body or texture, color, and package. If an expert grader scores the butter ninety-three, it may be labeled USDA Grade AA. This usage refers to a *commodity standard.* A second use of the concept is in reference to a *standard budget:* the amount, calculated at local current prices, required to sustain at a determined level of living (minimum standard) for a stated period, a family of given composition as to members and ages. A *budget* is consequently a plan for the use of resources to provide the needs and wants of the family group.

Standard of living: an ideal or desired norm of consumption, usually defined in terms of quantity and quality of goods and services. Investigators have utilized three slightly different definitions. *Typological* standard of living is the type of behavior which most adequately expresses the dominant values found in the associated manner of living. It is a species of the systems of living. This behavior is neither average nor extreme: it is the type of behavior common to those who successfully represent the habits and values of the given group. For example, in a society where frugality is highly regarded, the individual who avoids consumption and accumulates capital exemplifies the behavior characteristic of the standard of living. (Marshall; Weber.)

The *scientific* standard of living is the ideal level of expenditures set up by social scientists as a means to a sanctioned social end, that is, as a means to removal of poverty. This form of the concept differentiates between *plane of living* (what people actually consume) and *standard of living* (what those who attempt to reform society consider the theoretical level of living). An example of the latter would be the examination of what will happen in terms of living efficiency if the family regulates its expenditures according to a scientifically determined budget which is planned with reference to efficiency. This concept gives rise to standard budgets.

The third approach is the *attitudinal* standard: a standard of living that is wanted: the attitudes which govern spending, rather than the actual consumption of goods and services. (Zimmerman, 1936, pp. 4–5.) Kyrk (1953) defines standard of living as the things which one insists upon having.

Reid (1938) defines a standard of living as the sum total of things that families consider essential as revealed through expenditures, status of housing, and numerous possessions. The standard of living in this sense is the result of economic behavior of the group and is more closely related to plane of living than the previous definitions. A plane of living represents the purely economic aspect of standard of living. It is the materially measurable form of the standard of living, the goods and services actually consumed. (Hoyt; Zimmerman.)

Minimum standard of living: the minimum standard consistent with health and decency. Minimum *social* standard of living is the minimum regarded by society as consistent with health and decency. Rates of pensions and unemployment compensation as well as welfare measures in legislation use this approach to the minimum standard. Poverty exists below this standard, the satisfaction of which the community regards as justified or necessary. Minimum *personal* standard of living: the minimum standard regarded by the individual as consistent with the health and decent living of his family. This is what is called the *felt* minimum standard. The standard of felt poverty always includes not only the necessities of health and decency, but also the necessities of efficiency and skill which would enable the worker to work at a high level of productivity. It includes psychological necessities which give the sense of respectability. The social poverty line or minimum standard of living operates on averages rarely going beyond the distinction of age, sex, and health. The felt or personal minimum standard is expressed in comparison to personal expectations, and the diversity of living conditions in the community.

The *scientific* minimum standard is based on measured needs for meeting requirements of consumption standards of health and decency. It calls for calculations of requirements by physiology or biology as well as economics and sociology. The aim of such a standard is to furnish a measuring-rod for the requirements of a family per consumption unit, reducing the differences of age, sex, and sometimes occupation (where the occupation involves differentials of food requirements as in heavy work) of members of the family to a consumption unit. (Zweig, 1949.)

Poverty: economic insufficiency, evident when a person or family is unable to maintain that standard of living which is regarded by the community (or the family) as adequate or socially desirable. Such a definition implies that the standard of living varies from one community to another. Therefore, poverty is relative to a minimum standard of living and relative to the community social standard. Galbraith considers people as poverty-stricken when their income, even if adequate for survival, falls markedly below that of the community. Families whose total earnings are insufficient to obtain the minimum necessities for the maintenance of mere physical efficiency are said to be in *primary poverty*. (Rowntree, Zweig, Kyrk.) Families whose total earnings would be sufficient for the maintenance of physical efficiency were it not that some portion is absorbed by other expenditures, either useful or wasteful, are said to be in *secondary poverty*. Poverty caused by factors such as bad health, incapacity, emotional instability, or old age is called *natural poverty* or *case poverty*. *Structural poverty* caused by unemployment and starvation wages is referred to as *social poverty*. *Insular poverty* manifests itself in an "island" of poverty, where nearly everyone is poor. (Galbraith, 1958.)

Deprivation: that stage of family welfare lying between poverty and adequacy as judged by the standard of living in the community. The deprivation level for families in the United States in 1960 as determined by the Conference on Economic Progress, for example, includes families of four persons with income between $4,000 and $5,999, the median income of the population at that time. Below $4,000 a family would be considered in poverty by this source; above $5,000 the family's income would be considered adequate to allow decent and comfortable but not affluent living.

Affluence: an elusive concept introduced into popular economic usage by Galbraith (1958), with a meaning somewhat synonymous with wealth and comfortable living. The Conference on Economic Progress defined affluent families as ones with incomes of $15,000 and over in 1960.

Status (as defined in the structure-functional approach): position plus the connotation of invidious evaluation, differential prestige, and hierarchy. Its primary use in the economic approach is in classifying the relative welfare of families in the *socio-economic structure* of the society. Socio-economic structure involves the concepts of (1) *economic stratification:* gratifications of wealth and income status that exist within a community including not only the amount of income and wealth but also the nature of the income and its sources and (2) *occupational stratification:* a ranking of occupational groups within a society based upon authority, skill, amount of responsibility, degree of complexity of work, and so on. *Occupation* is a classification of jobs usually following the census classifications. *White-collar workers* include professionals, technical workers, managers, officials, self-employed businessmen, clerical help, and salesworkers. *Blue-collar workers* include craftsmen, foremen, operatives, laborers, service workers, and government workers in protective jobs. *Skilled workers* are craftsmen and foremen. *Unskilled workers* are laborers, service workers, and government protective workers.

Income: family income is that stream of money, goods and services, and satisfactions that come under the control of the family to be used by them to satisfy needs and desires and to discharge obligations. (Nickell, Dorsey, and Budolfson, 1959, p. 208.) *Real income* is used in a nonmonetary concept as the flow of goods and services available for any given period of time. Real income is derived from the use made of money income including the services derived from owned property and possessions. It includes such things as food furnished by a garden, the use of a house, automobile, and all other equipment and durable goods. *Psychic income* is the flow of satisfactions that arise out of every-day experiences, derived largely from the use of money and real income and making for psychic and physical well-being. *Permanent income* is the mean income regarded as permanent by the consumer unit in question, which in turn depends on the horizon and foresightedness of the consumer unit. (Friedman, 1957, p. 93.) *Windfall* (*transitory income*) is an accidental or chance occurrence of income not giving rise to anticipations of further income from the same source. (Jones, *et al.*, 1960.)

Parsimony: abstinence from expenditure on consumable commodities leading to accumulation of savings. The result of parsimony is considered as capital investment and thereby economic growth by those who stress the savings function.

Consumption: the use of economic resources by ultimate consumers. (Hoyt, 1938, p. 5.) Consumption is the use made of wealth. *The consumption function* considers consumption as spending for consumer goods. Consumption in this use causes *demand*, bringing into existence both production and capital, the latter as a factor of production. The consumption function, then, is the economic effect of consumption. *Conspicuous consumption:* the consumption of a high proportion of economic goods, services, and advantages, particularly those considered by society as luxuries, for the purpose of demonstrating pecuniary power, of satisfying sensations other than organic or cultural wants. In this type of consumption, wealth is considered to arouse esteem only as others know about it. (Zimmerman, Hoyt, Veblen, Hobson.) *Consumer behavior* includes behavior in the use of money and in the choice between leisure (time) and money. It involves also the motivating forces behind consumption—wants and needs and consumer attitudes and preferences as well as behavior.

Needs: the lack of something which, if allowed to continue, will result in harm to an individual. *Wants* are the desires for goods people learn to use to meet needs. Wants are learned and are largely psychological, highly influenced by the opinions of the groups to which the individual belongs. (Fitzsimmons, 1961.) Wants are tendencies born of social life and evolving with it, and as such can be extended indefinitely. (Halbwachs.) *Necessities* are needs: those goods and services which are essential to the health and strength of habitual activities of an individual or group including food, shelter, and clothing. *Decencies* are those things which a given individual must use in order to preserve his existing rank in society. (Senior, 1872.) *Luxuries* are wants and differ from one society to another and from one family to another. The satisfaction of consumer needs and wants is the ultimate purpose of the economic system. *Demand* exists when wants are accompanied by the means to pay for the goods and by the willingness of consumers to part with the money or expend the time and energy needed to get the goods. Willingness of the consumer to buy depends upon the value of the goods and their utility to him.

Value: the power of one good to command other goods (or money) in exchange. Three types of value are recognized by Gordon (1961): survival, prestige, and welfare. The group concept of what constitutes and promotes its welfare (as education, religion, military prowess, artistic achievement) constitutes *welfare value*. *Utility* is the want-satisfying power of goods and may take any of several forms: time, place, form, or possession utility. *Marginal utility* is the utility to a consumer of any one unit of his available stock of a given commodity. It is what he would lose in ability to satisfy his want for that good if he had one less unit of it. (Bigelow, 1953.) The principle of *diminishing marginal utility* shows that each additional unit of a series of identical units adds to the sum of total utility a person expects to gain from a supply of the units, an amount which is less than that expected from the preceding unit.

Working wife: a married woman living with her husband who seeks income from sources other than her activities within her family. Because of the magnitude of research conducted on the working wife and her effect upon the modern American family, it is imperative that she be mentioned in a list of concepts forming the economic framework.

BASIC ASSUMPTIONS

The following assumptions are representative of those under which investigators have operated in viewing the welfare of the family. A few of the assumptions are conflicting in outlook; so are the theories of the investigators. Some assumptions have been changed and modified through time and in light of the society to which the assumption applies.

1. Man's desire to maintain and improve his condition is fundamental. Progress is linear. The general level of living of the masses can be and is rising. It is more difficult for a family to reduce its expenditures from a high level than for a family to refrain from having high expectations in the first place. (Zimmerman, Modigliani.)

2. Desires vary not only with time or place, but also according to the economic condition, social class, and experience of the individual. All wants are not equally important in the competition for recognition. Material wants are highly competitive and compelling in societies of high material wealth and in those in which there is no class structure based on family. It is natural for individuals and groups in a democratic society to emulate their social betters.

3. Man can control his station in life. To use a traditional economic

analysis: consumers are assumed to be "economic men" who consciously guide and control the economic system. Consumers are assumed to determine through the price system what shall be produced, how much, and what quality. Market price is assumed to adequately regulate prices in the consumer interest. (Gordon, 1961.) More recent economic analysis assumes that the money which individuals have to spend is a reasonably good indicator of the importance they attach to their needs. The justification for a market system relies on the assumptions that earned incomes are a fair measure of the value of the individual's contribution to production and that human needs are adequately represented by dollars available to be spent.

4. Measurement of socio-economic status is dependent upon three basic assumptions described by Hollingshead in establishing an index of social position: (*a*) there exists a status structure in society, (*b*) positions in this structure are determined mainly by a few commonly accepted symbolic characteristics, and (*c*) the characteristics symbolic of status may be scaled and combined by the use of statistical procedures so that a researcher can quickly, reliably, and meaningfully stratify the population under study. (Hollingshead, 1957, p. 2.)

5. There is close relationship between the level of consumption and the behavior of the people in which this level of consumption prevails. (This assumption has some weakness in that the level of consumption may be as much a determined, as a determining, factor, but it is subscribed to by many investigators.)

6. There is also assumed to be a close relationship between the schedules of consumption of economic goods and the other activities of man. Knowledge of the entire family budget can lead to knowledge of the family which in turn leads to understanding of the total social structure of which it is a part. (More recent investigators have modified this assumption of Le Play to include standard of living in place of the family budget.) It is this assumption which allows social objectives to be measured by scales of expenditure.

7. Receipt of economic assistance by a family lessens ambition, thrift, and aspiration. The assumption is one of the more controversial ones at the present time. Proponents of the assumption further assume in their research that economic autonomy of nuclear families in Western industrialized societies is the preferred form for the best functioning of the society and that parental as well as gov-

ernmental aid is potentially destructive to family independence. Opponents of the assumption believe that if families are guaranteed a subsistence level of income in time of unemployment, without a "means test" or loss of the assets acquired through savings, the family will not lose the will or desire to improve its status. This belief in the right of every family in a democracy to a minimum standard of living is the foundation for OASI, poverty improvement programs, and other "civil rights income" such as veterans benefits, and points to the difference between Kerr-Mills Medical Assistance and Medicare.

8. The welfare of the family is related to the economic conditions of the society. Poverty is relative, not only to the society in which it occurs but relative to its cause and the standards of those who experience it. (Galbraith, Harrington, Eliot.)

9. Saving (abstaining from present consumption) is a virtue, which should and can be taught to children and adults. Reducing future income by incurring debt lowers families' level of living and is likely to lead to family dissension and perhaps financial disaster.

PRODUCT

Theory

The economic school has produced numerous theories and volumes of laws, some of which may be considered highly scientific contributions to the body of knowledge about families and their societies. Aside from the early theories of the founders of the school, three general theories based on research have emerged as determinants of consumer spending: the absolute-income hypothesis, the relative-income hypothesis, and the permanent-income hypothesis. Each of these theories was advanced as a hypothesis in terms of individual behavior and then generalized to aggregate behavior, accounting for the use of the word *hypothesis* in the title of the theory. Each postulates a relationship between consumption and income, although the assumptions underlying the hypotheses vary considerably.

The absolute-income hypothesis: (men are disposed, as a rule and on the average, to increase their consumption as their income increases, but not by as much as the increase in their income) was originated by Keynes (1936), and through this theory he derived the consumption function. The adequacy of this theory was ques-

tioned by Kuznets (1946) and by Goldsmith (1955) primarily
because of its apparent inability to account for budget data on
saving with observed long run trends.

The relative-income hypothesis: an answer to this inconsistency,
was substituted by Brady and Friedman (1947). Its underlying assumption is that the saving rate depends not on the level of income
but on the relative position of the individual (or family) on the income scale. The hypothesis was further modified by Modigliani
(1949), Deusenberry (1949), and Davis (1952) on the basis that
families become adjusted to a certain standard of consumption
rather than to a certain level of income, so it is past spending that
influences current consumption rather than past income. Numerous
investigators have tested the theory for differences in rural and
urban families, white and non-white families, and for geographical
location with validating conclusions.

The permanent-income hypothesis grew out of a concern by Reid,
Kuznets, and Friedman for the adequacy of current income as the
most appropriate determinant of consumption expenditures. According to this theory a family is said to determine its standard of living
on the basis of expected returns from its resources over its lifetime.

There are likely to be further modifications of these theories.
Family size and composition, as well as the sources of family income,
are important factors in consumer behavior. So are habit persistence,
emulation, and custom. Assets, both inherited and acquired, which
are relatively neglected in the theories, are actually and clearly
highly relevant.

Economic welfare research has contributed a number of laws of
consumption which help to explain the economic behavior of families and the standards of living they seek. Zimmerman (1936, pp. 51–
55) collected twenty-six of these theories developed by early pro-
pounders of consumption economics who are well respected in the
schools of economic thought. Several from this list are:

AUTHOR	THEORY
Gregory King	The demand for food is such that a short-age causes extreme modification in the other fields of consumption.
Ernst Engel	Percentages spent for food decrease with increased income and vice versa.

AUTHOR	THEORY
Ernst Engel	The proportion of the outgo used for food, other things being equal, is the best measure of the material standard of living of a population.
M. Halbwachs	Laborers spend more per adult unit for food than white-collar employees of the same income class.
E. Laspeyres	The lower the income, the higher are the proportions for rent within any given social class, and vice versa.
Zimmerman	Not only do expenditures of the lower-class families indicate a greater nearness to physiological requirements, but their homes are so organized that more of the space is devoted to eating, sleeping, and the physical needs of the group.
F. Le Play	The level of future consumption is guided by mores and customs which constitute an important part of the nonmaterial standard of living.
American Engel School	The proportion of expenditures for sundries (advancement goods) is the best measure of the standard of living of the population.

Research

Recent contributions of the economic school to research have been made first in the refinement of data-gathering and cross-sectional representative sampling techniques, and second in the building of bodies of useful demographic and expenditure data on families throughout the country which are available over a period of consecutive years. Widespread use of such data by researchers is encouraged as a result of storing the data on magnetic tapes or in decks of data cards which facilitate scientific analysis by machine.

Development of the Lorenz Coefficient of Inequality (the Gini Index), which is highly useful in comparing departure from equality of two distributions, has facilitated the measuring of inequality in the distribution of incomes, a necessary step in determining family welfare.

The economic approach has provided the basis for the development of indices of socio-economic status so frequently used in research by other disciplines to control variables. The numerous studies of families in crises, reactions to working wives, and the development of cost-of-living estimates for families and development of standard family budgets have facilitated the testing of hypotheses and the development of theories of family welfare. Thus, these studies serve as bases for analysis and prediction of noneconomic family reaction.

Morgan (in Clark, 1958) classifies research on consumer behavior according to the theories which are utilized in the research: reference-group theories, habits, standards of living, resistance to change, social and economic mobility, irrational behavior, clinical psychology and psychoanalysis (needs and personality factors which motivate choice), the family as the primary reference group, perception, personality, learning, and attitude and attitude changes. Obviously not all such research has been directed specifically at understanding the family, but it has contributed to the body of knowledge regarding the habits and activities of families. Such theories indicate the recent trend in economic research to question not only the economic phenomenon being measured, but to seek also what causes attitudes to change and how needs, incentives, and expected outcomes affect attitudes and behavior within the family reference group.

We know far too little about the very wealthy and the very poor and the effect of wealth and poverty upon the dynamics of the family. A continued emphasis is needed on studies relating economic to familial factors. Such studies as those made by the Bureau of the Labor Statistics and described by Lamale (1958 and 1963) which analyze changes in consumption expenditures, and those conducted on income and welfare at the Michigan Survey Research Center and described by Morgan, *et al.* (1962) point the direction for analysis on a national scale and future research within the economic welfare framework.

Practice

Knowledge of the characteristics of financial decisions, income and consumption habits, and aspirations for standards of living at each of the socio-economic levels and during each stage of family life form a necessary background of knowledge and reference point for marriage counselors as well as for teachers of courses in family living.

Research on consumer behavior, motivation, and intentions has produced data of value in predicting consumer spending and saving —data used freely by the advertising, manufacturing, and merchandising industries.

Knowledge of how many and which ones of the families in the society are unable to provide the decencies of living is an aid to the government and to agencies planning for welfare and social-security measures. The economic school has served society as a tool for discovery of the level of welfare of its members. It has guided the action of other scientific groups carrying out reform programs.

VALUES

Obviously, values do exist within the framework of the economic approach, but these values differ from one investigator to another. One researcher may be convinced of the value of individualism or atomism as opposed to familism, as can be seen in the works on development of underdeveloped countries. For them, the general value system under which they operate is stated thus: The good of the group is more important than that of the individual; in the long run, the individual will benefit greatest by what benefits the society as a whole. But in the short run, individualism, principally in the form of occupational mobility and entrepreneurship, will bring greatest rewards to the individual who, as a consequence, imparts his rewards to society.

There was an undertone in the approach of earlier writers—which is still evident in the works of followers of Marxism and socialism—of placing higher value upon materialistic goods than nonmaterial ones, but this value is *not* inherent in the total framework of the economic approach. It is true that Marxist theory (that the mode of production in material life determines the general character of the social, political, and spiritual processes of life) is based on this value, but Marxist theory is not the accepted foundation for the economic-welfare framework.

Rather, the free-world proponents of the economic-welfare approach to the study of the family appear to value family welfare highly, believing that a minimum standard of living is the due of all families.

THE FRAMEWORK

Within the economic framework the family is viewed as an economic unit composed of individuals each with a set of mutual economic rights and responsibilities as well as relationships. There is no family, according to this viewpoint, unless the related members live together in a common dwelling-place and share in the returns of their labors and consumption of common goods. This view of the family accounts for the use of the household or consumer unit as a unit of reference in current economic surveys. Such usage is not far from earlier references to the family as a productive unit. Economic conditions of the society have changed production to consumption as the mutual right and responsibility of family members.

The economic framework consists of a network of inter-related economic concepts and assumptions which focus upon discovery, measurement, and analysis of family welfare. Through it economic factors are related to family phenomena and vice versa. Consumption emerges as a key concept in the economic framework, linking together the four areas of concentration: (1) *standards* of living, which depend upon custom, habit, emulation, tastes, and the means of financing consumption: occupation and income; (2) socio-economic *status* and its numerous indices of rank: occupation, source of income, education, housing, and material goods and services, which are the product of consumption; (3) consumer *behavior* and the wants and needs that are the motivating forces behind consumption; and (4) economic *conditions* of the society: the relative well-being of the society and the circumstances which it imposes upon the family.

In the economic approach, welfare depends upon the use made of resources to provide physical necessities, goods and services deemed necessary by the consensus of opinion, and psychic necessities which grow out of the relationship of an individual to the family or of the family to its society. The standard of living is generally accepted as meaning the sum total of things families consider essential as revealed through their consumption or aspirations. Consumption is the use made of whatever wealth the family possesses, and is directed toward the satisfaction of needs and wants. Demand exists when wants are accompanied by the means to pay for the good(s), and value is the power of one good to command other goods (or money) in exchange. Utility is the want-satisfying power of goods. The diagram shows the relationship between these economic concepts.

ECONOMIC CONCEPTUAL FRAMEWORK

Use of Family
RESOURCES

is determined by
WANTS, NEEDS, ATTITUDES, CUSTOMS, HABITS

leads to
CONSUMPTION

of
GOODS and SERVICES

which determines or is determined by

STANDARDS	STATUS	BEHAVIOR
Values Income	Occupation Education Income	Utility Value

producing

STANDARD OF LIVING   SOCIOECONOMIC STATUS   LEVEL OF LIVING AND
CONSUMER BEHAVIOR

considered in relation to
ECONOMIC CONDITIONS OF THE SOCIETY

leads to
FAMILY WELFARE

There appears to be developing in the economic approach a continuum of concepts forming a measuring stick for reference to family welfare. The following diagram of such a continuum is admittedly premature, but may serve to clarify the relatedness of certain concepts underlying the economic framework.

POVERTY	DEPRIVATION	THE COMMON MAN	AFFLUENCE	SATIETY
(Destitution)	(Insecurity)	(Adequacy)	(Wealth)	(Luxury)

Dominant values held by researchers within the economic framework differ. The free-world proponents of the approach appear to value family welfare highly, believing that all families in the society are due a minimum standard of living. Such a value is highly questioned by researchers who believe that receipt of economic assistance to a family member lessens ambition, thrift, and aspirations.

What families do economically—the standards they stress, the status they seek, and the behavior they exhibit—is a highly useful analytical tool in the study of the family.

CRITIQUE AND DISCUSSION

Economic theories came early in the development of literature regarding society and the family. The means of testing these theories came late. Economists have therefore tended to philosophize, to produce laws before the groundwork has yet been laid, to think in terms of laws rather than hypotheses or postulates. This is a result not of indiscretion or lack of sophistication in research technique, but rather of overzealousness and preoccupation with the material aspects of economics as a result of the mathematical and philosophical origin of economic thought.

The economists, statisticians, home economists, sociologists, and others interested in economic phenomena as they relate to the family have contributed a wealth of factual material about families and societies past and present. Their views and findings have stimulated research into understanding behavior and motives that may have not been satisfactorily explained elsewhere. Without the use of economic concepts, control for status or class would be extremely difficult in determining relationships of a noneconomic character. Without the use of economic concepts, wants and drives would be difficult to explain fully. Economic concepts contribute to the very form and family system which a society follows. Determination of consumption patterns over long periods of time is crucial to full analysis of the family-cycle concept. Power structure and role are affected by economic concepts such as those relating to income, control of expenditures, and division of labor within the household. Child-care training practices are related to the educational attainment and economic status of the mother. Consumer-expenditure studies provide knowledge of what happens to families during crises and in periods of poverty and of affluence.

In recent years interest has turned toward the development of methods of analysis of economic concepts. A most useful innovation was made in methods of producing representative sampling of populations by using area probability techniques. The results of surveys are principally descriptive data. Often surveys are conducted at the expense or with backing of government agencies for data-gathering purposes without analysis by the usual social-research methods. In view of this, it is not surprising that Hill and his associates discredited "budget studies" as lacking a conceptual frame-work. But descriptive works such as budget studies and estimates of consumer expenditures, as well as measures of income and welfare, serve an essential purpose—furnishing factual knowledge upon which governments establish welfare measures. Such works are essential in measuring the extent of unemployment as the basis for corrective measures, and discerning consumption habits as the bases for cost-of-living indexes. It is descriptive research which furnishes the data from which analyses and even predictions can be scientifi-cally made.

That writers of economic studies have, as a whole, become pre-occupied with refinement of techniques for gaining accurate descrip-tive data and, in many cases, have stopped short of analysis of family phenomena, may still constitute a weakness of the economic approach. A large number of economic studies have examined economic phenomena of the family and not the family itself. A large number have stopped short of the analysis stage, concentrating on the descriptive. It is hoped that more and more research will reach beyond the descriptive stage into interpretation, analysis, and prediction. Future employment of economic concepts should (and, it is to be hoped, will) be directed toward deductive explanation of inequalities of family welfare and toward new theoretical analysis of the family.

It is felt, however, that there does exist a large enough body of studies relating economic phenomena to the family to allow formu-lation of an economic framework at this time. The time is ripe for putting into a logical conceptual framework the separate compo-nents of economic theory, the economic variables used in analysis of the family, and the economic phenomena measured in descriptive family surveys. The present paper is such an attempt. It is certain that this attempt will need alterations and changes before its form is crystallized, but it is hoped that this organization and statement of relationship of components focusing on family welfare will serve as a stimulant to the formulation of further family economic theory.

REFERENCES

ABINGTON, FLORENCE. "Money Management Experiences of a Selected Group of Louisiana Youth as Related to Subculture, Sex, Social Status and Age." Uupublished dissertation (Florida State University, 1958).
ANGELL, R. C. The Family Encounters the Depression. New York: Charles Scribner's Sons, 1936.

ATELSEK, F. J. "Characteristics of Older Job Seekers: An Analysis in Terms of Their Unemployment History." Unpublished dissertation (University of Minnesota, 1958).

BAKKE, E. W. *The Unemployed Worker. A Study of the Task of Making a Living Without A Job.* Nos. 1. and 2. New Haven: Yale University Press, 1940.

BARRY, H., CHILD, I. L., and BACON, M. K. "Relation of Child Training to Subsistence Economy," *American Anthropologist,* (Jan. 1959), pp. 414–63.

BIGELOW, H. F. *Family Finance.* Philadelphia: J. B. Lippincott Company, 1953.

BILKEY, W. J. "Consistency Test of Psychic Tension Rating Involved in Consumer Purchasing Behavior," *Journal of Social Psychology,* **45** (Feb. 1957), pp. 81–91.

———. "A Psychological Approach to Consumer Behavior Analysis," *Journal of Marketing,* **18** (July 1953), pp. 18–25.

BODKIN, R. "Windfall Income and Consumption." *American Economic Review,* **49** (Sept. 1959), pp. 602–14.

———. "Windfall Income and Consumption," in I. Friend and R. Jones, eds. *Proceedings of the Conference on Consumption and Saving,* Vol. II. Philadelphia: 1960, pp. 175–87.

BRADY, DOROTHY S. "Influence of Age on Saving and Spending Patterns," *Monthly Labor Review,* **78** (Nov. 1955), pp. 1240–44.

———. "Family Budgets: A Historical Survey," *Monthly Labor Review,* **66** (Feb. 1948), pp. 171–75.

———. "Individual Incomes and the Structure of Consumer Units," A.I.A. Papers and Proceedings, May 1958.

———. "Family Saving, 1888–1950," in Goldsmith, Brady, and Mendershauser. *A Study of Saving in the United States,* Vol. III. Princeton, N.J.: Princeton University Press, 1956, pp. 139–276.

———, and FRIEDMAN, ROSE. "Savings and the Income Distribution," *Studies in Income and Wealth,* Vol. X, New York: National Bureau of Economic Research, Inc., 1947, pp. 247–65.

BRONFENBRENNER, URIE. "Socialization and Social Class Through Time and Space," in Eleanor Maccoby *et al. Readings in Social Psychology.* New York: Holt, Rinehart & Winston, Inc., 1958.

BROOM, L., and SELZNICK, P. *Sociology.* New York: Harper & Row, Publishers, 1958.

CARROLL, MARGARET. "The Working Wife and Her Family's Economic Position," *Monthly Labor Review,* **85** (April 1962), pp. 366–74.

CAUDLE, ANN. "Financial Management Practices of Employed and Nonemployed Wives," *Journal of Home Economics,* **56** (Dec. 1964), pp. 723–27.

CAVAN, RUTH SHONLE. *Marriage and Family in the Modern World*. New York: Thomas Y. Crowell Company, 1960.

————. "Unemployment—Crisis of the Common Man," *Marriage and Family Living*, 46 (May 1959), pp. 139–46.

————, and RANCK, KATHERINE. *The Family and the Depression*. Chicago: University of Chicago Press, 1938.

CENTERS, RICHARD. *The Psychology of Social Class*. Princeton, N.J.: Princeton University Press, 1949.

CHRISTOPHERSON, VANDIVER J. S., and DREUGER, MARIE. "The Married College Student," *Marriage and Family Living*, 22 (May 1960), pp. 122–28.

CLARK, ALMA B. "Economic Contributions Made by Families to Their Newly Married Children," *Journal of Home Economics*, 54 (March 1962), pp. 229–30.

————, and WARREN, JEAN. *Economic Contributions Made to Newly Married Couples by Their Parents*. Memoir 382. Ithaca, N.Y.: Cornell University Agricultural Experiment Station, May 1963.

CLARK, L. H. *Consumer Behavior: Research on Consumer Reactions*. New York: Harper & Row, Publishers, 1958.

————, ed. *The Life Cycle and Consumer Behavior*. New York: New York University Press, 1955.

CLAWSON, J. W. "Family Composition, Motivation, and Buying Decisions," in N. Foote, ed. *Household Decision-Making*. New York: 1960, pp. 200–17.

COHN, W. "Social Status and the Ambivalence Hypothesis: Some Critical Notes and a Suggestion," *American Sociological Review*, 25 (Aug. 1960), pp. 508–13. Reply, 26 (Feb. 1961), pp. 104–05.

COLES, JESSIE. *Standards and Labels for Consumers' Goods*. New York: Ronald Press Company, 1949.

Conference on Economic Progress. *Poverty and Deprivation in the United States*. Washington, D.C. Conference on Economic Progress, 1962.

CUBER, J. F., and KENKEL, W. F. *Social Stratification in the United States*. New York: Appleton-Century-Crofts, 1954.

CUSHING, H. M. "Economic Status of Married College Students," *Journal of Home Economics*, 40 (Jan. 1948), pp. 25–26.

DANLEY, R. A., and RAMSEY, C. E. *Standardization and Application of a Level-of-Living Scale for Farm and Nonfarm Families*. Ithaca, New York: Cornell University Agricultural Experiment Station, New York State College of Agriculture, July 1959.

DAVID, M. "Welfare, Income and Budget Needs," *The Review of Economics and Statistics*, 41 (Nov. 1959), pp. 393–99.

DAVIS, T. E. "The Consumption Function as a Tool for Prediction," *Review of Economics and Statistics*, 34 (Aug. 1952), pp. 270–77.

DEUSENBERRY, J. S. *Business Cycles and Economic Growth.* New York: McGraw-Hill, Inc., 1958.

———. *Income, Saving and the Theory of Consumer Behavior.* Cambridge, Mass.: Harvard University Press, 1949.

DICKINS, DOROTHY. *Food Use and Gainful Employment of the Wife.* Bulletin 558. Mississippi Agricultural Experiment Station, 1958.

EASTERLIN, R. A. "The American Baby Boom in Historical Perspective," *American Economic Review,* **51** (Dec. 1961), pp. 869–911.

ELIOT, T. D. *American Standards and Planes of Living.* Boston: Ginn and Company, 1931.

"Estimating Equivalent Incomes or Budget Costs by Family Type," *Monthly Labor Review,* **83** (Nov. 1960), pp. 1197–1200.

EVERSLEY, D. E. C. *Social Theories of Fertility and the Malthusian Debate.* London: Oxford University Press, 1959.

FARRELL, J. "The New Theories of the Consumption Function," *Economic Journal.* **69** (Dec. 1959), pp. 678–95.

FELDMAN, FRANCES. *The Family in a Money World.* New York: Family Service Association of America, 1957.

FERBER, R. "Research on Household Behavior," *American Economic Review,* **52** (March 1962), pp. 19–63.

———. "The Role of Planning in Consumer Purchase of Durable Goods," *American Economic Review,* **44** (Dec. 1954), pp. 854–74.

FISHER, JANET. "Family Life Cycle Analysis on Research on Consumer Behavior," in L. H. Clark, ed. *The Life Cycle and Consumer Behavior.* New York: Harper & Row, Publishers, 1955, pp. 28–35.

———. "Income, Spending, and Saving Patterns of Consumer Units in Different Age Groups," in National Bureau of Economic Research. *Studies in Income and Wealth,* Vol. 15. New York: 1962, pp. 75–102.

FITZSIMMONS, CLEO. *Consumer Buying for Better Living.* New York: John Wiley & Sons, Inc., 1961.

FOOTE, N. N., ed. *Household Decision-Making.* New York: New York University Press, 1961.

FRIEDMAN, M. "Comments on Windfall Income and Consumption," in *Proceedings of the Conference on Consumption and Saving,* Vol. 2. Philadelphia: 1960, pp. 191–206.

———. *A Theory of the Consumption Function.* National Bureau of Economic Research, General Series No. 63. Princeton, N.J.: Princeton University Press, 1957.

———. *Studies in the Quantity Theory of Money.* American Institute for Economic Research. Chicago: University of Chicago Press, 1956

———. "A Method of Comparing Incomes of Families Differing in Composition," *Studies in Income and Wealth,* Vol. XV. New York: National Bureau of Economic Research, 1952.

———, *et al.* "Socio-Economic Factors in Religious Differences i

Fertility," *American Sociological Review*, **26** (Aug. 1961), pp. 608–14.

GALBRAITH, JOHN K. *The Affluent Society*. Boston: Houghton Mifflin Company, 1958.

GIANOPULUS, A. and MITCHELL, H. E. "Marital Disagreement in Working Wife Marriages as a Function of Husband's Attitudes Toward Wife's Employment," *Marriage and Family Living*, **19** (Nov. 1957), pp. 373–78.

GILMORE, H. W. *The Beggar*. Chapel Hill, N.C.: University of North Carolina Press, 1940, pp. 168–82.

GLENN, HORTENSE. "Attitudes of Women Regarding Gainful Employment of Married Women," *Journal of Home Economics*, **51** (April 1959), pp. 247–52.

GOLDSMITH, R. *A Study of Savings in the United States*. Princeton, N.J.: Princeton University Press, 1955.

GORDON, L. J. *Economics for Consumers*. New York: American Book Co., 1961.

GREENFIELD, S. M. "Socio-Economic Factors and Family Form," *Social and Economic Studies*, **10** (March 1961), pp. 72–85.

GUILFORD, J. D. "A Survey of Consumption Theory—from Keynes Through Friedman," *The American Economist*, **6** (May 1962), pp. 12–20.

GUTHRIE, H. W. "Consumers' Propensities to Hold Liquid Assets," *Journal of American Statistical Association*, **55** (Sept. 1960), pp. 469–90.

HAER, J. L. "Predictive Utility of Five Indices of Social Stratification," *American Sociological Review*, **22** (Oct. 1957), pp. 541–46.

————. "A Comparative Study of the Classification Techniques of Warner and Centers," *American Sociological Review*, **20** (Dec. 1955), pp. 689–700.

HAGEN, E. E. "Population and Economic Growth," *American Economic Review*, **49** (June 1959), pp. 310–27.

————. "The Consumption Function: A Review Article," *Review of Economics and Statistics*, **37** (Feb. 1955), pp. 48–54.

HALBWACHS, M. *The Psychology of Social Class*, trans. by Claire De Lavenay. New York: Free Press of Glencoe, Inc., 1958.

HALL, J., and JONES, D. C. "Social Grading of Occupations," *British Journal of Sociology*, **1** (March 1950), pp. 31–55.

HARP, J. "Socio-Economic Correlates of Consumer Behavior," *American Journal of Economics*, **20** (April 1961), pp. 265–70.

HARRINGTON, M. *The Other America*. New York: The Macmillan Company, 1962.

HEAL, F. D. "Values in a Group of Lower-Socio-Economic Students," *Marriage and Family Living*, **22** (Nov. 1960), pp. 370–72.

HETZLER, A. S. "An Investigation of the Distinctiveness of Social Classes," *American Sociological Review*, 18 (Oct. 1953), pp. 493–97.

HILL, R. "A Critique of Contemporary Marriage and Family Research," *Social Forces*, 33 (Mar. 1955), pp. 268–77.

HILL, R. and HANSEN, D. "The Identification of Conceptual Frameworks Utilized in Family Study," *Marriage and Family Living*, 22 (Nov. 1960), pp. 299–311.

HILL, R., KATZ, A., and SIMPSON, R. "An Inventory of Research in Marriage and Family Behavior: A Statement of Objectives and Progress," *Marriage and Family Living*, 19 (Feb. 1957), pp. 89–92.

HOFFMAN, LOIS. "Effects of the Employment of Mothers on Parental Power Relations and the Division of Household Tasks," *Marriage and Family Living*, 22 (Feb. 1960) pp. 27–35.

HOLLINGSHEAD, A. B. *Two Factor Index of Social Position*. New Haven: Yale University Press, 1957.

HONEY, RUTH. "Family Uses of Financial Resources," *Journal of Home Economics*, 48 (May 1956), pp. 347–48.

HOUTHAKKER, H. S. "An International Comparison of Household Expenditure Patterns, Commemorating the Centenary of Engel's Law," *Econometrica*, 25 (Oct. 1957), pp. 532–51.

———. "The Permanent Income Hypothesis," *American Economics Review*, 48 (June 1958), pp. 396–404.

HOYT, ELIZABETH. *Consumption in Our Society*. New York: McGraw-Hill, Inc., 1938.

———, et al. *American Income and Its Use*. New York: Harper & Row, Publishers, 1954.

HUGHES, E. C. "Personality Types and the Division of Labor," *American Journal of Sociology*, 33 (Mar. 1928), pp. 754–68.

———. *Men and Their Work*. New York: Free Press of Glencoe, Inc., 1958.

INKELES, A. "Industrial Man: The Relation of Status to Experience, Perception, and Value," *American Journal of Sociology*, 66 (July 1960), pp. 1–31. Rejoinder, 66 (Jan. 1961), pp. 367–68.

International Labour Office. *Family Living Studies: A Symposium*. Geneva, 1961. Available at United Nations, 345 East 40th St., New York.

JONES, ROBERT C. "Transitory Income and Expenditures on Consumption Categories," *American Economic Review, Papers and Proceedings*, 50 (May 1960), pp. 584–92.

JUSTER, F. T. "Predictions and Consumer Buying Intentions," *American Economic Review*, 50 (May 1960), pp. 604–17.

———. *Consumer Expectations, Plans, and Purchases: A Progress Report* National Bureau of Economic Research, Occasional Paper 70. New York: 1957.

KAHL, J. A., and DAVIS, J. "A Comparison of Indexes of Socio-Economic Status," *American Sociological Review*, 20 (June 1955), pp. 317–25.

KATONA, G. "Analysis of Dissaving," *American Economic Review*, 39 (June 1949), pp. 673–88.

———. *The Powerful Consumer*. New York: McGraw-Hill, Inc., 1960.

KELSO, R. W. *Poverty*. London: Longmans, Green and Co. Ltd., 1929.

KENKEL, W. F. "A Sociological Study of Married Student Veterans at the University of Maryland" Unpublished M.A. thesis University of Maryland, 1950, pp. 56–75.

KEPHART, W. "Occupational Level and Marital Disruption," *American Sociological Review*, 20 (Aug. 1955), pp. 456–65.

KEYNES, J. M. *The General Theory of Employment, Interest, and Money*. New York: Harcourt, Brace and World, Inc., 1936.

KLEIN, L. R. "Statistical Estimation of Economic Relations from Survey Data," in Katona, *et al. Contributions of Survey Methods to Economics*. New York: Columbia University Press, 1954, pp. 189–240.

KNOLL, MARJORIE. "Toward a Conceptual Framework in Home Management," *Journal of Home Economics*, 55 (May 1963), pp. 335–39.

KOMAROVSKY, MIRRA. *The Unemployed Man and His Family*. New York: The Dryden Press, Inc., 1940.

Koos, E. L. *Families in Trouble*. New York: Columbia University Press, 1946.

KREININ, M. E. "Analysis of Liquid Asset Ownership," *Review of Economics and Statistics*, 43 (Feb. 1961), pp. 76–80.

———. "Windfall Income and Consumption," *American Economic Review*, 51 (June 1961), pp. 388–90.

KUZNETS, S. "Economic Development and Cultural Change," *American Economic Review*, (April 1961), pp. 225–48.

———. "The Why and How of Distributions of Income by Size," National Bureau of Economic Research *Studies in Income and Wealth*, Vol. 5. New York: 1943, pp. 5–29.

KYRK, HAZEL. *The Family in the American Economy*. Chicago: The University of Chicago Press, 1953.

———. *Economic Problems of the Family*. New York: Harper & Row, Publishers, 1933.

———. *A Theory of Consumption*. Boston: Houghton Mifflin Company, 1923.

LAMALE, HELEN H. "Workers' Wealth and Family Living Standards," *Monthly Labor Review*, 86 (June 1963), pp. 676–86.

LAMPMAN, R. J. *The Low Income Population and Economic Growth*. Study Papers Nos. 12 and 13 of the Joint Economic Committee at the 86th Congress, United States Government Printing Office, Washington, 1959.

LAWSON, E. D., and BOEK, W. E. "Correlations of Indexes of Families' Socio-Economic Status," *Social Forces*, 39 (Dec. 1960), pp. 149–52.

LINTON, RALPH. "Women in the Family." *Women, Society and Sex.* J. E. Fairchild. ed. New York: Sheridan House, 1952, pp. 67–82.

LITWAK, E. "Occupational Mobility and Extended Family Cohesion," *American Sociological Review*, 25 (Feb. 1960), pp. 9–21.

LIVITAN, N. "Errors in Variables and Engel Curve Analysis," *Econometrica*, 29 (July 1961), pp. 336–62.

LYDALL, H. "Income, Assets, and the Demand for Money," *Review of Economics and Statistics*, 40 (Feb. 1958), pp. 1–14.

———. "The Life Cycle in Income, Savings, and Asset Ownership," *Econometrica*, 23 (April 1955), pp. 131–50.

MAGRABI, FRANCES. "Some Aspects of Decision as a System," *Journal of Home Economics*, 55 (Dec. 1963), pp. 755–62.

MAISEL, S., and WINNICK, L. "Family Housing Expenditures: Elusive Laws and Intrusive Variances," in I. Friend and R. Jones, eds. *Proceedings of the Conference on Consumption and Saving*, Vol. 1. Philadelphia: 1960, pp. 359–435.

MALTHUS, T. R. *An Essay on the Principle of Population*, 6th ed. Homewood: R. D. Irwin, Publishers, 1963.

MARSHALL, ALFRED. *Principles of Economics*, 9th ed. New York: The Macmillan Company, 1916.

MATTHEWS, A. and ABU-LABAN, B. "Job Satisfaction and Leisure-Time Activity," *Sociology and Social Research*, 43 (Jan.–Feb. 1959), pp. 189–96.

MAYNES, E. S. "The Relationship Between Tangible Investment and Consumer Saving," *Review of Economics and Statistics*, 41 (Aug. 1959), pp. 287–94.

MAYO, S. C., HAMILTON, C. H., and PETTUS, C. "Sources of Variation in the Level of Living of Farm Operators in the United States," *Social Forces*, 39 (May 1961), pp. 338–46.

MIDDLETON, R. and NIMKOFF, M. "Types of Family and Types of Economy," *American Journal of Sociology* (Nov. 1960), pp. 215–25.

MODIGLIANI, F. "Fluctuations in the Saving-Income Ratio: A Problem in Economic Forecasting," National Bureau of Economic Research *Studies in Income and Wealth*, Vol. 11. New York: 1949, 371–443.

MOORE, W. E. "Labor Attitudes Toward Industrialization in Underdeveloped Countries," *American Economic Review*, 45 (May 1955), pp. 156–65.

MORGAN, J. N. "A Review of Recent Research on Consumer Behavior," in L. H. Clark, ed. *Consumer Behavior: Research on Consumer Reactions.* New York: Harper & Row, Publishers, 1958, pp. 93–219.

———, et al. *Income and Welfare in the United States.* New York: McGraw-Hill, Inc., 1962.

MORGAN, WINONA L. *The Family Meets the Depression.* Minneapolis: University of Minnesota Press, 1939.

MUELLER, EVA. "Consumer Attitudes: Their Influence and Forecasting Value," *The Quality and Economic Significance of Anticipations Data.* Princeton, N.J.: National Bureau of Economic Research, 1960, pp. 149–75.

———. "The Desire for Innovations in Household Goods," in L. H. Clark, ed. *Consumer Behavior: Research on Consumer Reactions.* New York: Harper & Row, Publishers, 1958, pp. 13–37.

NELSON, H. A., and LASSWELL, T. E. "Status Indices, Social Stratification and Social Class," *Sociology and Social Research*, **44** (Jul.–Aug. 1960) pp. 410–13.

NERLOV, M. "Comments and Discussion," *American Economic Review* **50** (May 1960), pp. 618–22.

NICKELL, PAULENA, DORSEY, J., and BUDOLFSON, M. *Management in Family Living.* New York: John Wiley & Sons, Inc., 1959.

NYE, F. IVAN "Employment Status of Mothers and Adjustment of Adolescent Children," *Marriage and Family Living*, **21** (Aug. 1959), pp. 240–44.

———, and HOFFMAN, LOIS. *The Employed Mother in America.* Chicago: Rand McNally & Company, 1963.

OGBURN, W. F. "Implications of the Rising Standard of Living in the United States," *American Journal of Sociology*, **60** (May 1955), pp. 541–46.

———, and NIMKOFF, M. F. *Technology and the Changing Family.* Boston: Houghton Mifflin Company, 1955.

———, and THOMAS, DOROTHY, "Influence of the Business Cycle on Certain Social Conditions," Journal of American Statistical Association (Sept. 1922), pp. 324–40.

OLIVER, JOHN W. *History of American Technology.* New York: The Ronald Press Company, 1956.

ORENSTEIN, HENRY. "The Recent History of the Extended Family in India," *Social Problems*, 8 (Spring 1961), pp. 341–50.

PENNOCK, JEAN L. "Rural Family Spending and Consumption in a Low-Income Area in Kentucky." *Home Economics Research Report No. 26.* Washington, D.C.: Agricultural Research Service, USDA, August 1964.

RAINWATER, *et al. Workingman's Wife.* Dobbs Ferry, N.Y. Oceana Publications, Inc., 1959.

REID, MARGARET. "Consumption, Savings and Windfall Gains," *American Economic Review*, **52** (Sept. 1962), pp. 728–37.

———. "Effect of Income Concept Upon Expenditure Curves of Farm Families," National Bureau of Economic Research *Studies in Income and Wealth*, Vol. 15. New York: 1952, pp. 133–74.

————. *Consumers and the Market.* New York: Appleton-Century-Crofts, 1938.

REISSMAN, LEONARD. *Class in American Society.* New York: Free Press of Glencoe, 1959.

RICE, ANN S. "An Economic Life Cycle for Childless Families." Unpublished dissertation (Florida State University, 1964.)

————. "Social Consequences of Working Wives." Unpublished paper (Florida State University, 1963.)

ROGERS, E. M. "The Effect of Campus Marriages on Participation in College Life," *College and University,* **34** (Winter 1958), p. 195.

————, and SEBALD, H. "A Distinction Between Familism, Family Integration, and Kinship Orientation," *Marriage and Family Living,* Vol. 24 (Feb. 1962), pp. 25–30.

ROSEBOROUGH, H. "Some Sociological Dimensions of Consumer Spending," *Canadian Journal of Economics,* **26** (Aug. 1960), pp. 452–64.

ROSENBERG, M., SUCHMAN, E. A., and GOLDSEN, ROSE. *Occupations and Values.* New York: Free Press of Glencoe, Inc., 1957.

ROWNTREE, S. *Poverty: A Study of Town Life.* London: Macmillan and Co., Ltd., 1902.

————, and LAVERS, G. R. *Poverty and the Welfare State.* London: Longmans, Green and Co., Ltd., 1951.

RUSTGARD, J. *The Problem of Poverty: A Plain Statement of Economic Fundamentals.* New York: Appleton-Century-Crofts, 1936.

SCHWARZWELLER, H. K. "Values and Occupational Choice," *Social Forces,* **39** (Dec. 1960), pp. 126–35.

SENIOR, W. N. *Political Economy,* 6th ed. London: C. Griffin and Company, 1872.

SERVICE, E. R. "Kinship Terminology and Evolution," *American Anthropologist,* **62** (Oct. 1960), pp. 747–63.

SHARP, H., and AXELROD, M. "Mutual Aid Among Relatives in an Urban Population," in Freidman, *et al. Principles of Sociology.* New York: Holt, Rinehart & Winston, Inc., 1956, pp. 433–39.

SOROKIN, P. *Social Philosophies of an Age of Crisis.* Boston: Beacon Press, 1950.

————. *Contemporary Sociological Theories.* New York: Harper & Row, Publishers, 1928.

STEINER, P. O., and DORFMAN, R. *The Economic Status of the Aged.* Berkeley and Los Angeles: University of California Press, 1957.

STOLZ, LOIS. "Effects of Maternal Employment on Children: Evidence from Research," *Child Development,* **31** (Dec. 1960), pp. 749–82.

STOTZ, MARGARET. "The LBS Interim Budget for a Retired Couple," *Monthly Labor Review,* **83** (Nov. 1960), pp. 1141–57.

SUITS, D. B. "The Demand for New Automobiles in the United States

1929–1956," *Review of Economics and Statistics*, **40** (Aug. 1958), pp. 273–80.

SUSSMAN, M. B. "The Help Pattern in the Middle-Class Family," *American Sociological Review*, **18** (Feb. 1953), pp. 22–28.

———, and BURCHINAL, L. "Parental Aid to Married Children: Implications for Family Functioning," *Marriage and Family Living*, **24** (Nov. 1962), pp. 320–32.

SYDENSTRICKER, E., and KING, W. I. "The Measurement of the Relative Economic Status of Families," *Quarterly Publication of the American Statistical Association*, Series 135 (Sept. 1921), pp. 842–57.

TABAH, L. "A Study of Fertility in Santiago, Chile," *Marriage and Family Living*, **25** (Feb. 1963), pp. 20–26.

TOBIN, J. "Relative Income, Absolute Income, and Savings," in *Money, Trade and Economic Growth*. Essays in honor of John H. Williams. New York: The Macmillan Company, 1951, pp. 135–56.

United Nations. *International Definition and Measurement of Levels of Living*. UN Pub. Sales No.: 61. IV: 7, 1961.

———. *Report on International Definition and Measurement of Standards and Levels of Living*. Joint Committee of International Labor Office and UN Educational Scientific and Cultural Organization. UN Pub. Sales No.: 54. IV: 5, 1954.

VAN SYCKLE, CALLA. "Economic Expectations and Spending Plans of Consumers," *Review of Economics and Statistics*, **36** (Nov. 1954), pp. 451–55.

VAN VALEN, MARTHA. "An Approach to Mobile Dependent Families," *Social Casework*, **37** (April 1956), pp. 180–86.

VEBLEN, THORSTEIN. *The Theory of the Leisure Class*. New York: The Modern Library, 1931.

VICKERY, W. S. "Resource Distribution Patterns and the Classification of Families," National Bureau of Economic Research *Studies in Income and Wealth*, Vol. 10. New York: 1947, pp. 260–329.

WARNER, W. L., MEEKER, M., and EELS, K. *Social Class in America*. Chicago: Science Research Association, 1949.

———, and LUNT, P. S. *Social Life of a Modern Community*. New Haven: Yale University Press, 1941, pp. 277–79.

WATTS, H. W. *Long-Run Income Expenditure and Consumer Saving*. Cowles Foundation Paper No. 123, New Haven: 1958.

———, and TOBIN, J. "Consumer Expenditures and the Capital Account" in I. Friend and R. Jones eds. *Proceedings of the Conference on Consumption and Saving*. Vol. 2. Philadelphia: 1960, pp. 1–48.

WEISSKOPF, WALTER A. *The Psychology of Economics*. Chicago: University of Chicago Press, 1955. Chap. 12.

WESTOFF, CHARLES, et al. *Family Growth in Metropolitan America*. Princeton, N.J.: Princeton University Press, 1961.

WHYTE, W. H. "The Web of Word of Mouth" in L. H. Clark, ed. *The Life Cycle and Consumer Behavior*. New York: Harper & Row, Publishers, 1955, pp. 113–22.

WILLIAMS, FAITH. "International Comparisons of Patterns of Family Consumption," in *Consumer Behavior: Research on Consumer Reactions*. New York: Harper & Row, Publishers, 1958.

———, and ZIMMERMAN, C. *Studies of Family Living in the United States and Other Countries*. USDA Miscellaneous Publication 223, Washington: 1935.

WOLF, CHARLES. "Institutions and Economic Development," in Okun, B. and Richardson, R., eds. *Studies in Economic Development*. New York: Holt, Rinehart & Winston, Inc., 1962, pp. 349–64.

WOLGAST, ELIZABETH. "Do Husbands or Wives Make the Purchasing Decisions?" *Journal of Marketing*, 23 (Oct. 1958), pp. 151–58.

XENOPHON. *Oeconomicus*, English translation. London: William Heinemann, Ltd., 1918.

ZIMMERMAN, C. C. *Consumption and Standards of Living*. New York: D. Van Nostrand Company, Inc., 1936.

ZWEIG, F. *Labour, Life and Poverty*. London: Victor Gollancz, Ltd., 1949.

chapter 11

Is There a Legal Conceptual Framework for the Study of the American Family?

K. Imogene Dean

and

M. W. Kargman

The development of legal systems[1] brought a new form of recognition to certain existing rights belonging to individuals who live together in society. These rights (representing some power, interest, or privilege), having been singled out by the legal system as ones to be enforced by the political authority of the state, became "the law." The purpose of the law is to coordinate human behavior by authoritative patterns. (Timasheff, 1939, p. 321.)

The fundamental aim of the law is to maintain the general security. The definition of general security changes and therefore the rights that are recognized must change too. The interests which become law have been classified at different periods in history as rights pertaining to the person and rights pertaining to property.

[1] A legal conceptual framework requires a legal system. Until a society has developed to the point where it has a legal system, its law problems are undifferentiated from other relationship problems.

269

Many social rights, so called because people think that from the point of view of ethics they should be law, do eventually become legal rights.

The law is an instrument for social control, and because there is great need for people to feel secure about their knowledge of law, there is great resistance to change of the laws—that is, principles—themselves. Yet the law keeps changing all of the time. There is less resistance to changes in the social space within which the law operates. Thus, legal principles which the law said applied only to business relationships are today applied to family relationships. The principles have not changed, but the application of the principles to new classes of persons has brought about changes in the law—new legally enforceable interests.

During the feudal period in English history when it was important to keep the title to land unencumbered because the social system was based upon land ownership, the general security required the law to protect interest in property even at the expense of other interests which clamored for legal recognition. When land descent became less important, other social interests were given the force of law. Today we see somewhat the same situation with regard to private-property rights. Modern business practices rely upon particular certainties in title to property. The business community will resist attempts to change this balance of interests.

We can see from the above that there is a hierarchy of interests the law will protect, but that the hierarchy may change. There are distinctions between controlling acts which threaten the security of the state and acts which threaten the security of the rights of individuals.

Criminal law is concerned with acts which threaten the general security of the society. In criminal law, all actions are brought by the state against individuals who have interfered with the peace. In tort law, one private citizen brings a legal action against another.

Rights considered absolute at one time in history may no longer be considered as rights at all. The idea that when a man and woman marry they became one, and that one was the husband, belonged to an earlier period in history. At that time, a man had the right of life and death over his wife. It was considered an absolute right. Today the rights of married men and women are differently defined and enforced by the law. Today *absolute rights* refer to the inalienable rights of man stated in the Constitution of the United States and the

Charter of the United Nations. They are vague and subject to judicial interpretation. They are constantly being redefined in social space and social time. The whole concept of *civil rights* and the enforcement of them is coming into conflict with other longer-established rights in private property which grew out of the social climate of the industrial revolution. The legal system must therefore adjust the conflicting relations of men growing out of the changes in the law—growing out of the recognition of right plus the political force to back it.

Criminal law results in a judicial sentence: either fine or imprisonment. Tort law results in a judicial decision: the assessment of damages to repair the loss. We generally refer to the sentence as punishment: "To inflict punishment means to restore the ideal order defined by law. Legal power shows its force and the socio-ethical conviction is reinforced. Other sanctions restore natural order." (Timasheff, 1939, p. 266.)

The law recognizes and will enforce a variety of rights that grow out of relationships; for example, citizenship, marriage, birth, and lease. Relationship through contract recognizes the negotiability of certain legal rights. The law of contracts grew out of the need for security in trade relations. When trade was an important social value, the law concerning contracts was weighted in its favor. Thus slavery was allowed to flourish under contract law. Slavery can no longer be contracted. A person cannot indenture himself even if he wants to.

The limits of freedom to contract are defined by the law. As the President of Harvard University says, "the law is the pursuit of wise restraints that make men free."[2]

Since the essence of law is enforcement, perhaps a word about the legal system for enforcement is in order. American law is based upon the English common law. Common-law courts handled matters of contract and tort. When social interests not recognized by the common law were pressing for legal recognition because of the changes in the social composition of the society, courts of equity were established by the king—the king's bench. The king's bench said it was morally wrong not to enforce certain rights not recognized by the common law. Thus the courts distinguished between legal rights and moral rights. Along with the separate courts grew different rules of procedure and evidence. Today we have still

[2] Recited when the degree of law is granted at a Harvard commencement.

another form of tribunal for adjudication: administrative boards as, for example, the National Labor Relations Board and the Civil Aeronautics Board.

The history of family law is related to the development of these three courts: the law court, the court of equity, and the administrative board.

Family law is divided into two categories: (1) the protection of those interests which have to do with the relations of family members to each other within the family and (2) the protection of interests of family members in their relations to other persons or social institutions outside the family. The first group includes such matters as annulment, divorce, custody, paternity, adoption, and support. The second group refers to actions in which the family as a social unit has suffered a loss or injury either through tort or contract; for example, a husband can recover damages when his wife has been injured for the family's loss of that wife's services. Under common law, actions for the enforcement of rights falling within the second group were permitted. However, actions for rights falling within the first group were not recognized by common law. Individual family members, except the father-husband as head of the household, had no legally enforceable rights. While interests within the family were recognized as important, they were not legally secured. Women and children were for all practical purposes owned by the male head of the house; they were not *sui juris*, that is, not legally defined as persons. They were considered human property.

Household tensions and problems had a different forum: the ecclesiastical courts. Although marriage was a sacrament and considered indissoluble, the religious courts did recognize divorce "from bed and board." The parties were divorced for all purposes except remarriage. The church attempted to adjudicate the personal conflicts between members of the families.

Since there were no religious courts in the American colonies, family disputes concerning divorce, separation, and child custody were tried in the courts of equity. In handling such matters, the equity courts had no precedents to follow except the decisions of the ecclesiastical courts, by which they were not bound but which they generally followed. Different colonies and, later, states accepted as much or as little of these precedents as they chose, and there was no uniformity in the development of family law. The result has been that much of our family law reflects theological thinking rather than a balancing of interests, a spirit of compromise, or any sense of limitation. (Foster, 1962, p. 86.)

Although church courts had no jurisdiction to grant absolute divorce, the Holy See could annul a marriage and leave the parties free to marry again. In England Parliament could grant an absolute divorce, and in this country the task fell to the colonial legislatures. Later, this task too was transferred to the courts of equity.

With the growth of statutory law to take care of situations not covered by the comon law, the social regulation of marriage and the family increased. The married women's acts gave new legal status to women, and the state, to secure the general welfare, secured the rights of children: "The patriarchal regime of the old clan family often subjected children to extreme oppression but the matter was within the family and did not disturb the economic balance of the family. But as soon as the new family consisting of only the parents and children stood forth, society saw how many were unfit for parenthood and began to realize the need for community care." (Calhoun, 1945, p. 173.)

Voluntary choice has always been a precondition for a valid marriage under common law. Today there is a question as to whether or not the courts should recognize a voluntary dissolution because of change in the affectional environment of the marriage. In some jurisdictions, incompatibility is a ground for divorce. (Clarke, 1957, pp. 27, 28, 70.)

Regulations affecting the family grow out of a particular culture and in turn contribute to the making of that culture. Family law responds to the needs and pressures of the time, often with notable cultural lag.

Some class or group is eternally in process of working over its marriage practices; more slowly, much more slowly, its marriage-concept will work into the revision; a new concept of what "right" marriage is comes into conflict with the older normation of another class or group. First socially. And later, in the law. Slowly.

The tentative conclusion, society, law-in-action, legal doctrine, all of necessity sown with contradiction and divergent tensions; the older basic structure and ideology (touchingly oversimplified even as to the conditions which it mirrored) bedevilled with a kaleidoscopic miscellany of new patchings—

and of more ancient hold-overs imbedded. (Llewellyn, 1950, p. 32.)

Ogburn elaborates that the changing family is forcing the law to take cognizance of family problems. (1950, p. 127.) Legal concepts based on judicial decision and allocating fault and, in a sense, declaring a moral judgment are being replaced by the hallmarks of other professions—ideas calling for diagnosis, treatment, and guidance. Juvenile courts and family courts are prime examples. Preventive law is designed to anticipate, to nullify, or to circumvent behavior, conduct, and relationships which might involve persons or groups in conflict with the law.

Pound in his discussion of domestic-relations interests says the law must take into account and secure the individual spiritual existence of family members. "From the beginning the social interest in general security requires the law to secure adequately this feature of domestic relations since injuries to them touch men on their most sensitive side and no injuries are more certain to provoke self-redress and even private war." (Pound, 1959, p. 70.)

Today private wars within the family are seeking relief within the legal system. And the legal system is beginning to give force to domestic interests and give them the status of law, that is, make them interests enforceable in law. A good example is the Conciliation Court of Los Angeles. If we were to place this court in the previously-mentioned categories of law, equity or administrative board, it would fit neither. In essence, it is closer to an administrative board than a court, since it deals with matters never before heard in law or equity. The conciliation-agreement document which the parties sign after consultation with a court-appointed marriage counselor is in the form of a legal contract, but the subject matter—"the husband promises to take his wife to dinner once a week," "wife promises not to call her mother in front of her husband," "husband promises not to see third party any more," or "wife promises she will stop drinking"—involves situations within the family which threaten to create family war. Failure to abide by this conciliation agreement gives the injured party the right to appear before the judge and ask for relief. This procedure is singular. It is closely related to what probably happened when family members brought their internal problems before the ecclesiastical courts in England. It may be an answer to the question raised by Seagle, who says, "The state blunders when it intervenes in family affairs, for example, in the decree that husband and wife shall be one, the state has no methods for promoting this remarkable unity." (1946, p. 50.)

As the legal system changes and expands to protect the personal element in nonfamily relationships (rights of privacy), family members look to the law to expand and to secure through force what they consider legitimate domestic-relations interests. Through analogy, family members extend laws of the political state into the family and expect similar relief. The woman whose husband has acquired a love interest in a third party asks, "Don't I have the right to stop her just as much as labor unions have the right to seek an injunction against management for an unfair labor practice?" Under our present legal system, such a right does not exist in law or equity. If the wife lived within the jurisdiction of the California court, she could test her domestic interest.

Pound in his *Fifty Years of Jurisprudence* (Vol. I, p. 349) said:

Looking at the characteristics of the science of law of today, in comparison with that of 50 years ago, we may say,

1. It has developed a functional attitude, asking not merely what it is and how it came to be but what (in all its senses) it does, how it does it and how it may be made to do it better.

2. It has given over its exclusiveness and seeks what may be called team play with other social sciences.

3. It studies law in all its senses in relation to the whole process of social control.

4. It becomes conscious of the role of individualization—personal judgment and intuition derived from personal experience.

5. It takes up problems of values, of criteria for measurement weighing interests, making and shaping precepts and interpreting them where found.

With all of these changes, has there developed a legal conceptual framework for approaching the American family?

FOCI OF STUDY

Except for few articles reviewed for this survey the literature consists of treatments of family law rather than studies of the family from the view of law. Changes in the law reflect the decay of one conception of the family and the emergence of another. For example, English common law was concerned with legal rights and duties of individuals rather than social needs. As the concept of individual dignity gained headway the earlier concern became inadequate. (Hogan and Ianni, 1956, 182.)

The following topics appear to be the foci of concern of those who write in the field of family law:

1. The rights and duties of individuals who occupy given statuses (or those who aspire to occupy those statuses).
2. Historical and locational variability in family law.
3. Sociocultural interrelationships—changes which are reflected by law and changes which might be effected by changes in law.
4. The gaps between "real" and "ideal" values and practices in the family area.
5. Legal problems arising from *conflicts of laws*, conflicts between old and new cultural forms, and uncertainties about new forms. The focus here will be upon legal problems arising from conflicts of law—a term referring to a situation in which two legal decisions made in different states concern the status of the same family member. This occurs where the husband and wife separate and file separate law suits. *Conflicts in law*, on the other hand, refers to a situation in which legal problems arise out of conflicting legal decisions in one state. These conflicts occur when a new statute or decision is added to the body of family law and seems to create ambiguities in the established family law of that state.

CONCEPTS

Marriage: the establishment of the legal relationship of husband and wife in accordance with all of the legal requirements as set forth by the political entity charged with the enforcement of law.

Family: a concept used to designate many relationships. (Black, 1951, p. 727.) Relationships are specified: husband and wife, parent and child, cousins, and so on. Marriage laws regulate what degree of consanguinity is permissible for a legal marriage. The law also legitimizes certain procedures for adoption of new family members. Inheritance and descent of family members are defined and classified unless the common law applies in that state.

Separation agreements: disposition of marriage rights. Upon marriage, certain rights accrue. When the parties seek to separate and fulfill the legal requirements prerequisite to separation (being of sound mind, under no duress), they make disposition of certain rights that accrued upon marriage. They can negotiate support, residence requirements, lump-sum payments, insurance, and so on. They cannot, however, give each other the right to remarry. This right must come from the courts through the divorce decree.

Divorce decree: a judicial document reciting that the legal requirements for divorce have been fulfilled and that the plaintiff seeking the relief of divorce is being granted this relief. From the legal point of view, it rescinds the rights and obligations of the husband-wife relationship established by the marriage. If a separation agreement has been made by the parties, it will usually be incorporated into the divorce decree and thereby acquire certain legal privileges of enforcement different from a separation agreement not incorporated into a divorce decree.

Child-custody agreements are usually incorporated in the divorce decree where there are minor children. Some states require that the parent who receives custody refrain from taking that child out of the state without the permission of the other parent or the court. In common law, there was no duty to support children. In the colonies, children of divorced parents were often indentured out.

Coverture: the bundles of rights residing in the wife under common law; the condition or state of a married woman. (Black, 1933, p. 473.) A married woman is entitled to dower on the death of her husband. Dower includes a one-third interest in the real estate and half of the personal property. The right to dower attaches upon marriage and the wife's inchoate right becomes a lien upon the real estate. The real property (land and the buildings attached to it) cannot be sold during her lifetime without a release by her. No such lien attaches to the personal property, which a husband can convey without the wife's release. Today a married woman has the right to pledge her husband's credit for the necessities of life. In community-property states, her status as a married woman has specific attributes regarding property.

Divorce: the legal separation of man and wife effected, for cause, by the judgment of a court and either totally dissolving the marriage relation or suspending its effects so far as concerns the cohabitation of the parties. (Black, 1933, p. 602.) *Absolute divorce,* which was unknown under common law, places the parties in the same position as the single person and does not restrict remarriage. In the United States today, some jurisdictions issue divorces in stages, part one authorizing the persons to live separate and apart as though divorced (an interlocutory decree) but without the right to remarry until the decree becomes final. Before the decree becomes final, they can decide to live as husband and wife and do not need to remarry. When the decree becomes final, they must remarry if they want to be married legally.

Partial divorce: a legal separation which the parties have had legitimized through court action.

Annulment: a legal action to rescind the marriage and return the parties to the same legal status they had before the marriage. It differs from divorce, because in a divorce the parties must make legal disposition of the rights and duties acquired upon marriage. In annulment, the theory is that marital rights and duties never attached.

Limited divorce (a mensa et thoro—"from bed and board"): the divorce granted by the ecclesiastical courts in England and in this country. Its effect upon the relationship of the parties is very similar to the legal separation: no right to remarry.

Defenses: legal denials of charges. Divorce is a right enforceable only in equity. Certain equitable defenses will invalidate the right. A person must come into equity with clean hands or the court will not grant relief. Collusion, connivance, condonation, and recrimination are all equitable defenses. Collusion and connivance are related to the validity of the grounds for divorce. If a defendant says, "I hit my wife only because she wanted grounds for divorce and I said I would give her the divorce," this is collusion and a good defense to the wife's action for divorce. If a husband sues a wife for adultery and the wife proves that she never intended to commit adultery but that her husband forced her by his actions into the relationship, the wife's defense of connivance will bar the divorce.

Condonation: action which erases the ground for divorce. Where a wife sues for divorce on the grounds of physical cruelty and the husband proves that after the alleged cruel acts, they lived as husband and wife, the courts hold that the living together has condoned the cruelty.

Recrimination: action which nullifies the ground for divorce. If a wife sues for divorce on the ground for cruelty and the husband defends and proves adultery on the part of the wife, the court will not grant a divorce to the wife. Recrimination as a defense says the plaintiff has committed acts which would be grounds for divorce if the defendant were to sue.

Grounds for divorce: what the statutes define as sufficient reason for a "cause of action" to accrue against the defendant. Because divorce is a statutory right, the statutes alone can define its causes. At one time, the only ground was adultery. Vernier lists eight major grounds: cruelty, desertion, impotence, imprisonment or conviction of a crime, intoxication, nonsupport, and insanity. (p. 3.) One plaintiff may have a choice of grounds depending upon the facts.

Conjugal fidelity: interest prejudiced by adultery. The law intends to discourage infidelity by allowing actions for alienation of affections and for adultery.

BASIC ASSUMPTIONS

1. Freedom exists only in a social climate of wise restraints.
2. The state is best able to designate the order of those restraints which will inure to the general welfare. Some restraints not specifically designated by the state are acknowledged by it to be important to the general security. These are ethical but not imperative.
3. The interests of individuals must be weighed against the interests of social groups.
4. The state is an interested third party in all matters affecting the husband-wife relationship and in all matters affecting the parental relationship. The state delegates to the husband and wife certain responsibilities necessary for the carrying out of the functions of the state, the most important being custody of children and their socialization. When parents fail, the state must designate substitutes.
5. The welfare of individual family members must be considered relative to the needs of the basic relationships upon which the family is founded. The law will carefully consider all of the factors. "It is important to distinguish the individual interests in domestic relations from the social interest in the family and marriage as social institutions. This social institution must play an important part in weighing it with the social interest in individual life to determine what individual interests in such relations are to be secured and how they are to be secured." (Pound, 1959, p. 68.) "The law has to give effect to the right of the one party to the relationship against the other and enforce the corresponding duty. The law has never attempted to deal fully with this task. Religion, boni mores and the internal discipline of the household have largely sufficed to

secure the interests of members of the household as among themselves." (Pound, 1959, p. 71.)

6. Where the custody of a child is before the court, the judge will try to do whatever is in the best interests of the child. In the United States, there has been a tendency to give custody to the mother even if she is at fault in a divorce proceeding. However, this is changing (as in the recent Rockefeller case).

7. Marriage laws should encourage responsible marriages, and the law is constantly seeking new regulations to encourage this attitude: for example, health requirements, waiting periods between license and marriage dates, raising age of marriage.

8. The law concerning divorce will change because the need to resort to legal fictions in order to have grounds for divorce offends the ethical nature of man.

9. The law assumes that the child has a right to the natural love and affection of his parents and that he will receive these from living with his parents. The law will not disturb custody unless the court feels this assumption in a particular case is not true.

PRODUCT

The literature which approaches marriage and the family from the legal aspect is heavily weighted toward practical matters. It is written for two purposes: to be used as teaching material in the law schools and to help practicing lawyers better represent their clients. The judicial administration of family law has recently been discussed more frequently, however, since there is a movement for specialized domestic-relations courts with specially trained judges. There are increased attempts to consolidate all family matters in one court. There is as yet no uniformity of meaning to the term *family court*. In some jurisdictions such courts have very broad powers: in others, they are limited juvenile courts. Recommendations for better trained legal counselors in domestic matters; recommendations for uniformity and greater clarity of marriage and divorce laws; and recommendations for changes in adoption, legitimacy, support, alimony, and annulment laws have resulted from special conferences on illegitimacy, marriage, divorce, and family life.

States have codified their family law after study. (In 1959 Wisconsin did this following a study committee's recommendations toward improvements. (See Appendix 1.)

As Pound said, the law has never attempted to deal fully with the problems raised by family disputes. (p. 71.) Yet the changing social order and the change of the family from a basic economic unit to a multifaceted social unit is making heavy demands upon the courts and the legislatures. There is agitation for a better fit between the ethical interests and legal interests of family law. The law is uncertain as to the rights and statuses of the divorced, the children of the divorced, the children born through artificial insemination, the status of the wife artificially inseminated (is it adultery?), the rights of stepfathers by divorce, and so on.

Contributors to research in family law are concerned with drawing better agreements; creating less hostility between parents by requiring fewer admissions in the legal papers; clarifying conflicts in laws so as to prevent illegitimacy; experimenting with new adoption laws; experimenting with safeguards in child-custody cases—even requiring counsel for the child in some jurisdictions.

Lawyers believe better skills in these areas will be beneficial to parents and children and the community.

Contributions to theory in the field of the family via the legal approach have been very limited. (Kargman, 1959.)

To insure stability each society constructs a web of regulations to pattern the relationships among family members: between marital partners, between parents and their offspring, among siblings, and between the family and the larger community. This ordering is vested in the mores, folkways, and laws as a normative system and is inherent in the value system. The literature of today is directed to the parallel controls of the state as an enforcing unit and the family as an enforcing unit.

VALUES

1. Marriage is sacred and the courts should not dissolve it except where divorce is for the best interests of the members of the family and the total community.
2. The courts do weigh possible psychological injuries to children in evaluating their decisions concerning the parents.
3. Lawyers must respect their clients' wishes in representing them. (O'Gorman, 1963.)
4. It is the purpose of matrimonial law to carry out the current values in the total society as they affect marriage.
5. The courts will not interfere with decisions of parents concern-

ing the custody of their children in divorce except where there is a fraud on the court. The court assumes parents will act in the best interests of their children.

6 Although the welfare of the children is paramount, this must be balanced against the interests of the parents. Parents have a right to lead normal lives: for example, a man must be left with sufficient income to care for himself and perhaps to remarry.

7. The lawyer's professional responsibility is to advise his client to the best of his ability about his legal rights, the legal courses of action open to him, the legal consequences of his behavior and possible effects on future legal action (remarriage).

To do a thorough job, the lawyer needs to explore with his client the social interaction that gave rise to the legal right.

THE FRAMEWORK

The law accepts the family as a working social group whose members have competing interests which do not need legal enforcement because there are other cultural forces working to keep the family together. Where parents within a common household so disregard the rights of children as to endanger the general security, the state will either protect the children within the family or will remove them. When the competing forces cause the household members to separate, the law will enforce those family interests which concern the general security.

Today, the general security places value upon the need for individuals to separate rather than live in conflict. However, the general security also includes the right of the state to prevent children from becoming public charges economically and psychologically, and includes the rights of children to receive the equivalent, if possible, of what they would have received had their parents not dissolved the common household.

Appendix 1.

Conclusions and Recommendations of the Family Law
Committee of Wisconsin

The 1957 legislature of Wisconsin recommended a study of the statutes of the state relating to family law, divorce, and domestic relations for the following reasons: (1) these statutes had not been revised for many years except through piecemeal amendments, (2) amendments had only made the statutes increasingly more complicated, (3) modern sociological advances and innovations had made it highly desirable that the family and domestic relations laws be in accord with modern conditions.

The family law committee was made of persons representing lawyers, judges, the clergy, welfare agencies, and the general public. The following topics were studied: (1) marriage, (2) divorce, limited divorce, annulment and proceedings to affirm marriage, (3) support of dependents, (4) property rights of married women, (5) breach of promise actions, (6) presumption of legitimacy, and (7) family court provisions. In relation to all of these topics the committee recommended changes in Wisconsin laws. (Report of the Wisconsin Legislative Council, 1959, pp. 67–68.) Conclusions and recommendations of the committee follow:

1. Since the family is the basic unit of society, laws relating thereto should be designed to maintain family stability.
2. Laws relating to marriage should establish high standards as a means to avoid unstable marriages.
3. The minimum marriageable age for females should be raised from 15 to 16.
4. Procedures in obtaining a license should be formalized in keeping with the seriousness of marriage.
5. Premarital counseling should be urged upon parties contemplating marriage.
6. Documentary proof of identity, residence, and dissolution of prior marriages should be required when application is made for a license.
7. There should be an opportunity to counsel a divorced person who is about to remarry and who has obligations to support the children of his former marriage.
8. Secret marriages should be discouraged. They are not in harmony with the principle that marriage is a serious undertaking of great concern to society.
9. Authority to perform a civil ceremony should be limited to judges of courts of record in order to lend greater dignity to the ceremony.
10. Parents should have the right to bring suit for annulment when children have married without parental consent (when required) or when the children are under marriageable age.

11. Statutes relating to marriage should be arranged in a logical sequence, correlated with actual procedure in getting married.
12. The complaint in a divorce action should not be served until 60 days after service of the summons in order to enhance possibilities of reconciliation.
13. An attorney empowered with the authority of a regular court commissioner should be employed by each county as a family court commissioner to safeguard the interest of the family and society whenever divorce proceedings are commenced.
14. The doctrine of recrimination should be abolished except in those divorce actions based on grounds of adultery.
15. The common law action for breach of promise has no place in modern family law and it should be abolished.
16. Statutory chapters relating to family law should be a part of a family code to assure uniform interpretation of this body of law.
17. Where the workload warrants specialization, permanent family court branches should be established as a means of best safeguarding the interests of the family and society.

REFERENCES

Abbott, Edith. "Poor Law Provision for Family Responsibility," *Social Service Review*, 12 (Dec. 1938), pp. 598–618.
Abbott, Grace. "Child Marriages in the United States," *Journal of Social Hygiene*, 17 (May 1931), pp. 299–300.
———. "Federal Aid for the Protection of Maternity and Infancy," *American Journal of Public Health*, 12 (Sept. 1922), pp. 737–42.
Alexander, Paul W. "The Family Court of the Future," *Journal of the American Judicature Society*, 36 (Aug. 1952), pp. 38–46.
———. "A Therapeutic Approach," *Conference on Divorce*. Conference series No. 9 of the University of Chicago Law School. (Feb. 29, 1953).
Association of American Law Schools. *Proceedings*, 1960, p. 186. Announcement that the University of Louisville Law School will publish the *Journal of Family Law* at least on a semiannual basis.
———. *Proceedings*, 1958, p. 179. Recognition of the creation of a section on family law of the American Bar Association. This "indicates a coming of age of the movement to improve the field of family law."
———. *Proceedings*, 1956, p. 162. A bibliography of materials published during the past ten years in the field of family law.
Bates, Alan, Cohen, Julius, and Robson, R. A. H. *Parental Authority,*

the Community and the Law. New Brunswick, N.J.: Rutgers University Press, 1958. Reviewed in *American Anthropologist,* 61 (Aug. 1961), p. 689. The researchers ask: "To what extent is the law in selected areas (in this study) of child-parent relationships in agreement or at variance with the views (expressed moral sense) of the community?" Thus the research is in the field of legal norms and their relation to basic social values.

The State of Nebraska is used as community; the law of the state is the legal norm. The moral sense of the community is what a stratified, random sample (1 in 1,000 of the total population of the state) says should be allowed or prevented by law.

Fundamentally, the law of Nebraska, in common with Anglo-American common law, postulates that morally fit and competent parents should have overriding authority vis-a-vis their children. (In law, all earnings of a child "belong" to the parents who may dispose of such earnings as they wish, and anyone under 21 and unmarried is a child.) The "fit" of legal prescription to community moral sense was tested on seventeen "issues" of parent-child relationships on which the law is determinate. Only on five of these did the legal norms and the moral norms agree. Sharp disagreement was seen on ten. The law definitely posits family values not held by the people whose law it is.

The aim of the research was to demonstrate a method for determining community values relevant to matters of legal policy in a restricted field.

BLACK, HENRY CAMPBELL. *Black's Law Dictionary,* 3rd ed. St. Paul, Minn.: West Publishing Co., 1933. Since the first edition in 1891, a reliable dictionary of legal terms.

BRADWAY, JOHN S. "The Family Watchdog," in Association of American Law Schools. *Selected Essays on Family Law.* Brooklyn: The Foundation Press, Inc., 1950, pp. 254–73. The volume containing this article is a collection of readings selected for their scope and richness of interpretation of the various parts of family law. Following each of the twenty-one sections of the book there is a list of additional suggested readings. The volume of 1122 pages is divided into four parts: The Place of Family in Civilization; The Creation of the Family Unit; The Family As a Going Concern; and Family Disorganization.

―――. "Forgive and Forget—Condonation Today," *Journal of Family Law,* 2 (Fall 1962), pp. 116ff. In a family crisis Bradway suggests that a useful device might be for the court to declare the family unit itself a ward and then go forward to find out what solution in its opinion is in the best interest of the family concerned.

―――. "Legal Peg and the Social and Economic Hole." *Law and Contemporary Problems,* 10 (June 1944), pp. 855–64.

―――. "New Techniques in the Law," in Association of American Law

Schools. *Selected Essays on Family Law.* Brooklyn: The Foundation Press, Inc., 1950.

———. "Some Domestic Relations Laws that Counselors in Marital Difficulties Need to Know," *Social Forces,* 17 (Oct. 1938), pp. 83–89. To familiarize the marriage counselors with all the multitude of rules of law is a project as useless as it is enormous. The author recommends that marriage counselors (1) secure a general picture of the area of contact, (2) learn something about the resources of the law and the method of functioning of the legal mind, (3) utilize recurring experiences as a basis for molding rules of law which are proven inadequate. He recommends that each marriage counselor arrange the individual cooperation of a lawyer on the legal aspects of cases.

BRANSCOMBE, MARTHA. "Poor Law Policy of Liability of Relatives to Support and the New York Courts, 1784–1929," *Social Service Review,* 17 (Mar. 1943), pp. 50–66.

BRECKINRIDGE, SOPHONISBA. *The Family and the State, Select Documents.* Chicago: The University of Chicago Press, 1934. A "classical" collection of documents illustrating problems presenting themselves in relation to the marriage relationship and the institution of the family.

CAHN, EDMOND N. "Madison and the Pursuit of Happiness," *New York University Law Review,* 27 (1952), pp. 205–76.

CALHOUN, A. W. *A Social History of the American Family,* Vol. 3. New York: Barnes & Noble, Inc., 1945.

CHRISTENSEN, HAROLD T. "Development of the Field of Family Study," in his *Handbook of Marriage and the Family.* Chicago: Rand McNally & Company, 1964, Chap. 1. pp. 3–32.

CLARKE, HELEN I. *Social Legislation,* 2nd ed. New York: Appleton-Century-Crofts, 1957. This book "offers an up-to-date analysis of the legal relationships of husband, wife, and the state; parent, child and the state; and needy persons and the state. It is primarily concerned with public policy as defined by legislatures, but it also considers the effects of judicial decisions upon such policy and some of the administrative problems associated with its implementation."

COHEN, EMMELINE. "The Family and the State," *Political Quarterly,* 11 (Oct. 1940), pp. 396–404.

Conference on Divorce. Conference series No. 9 of the University of Chicago Law School (Feb. 28, 1953).

DAGGETT, HARRIET SPILLER. *Legal Essays on Family Law.* Baton Rouge, La.: Louisiana State University Press, 1935. Discusses legal aspects of amalgamation in Louisiana, action for breach of promise, and the problem of the wife's interest in community property.

DEMBITZ, NANETTE. "Ferment and Experiment in New York: Juvenile Cases in the New York Family Court," *Cornell Law Quarterly,* 48 (Spring 1963), pp. 499–523.

Dix, Dorothy K. "Legal Dissertation for Parents and Those 'in *Loco Parentis,*'" *Journal of Family Life,* 2 (Spring 1962), pp. 6ff.

Drinan, Robert. "The Rights of Children in Modern American Family Law," *Journal of Family Law,* 2 (Fall 1962), pp. 101–09.

Ehrenzweig, Albert A. " 'Bastard' in the Conflict of Laws, A National Disgrace," *University of Chicago Law Review,* 29 (Spring 1962), pp. 498ff.

————. "Alienation of Affection in the Conflict of Laws," *Cornell Law Quarterly,* 45 (Spring 1960), pp. 514–18.

————. "Miscegenation in the Conflict of Laws," *Cornell Law Quarterly,* 45 (Summer 1960), pp. 659–78. "Marriages between persons of different races" are exempt from the new regime of the "state of paramount interest."

Elliot, Sheldon D. "Legal Aspects of Casework Practice and Marital Problems in Families," in National Conference of Social Work. *Proceedings,* 1938, pp. 133–45.

Foster, Henry H., Jr. "Procrustes and the Couch," *Journal of Family Law,* 2 (Fall 1962), pp. 85–95.

Goode, William. "Pressures to Remarry: Institutionalized Patterns Affecting the Divorced," in N. W. Bell, and E. F. Vogel, *A Modern Introduction to the Family.* New York: Free Press of Glencoe, Inc., 1960, pp. 316–26. The divorced person in American society does not have the standard set of ties, obligations, and identity expected of adults which make it easy for others to relate to them. This situation puts pressure on the divorced to remarry. Some of the normative guides for the divorced are to be found in the extensive body of marriage and divorce laws, for example, the legal responsibility of the husband for the care of the wife, and care of the child. Law also defines the responsibilities of the wife toward the children.

————. *After Divorce.* New York: Free Press of Glencoe, Inc., 1956.

Goodsell, Willystine. *A History of Marriage and the Family.* New York: The Macmillan Company, 1935.

Green, Leon. "Protection of the Family Under Tort Law," *The Hastings Law Journal,* 10 (Feb. 1959), pp. 237–49.

Hager, John W. "Artificial Insemination: Some Practical Considerations for Effective Counseling," *North Carolina Law Review,* 39 (April 1961), pp. 217–37. A University of Oklahoma professor of law supplies information for the use of practicing attorneys in helping clients decide whether a "test-tube baby" will cure or curse them. He states that cases of AIH (artificial insemination husband) present few, if any, legal problems. CAI (combination artificial insemination) and AID (artificial insemination donor) present the same kinds of legal problems, that is, questions of adultery, legitimacy, inheritance rights, and dependency for income-tax purposes.

HALL, FRED S. "Marriage and the Law," *Annals of the American Academy of Political and Social Science*, 160 (March 1932), pp. 110–15.

HARMSWORTH, HARRY C., and MINNIS, MHYRA S. "Non Statutory Causes of Divorce; The Lawyers Point of View," *Marriage and Family Living*, 17 (Nov. 1955), pp. 316–21. Two hundred eighty-two Idaho lawyers report statutory reasons for divorce to be markedly different from the real causes. Most lawyers are reported to be aware that finances, adultery, drunkenness, and basic incompatibility are the real causes.

HARNO, ALBERT J. "The Precepts We Live By," *South Dakota Law Review*, 2 (Spring 1957), pp. 19–35. The author defines three domains of human action: (1) area of free choice, (2) domain of obedience to the unenforceable—duty, sympathy, taste, fairness, tolerance, and (3) domain of the law.

HARPER, FOWLER V. *Problems of the Family*. Indianapolis: The Bobbs-Merrill Company, Inc., 1952. Cases and notes on law and readings from the literature of anthropology, sociology, and psychiatry. This material has been used in the Yale Law School course on domestic relations.

HILL, REUBEN, and HANSEN, DONALD A. "The Identification of Conceptual Frameworks Utilized in Family Study." *Marriage and Family Living*, 22 (Nov. 1960), pp. 299–311.

HOGAN, JOHN D., and IANNI, FRANCIS, A. J. *American Social Legislation*. New York: Harper & Row, Publishers, 1956. The book is about social legislation in the United States and the forces which have given it its present structure. A part of the book deals with "the area of family legislation in functional terms, with discussion centering on role changes, need satisfaction, and goal fulfillment."

ISAAC, S. M. "Family Law and the Lawyer," *Journal of Family Law*, 2 (Spring 1962), pp. 43ff.

JONES, SYBIL M. "The Problem of Family Support: Criminal Sanctions for the Enforcement of Support," *North Carolina Law Review*, 38 (Dec. 1959), pp. 1–61.

KARGMAN, MARIE W. "A Socio-Legal Analysis of Family Role Conflict," *Marriage and Family Living*, 21 (Aug. 1959), pp. 275–78. As the states' interest in the family changes, new laws are put on the books; for example, at one time the father was considered absolute head of the household and could punish the child even to the point of taking the child's life. Now, a minor child is considered the ward of the state and is under the jurisdiction of the father only so long as he does not abuse his rights. These changes imposed from the outside do not create as much disruption in the family as the changing expectations within the family caused by changes in the life cycle.

KNOX, SARAH T. *The Family and the Law*. Chapel Hill, N.C.: University of North Carolina Press, 1941. Concise summary of legal information which the student of the family and the social worker may desire.

LAURITZEN, CHRISTIAN MARIUS, II. "Only God Can Make an Heir," *Northwestern University Law Review*, 48 (Nov.-Dec. 1953), pp. 568–89. English law concerning inheritance acquired that the descent be cast upon the heir regardless of his own desire. The title came to him by "the single operation of law and the heir could not refuse to accept."

LEMKIN, RAPHAEL. "Orphans of Living Parents: A Comparative Legal and Sociological View," *Law and Contemporary Problems*, 10 (June 1944), pp. 834–54.

LEVI, WERNER. "Family in Modern Chinese Law," *Far Eastern Quarterly*, 4 (May 1945), pp. 263–73.

LICHTENBERGER, J. P. "Divorce Legislation." *Annals of the American Academy of Political and Social Science.* 160 (Mar. 1932), pp. 116–23.

——. *Divorce.* New York: McGraw-Hill, Inc., 1931.

LITWAK, EUGENE. "Three Ways in Which Law Acts as a Means of Social Control: Punishment, Therapy and Education," *Social Forces*, 34 (March 1956), pp. 217–23. The idea of divorce as punishment rests on the general Christian doctrine that marriage is a good *per se* which can be broken only by a sinner. The paper indicates that a single set of laws—divorce laws—have different ways of effecting social control: through punishment, therapy, and education. The dependent variable which the law seeks to control, family break-up, is complex. Break-up may be one of many different kinds: by conflict, indifference, opportunity, and marital fiat. The matching of type of law and type of break-up will lead to the maximum form of social control.

LLEWELLYN, K. N. "Behind the Law of Divorce," in Association of American Law Schools, *Selected Essays on Family Law.* Brooklyn: The Foundation Press, Inc., 1950.

Law and Contemporary Problems. 18 (Winter 1953). Special issue on divorce with a re-examination of basic concepts. Nine articles on various aspects of divorce. The theme is that there should be something done to guide those entering marriage so as to eliminate many unsuitable unions, thus preventing marital discord and divorce action.

MACKAY, RICHARD. *Law of Marriage and Divorce.* Dobbs Ferry, N.Y.: Oceana Publications, Inc., 1959.

MADDEN, JOSEPH W. *Persons and Domestic Relations.* St. Paul, Minn.: West Publishing Co., 1931.

MANDELL H. *Law of Marriage and Divorce Simplified*, 2nd ed. Dobbs Ferry, N.Y.: Oceana Publications, Inc., 1957.

MONAHAN, THOMAS P. "State Legislation and Control of Marriage," *Journal of Family Law*, 2 (Spring 1962), pp. 30–42. The American Bar Association and the legal profession hold a strategic position in the

field of family regulation and direction, and they could mount, therefore, "a dynamic and effective program of an interprofession kind
which could do more for the betterment of the American family than
we have witnessed so far." In such a program is recommended: (1) a
positive approach, (2) interprofessional liason, (3) a good system of
accounting, (4) scientific efforts to test the effectiveness of the measures adopted.

————. "Family Fugitives," *Marriage and Family Living,* 20 (May 1958),
pp. 147–51. An overview of the nature and consequences of family
desertion and nonsupport in which the policies, procedures, and costs
of amelioration of its effects are touched upon. Reciprocal legislation
for family support responsibility is discussed.

MORLAND, JOHN W. *Keezer on the Law of Marriage and Divorce,* 3rd
ed. Indianapolis: The Bobbs-Merrill Company, Inc., 1946.

MULLINS, CLAUD. "Illegitimate Child in Relation to Society and the Law,"
Quarterly Review, 275 (July 1940), pp. 13–27.

OGBURN, CHARLTON. "The Role of Legal Services in Family Stability."
Annals of the American Academy of Political and Social Science, 212
(1930), pp. 127–33.

O'GORMAN, HUBERT J. *Lawyers and Matrimonial Cases—A Study in
formal Pressures in Private Professional Practice.* New York: Free
Press of Glencoe, Inc., 1963.

PERKINS, ROLLIN M. "The Vagrancy Concept," *The Hastings Law
Journal,* 9 (May 1958), pp. 237–61. "A man has a common-law duty
to support and protect his wife (State v. Smith, 65 Me. 257, 1876) and
any child of his too young to supply his own needs; (Regina v. Senior,
19 Cox C. C. 219, 1898) but while the duty is well recognized the
breach thereof does not bring him within the toils of the law (in the
absence of special statute) unless some serious consequence ensues. If
death results from his malicious or criminal negligent failure to give
such needed support, he is guilty of criminal homicide (Regina v.
Conde, 10 Cox C. C. 547, 1867.)

PHILPEL, HARRIET F., and ZAVIN, THEODORA. *Your Marriage and the Law.*
New York: Holt, Rinehart & Winston, Inc., 1952. "Because sex, marriage and reproduction always involve other people, many laws have
been enacted to control marital and sex behavior and to protect individuals' rights. Some of these laws are expressive in nature, while
others are merely repressive in character, the result not of social needs
but of the attitude of certain groups and factions within society." This
book concerns itself with these various kinds of laws on marriage and
family life.

PLOSCOWE, MORRIS. "Family Law," in New York School of Law, *Annual
Survey of American Law,* 1959, pp. 465–77. Indicates decreasing sympathy to women in marital controversies and greater realism in dealing

with adoptions and custody problems of children. Considers dilemmas in the areas of breach of promise, common-law marriage, annulment, divorces, alimony, custody of children, adoption and illegitimacy.

———. *The Truth About Divorce.* Hawthorne Books, Incorporated, 1955.

POUND, ROSCOE. *Jurisprudence,* 5 Vols. St. Paul, Minn.: West Publishing Co., 1959. References are to Vol. III unless otherwise stated.

———. "Individual Interests," in Association of American Law Schools. *Selected Essays on Family Law.* Brooklyn: The Foundation Press, Inc., 1950.

———. *Interpretations of Legal History.* New York: The Macmillan Company, 1923.

SAYRE, PAUL. "Awarding Custody of Children," in Association of American Law Schools. *Selected Essays on Family Law.* Brooklyn: The Foundation Press, Inc., 1950, pp. 588–620.

SCHMIEDELER, EDGAR. "Some Social Values of Ecclesiastical and Civil Marriage Legislation," *Social Forces,* 10 (May 1932), pp. 587–93. Cites marriage laws of church and state that are commonly used and states the social purposes which they serve. Laws, briefly considered, are those (1) demanding a minimum marriage age or parental consent (2) forbidding marriage of near kin, (3) demanding advance notice to provide a delay before marriage and give publicity to it, (4) demanding public rather than secret or clandestine marriages. The article points out the need for creating laws peculiar either to the church or the state rather than common to both.

SEAGLE, WILLIAM. *The History of the Law.* New York: Tudor Publishing Company, 1946.

STEVENS, R. B. "Illegal Families Among the Clients of Family Agencies: Relationship to Divorce Laws," *Social Forces,* 19 (Oct. 1940), pp. 84–87.

STRANGER-JONES, L. I. *Eversley's Law of Domestic Relations,* 6th ed. London: Sweet & Maxwell, Ltd., 1951.

"Symposium on the Law of Domestic Relations in Oklahoma," *Oklahoma Law Review,* 14 (Aug. 1961), pp. 281–436.

TAPPAN, PAUL W. "Family Relations and Persons," *New York University Law Quarterly Review,* 24:1288–97 and 25:1255–33.

TIMASHEFF, N. S. *An Introduction to the Sociology of Law.* Cambridge, Mass.: Harvard University Committee on Research in the Social Sciences, 1939.

United States Department of Labor. *Legal Status of the American Family.* Washington, D.C.: Women's Bureau, 1950.

VERNIER, CHESTER, et al. *American Family Laws.* Stanford, Cal.: Stanford University Press, 1931–1938. Five volumes in which the family law of forty-eight states, Alaska, the District of Columbia, and Hawaii (to

Jan. 1, 1931) is compared. The attempt is made to (1) briefly summarize the common law, (2) state in summary and detail the statutory law showing variations, resemblances, and omissions, (3) comment and criticize, (4) collect references for each topic.

WATSON, ANDREW S. "Family Law and Its Challenge for Psychiatry," *Journal of Family Law*, 2 (Fall 1962), pp. 71–84.

WESTERMARCK, EDWARD. *A Short History of Marriage and the Family.* New York: The Macmillan Company, 1926.

WHERRY, WILLIAM M. "Preventive Law and Justice to Children," *Journal of the American Judicature Society*, 36 (Dec. 1952), pp. 114–19.

Wisconsin Legislative Council. *General Report*, Vol. V. Report submitted to the governor and the 1959 legislature, Jan. 1959.

WOLFF, HANS J. *Written and Unwritten Marriages in Hellenistic and Postclassical Roman Law.* Lancaster, Pa.: Lancaster Press, Inc., 1939. A discussion of (1) why provincial law in contrast with Roman law made legal recognition of the marriage dependent upon drawing up a document with property matters, and (2) why there existed both (*a*) written and unwritten marriages and (*b*) double documentation of the same union.

chapter 12

Western Christian Conceptual Framework for Viewing the Family*

Stanley R. Reiber

From the earliest times, religion and the family have been intimately related. Each has had an influence upon the other. According to Moberg, "many of the deepest concepts of religion may be traced to family relationships. The church and the family are inter-related in a never-ceasing process of reciprocal interaction. Neither can be fully understood apart from the other." (1962, p. 367.)

Although, admittedly, it would be interesting and valuable to compare the various religious systems of the world and attempt to ascertain the type of interaction that each of them may have with the families who claim allegiance to the particular system, this is impossible within the scope of one paper. We have, therefore, limited ourselves to the Western Christian religious teaching. Since the Christian faith is so intimately related in its conceptual framework with that of the Hebrew thought as it is presented in the Old Testament, it will be necessary at times to refer to the ancient Jewish teachings. The main emphasis, however, will be directed toward the

* Grateful acknowledgment is made of the contribution of Seward Hiltner, who served as editorial consultant for this framework and who read and critically reviewed the manuscript prior to its final revision. Many, although not all, of his suggestions have been incorporated into the final manuscript. Inadequacies and errors in the chapter as published, however, are entirely the responsibility of the author and the editors.

teachings of the New Testament and the religious thought and beliefs founded upon it.

Christianity, like all religions, operates primarily within a particular value matrix. It is an organized value system. To work within this framework presupposes an acceptance of truth regarding the teachings and assumptions inherent within the system: "whether religious ideas are 'true' hinges on one's definition of the truth, and hence becomes a metaphysical, not a scientific problem." (Yinger, 1957, p. 56.)

Here we will look at the family, including family research, from the Western Christian point of view. It will be necessary upon some occasions to differentiate between the Roman Catholic and Protestant points of view. Although there are other Christian groups such as Mormons and the Eastern Orthodox rite, this paper will be primarily limited to the general Protestant and Roman Catholic groups.

It will be evident to all that certain ideas here viewed as assumptions would, in another context, be viewed as values. It will be equally obvious that not all Christians will agree with certain of the interpretations presented. An attempt has been made, however, to give as representative or modal a view of Christian beliefs as possible.

The churches have turned to the systematic use of research only in the past few years. (Fairchild and Wynn, 1961, p. 8.) This may be partly due to the fact that there has been no clearly delineated framework from which to operate. What little research has been accomplished has not followed any organized pattern, but rather has apparently been influenced by the degree of ease to which the data would be susceptible to statistical analysis. (Moberg, 1962, p. 350.)

Since the culture of our society is influenced considerably by certain aspects of the Christian ethical system, and since the majority of the people living in our country would not deny at least a minimal allegiance to the broad concepts of the Christian faith, it appears that the attempt to formulate a Western Christian conceptual framework is indicated. To study the family in our culture today without taking into account the religious factor is to ignore one of the most persistent of all social forces: "a person's religion is his framework of meaning, the source of his priority scale of values, the measure of his hopes, the well spring of his most secure joys." (Pike, 1954, p. 10.) When two people decide to pool for a lifetime their strengths and weaknesses, their hopes and fears, then the religious dimension, of necessity, plays its part in the personality of each—whether the people are conscious or unconscious of it—in their most significant relationships, decisions, and responses to each other.

History of the Development of the Approach

Hiltner points out that a principal characteristic of the Western Christian framework for viewing the family as well as other subjects of social significance, includes but transcends the religious convictions, ideas, and institutions from which the viewpoint arises.

Professing to be based on a revelation from God himself, in Jesus Christ, that is intended for the salvation of all mankind, the Christian point of view includes the declared implication as well as the alleged source. As Archbishop William Temple, of the Church of England, once noted, 'God is interested in a great many things besides religion.'

Christian faith is clearly founded upon the Judaism of the Old Testament, in addition to some Hellenistic elements and the declaration of the revelation in Jesus Christ as the Messiah of God. The early Jewish view of the family had been both patriarchal and polygamous; but by the time the Christian era began it had become monogamous, and slightly less patriarchal through increased recognition of feminine rights. The Old Testament is filled with family metaphors to explain the relations of man and God.[1]

Hastings refers to the intensity of the family feeling of the ancient Israelites (1955, p. 723.), but this feeling was for the larger family rather than for the nuclear family as we conceive of it today. This family was expanded to include the whole tribe, and even in some instances to include all human beings. The basic unit was the family, and the individual had little identity. With the beginning of the Christian movement, the emphasis changed to more of a person-centered interest, and this emphasis persisted for many generations. It is, in fact, evident in our own time.

Theories concerning the family were not a concern of earlier generations of Christians. The family and family life were taken largely for granted, even though from the earliest times the Christian religion has been passed on through families. New Testament references to families and family life are frequent, but in most situations

[1] Personal correspondence with Seward Hiltner.

families appear only as they aid the forward progress of the Christian movement.

Even at the time of the Reformation, Luther showed a general lack of understanding of the relationship between Christianity and family life when he complained that marriage relations took so much time that he could "hardly read, preach, or study." (Plass, 1961, p. 900.) As late as the nineteenth century, little of the church's direct interest was devoted to the family.

In the past few generations this emphasis has changed to the point where a great amount of the thought and interest of the church is now devoted to the relationship between faith and family. In one study (Reiber, 1961) it was found that the leaders of thirty-eight Protestant denominations comprising altogether forty-five million adherents felt that a total of twenty-two changes had taken place in the church in the past century in the relationship between families and the church; nearly all of these were in the direction of the church focusing on more adequate methods of meeting the needs of the family. During this same period, the churches were attempting to formulate a philosophy of church-family interaction. This has given rise to a series of family-centered curricula in many of the denominations. Family-life departments have been instituted and special programs relevant to the family have been inaugurated.

As an example, when legal divorces became common in the United States in the 1920's, there was immediate reaction in the Christian churches. A Commission on Marriage and the Family was instituted in what was then the Federal Council of Churches. This body promoted the proper education of couples by clergymen who were to marry them, considered the responsible ethics of birth control, fostered education of young people about sex, marriage, and family life, and urged on the churches the serious consideration of educating even the married about family life.

During the past fifteen years the Roman Catholic Church in this country, through such means as the Cana Conferences, has also tried to reconsider for itself and educate couples on the meaning of marriage and family life.

In 1947 the Congregational-Christian Church and in 1948 the Presbyterian Church in the United States of America (now known as the United Presbyterian Church U.S.A.) prepared new series of family-centered religious-education materials. Several other denominations have followed their lead. At the present time, the Presbyterian Church is developing such a program. In one of its publications preparatory to this program, we find the following statement concerning one aspect of the work: "the divorce rate is increasing at an alarming pace. The church should accept responsibility for a strong program of sex and family education to develop in its people an understanding of the meaning of the Christian family, and to prepare them for the kind of fidelity demanded by the marriage vow." (Foundation paper IX, 1961.)

Throughout all of this work, however, little in the way of any specific conceptual framework has appeared. This is rather surprising in the light of what many hold to be the very center of the New Testament ethical system. Grant, for instance, points out that, "If we are to isolate one idea which is more basic to New Testament ethics than the rest, it will be the idea of the family." (1952, p. 315.)

Although no spelled-out framework has been produced, the churches have been operating within a certain frame of reference.

This century has seen the initiation of considerable inter-church cooperation rising out of the ecumenical movement. Although this movement, for the first part of its history, concerned mainly the various Protestant groups' attempts to come back into contact with one another, with increasing participation by the Eastern Orthodox Churches, it has latterly been aided by Popes John and Paul into discussions and common activities with Roman Catholics as well. Sober analysts warn us not to expect radical changes as a result of these 'ecumenical' concerns, and they are correct. But they have freed Christian scholars from all groups to talk and work together as never before in history; and even the most perplexing questions about the family are being included in these discussions. Although differences on matters such as the ethics of contraceptive devices became plainer in this new era of discussion, many other matters about the family appear to be shared. Hence, there probably is a closer consensus to a 'Western Christian' view of the family now than at any time since the late middle ages. And the working out of the present view, if not necessarily its roots, has been influenced in every quarter by the findings of the modern behavioral sciences including sociology. (Hiltner, 1964.)

Christian philosophies of marriage and family are in existence. Many doctrines concerning marital life have been promulgated.

Specific teachings relating to different aspects of marriage and family relationships have been issued. It is our purpose in this paper to attempt to formulate them into a more explicit conceptual framework.

FOCI OF STUDY

In the area of marriage and family relationships, the primary interest of the Christian churches has appeared to be centered about the value and stability of the marital vows, especially for the protection and rearing of children.

> The centrality of this concern is reinforced when it is noted that there has never been a marital ethic set forth for persons who have completed their child-rearing duties. Instead, the same principles have simply been assumed to apply. Until a century ago, of course, very few persons lived long beyond the time of completing child-rearing tasks. (Hiltner, 1964.)

While the Roman Catholic and some Protestant denominations hold that the marital vows cannot be dissolved by divorce except under a limited set of circumstances, other denominations hold to a slightly more liberal view of divorce. Without exception, however, the Western Christian churches have held that the New Testament teachings point to the desirability of permanence in the marital union. Even those churches which do sanction divorce do so with reluctance and a feeling that it is only to be granted under extreme circumstances. The United Presbyterian Church in 1959 issued this statement:

> When marriage seems in danger of breaking for any cause, permanent separation or divorce must be regarded as a last resort. Neither can rightly be sanctioned by the church except where a continuation of the legal union would endanger the physical, moral, or spiritual wellbeing of one or both of the partners or that of their children.

The United Lutheran Church (now The Lutheran Church in America) carries this thought yet further:

> Undoubtedly, infidelity and malicious desertion do actually break the marriage in the most obvious way. . . . The nature of the marriage bond and love would both demand exploration of every alternative in an effort to preserve the union. Neverthe-

less, it may be in any given instance the clear demand of love that a marriage should be dissolved, out of Christian love for all concerned. In the actual human situation, frequently the only possibility is to choose the lesser of these evils. (1956, p. 22.)

Closely related to this has been the problem of the remarriage of divorced people. The Roman Catholic church holds that divorced people cannot be remarried (although marriages may be annuled for certain reasons, and this permits the members to remarry), but the Protestant churches have devoted much attention and interest to the permissibility or advisability of the remarriage of divorced members. As an example, the United Lutheran Church says: "Having recognized the possibility of separation and divorce, the church must make clear to its people that remarriage, while violating the order of God, may in some specific instances be in accordance with the will of God." (1956, p. 20.)

The opinion of the churches has been almost unanimous concerning the prohibition or inadvisability of interfaith or interreligious marriage. The Protestant Episcopal Church meeting in General Convention at San Francisco, California in 1949 passed a resolution: "This Convention earnestly warns members of our Church against contracting marriages with Roman Catholics under the conditions imposed by modern Roman Canon Law." Pike quotes: "The Catholic Church's attitude towards mixed marriages may be summed up briefly, writes Rev. John O'Conner, S.J. in a syndicated article for the Catholic press, She strongly disapproves of them and strives to dissuade her children from contracting them." (1954, p. 100.) Landis states that the orthodox Jewish group prohibits mixed marriage altogether. (1960, p. 230.)

In recent years the range of concern about marriage and family matters has tended to become broader. Especially important are the attempts to reconsider the Biblically-rooted principles about the family, at the same time bringing them up to date in relation to the present social situation.

A review of the literature indicates that in the majority of research studies, religion is conceived of as merely one among many of the variables which have an influence on individuals or families. There appears to be no body of literature in which the family has been studied specifically from the framework of the Western Christian belief system. Individual Christian teachings such as the necessity for fidelity in marriage or prohibitions against premarital intercourse have been studied in relation to patterns of adjustment or happiness (Dedman, 1959, and Bell and Blumberg, 1959); interreligious dating and marriage has been investigated (Heiss, 1961); the effect of religion on family values has been researched (Landis, 1960); and various other aspects of religion and family interaction have been studied. In most of these studies, the data have been examined from a sociological or psychological framework that was not specifically of a religious nature. Even here, however, the particular religious beliefs or biases of those performing the research have been frequently in evidence.

Some of the principal concerns, beyond those just mentioned, continue to be:

1. Cultivation of factors making for stable and fulfilling family life.
2. Encouragement of both fidelity and fulfillment in married life.
3. Encouragement of family stability for both the mental health and the Christian education of the children.
4. Discouragement of premarital intercourse through education concerning the seriousness of such practices.
5. The proper place and meaning of sex in human life.
6. The bases of family limitation.

CONCEPTS

One of the factors which increases the difficulty of creating or formulating a Western Christian framework lies in the multiplicity of definitions and beliefs concerning the most basic concepts.

In order to avoid lengthy and involved mental gymnastics, a few concepts are presented with the thought that they may serve as a starting point for a more complete delineation in the future.

Religion. Every religion contains the idea of a "religious blessing from a divine power, a conviction as to the nature of this divine power, and a set of conditions which this divine power lays down which must be fulfilled if an individual is to secure this blessing." (Dickie, 1931, p. 15.)

Christianity. An ancient and classifical definition of Christianity is that of Schleiermacher: "Christianity is a monotheistic faith belonging to the teleological type of religion, and is essentially distinguished from other similar faiths in that everything in it is related to the redemption accomplished in Jesus of Nazareth." (1928, intro-duction.)

Sovereignty of God. God is supreme in power and authority and is not bound in any way.

Man. The Christian view holds that man is a creature made in the image of God. (This points up most clearly the Christian teaching of the worth of the individual human life).

Kingdom of God. Although the kingdom of God is an other-worldly or spiritual kingdom, it has authority over all men here upon earth, and they have obligations to it.

The meaning of sex in human life. The function of sex in human relationships is frequently commented upon in theological literature. Hiltner represents one major viewpoint in stating that through sex one comes to "know" another and thereby to know something of the secret of his own existence.

> The use of the term "know" (in the Bible) as a synonym for sexual intercourse is not a matter of delicacy. Through sex, one discovers something he can explore in no other way. He is a physical being; and through sex he discovers something of an-other being, and thus also of himself that he had not from the inside "known" before. (1957, p. 35.)

Familial Concepts

Of the many familial concepts of the Christian religion, the fol-lowing are particularly important:

Christian family. Hastings says: "By consecrating marriage, by emancipating womanhood, by sanctifying childhood, by expanding brotherhood, and making the domestic group the type of the Divine social order which is to be, Jesus created what may distinctively be called the Christian Family." (1955, p. 726.) The General Conference of the Methodist Church in its meeting of 1956 defined the Chris-tian family as:

> one in which parents so live the Christian life and practice the presence of God that children come to accept God as the great-est reality in life. The Christian family is one where each mem-ber is accepted and respected as a person having sacred worth . . . one which manifests faith in God. . . . It is committed to behavior in keeping with Christian ideals for family relations, community life and national and world citizenship.

Male and female. The male and female are considered to be not independent but complementary. According to Bailey they are "individually incomplete until they have achieved the union in which each integrates and is integrated by the other." (1952, p. 44.)

One flesh. This is closely allied with the immediately preceeding concept. Bailey points out that "the singleness of which 'one' stands . . . is organic, not arithmetical . . . it is exemplified at its highest in the mysterious triunity of God, of which the biunity of husband and wife is an analogue." (1952, p. 43.) Clearly this concept has deep relevance to the Christian teaching concerning the necessity for sexual fidelity in marriage.

Marriage. Marriage is a union between one man and one woman. According to many Christian marriage ceremonies, it is "instituted by God, regulated by his commandments, to be held in honor by all men, and it is until death parts the married couple."

Infidelity. Because of the intimate relationship between marriage and God, any infidelity is not just against another human but also involves unfaithfulness to God.

BASIC ASSUMPTIONS

General Assumptions

The most general basic assumptions upon which could be built a religious framework for viewing the family are these:

1. Religious ideas as related to human life. Yinger states that, "once started, religious ideas and structures are continuously involved in the interactions of human life." (1957, p. 306.)
2. The influence of ideas in life. Religious ideas, like all other ideas, not only enter the lives of individuals but also influence the individuals' responses to their environment.
3. Truth of the Christian ideas and teachings. In some unique way, the teachings of the Christian religion are assumed to be true, since they are conceived of as having been created by God.
4. God the Creator. Not only does God create all things, but, because He has created them, they are basically good.
5. Universe in the hands of God. God did not just create the world and then abandon it; rather, He remained active and concerned in the life of the world and of individuals within the world.

6. Moral order of reality. The universe of God is subject to a moral order as expressed in the Ten Commandments. These were God-given and hold sway over all of life including pre-marital, marital, and family interaction.
7. New Testament view of marriage and family life. A publication of the United Church of Canada expresses the New Testament view of marriage and family life as follows: "A Christian un-derstanding of sex and marriage must avoid the temptation to find its basis in isolated passages in the Bible, especially if they support a literalism and legalism which Jesus denounced. . . . Although there are a number of allusions to betrothal, marriage and wedding customs in the New Testament, explicit teaching about the essential nature of marriage is not extensive." (United Church of Canada, 1960, p. 5.) As is true of other aspects of life, so it is true of Christian marriage and family life that the primary teachings are to be obtained from the New Testament.

Specific Assumptions

Among the most important specific assumptions of Christianity in regard to the family are the following:

1. Family as ordained by God. The family is ordained by God, planned and instituted by Him, for the enrichment of personal life and the life of society. Thus, God's place in its life cannot be ignored.
2. Family relations as symbols of relationships to God. Tillich says, "Jesus uses the family relations as symbols for a relation of a higher order, for the community of those who do the will of God." (1955, p. 106.)
3. Family as the basic democracy. Although this concept of the family as the basic democracy was not clearly understood until recent times, it has been an essential element in the Christian framework from the early days. It grew out of the concept of the worth of the individual.
4. Sacredness of the individual. Baber writes, "the teachings of Jesus as to the sacredness of the individual were so insistent that they were bound to break through the restraints of dogma which appeared after His death. The sanctity of life and of the person—any person—was the idea from which developed the opposition to abortion, infanticide, prostitution,

illegitimacy, and any other practice that did not recognize the dignity of human life." (1948, p. 97.)

5. Monogamy as a divine institution. Founded upon the teaching of the New Testament, monogamy was likened to the relationship between Christ and the church, and thus was divinely instituted.

6. Loyalty of spouses to each other. The loyalty of spouses to each other takes precedence over their loyalty to their parents.

7. Parent-child relationships. Children owe unquestioning obedience and loyalty to their parents.

8. Sacredness of the family. The family was ordained by God at the time of creation and was supported by Jesus.

9. Limitation of sexual intercourse. It is generally recognized that sexual intercourse is limited to marriage, although there are certain societies where sexual intercourse is permitted for a couple during the period of their engagement. It should be noted, however, that in cultures where this is permitted, engagement is a much more binding contract than it is in our own culture, and hold much the same meaning as marriage. (This refers to Christian cultures only.)

10. Uniqueness of family relationship. The unique family relationship represents the marital unity of God's creation. It is He who is the source of love and power which enables the couple to fulfill the duties of marriage, which include happiness and the procreation and rearing of children. The Western Christian teaching is that there is no other institution which can successfully substitute for the family as the medium for providing the right milieu for the early years of the life of a child.

PRODUCT

At first glance, the primary impact of the Christian religious system on the development of family theory has been that of a retarding force. Sociological and psychological theories of man's origin or development have frequently experienced opposition and/or hostility from the forces of organized religion.

That this retarding effect has not been entirely of a negative nature can be seen in the fact that it forced theoreticians into active research to attempt to overcome this opposition. Unfortunately it is difficult to compare or correlate philosophical or spiritual truths and empirical research findings. As yet, measurement process are not sufficiently well defined or sensitive enough to measure the facts of the spiritual realm. Possibly a motivation toward an attempt to do so will be one of the major contributions of the Christian religious system to the field of sociological or psychological theory.

Impact on Research

The impact of the Western Christian theoretical framework on research is difficult to appraise, due in part to the fact that there has been no organized school of social researchers who operated from this framework.

As the social scientists attempted to study the family they discovered religious taboos which were not always easy to overcome. An example can be seen in the negative reaction which was manifested by many toward the early sex researchers. Many Christian families felt that such research was an invasion of privacy and family life. The religiously engendered guilt which many felt over certain aspects of sexual life (such as the early church teachings regarding the sin of masturbation) undoubtedly presented difficulties to researchers who were working in this area.

An additional factor is that most researchers, having been oriented to a culture with many Christian roots, are not always able (whether they are pro or con) to distinguish Christian elements from others, in their assumptions (for example, concerning the "worth of the person").

On the other hand, much research has been concerned with the interaction of religion and the individual or the family. It has been investigated from many aspects as an important variable in family life. This is likely due to the fact that, "religion has helped set the standards for every phase of marriage and family life." (Baber, 1962, p. 98.)

Perhaps some of the most effective research work in this area has been that in 1962 of Lenski, who feels that religion is as great an influence on the behavior of individuals (and hence families and society as a whole) as is social class. He has advanced the idea that the person's religious life affects not only his family ties but also may affect such things as economic mobility.

At least one additional study has been motivated by the desire to ascertain the power of the Christian religious element in family life. In this study by Reiber in 1961, the religious behavior of the family was viewed as the independent variable in its effects upon the life and activity of the organized work of the Christian Church. Perhaps this indicates the possibility for a new line of approach. It would appear that such an approach would open new areas of research. Religion is viewed as something more than merely a sociological system or a verbal appellation given to a particular grouping of ideas or thoughts. It exerts an influence and is a motivating source to some degree in the life of the family. It affects the family behavior in some respect for a great number of families in our nation. (According to the most recent figures, well over half the population of the United States stated that it had an affiliation with some church.)

Many aspects of family-society-religion interaction might be profitably studied within this framework. Religious differences in mixed marriages may be more incisively determined. The effect of religion on the stability of marriage provides a fruitful field of endeavor. The relationships between types and degree of religious beliefs to patterns of family interaction may provide useful information.

Impact on Practice

Most likely it is in the area of practice that the Western Christian framework, though unformalized, has had the greatest effect. Various studies have found that a person's religious beliefs have an effect upon his mate selection, the happiness of his marriage, his attitudes toward others, his system of values, and much of the action of his daily life.

Many of the values held by other frameworks find their origin in the Judeo-Christian religious systems. The teachings of the Judeo-Christian religions have been of interest to many researchers operating within various theoretical contexts. Burgess and Cottrell interpret some of their findings concerning the relationship between religion and marital happiness by saying that "the constant emphasis upon the church doctrines of love, kindness, forgiveness, and tolerance should play at least some part in the formation of attitudes that later affect marriage." (1939, pp. 122–25.)

Many of the assumptions of the legal profession rest upon these teachings. For example, value is traditionally placed upon the stability of the marital vows, and divorce is to be used as a last resort in marital difficulty. In fact, it would be difficult to find many ethical values held by family theorists of any discipline that do not trace their genesis to the Biblical teaching.

In the family-counseling area the impact of the Christian faith is especially evident. Christian mores of monogamy, fidelity, love, and concern for other family members permeate the lives of even non-Christian individuals living in the Western world. Most of these ethical principles are in complete accord with the teachings of the founder of the Christian religion.

It is against this background of concern that many clergymen of all faiths and sects identify specific needs and problems which impel them into the family-counseling activity. In one study clergymen responded that they felt the pastoral-counseling phase of their work to be the most important aspect. The great majority of this counseling is in the family-life area. (Fairchild and Wynn, 1961.)

An additional element in religious thought that has had a practical effect has been the belief that man can change. His existence is not a static one. In this change he can make use of both human and divine help. If such change were not possible, counseling would be a well-nigh useless endeavor.

Although, as was previously mentioned, little research has been undertaken directly within this framework, the number of theoretical or teaching publications is almost endless. This would include works such as the following few examples:

1. Seward Hiltner. *Sex and the Christian Life.* This book points out the need for understanding sex as a vital factor in the life of the Christian and attempts to correct some of the mistaken ideas many Christians have regarding sex.
2. J. A. Pike. *If You Marry Outside Your Faith.* Although primarily devoted to the problems of Protestant-Roman Catholic marriage, the book also includes other types of intermarriage as well.
3. L. R. Smith. *This Love of Ours.* This is a manual of methods by which to put more Christian meaning into the marriage and family life.
4. H. G. Werner. *Christian Family Living.* This brief book resembles a primer in its approach to family life. The purpose is to enable the reader to see possibilities for better Christian living within his own family.

In addition to books such as the above each of the denominations has published study books and pamphlets concerning all aspects of family life from birth until death.

VALUES

In the preface to the book, *Religion, Society, and the Individual,* Yinger in 1957 refers to the necessity for the student of sociology to be also a student of religion. He feels that one of the best ways in which to study a man is through his religion.

Admittedly, this is a difficult task. Religions vary greatly. Even within one general framework of a particular religion are many shades of belief and opinion.

Since any religious system is deeply concerned with values, in fact, it is in many respects a value system, the attempt to formulate any theoretical framework based on religion must take account of the values most basic to that system. The task is complicated by the fact that values cannot be empirically investigated, that is, they can only be inferred. This does not, however, automatically mean that they have no effect and can therefore be ignored. The effect of the Western Christian belief system and the values inherent in it and basic to it can be seen in many aspects of personal and family life in the Western world.

A brief quotation from Bainton affords an example of some of the spheres in which the Western Christian values have influenced our life: "the church then from the outset and throughout her history and in the midst of her own divisions has consistently taught that marriage is good, ordained of God for the propagation of the race, sex is not evil, marriage should be to a single partner and for life. Both parties are obligated to be faithful to the bond." (1956, p. 16.)

It is evident that the foregoing set of values has actually progressed beyond the level of values and has become a set of basic assumptions upon which the Christian framework stands. This will be seen to be the case with many of the values which we will mention.

Brotherhood of All Men

The United Church of Canada report of 1960 expresses the value of the brotherhood of all men as follows: "The conviction that all men are brothers rests upon the faith that God is the Creator-Father and that the world of men is or should be a family, a household of faith, inspired by family loyalty."

Normalcy of Sex

Sex is a normal aspect of all of life, a gift of God. This gift may be used correctly or incorrectly in relation to man's concept of his fellow human beings: "Since man is a whole or total being, sex is good if it serves the fulfillment of man as a total being, that is, if it serves God's will for man. . . . Man's total self or being has its very existence in the community of other selves; and it is the aim of all human inter-relationships in all their aspects (including sexual) to foster the love in which spiritual or organismic selfhood is nurtured." (Hiltner, 1957, pp. 72, 75.)

Sanctity of Human Life

Hiltner illustrates Jesus' teaching concerning the sanctity of human life by referring to His comments about a man who lusts after a woman: "If a man 'lusts' after a woman, such a limited perspective upon people has become so basic a part of his character that he does not see the whole person who is there. This is the sin . . . the rejection of a personal relationship, the use of another person (even symbolically) as if she were not a person or child of God." (1957, p. 39.)

Divorce

Concerning divorce there is some diversity of thought and practice between the Protestant and Roman Catholic value matrices. To the Protestant, "maintenance of the unbroken family unit is a means to an end, the happiness of the individual members of the family. To Catholicism, however, it is an end in itself, to be served even at the cost of the happiness of the individual members." (Pfeffer, 1958, p. 113.)

Purpose of Intercourse

The Protestant and Catholic divergency of teaching concerning the purpose of sexual intercourse has relevance to the attempt to formulate a theoretical framework for working with families. To the Protestant, sexual intercourse is properly a source of pleasure and enjoyment as well as a necessary factor in the procreative process. It may be enjoyed for its own sake with no intention of procreation. To the Catholic, however, any mechanical process which interferes with the procreative act is a sin. This is clearly stated by

O'Connor: "The Holy Father makes it abundantly clear that the primary end of marriage is the 'procreation and the education of new life,' and that other ends, such as the pleasure and satisfaction of the married couple, are secondary and subordinate to the primary end." (1956, p. 181.)

Intermarriage

All Christian groups point out that intermarriage is less likely to make for a happy life and a strong religious faith than is a religiously homogeneous marriage, and therefore religious intermarriage is to be avoided.

Family Worship

The worship by the family members together will strengthen family ties and will help to bring about a happy and meaningful family life.

Although all Christian religious groups hold many values in common, there are certain divergencies created by varying theological interpretations in certain areas. These include such things as the purpose of intercourse, the grounds for divorce, the methods of contraception. (O'Connor, 1956, p. 181; Report on the Actions of the 1960 General Assembly on Social Problems of the Presbyterian Church in the United States; and Sheed, 1963, p. 4.)

THE FRAMEWORK

The Christian framework depends on the idea of the sovereignty of God: that it is He who has made us and not we ourselves. It is He who has established the universe and all that is in it. He has set up a moral order in reality which has relevance for all of life.

Each individual is a child of God and his life is sacred to God. Each individual, therefore, has worth within himself. This is the primary factor behind the prohibition concerning sexual intercourse outside of the bonds of marriage.

The family is ordained by God, regulated by His commandments, and is to be a monogamous union entered into for life, unless certain special circumstances alter the situation. The earthly family is symbolic of the wider family of all the children of God, and hence is sacred. The life of the family is to benefit the individual members but above that, it is to serve the kingdom of God.

CRITIQUE AND DISCUSSION

The western Christian conceptual framework differs from most others in certain significant ways. Most theories have developed gradually as a result of a series of research projects viewing the family from a specific type of approach. Frequently, it was only after several studies had been accomplished that a delineation of the theory surrounding them was formulated. In the Western Christian tradition, we have a basic framework as it is promulgated in the New Testament and interpreted by Christian theologians. This framework was in existence for centuries before any use was made of it in empirical research. Theoretical or teaching tasks find in it a satisfactory foundation from which to work, but since this foundation is abstract rather than concrete in nature, it poses certain problems for researchers.

This is not to say that research under this system is impossible, but merely to point out that specific methods to do so adequately have not, as yet, been identified. The Western Christian philosophy has had an effect upon research in other related groups concerned with the family. It has forced finer delineation of research methods, it has provided an important variable which has had a profound effect upon family life, it has been the initiating factor in many research problems, and it has motivated certain individuals in related disciplines of study to search for its impact upon the family life of the entire culture.

In a discussion concerning organized religion in America Abrams observed that: "Religion is one of the most powerful and persistent of all social forces . . . organized religion plays an important role in our society. These institutions and thought have influenced to a considerable extent our economic and political structure, the nature of our educational institutions, and the norms and values in family life," (1948, p. vii.) This reason, among others, points up the need for attempting to formulate and delineate a religious framework from which to study the family.

Such a framework stands or falls upon the ability of the individual to accept the truth of the Christian religious teachings. Yinger argues that the important question is not whether or not religious beliefs represent reality, for in fact they do exist and influence human beings. To him, the important question is rather how they are used and the manner in which they do influence men: "Whether religious ideas are 'true' hinges on one's definition of the truth, and hence becomes a metaphysical, not a scientific problem." (1957, p. 56.)

If a particular student of the family can believe that the Christian faith has a type of objective existence, one which is real although it cannot be put to any empirical tests except those which examine its functions, he may find the Christian framework a worthwhile one from which to view human interaction in the family. This may be difficult for some social scientists to do, yet there are similarities between social science and religion which should facilitate this process:

"The social scientist discovers that religion on its human side deals with the same social facts and conditions which he himself studies. To be sure, it deals with them differently. It aims not to understand them but to control them. But as understanding must be the basis for wise control, and inasmuch as the social scientists know that understanding is for the sake of control, they see that the ultimate aim of both religion and science must be the same . . . to benefit man." (Elwood, 1923, p. 2.)

REFERENCES

ABRAMS, R. H. *The Annals of the American Academy of Political and Social Science*, **256** (March 1948) p. vii. A complete issue devoted to a presentation of a series of articles concerning organized religion in the United States.

AMES, E. S. "Religion and Childhood" in Orlo Strunk, Jr., ed. *Readings in the Psychology of Religion*. Nashville: Abington Press, 1959.

BABER, R. E. "Religion and the Family," *The Annals of the American Academy of Political and Social Science*, **256** (March 1948), pp. 92–100.

BAILEY, D. S. *The Mystery of Love and Marriage*. New York: Harper & Row, Publishers, 1952.

BAINTON, R. H. *What Christianity Says About Sex, Love, and Marriage*. New York: Association Press, 1957. An historical survey of Christian teaching concerning sex, love, and marriage.

———. "Christianity and Sex," in Simon Doniger, ed. *Sex and Religion Today*. New York: Association Press, 1953.

BELL, R. R., and BLUMBERG, LEONARD. "Courtship Intimacy and Religious Background," *Marriage and Family Living*, **21** (Nov. 1959), pp. 356–60.

BURGESS, E. W., and COTTRELL, L. S. *Predicting Success or Failure in*

Marriage. Englewood Cliffs, N.J.: Prentice-Hall, Inc., 1939. One of the classic studies in the area of marital prediction.

COLE, W. G. *Sex and Love in the Bible*. New York: Association Press, 1959. A review of all major incidents of sexual activity of all types as recorded in the Bible, as well as an account of Biblical teachings concerning sexual practices.

Congregational-Christian Denomination. "Christian Nurture in the Family and the Relation of the Church to the Family." An unpublished paper circulated within the Congregational-Christian denomination.

DEDMAN, JEAN. "The Relationship Between Religious Attitude and Attitude Toward Premarital Sex Relations," *Marriage and Family Living*, 21 (May 1959), pp. 171–76.

DICKIE, JOHN. *The Organism of Christian Thought*. London: James Clarke, & Company, Ltd., Publishers, 1931.

DUVALL, E. M., and DUVALL, S. M., eds. *Sex Ways in Fact and Faith*. New York: Association Press, 1961. A collection of research reports presented at the North American Conference on Church and Family Life at Green Lake, Wis., in 1961.

ELLWOOD, C. A. *Christianity and Social Science*. New York: The Macmillan Company, 1923.

GRANT, F. C. *An Introduction to New Testament Thought*. Nashville: Abington Press, 1950. A comprehensive survey of key ideas in New Testament theology. Of particular interest to the focus of family life is the section concerning New Testament ethics.

HASTINGS, JOHN, ed. *Encyclopedia of Religion and Ethics*. New York: Charles Scribner's Sons, 1955.

HEISS, J. S. "Interfaith Marriage and Marital Outcome," *Marriage and Family Living*, 23 (Aug. 1961), pp. 228–33.

HILTNER, SEWARD. *Sex and the Christian Life*. New York: Association Press, 1957. A discussion of the different views of sex, a review of the Biblical and historical Christian attitudes and teachings regarding sex, and the attempt to formulate a modern Christian view.

JACKSON, S. M., ed. *The New Schaff-Herzog Encyclopedia of Religious Knowledge*. New York: Funk & Wagnalls Company, Inc., 1909.

KILDAHL, H. B. *Family Affairs*. Minneapolis, Minn.: Augsburg Publishing House, 1948. A presentation of the contemporary situation of the family against the historical background of Biblical teaching. A discussion of the ideals of the modern Christian family is also presented.

KOLB, W. L. "Images of Man and the Sociology of Religion," *Journal for the Scientific Study of Religion*, 1 (Oct. 1961), pp. 5–29.

LANDIS, J. T. "Religiousness, Family Relationships, and Family Values in Protestant, Catholic, and Jewish Families," *Marriage and Family Living*, 12 (Nov. 1960), pp. 341–47.

LENSKI, GERHARD. "Religions's Impact on Secular Institutions," *Review of Religious Research*, 4 (Fall 1962), pp. 1–16.

——. *The Religious Factor*. New York: Doubleday & Company, Inc., 1961. A report of the 1958 survey of the Detroit area which was concerned with measuring the effect of religious commitment on daily life.

MOBERG, D. O. *The Church as a Social Institution*. Englewood Cliffs, N.J.: Prentice-Hall, Inc., 1962. A sociological survey of those aspects of the church which can be observed and interpreted by sociological methodology.

O'CONNOR, D. A. *Catholic Social Doctrine*. Westminster, Md.: The Newman Press, 1956.

PFEFFER, LEO. *Creeds in Competition*. New York: Harper & Row, Publishers, 1958.

PIKE, J. A. *If You Marry Outside Your Faith*. New York: Harper & Row, Publishers, 1954. A presentation of the problems of mixed marriage with particular relevance to the Protestant-Roman Catholic marriage.

Presbyterian Church in the United States. "Actions of the 1960 General Assembly on Social Problems." An unpublished paper circulated among the members of the denomination.

——. "The Impact of Culture upon the Educational Work of the Church." Richmond, Va.: Board of Christian Education, 1961. One of a series of study pamphlets in preparation for the issuance of a new teaching curriculum.

PROTESTANT EPISCOPAL CHURCH. *The Book of Common Prayer*. New York: The Church Pension Fund, 1945.

REIBER, S. R. "How Family Changes in the United States Between 1860 and 1960 Have Affected the Church." Unpublished study, Department of Sociology, Florida State University, 1961.

SALISBURY, W. S. "Religiosity, Regional Sub-Culture, and Social Behavior," *Journal for the Scientific Study of Religion*, 2 (Fall 1962), pp. 94–101.

SAMENFINK, J. A. "A Study of Some Aspects of Marital Behavior as Related to Religious Control," *Marriage and Family Living*, 20 (May 1958), pp. 163–69.

SCHLEIERMACHER, FRIEDRICH. *The Christian Faith*. London: James Clarke & Company, Ltd., Publishers, 1928.

SHEED, F. J. "Church's Position Stated on Marriage Act Teaching," *The Florida Catholic*, 24, No. 31 (May 31, 1963).

SMITH, L. R. *This Love of Ours*. Nashville: Abington Press, 1947. A book written for newly married couples to help them to face some of the problems of married life and to help them to establish those elements in their home which will bring harmony and happiness.

TILLICH, PAUL. *The New Being.* New York: Charles Scribner's Sons, 1955.

United Church of Canada. *Toward a Christian Understanding of Sex, Love and Marriage.* Edmonton, Al.: United Church of Canada Press, 1960.

United Lutheran Church. *Christian Guidance on Marriage and Family Life.* New York: The Lutheran Church, 1956.

United Presbyterian Church in the U.S.A. *The Constitution of the United Presbyterian Church.* Philadelphia: United Presbyterian Church, 1960.

WERNER, H. G. *Christian Family Living.* Nashville: The Graded Press. 1958. One of a series of non-technical books interpreting various aspects of the Christian faith.

WYNN, J. C., and FAIRCHILD, R. W. *Families in the Church.* New York: Association Press, 1961. The report of a research study within the Presbyterian Church concerning family-church interaction.

YINGER, J. M., ed. *Religion, Society, and the Individual.* New York: The Macmillan Company, 1957. A systematic analysis of religion from the point of view of sociology, and a collection of readings in the sociology of religion.

AUTHOR INDEX

317

SUBJECT INDEX

ABOUT THE EDITORS AND CONTRIBUTORS

DR. F. IVAN NYE is senior visiting scientist at the Boys Town Center for the Study of Youth Development, Boys Town, Nebraska. He received his M.A. from Washington State University and his Ph.D. from Michigan State University, both in sociology. After initial appointments at Ohio State University, University of Missouri, and Bucknell University, he served as director of the Sociological Research Laboratory at Washington State University (1954–60) and as director of the Inter-Divisional Ph.D. Program in Marriage and the Family at Florida State University (1960–63). Between 1963 and 1976 he returned to Washington State University as professor of sociology and rural sociology and as extension sociologist (1974–76), returned briefly to Florida State University before going to Boys Town in 1979. Dr. Nye, who has authored and edited numerous books and journal articles (the most recent being the 1979 publication of *Contemporary Theories about the Family, Volumes I and II*, edited with Wesley R. Burr, Reuben Hill, and Ira Reiss), is a past editor of the *Journal of Marriage and the Family* and a past president of the National Council on Family Relations.

DR. FELIX M. BERARDO is professor of sociology at the University of Florida, where he formerly served as associate chairman of the department. He completed his undergraduate degree at the University of Connecticut (1961) and his Ph.D. in sociology at Florida State University (1965). He came to the University of Florida in 1969 from Washington State University where he was on the faculty of both the departments of sociology and rural sociology. Dr. Berardo's teaching, research, and publication efforts are within the fields of family sociology and social gerontology. He has published widely in both areas. Besides *Conceptual Frameworks*, he is also a coauthor with Dr. Nye of a family textbook, *The Family: Its Structure and Interaction*. For the past several years he has been the editor of the

329

Journal of Marriage and the Family. He is also an associate of the University of Florida's Center for Gerontological Studies, and coordinator of its Summer Institute.

DR. JENNIE MCINTRYE is associate professor of sociology at the University of Maryland. She received her M.A. and Ph.D. in sociology from Florida State University (1966). Dr. McIntrye has published numerous journal articles, and is currently at work on an interview study of rape victims and a survey of sexual harassment in the workplace.

DR. DANIEL J. KOENIG is associate professor of sociology at the University of Victoria. He received his M.S. from Florida State University (1964) and his Ph.D. in sociology from the University of Illinois at Urbana-Champaign (1971). Dr. Koenig has published numerous monographs and journal articles, and is the director of the Canadian Association for Criminological Research and a regular guest lecturer in the training programs of the Royal Canadian Mounted Police.

DR. ALAN E. BAYER is senior visiting scientist at the Boys Town Center for the Study of Youth Development, Boys Town, Nebraska, and professor of sociology and director for the Center for Research on Educational and Scientific Systems at Florida State University. He received his Ph.D. from Florida State University in 1965. Dr. Bayer is the author of more than 75 monographs and journal articles, and is coauthor of *Human Resources and Higher Education* and *Power of Protest.*

DR. JAY D. SCHVANEVELDT is professor of family and human development at Utah State University, where he served as chairman of the department from 1973–80. He received his Ph.D. from Florida State University (1964) and did post-doctoral work at the University of Minnesota (1972–73). Dr. Schvaneveldt has published widely in the areas of family interaction, parent-child relations, adolescent development, and family theory and is currently finishing a book with Gerald R. Adams entitled *Understanding Research Methods.*

DR. E. M. (BUD) RALLINGS is associate professor of sociology at the University of North Carolina at Greensboro. He received his B.S. and M.S. from Clemson University and his Ph.D. from Florida State

University. His major teaching and research interests are in the areas of marriage and the family and group dynamics.

DR. WILLIAM D. BROWN is a psychologist in private practice in Washington, D.C. He received his M.A. from Texas Christian University (1962) and his Ph.D. from Florida State University (1965), both in psychology. Dr. Brown has authored numerous journal articles and two books, *Families under Stress* and *Welcome Stress it Can Help You to Your Best.* In addition, he is active on the lecture circuit and writes a syndicated newspaper column on stress.

DR. GEORGE P. ROWE is associate professor of human development and the family at the University of Nebraska. Since receiving his Ph.D. from Florida State University in 1966 he also has taught at the University of Missouri and North Dakota State University. Currently Dr. Rowe is involved in research on preretirement planning and marriage and kin relationships in the later stages of the family life cycle.

DR. ANN SMITH RICE is currently doing consulting work for a private firm, Resources in Consumer Education, Santa Barbara, California, and is teaching a course in consumer math for the Santa Barbara school district. She received her M.A. in education from the University of Georgia (1951) and her Ph.D. in home economics, economics, and sociology from Florida State University (1964). In addition, she did post-doctoral work in economics at the University of Miami. Formerly of the University of California at Santa Barbara, Dr. Rice is coauthor (with Drs. Nickells and Turner) of a textbook, *Management in Family Living,* now in its fifth edition, as well as author of numerous journal articles.

DR. K. IMOGENE DEAN is associate professor of sociology at the University of Georgia. She received her Masters of Social Work from Louisiana State University (1954) and her Ph.D. in sociology from Florida State University (1970). Dr. Dean is the author of numerous journal and editorial publications and is involved in helping to develop undergraduate interdisciplinary programs in social work, gerontology, and criminal justice.

MARIE WITKIN KARGMAN is a family therapist, trained as a counseling sociologist. She is also a lawyer who represents children

331

before the court in custody disputes. She received her M.A. from Harvard University and her J.D. from DePaul University. Dr. Kargman, whose major areas of interest are in the impact of judicial decisions on family life and the representation of children in the courts, has authored over 25 publications in legal and sociological journals.

DR. STANLEY ROBERT REIBER is professor and chairman of sociology and social work at Carroll College, Waukesha, Wisconsin. He received his A.B. from Grove City College, his B.D. from Yale Divinity School, and his M.Sc. and Ph.D. from Florida State University. Dr. Reiber, whose major areas of interest are in the sociology of the family and social gerontology, is the author of *Toward Understanding Sex.*